FROMMER'S
EasyGuide
TO
NEW YORK CITY

By
Pauline Frommer

EasyGuides are ✦ Quick To Read ✦ Light To Carry
✦ For Expert Advice ✦ In All Price Ranges

FrommerMedia LLC

JLarkin (signature)

Published by
FROMMER MEDIA LLC

ISBN 978-1-62887-012-1 (paper), 978-1-62887-042-8 (e-book)

Editorial Director: Pauline Frommer
Editor: Arthur Frommer
Production Editor: Donna Wright
Cartographer: Roberta Stockwell
Cover Design: Howard Grossman

For information on our other products or services, see www.frommers.com.

FrommerMedia LLC also publishes its books in a variety of electronic formats. Some content that appears in print may not be available in electronic formats.

Manufactured in the United States of America

5 4 3 2 1

CONTENTS

ABOUT THE AUTHOR

Pauline Frommer is a lifelong New Yorker who enjoys nothing more than exploring her hometown. She is the author of several award-winning guidebooks to New York, as well as books on Las Vegas and Hawaii. She's the Co-President of FrommerMedia, the co-host of the nationally syndicated radio show *The Travel Show*, and a syndicated newspaper columnist. Pauline would like to thank her patient and loving husband Lonnie, and dedicate this book to her daughters Veronica and Beatrix.

ABOUT THE FROMMER TRAVEL GUIDES

For most of the past 50 years, Frommer's has been the leading series of travel guides in North America, accounting for as many as 24% of all guidebooks sold. I think I know why.

Though we hope our books are entertaining, we nevertheless deal with travel in a serious fashion. Our guidebooks have never looked on such journeys as a mere recreation, but as a far more important human function, a time of learning and introspection, an essential part of a civilized life. We stress the culture, lifestyle, history and beliefs of the destinations we cover, and urge our readers to seek out people and new ideas as the chief rewards of travel.

We have never shied from controversy. We have, from the beginning, encouraged our authors to be intensely judgmental, critical—both pro and con—in their comments, and wholly independent. Our only clients are our readers, and we have triggered the ire of countless prominent sorts, from a tourist newspaper we called "practically worthless" (it unsuccessfully sued us) to the many rip-offs we've condemned.

And because we believe that travel should be available to everyone regardless of their incomes, we have always been cost-conscious at every level of expenditure. Though we have broadened our recommendations beyond the budget category, we insist that every lodging we include be sensibly priced. We use every form of media to assist our readers, and are particularly proud of our feisty daily website, the award-winning Frommers.com.

I have high hopes for the future of Frommer's. May these guidebooks, in all the years ahead, continue to reflect the joy of travel and the freedom that travel represents. May they always pursue a cost-conscious path, so that people of all incomes can enjoy the rewards of travel. And may they create, for both the traveler and the persons among whom we travel, a community of friends, where all human beings live in harmony and peace.

Arthur Frommer

THE BEST OF THE BIG APPLE

There is simply no place in the United States as brimming with opportunities as New York City. Those of us who live here open our doors to incredible options each and every day: The chance to experience the best and newest in the worlds of art, theater, dance, and music; the ability to feast on expertly prepared foods from all over the world; the belief that we can make our voices heard on political issues, in this news media capital of the nation; and the opportunity to meet today's movers and shakers. The ambitious come here because they know that if they want to achieve a certain level of prominence in their careers or in the eyes of the world, New York is the place to do it (are you humming "If I can make it there, I'll make it anywhere, right now?).

There's a factual basis to this New Yorker's pride. Because of the density and diversity of our population; our long history as a center of commerce and ideas; our access to the United Nations, Wall Street, and the opinion makers of Madison Avenue; and endless other resources, there's simply *more* here than in other places. And if that claim seems extreme, well, you'll just have to regard boastfulness as another unavoidable characteristic of "the Big Apple." What would New Yorkers be without our big mouths?

In visiting New York, you, too, are opening yourself up to a world of wonderful opportunities. In fact, that's what can make New York so intimidating to visitors: There are just so many darn choices. In this chapter, I've sorted through a book's worth of options, selecting some favorites to help you hit the city's highlights.

MOST unforgettable NEW YORK CITY EXPERIENCES

o **Seeing the City from On High:** And it doesn't really matter if you do so from the **Top of the Rock** (p. 132), the **Empire State Building** (p. 124), the **Stone Rose Lounge** (p. 220) or one of the many other venues where one can get a bird's eye view. What's important is that you get a feeling for the immensity of the city; with its wonderful order of the grid system of streets (which plays off the chaos on the streets themselves); and the dizzying variety of building types (many of which can't be adequately seen from the sidewalk). Try and get somewhere high early in your trip as there's no better way to orient yourself.

o **Walking the Brooklyn Bridge:** The bridge, too, offers glorious views of the city. But that's not the only reason you stroll here: walking the span allows you to see this marvel of engineering up close. (It was the longest suspension bridge in the world when it was build in 1883.) And it gives you an excuse to stop by Jacques Torres scrumptious ice cream store in Brooklyn for a post-walk treat. See p. 108.

o **Going to a splashy, big Broadway musical:** When they're done right—and they're not always—there are few experiences as life affirming (no, truly!) as seeing ridiculously talented people sing and dance their hearts out in a show that makes you laugh, cry, and think about your own life story. See p. 196.

o **Staying out late:** The city changes its face after dusk. All the people who were rushing by you during the day, slow down and take to the city's bars, restaurants, and clubs to socialize. Even if you're not normally a nightlife person, try it while in NYC. If you're outgoing, you may be rewarded with some great conversations (despite our reputation, this is actually one of the friendliest cities on the planet); and if you're shy, well, the eavesdropping can be informative, too.

o **Touring Ellis Island:** You'll see the **Statue of Liberty** (p. 115) first (also a thrill) and then spend several hours in the place so many of our ancestors passed through in order to settle in the "New World." Hearing the tales of what went on here is a tremendously moving experience. See p. 109.

o **Traveling Underground:** Don't be afraid of the subways! Not only will they zip you anywhere you need to go at nearly the speed of light (okay, maybe not that fast, but they're efficient), but there are few better places to feel the intense energy of this always-on-the-go metropolis. The people watching is primo, too, and some of the musicians who perform underground are darn good, meaning you get a show with your ride.

best FREE NEW YORK ACTIVITIES

o **Ride the Staten Island Ferry:** The Staten Island Ferry is used daily by thousands of commuters. Ride it for a great view of the Statue of Liberty, Ellis Island, New York Harbor, and the lower Manhattan skyline. You can't beat the price: free. See p. 115.

o **Visit a museum for free (or nearly free):** A number of museums allow free entry on Fridays. The **Museum of Modern Art** (p. 130) is free from 4 to 8pm on that day as is the **Museum of the Moving Image** (p. 149). The **Rubin Museum**'s (p. 120) free Fridays runs from 6 to 9pm, the **Whitney**'s (p. 137) from 6 to 9pm, and the **New-York Historical Society** (p. 141) from 6 to 8pm. Remember that a number of museums—most prominently the **Metropolitan Museum** (p. 135), the **Brooklyn Museum** (p. 146), and the **Museum of Natural History** (p. 138)—charge a "suggested donation," meaning you could, without shame, pay just a nickel for entrance. See chapter 5 for more.

o **Attend a TV taping:** You'll get a behind the scenes peek at how David Letterman, Jon Stewart, Stephen Colbert, and the other NYC-based TV stars work their magic. And you won't pay a cent more than you have to see the show on TV in your own home. See p. 205 for full details.

○ **Take a tour with a Big Apple Greeter:** Volunteers who love their hometown and love showing it to outsiders even more lead these unique tours. You'll need to sign up well in advance, but when you do you'll be assigned a local with similar interests to yours who can show you the neighborhood of your choice. Possibly the best tours in the city and absolutely free. See p. 19.

○ **Kayak the Hudson River:** From May through October, the Downtown Boathouse organization (www.downtownboathouse.org) offers both lessons and boats, gratis, to anyone who's interested. It's a thrilling, remarkably easy-to-learn activity, and a great way to get a bit of exercise.

○ **Gallery Hop in Chelsea:** Go in the early evening hours, and you may score free wine and nibbles at a gallery opening. But even if you don't, wandering through these galleries—the biggest concentration in the world—is an intriguing, intellectually rich experience, as you'll see what the current zeitgeist of the art world is, as expressed by hundreds of would-be Picassos. See p. 122.

○ **Walk. Everywhere:** New York City is one of the world's greatest walking cities. Since most of it is planned on the grid system, it's hard to get lost (except below 4th street, where getting lost is part of the fun). Avenues go north and south, streets go east and west. You can actually walk the entire length of Manhattan—a walk that, done briskly, takes upwards of 6 hours. That's a 13½-mile hike, by the way!

THE best WAYS TO SEE NEW YORK CITY LIKE A LOCAL

○ **Watch the sun set over Central Park from the roof garden of the Metropolitan Museum:** Though the museum is jammed with tourists during the day, locals take over at dusk, on Fridays and Saturdays (when the museum is open until 8:45pm). They head up to the art-filled roof—a different contemporary artist is given the commission to decorate it each year—to sip wine, socialize and (often) pick up each other. It's a great time to look at the art downstairs, too, as the galleries are a quarter as crowded as they are during the daytime.

○ **Ride the Roosevelt Island Tram:** It may just be a 4-minute ride, but the views are spectacular, and you'll head to an island very few outsiders ever visit. A shame, especially now that the new **FDR Four Freedoms Park** has opened at Roosevelt Island's tip (an architectural achievement that should be seen). See p. 126.

○ **Stand in line for Shakespeare in the Park:** Shakespeare performed by stars, under the stars, in Central Park—for free! Even though you can put your name into an online lottery for tickets, every summer, thousands of New Yorkers make a day out of waiting in line (and chatting, picnicking, and people-watching) for the tickets to be distributed. While you won't find a real New Yorker at Times Square on New Year's Eve, you will find lots of them on a summer's day waiting for the Bard. See p. 154.

○ **Get from here to there by Citibike:** The city's new bike sharing program has shown locals just how much fun it is to get around on two wheels. Join them! The program is affordable, and thanks to all the new bike lanes in the city, getting around by bike is easier—and safer—than ever. See p. 237.

○ **Browse the Greenmarket:** Union Square's farmer's market has to be one of the best of its kind in the U.S. You'll meet the farmers and get to sample all sorts of treats—from jams to artisanal beers to pickles—when you wander through this bustling market. See p. 160.

best FAMILY EXPERIENCES

o **Central Park:** With its carousel, a zoo, two ice-skating rinks and pools (depending on the season), playgrounds, and ball fields, Central Park is a children's wonderland. See p. 152.

o **Bronx Zoo:** This is one of the great zoos in the world, and you don't have to be a kid to love it. See p. 145.

o **Coney Island:** It's not a theme park (yet!), but you can still enjoy longtime survivors of what was once New York City's favorite summer playground, including the land-marked Wonder Wheel and Cyclone roller coaster. Nearby is the New York Aquarium, MCU Park (home of the minor league baseball team Brooklyn Cyclones), and Nathan's Famous hot dogs, and, of course, the beach! See p. 147.

o **Museum of the Moving Image:** Make your own photo flip-book, dub your voice over Julie Andrew's in a clip from Mary Poppins, or play classic video games from the 80s together. This highly interactive museum—it's dedicated to the craft of making movies, TV shows, and video games—is a blast for people of all ages. See p. 149.

best OFFBEAT NEW YORK EXPERIENCES

o **Attend a poetry slam:** The talent you'll see up on the stage, and the passion with which the spoken word is greeted here, is inspiring. See p. 215.

o **Spend the evening at Sammy's Famous Roumanian Restaurant:** The closest New York City comes to an old-time Catskills resort experience, you'll listen to the hoariest of jokes and songs from Fiddler on the Roof while eating chopped liver and downing glasses of vodka from a bottle encased in a block of ice. See p. 71.

o **Ride the International Express:** The no. 7 train is known as the "International Express." Take it through the borough of Queens (where it runs aboveground for most of its length), and you will pass one ethnic neighborhood after another, from Indian to Thai, from Peruvian to Colombian, from Chinese to Korean.

o **Take a "performance art" tour:** The company that runs these programs is known as **Elastic City,** and it uses artists of all sorts to take visitors on experiential tours. You might find yourself etching poetry into the sands of Brighton Beach, Brooklyn or experiencing what it's like to walk down a block blindfolded. This tour is for those who enjoy pushing the boundaries. See p. 164.

o **Head to a Russian nightclub:** At **Tatiana** (p. 221) or one of Brighton Beach's other supper clubs, you get a multi-course feast and a show in Russian featuring acrobats, showgirls, and lots and lots of feathers. It's a wacky way to spend the evening.

NEW YORK'S best MUSEUMS

o **Best All-Around Museum: The Metropolitan Museum of Art.** It's a case of more is more; the largest museum in the Western Hemisphere is also the finest museum-going experience in New York. How could it not be with the variety of treasures this fabled institution holds, from an actual ancient Egyptian temple to murals from a Pompeian villa, to masterworks by Rembrandt, Vermeer, Van Gogh, and on and on. See p. 135.

o **Best History Museum: The Tenement Museum.** Usually historic sites tells the tales of the rich and powerful. This tiny museum recalls a more moving story: that of immigrants who made their first "New World" homes in this actual tenement. Visiting here is an emotionally powerful experience. See p. 119.

o **Best Art Museum that People Outside New York Love to Tell You They Love the Most: The Frick.** The Frick is stately, restrained, elegant, and humble. It's also home to an unrivaled collection that focuses on quality over quantity—making visitors feel like they discovered a secret art haven. See p. 133.

o **Best New York Museum About New York: The New-York Historical Society.** The introductory film alone is worth the cost of admission. Along with the ever-changing exhibits on New York history, be sure to head to the third floor for eye-popping displays of fine furniture, Tiffany lamps, paintings, and more. See p. 141.

o **Best Museum for Hipsters: PS 1.** The Queen's off-shoot of the Museum of Modern Art not only displays the most adventurous of contemporary art, it holds a groovy series of outdoor parties each summer and houses a dazzling restaurant (M. Welles Dinette) on its ground floor. Coming here is always an adventure. See p. 150.

o **Best Home Posing as a Museum: The Louis Armstrong House Museum.** This unassuming house in Queens was Satchmo's home for almost 30 years, and it's been preserved almost exactly as it was when he died in 1971. See p. 149.

best NEW YORK CITY BUILDINGS

o **Best Historic Building: Grand Central Station.** A Beaux Arts gem, this railroad station was built in 1913 and restored in the 1990s to its original brilliance. You can take a tour with the help of a smart phone once you're in the building. See p. 125.

o **Best Skyscraper: The Chrysler Building.** Its cap is iconic and as jaunty as ever, a heartening site to behold. Alas, the Chrysler has no observation deck, but this Art Deco masterpiece can be viewed from outside or from nearby observation decks, such as the Empire State Building's. See p. 123.

o **Most Impressive Place of Worship: Cathedral of St. John the Divine.** Construction began on the world's largest Gothic cathedral in 1892—and it's still going on. This is one structure that benefits from being a work in progress. See p. 140.

best NEW YORK CITY PARKS

o **Central Park:** This park inspired others across the United States and abroad. As one of the world's great urban refuges, it remains a center of calm and tranquility on this clamorous island. See p. 152.

o **Prospect Park:** The *other* masterwork by Frederick Law Olmstead and Calvert Vaux (designers of Central Park), seeing it is a delightful exercise in compare and contrast. See p. 148.

o **High Line:** Located in the Meatpacking District of Manhattan, this quirky, handsome park (opened in 2009, with an additional section that debuted in 2011, and another section set to open in 2013–14) was once an elevated structure for freight trains. It's immensely popular and a good object lesson in how New York City is constantly reinventing itself. See p. 159.

best NEIGHBORHOODS TO STROLL IN NEW YORK CITY

o **Brooklyn Heights:** This was the very first designated historic district in New York City, and you'll understand why when you stroll through its blocks of pristine 19th-century row houses, brownstones, and mansions. Plus there is no better view of Manhattan and New York Harbor than from the Heights' famous promenade.

o **Brighton Beach and Coney Island:** Explore the all-Slavic Brighton Beach first, with its stores selling Russian-nesting dolls, elaborate samovars and all sorts of Russian food items. Then hit the boardwalk and walk half a mile to the classic fun fest that is Coney Island.

o **Greenwich Village:** With its historic winding streets, cozy restaurants, and eccentric characters, Greenwich Village lives up to its reputation.

o **Chinatown:** You don't so much stroll here as push your way through crowds, peer in the windows of herbal medicine stores and jewelry marts, and fend off counterfeit bag sellers. But if I've made this walk sound like a drag, I've done my job poorly, as there are few areas as fascinating to explore despite its teeming streets.

o **The Upper East Side:** Madison Avenue from the upper 60s to the mid-80s is still one of the best window-shopping stretches on the planet, and when you get tired of staring at overpriced baubles, you can duck into the side-streets between Fifth Avenue and Madison for an array of historic townhouses just as dazzling.

o **Harlem:** Harlem encompasses a large area where historic homes, lovingly preserved, abound. I think you'll be impressed by the architectural beauty, but beyond that, by the local spirit, which you'll experience in the area's restaurants, bars, churches, and stores.

THE best FOOD

o **Best cheap eats:** Yes, the line to get in can be long (they do take some reservations, so try), but hey, not only is the food delicious and inexpensive at **Mission Chinese** (p. 72), they give out unlimited beer from a keg, for free, to those waiting to come in.

o **Most romantic restaurant:** I'll have to go classic French on this one and suggest **Daniel** (p. 97). The food is exquisite, as is the décor, and the waitstaff are veritable cupids, who seem to know, instinctively, when to top off a glass and when *not* to interrupt a conversation.

o **Most family-friendly restaurant for those with kids over 8:** Why not give your children a cultural experience along with a feeding? At **Robataya** (p. 74) they'll experienced the best of cooked Japanese cuisine (almost no sushi here), while being served by a genuine Japanese chef who grills all the food in front of you with an intensity of concentration that's fascinating to behold.

o **Most family-friendly restaurant for those with kids under 8:** **Bubby's**(p. 93) has classic American comfort food, a photo booth in the basement, and a shelf of kid's toys and books.

- **Most exotic eating experience:** Brooklyn's **Aska** (p. 101) prepares its food in some pretty wacky ways—dehydrating scallops, cooking fish with pine needles, and creating meatballs out of pig's blood—but 90% of what's served, though unusual, is absolutely scrumptious.

- **Best place to go with a group:** Dive into the tapas and paella at NYC's finest Spanish restaurant, **Tertulia** (p. 75). All the food is meant to be shared and with a group, you'll have the numbers to try more of it.

- **Best splurge:** This is a tough one, but I'll have to go with the endless, unusual and delicious tasting menu at **Chef's Table at Brooklyn Fare** (p. 101). You'll see it all cooked in front of you, and many of the ingredients are over-the-top decadent. Dress appropriately though; they don't let in people in jeans, sandals, or shorts.

- **Best old school Gotham dining experience:** Still a classic, and still serving the tenderest steaks in town, **Peter Luger Steakhouse** (p. 102) is the place to come when you want a taste of olde New York.

- **Best new school Gotham dining experience:** At **Marea** (p. 86) you'll be digging into the most creative Italian food you've likely ever tasted, in a chic and contemporary dining room filled with the biggest of bigwigs.

best CULTURE & NIGHTLIFE IN NEW YORK

- **Best Concert Hall: Carnegie Hall.** There's a reason every musician dreams of playing here some day. The acoustics are exquisite, the look of the place lovely, and the ghosts of stars past ever-so-friendly. See p. 204.

- **Best Children's Theater: The New Victory Theater.** Savvy programmers bring in the top children's productions from around the globe, from circus shows to plays to dance and performance art works. See p. 201.

- **Best Jazz Club: The Village Vanguard.** It's the real thing. All of the greats have performed here, and because of the Vanguard's savvy bookers, this is where the current generation's stars (often up-and-coming) play, too. See p. 212.

- **Best Gay Bar: The Monster.** Sure, the overall scene is hotter in Hell's Kitchen than it is in the Village nowadays. But men have rediscovered this classic Village bar in the last 2 years, and are flocking to its weekend tea dances and second floor piano bar. See p. 224.

- **Best Comedy Club: Upright Citizens Brigade.** The brilliance of the performers here, who are walking the tightrope of making up everything as they go along, will blow you away. See p. 213.

- **Best Brooklyn Bar: The Shanty.** The cocktails here are made with liquors distilled on site, along with artisanal brands from around the globe. Grab a perfectly mixed Dorothy Parker gin martini, sit back, and enjoy life. See p. 221.

- **Best Cocktail: Death & Co.** This one's a close race, because the bartenders at this joint, Pegu Club, PDT, The Shanty, and Employees Only are friendly and swap recipes. But I'm going out on a limb to say that the cocktails here are both the most balanced and the most inventive. See p. 217.

- **Best Dive Bar: Winnie's.** If seedy—but friendly—is your scene, you can't do better than Winnies. The drinks here pack a wallop, and with the karaoke machine cranking out Mandarin pop tunes, you're guaranteed surreal, but real, entertainment. See p. 215.

- **Best Speakeasy: PDT.** Hidden behind a secret-panel in the phone booth of a hot dog stand, PDT (it stands for Please Don't Tell) serves some of the most expertly (and creatively) mixed cocktails in the city, in a hidden space that feels oh-so-exclusive. See p. 217.

- **Best Hotel Bar: Bemelman's Bar in the Carlyle.** It's not a cheap experience, but enjoying an excellent jazz trio, Manhattan in hand, in this hoity toity watering hole, is one of those experiences that seem taken right from a Woody Allen movie. Classic. See p. 220.

SUGGESTED ITINERARIES & NEIGHBORHOODS

ow fast the time flies on a visit to New York! With so many
sightseeing and entertainment options, the job of organizing a
day of touring can be a daunting task. That's why I've inserted
this chapter at an early point in your reading. In it, I've suggested
several workable ways to organize your time: several different itineraries from which to choose, several different tastes and interests to satisfy. Each one hits many of the "bucket list" sights (and some of the
more unique ones). And each one, I hope, will lead to an enjoyable
New York vacation. Along the way, I'll also explain how NYC is laid out
and what you'll find in the various neighborhoods, so that, if you
decide to skip our suggested itineraries, you'll at least be able to create a logical alternative designed to satisfy your own particular wants.

ICONIC NYC IN 1 DAY

If you have just 1 day in New York, you have my condolences. First thing
you're going to want to do is slam your shoe into your fanny for giving
yourself far too little time to experience the city. When you're done with
that, try the following itinerary: ***Start: 34th Street and Fifth Avenue.***

1 The Empire State Building ★★★

Start your day with a Kong's eye view of the city. It will help you
immensely to understand the layout and is a heckuva lot of fun (especially if you can skip the lines, which you'll do by arriving first thing
in the morning). See p. 124.

Walk uptown, gazing into the window of Lord and Taylor and Saks Fifth
Avenue until you get to:

2 New York Public Library ★★

You'll recognize this building by the lion sculptures guarding its
gates. Step inside to see the grand interior; usually one or two free
exhibits will be taking place, drawn from the library's vast collections. See p. 127 for more.

Continue walking uptown until you get to 48th Street, home to:

3 Rockefeller Center ★★

There are scores of complexes across the U.S. housing a mix of offices
and arts buildings, but none have the visual wallop of Rockefeller

Center. That has partially to do with the harmony and grandeur of the Art Deco skyscrapers; and partially because there's always so much to see and do here. You may just have time to stroll around, or, if you're here in the right season, you could skate below the massive Christmas tree. I'd also recommend the tour of **Radio City Music Hall** ★ or the **NBC Tour.** Since you've just come from the Statue of Liberty, it doesn't make sense to go to the **Top of the Rock** ★★, the observation deck of the RCA Building in Rockefeller Center (but do so if you skipped stop #1). If you have time, stroll uptown on Fifth Avenue for primo window-shopping. See p. 131.

Hop a bus, or walk back downtown to 42nd and Fifth Avenue. Then walk east until you get to:

4 Grand Central Terminal ★★

Before stepping into the station, take a look east towards Lexington Avenue and up, up, up you'll see the famed scalloped spire of the **Chrysler Building** ★★★. Then enter the terminal, one of the most justifiably famous train stations in the world. If you have time, take the audio tour (see p. 123) for insights into the building's architecture and decor. See p. 125 for more.

Grand Central Terminal for Lunch 🍴

Head downstairs to the Oyster Bar if you like seafood (take a peek at it even if you don't, as it's a lovely space) or head to the excellent food court, offering most every cuisine known to man.

In the station are the 4, 5, and 6 subway trains. Grab one of them and head uptown to 86th Street. When you exit, walk west towards Central Park and then downtown until you come to:

5 The Metropolitan Museum ★★★

Since this is the largest museum in this hemisphere, and a wondrous one at that, you're going to spend the rest of the afternoon here. See p. 135.

Walk back to the subway station, going downtown this time, back to 42nd Street where you'll hop the S train to:

6 Times Square ★

Try and get your first glimpse of this famed square after the sun has set, when all the lights are glittering. Otherwise it looks a bit, well, tawdry. But when it's aglow and the crowds are pulsing, it can feel like the most exciting place on the planet. Hopefully you've gotten theater tickets in advance, the perfect capper for a day on the town. See p. 132.

ICONIC NYC IN 2 DAYS

On your second day, head downtown to see where the city began, Lady Liberty and its most sobering, but popular, sight: Ground Zero. *Start: Subway: 1 to South Ferry or 4 or 5 to Bowling Green.*

1 Statue of Liberty ★★ and Ellis Island ★★★

Whether or not you'll get to tour both depends on how early you can get to the ferry terminal and how large are the crowds. Having advance tickets up to the crown is a good reason to get off at Liberty Island. But if the stars aren't aligned or you miss the first ferry of the day, take in the view of Lady Liberty from the ferry (without disembarking) so you can spend the bulk of your time at Ellis Island, the famed portal to the "New World" for millions of immigrants. It's the more compelling visitor experience of the two. See p. 109.

2 Wall Street ★

Back on the isle of Manhattan, walk uptown to the Financial District. Along the way you'll see structures such as **Castle Clinton National Monument** in Battery Park—it's what's left of a fort built in 1808 to defend New York Harbor against the British—and the impressive **U.S. Customs House,** which houses the Museum of the American Indian (p. 114). Once on Wall Street, stop for a photo op at the **Federal Hall National Memorial,** where George Washington took the oath of office as our first President (his statue is in front), and the **New York Stock Exchange,** across the street. Unfortunately, the Exchange is no longer open for tours. See p. 118.

Walk west past Broadway to Rector Street and turn right, walking uptown until you reach Ground Zero. Follow the signs to the entrance (which will be changing after this book goes to press).

3 9/11 Memorial ★★★

Be sure to get advance tickets to the National September 11 Memorial, as the line for day-of entry admission can take up to an hour, and that's on top of the 20 minutes it takes to get through security here. Still, the opportunity to pay your respects to all those who perished, and see "Reflecting Absence," the design that movingly commemorates the dead, is not one to be missed.

Exit the site and head east towards Broadway and Fulton Street, to the Fulton Street subway stop. There, you'll hop a 4 or 5 train to Brooklyn Bridge, switching to the 6 train to the Canal Street stop. Get off the train and start walking east on Canal to:

4 A Chinatown Lunch ☕

If you'll flip to the restaurant section, chapter 4 of this book, you'll find four top recommendations in Chinatown, all of which are open for lunch. Grab a bite at one of these, and then wander through this fascinating neighborhood for a bit. See p. 69.

Walk or take the M103 bus uptown to Delancey Street, at Delancey turn right and walk to Orchard Street, passing Chrystie, Forsyth, Eldridge, and Allen streets to the:

5 Lower East Side Tenement Museum ★★★

The perfect follow up to Ellis Island, this time capsule of a Lower East Side tenement is now an innovative museum that explores what it was like to be an immigrant in New York City between 1863 and the early 1930s. It's an extremely moving place to visit. You'll need advance reservations to take the 1-hour guided tour of the museum (the only way to see it). See p. 119.

6 Il Laboratorio del Gelato

About 3 blocks north of the Lower East Side Tenement Museum is a wonderful ice-cream-and-gelato shop where you can experience a multitude of homemade ice cream and sorbet flavors. Pick up a cone or cup for the walk to the subway. 188 Ludlow St., at Houston Street. ✆ **212/343-9922.**

SOME THINGS not to do IN NYC

Despite what you have heard, the following experiences are best avoided:

New Year's Eve in Times Square: You won't find any New Yorkers in this crowd. They know better than to show up in the frigid cold at 6am (get there any later and you won't see the ball drop), and stand around all day long in a massive crowd of people, with few eating options nearby and even fewer bathroom facilities. Did I mention they don't allow champagne or other alcoholic drinks in Times Square that night? 'Nuf said.

Chain Restaurants: Yes, we have them. But why would you eat at a place you can find in your home town when right next door to these chains are restaurants lovingly created by some of the most talented chefs in the nation. And I'm not just speaking of haute cuisine! We have some of the most wonderful cheap eats, too, so don't resort to Mickey D's. You're missing a great opportunity if you do.

Driving: Most New Yorkers don't own cars. They know that the traffic is impossible, finding affordable parking even more so, and one can get anywhere, much quicker, on the subway. So don't drive yourself crazy by bringing your own car to Gotham. If you must get around in a private car, hail a cab. Even with the recently increased rates, getting around that way will be cheaper than paying for parking.

Take the F train at Second Avenue and Houston Street two stops uptown to West 4th Street.

7 Washington Square Park ★★

As the sun starts to set, head to this carnival of a park, where street musicians are always performing and crowds of Villagers and NYU students gather. Spend some time relaxing here before heading somewhere in the vicinity for a terrific dinner (the restaurants downtown are the best in the city). See p. 67 for suggestions on where to dine.

ICONIC NYC IN 3 DAYS

If you've followed the first 2 days' suggested itineraries, you've experienced a slice of the best of Manhattan, but there's still plenty to see (more than can be done in just 3 days, sadly). Note that this day should only be attempted if the weather is nice. If not, head inside to one or two of the city's great museums. *Start: Subway B or C to 72nd Street.*

1 The Dakota

The day begins in front of this 1884, French Renaissance–style apartment building (corner of 72nd Street and Central Park West). Besides being used for several films, the Dakota is in many ways a shrine for visitors, as this is where John Lennon lived (and where Yoko Ono still lives), and where he was shot and killed. After seeing the building, head across the street to Central Park and **Strawberry Fields ★**, named in honor of the former Beatle; fans gather to leave flowers, play music, and commune together. See p. 157.

Manhattan Neighborhoods

HARLEM

W. 79th St.
American Museum
of Natural History

E. 79th St.
YORKVILLE

W. 72nd St.
UPPER
WEST SIDE

E. 72nd St.
UPPER
EAST SIDE

CENTRAL
PARK

LINCOLN
CENTER
Columbus
Circle

Central Park
Zoo
Central Park So.

W. 57th St.
Carnegie
Hall

E. 57th St.
MIDTOWN
EAST

MIDTOWN
WEST
Radio City
Music Hall
ROCKEFELLER
CENTER

St. Patrick's
Cathedral E. 50th St.

Intrepid
Sea, Air & Space
Museum

Grand Central
Station

United
Nations

QUEENS

TIMES
SQUARE

W. 42nd St.
E. 42nd St.

Port Authority
Bus Terminal
E. 40th St.
N.Y. Public
Library

Queens-Midtown
Tunnel

MURRAY
HILL

Lincoln
Tunnel

Jacob Javits
Convention
Center
W. 34th St.
Macy's

E. 34th St.

GARMENT
DISTRICT
Penn
Station

Empire State
Bldg.

GRAMERCY
PARK

W. 23rd St.
Madison
Square Park
E. 23rd St

CHELSEA
Flatiron
Bldg.
FLATIRON
DISTRICT

MANHATTAN

W. 14th St.
Union
Square Park
E. 14th St.

MEATPACKING
DISTRICT
EAST
VILLAGE

Tompkins
Square Park

GREENWICH
VILLAGE
Washington
Square Park

East
River
Park

NOHO

W. Houston St.
SOHO
NOLITA

E. 1st St.

LOWER
EAST SIDE

Delancey St.

Williamsburg
Bridge

Canal St.
LITTLE
ITALY

TRIBECA

CHINATOWN

Holland Tunnel

Brooklyn Bridge

DUMBO

9/11 Memorial
FINANCIAL
DISTRICT
South Street
Seaport

NEW JERSEY

Wall St.
New York
Stock Exchange

BROOKLYN
HEIGHTS

Battery
Park
Brooklyn-Battery
Tunnel

BROOKLYN

ASTORIA

ROOSEVELT ISLAND

Queensboro
(59th St.) Bridge

LONG
ISLAND
CITY

Long Island
Expwy.

GREENP

East River

FDR Dr.

Henry Hudson Pkwy.

Hudson River

West Side Expwy.

High Line Park

0   1/2 mi
0   0.5 km

2 Central Park ★★★

Wander deeper into the park. If you keep walking straight from Strawberry Fields, you'll hit the park's grand promenade area and boat pond. Another option is to take one of the Central Park Conservancy's terrific tours; you'd head towards **The Dairy** (p. 156) if that's your plan. For instructions on what else to see in the park—and you should allot the morning to that (unless the weather is bad). See p. 152.

Make your way back to the west side of the park and exit at 81st street, walk west to Columbus and walk downtown one block to:

Lunch at Shake Shack ☕

Time is short, so you'll want to just grab a burger and perhaps one of the Shack's famed milkshakes. See p. 85 for more.

3 American Museum of Natural History ★★★

Head across the street to one of the country's greatest science museums. I highly recommend the tours led by well-trained docents of the museum's highlights. If you'd rather do it on your own, don't skip the Fossils Hall, which has the world's largest dinosaur collection. See p. 138 for more.

Exit the museum and walk west to Amsterdam Avenue to catch an uptown M11 bus. Get off at 110th Street.

4 Cathedral of St. John the Divine ★

On the east side of Amsterdam Avenue, is the world's largest Gothic cathedral and a sight that's overlooked by too many tourists. Construction began in 1892 but because the builders are using medieval techniques, it's still unfinished. Tours are offered to the spectacular interior, or you can see it on your own (p. 140).

Take the M7 uptown bus to 125th Street.

5 Apollo Theater ★

Finish the day by touring the city's most famous theater and then head either to Red Rooster (p. 99) or Amy Ruth's (p. 100) for a soul food meal. You may then want to return to the Apollo to see a show. See p. 206.

AN ITINERARY FOR FAMILIES

The key to enjoying NYC with kids is to take it easy and choose a hotel outside of the overcrowded Times Square area. Many youngsters find the incessant bustle of midtown, and the city in general, tiring (as do adults!). So choose a hotel in a more residential area (the Upper West Side is a good choice). Also, build a lot of free time into your itinerary, especially if the kids are under the age of 8. Here's what this mom recommends for a 3-day visit.

Day 1: Park and Museum

Once the sun is up, **Central Park** is open, so if you have an early-rising tot, grab a bagel and explore the park over breakfast. With its zoo, playgrounds, and boating ponds (both for rentable toy boats and ride-able row boats), this should account for the entire morning. See p. 152 to 157 for more on visiting the park. Right before lunchtime, head out of the park on the east side near 59th Street and hop the subway (the N, Q, or R trains at 59th and Fifth Avenue) to 36th Avenue in Astoria, Queens. Your ultimate goal is **The Museum of the Moving Image** (p. 149), but right opposite it is **Five Napkins Burger** (35–01 36th St., at 35th Ave.; (C) **718/433-2727;** Mon–Fri 11:30am–midnight, Sat–Sun 11am–midnight) where you can have lunch. After lunch, head to this incredibly fun, interactive museum (people of all ages love it) and spend the afternoon there learning about how films, TV shows, and video games are created.

Day 2: Boats, a Big Statue, and Another Boat

What kid doesn't love a boat ride? You'll start day 2 on the very first ferry of the day (to avoid the lines) heading across the Hudson River to visit the **Statue of Liberty** (p. 115). Get advance tickets, so you can climb up to the crown (it's a narrow, winding staircase that most kids will find to be a great adventure). If your young ones are over the age of 8, continue to **Ellis Island** (p. 109); it was the point of entry for millions of immigrants, and older children will find the stories of how they were processed, with some turned away, both fascinating and moving. Once back on the isle of Manhattan, walk to **Stone Street** (p. 69) for lunch and then grab the A, C, or E subways nearby to 42nd Street. and then hop the M42 bus west to the **Intrepid Sea, Air and Space Museum** (p. 129). Set on a 40,000-ton aircraft carrier, it has all kinds of flight simulators your kids will like, as well as an actual space shuttle, a tourable submarine (for kids over the age of 6 only), and much more neat hardware and gizmos to view.

Day 3: A Museum and a Show

You may need to do this itinerary on day 1 or 2, as matinees are only on Wednesdays, Saturdays, and Sundays. But before you get to the theatrical part of your day, head to the **American Museum of Natural History** (p. 138, Central Park West at 79th Street), one of the finest science museums in the country. A terrific planetarium show, the massive dinosaur exhibit, and the huge whale that hangs from the ceiling of one gallery, enthrall most children, as does the interactive Discovery Center. Eat lunch at the cafeteria here, before heading downtown to see the matinee of either a Broadway show (p. 196, there will be a few that are appropriate for children); or a very fine kids show at the **New Victory Theater** (p. 201). After the show, explore all the sights of Times Square, including the huge Ferris wheel at **Toys "R" Us.**

A WEEKEND FOR ROMANTICS

Friday: A Stroll, a Gallic Lunch, Shopping, and a Cabaret

Sleep in—you're on vacation! Then grab a bagel and head to the Manhattan side of the **Brooklyn Bridge.** Saunter over it to Brooklyn, where you can stop at the **Jacques Torres Ice Cream Shop** at 62 Water St. Here the famous chocolatier (p. 176) sells scrumptious sundaes, as well as chocolates (peek at the factory to see it all being made). With treats in hand, hop the C subway at High Street to the

Spring Street stop so that you can have lunch at the oh-so-French **Balthazar Restaurant** (p. 72). Spend the rest of the afternoon shopping (or window-shopping) in Soho, and then head to midtown for a cabaret performance with dinner at the swank **54 Below** (p. 212).

Saturday: Picnic in the Park, a Matinee, and a Museum

Head to **Eataly** (p. 175) or **Zabars** (p. 175) to purchase the ingredients for brunch in Central Park (go to p. 152 to pick a spot). Then sightsee in the park for a few hours, before heading to a **Broadway matinee** (p. 196). After the show, hop the S subway to Grand Central and the 4, 5, or 6 uptown to the **Metropolitan Museum** (p. 135). It's open until 9pm on Friday and Saturday nights, and there are few better places to watch the sun set over Central Park than the terrace here (cocktails are served!). Then head to **Marea** (p. 86) for one of the cushiest, most delicious seafood meals of your life.

Sunday: Gospel, Brunch, and a Step Back in Time

Attend a **gospel service in Harlem** (p. 144), then head to the fabulous **Red Rooster** (p. 99) for lunch. For your last few hours in the city, head uptown even further to the exquisite **Cloisters Museum** (p. 144), which features art and arti-facts from the Middle Ages in a setting that seems airlifted from Europe.

CITY LAYOUT

Lots of people travel to New York, plop themselves down into Time Square, and never go anywhere else. They seem to fear venturing into neighborhoods that exist for pur-poses other than tourism.

You don't have to be among them. By devoting just a few minutes to the basic geography of New York and its distinctive neighborhoods, you can immensely enhance your enjoyment of this multifaceted city. And once you absorb the highly logical orga-nization of New York's transportation system, you'll find that you can zip from place to place with minimal fuss.

The Grid Plan of Manhattan

The city is comprised of five boroughs on four different pieces of land, only one of which is on the North American continent! When most people talk about "New York City," however, they are referring to the borough of Manhattan, which is a long, narrow island between New Jersey and Long Island, bordered by the Hudson and East Rivers.

Finding your way around Manhattan is easier than in almost any other city because of the careful plan that was adopted for laying out the city's avenues and streets. In the areas above 14th Street, the city fathers imposed a strict and unnatural grid upon Man-hattan, leveling hills and tearing down existing homes to create straight, evenly spaced thoroughfares in all but a few places. The grid consists of numbered streets and ave-nues that cross each other at right angles. If you can count up to 100 you can get around this surprisingly compact island.

Streets in Manhattan are numbered and run from east to west. So if you're on 23rd Street and wish to get to 42nd Street, you simply go 19 blocks north. To get from

80th Street to 75th Street walk 5 blocks south. **The avenues of Manhattan run north to south** with some bearing numbers and others names (which does complicate the picture but only a bit). Those that are numbered go from east to west with First Avenue being close to the East River and Twelfth Avenue on the far west side of the island. Interspersed between these numbered avenues are several named avenues, including (among others) Park, Lexington, and Madison. The named avenues live primarily on the east side between Fifth and Third Avenues in midtown and uptown. On the west side, Seventh, Eighth, and Ninth Avenues turn into Columbus Avenue, Central Park West, and Amsterdam Avenue above 59th Street.

The exceptions to the grid rule (all found below 14th Street) are the Financial District, Chinatown, Little Italy, the Lower East Side, Greenwich Village, Soho, and Tribeca. These southern parts of Manhattan were the first to be settled and therefore follow a haphazard non-system of the streets and alleys that curve and twist, sometimes doubling back on themselves (most famously in Greenwich Village where 4th Street collides with 4th Street). Because most of these southern section streets bear names rather than numbers (Delancey Street, Wall Street, Church Street), orientating yourself can be tricky. So it's important to carry a good map and to ask for directions when necessary. Even native New Yorkers can get lost down there.

New York City Neighborhoods in Brief

It never fails to amaze. I'm strolling along a pleasant street of small brownstones, I come to the corner, and suddenly, the landscape morphs. I'm a small ant in a canyon of skyscrapers, or else I'm a visitor to India, surrounded by cumin-scented restaurants and men with strong accents beckoning me into their curry joints. New York is a city of multiple personalities and like Sybil, they can shift on a dime, within the space of one block going from elegant to seedy, from industrial to chic, from ethnic to all-American.

It's this quicksilver quality, this constant metamorphosis, that endows even a simple stroll in New York with real excitement. I urge you to spend at least part of your vacation simply ambling around, window-shopping, eavesdropping on passing conversations and exploring places beyond the heavily touristed areas.

Here's what you'll find in the various—and strikingly different—neighborhoods of New York City.

DOWNTOWN

The Financial District

Best for: Museums, historic sites (like the 9/11 Memorial), architecture, and access to Ellis Island, the Statue of Liberty, and the Brooklyn Bridge

What you won't find: Great dining, evening entertainment

Parameters of the neighborhood: Everything south of Chambers Street

This is where New York City—then New Amsterdam—was born. The area packs the same historic punch as do colonial sections of Boston and Philadelphia. It was on Wall Street that George Washington took the oath of office as America's first president. It was here, at Fraunces Tavern, that the Sons of Liberty gathered to plot the overthrow of the British. It was at Castle Clinton and then Ellis Island that millions of immigrants flooded the city in the 19th and 20th centuries to get their first glimpse of a "promised land." The great financial movers and shakers also stalked the area (and continue to do so today), and a visit to these "canyons of greed" at the beginning of the day or at 5pm, when those men and women in suits and trader's smocks pour onto the streets, is an exciting sight. Recent history has overshadowed other sights and for many visitors this has become simply the place to pay respects at **Ground Zero.** Other top museums here include **The Police Museum** (p. 114) and **The Museum of Jewish Heritage** (p. 113).

Chinatown (& Little Italy)

Best for: *Affordable dining and shopping*

What you won't find: *Top museums, streets without gridlock*

Parameters of the neighborhood: *Chinatown is roughly bordered by Broome Street to the north, Allen Street to the east, Worth to the south, and Lafayette Street to the west.*

At points, Chinatown takes on the aspects of Shanghai or Beijing: the dense crowds on the streets, the awnings with Chinese characters, the pinging sound of Chinese conversation everywhere. It's a fun, truly transporting area to visit and one that's been voraciously swallowing up other neighborhoods—Little Italy, the Jewish Lower East Side—for the past few decades. In fact, except for two blocks of Mulberry Street (from Canal to Broome), strung with colored lights, Little Italy has ceased to exist and is really only a tourist-trapping shadow of its former self. There are a handful of worthwhile places to shop for Italian food, eat gelato or get Italian coffee, but no noteworthy restaurants and very few real Italian-Americans around anymore. For great, cheap eats (and shopping) stick with Asian restaurants and marts, for the most part.

TriBeCa, Nolita & Soho

Best for: *Dining, bars, star-sightings, architecture, shopping*

What you won't find: *Cutting-edge galleries (they're now in Chelsea), museums*

Parameters of the neighborhood: *Let's explain the names first. SoHo means "south of Houston Street." This fashionable neighborhood extends down to Canal Street, between Sixth Avenue to the west and Lafayette Street (one block east of Broadway) to the east. Nolita is the area just north*

of Little Italy (Mott, Mulberry Street and Elizabeth Street north of Kenmare Street). Bordered by the Hudson River to the west, the area north of Chambers Street, west of Broadway, and south of Canal Street is the Triangle Below Canal Street, or TriBeCa. To get here, take the 1 subway to Chambers Street.

Now that we've gotten *that* out of the way, comes the harder task of figuring out what it is about former factories and tenements that the ultra-rich find so appealing. They certainly wouldn't have wanted to work or live in this area back then, but these formerly industrial areas have been drawing a lot of boldfaced names lately. And with these *arrivistes* has come a welcome wagon of hot new restaurants, boutiques, spas, and *boites.* Which means simply wandering these (often) cobblestoned streets, by the cast-iron buildings (Soho has the most of any area in the world) can be a hoot.

The Lower East Side & East Village

Best for: *Dining, bars, dance and music clubs, innovative theaters, local designer-clothing shops*

What you won't find: *Museums (with the exception of the very fine **Tenement Museum** and the **Museum of Contemporary Art**)*

Parameters of the neighborhood: *Between Houston and Canal streets east of the Bowery*

For millions, these areas were once the portal to America. In fact, the buildings you see on the Lower East Side were built expressly to house the teeming masses of immigrants who flooded into New York between roughly 1840 and 1930. At the turn of the last century, this was the most densely populated area in the world, with a dozen to an apartment and pushcarts jamming the streets. While there are some remnants of that life in the old-world fabric and luggage stores along **Orchard Street,** these areas are mostly known today for bars, lounges, and

If you'd like to tour a specific neighborhood with an expert guide, call **Big Apple Greeter** (© 212/669-8159; www.bigapplegreeter.org) at least 4 weeks ahead of your arrival. You can also go to the website and fill in a visit request form. This nonprofit organization has specially trained volunteers who take visitors around town for a free 2- to 4-hour visit (with a $20 suggested donation) of a particular neighborhood. And they say New York isn't friendly!

music clubs. It's in these two neighborhoods that you're most likely to find young designers opening their own tiny stores and protégés of the town's great chefs trying out their own first restaurants. I may be prejudiced because I live in the East Village, but I find it one of the most vibrant areas of Manhattan—though many blocks have lost their gritty edges thanks to ever-rising real estate prices.

Greenwich Village

Best for: *Strolling, dining, historic sites, lovely architecture, specialty food shops, theater, live music clubs, star sightings*

What you won't find: *Museums, many hotels*

Parameters of the neighborhood: *From Broadway west to the Hudson River, bordered by Houston Street to the south and 14th Street to the north*

Greenwich Village has always been where the city's outsiders and oddballs have found a haven. In Dutch Colonial times, it was farmland set outside the walls of the city, and a number of slaves were given conditional freedom in return for providing the burghers with food (and fighting off the Native Americans). At the turn of the 20th century, the area became known as a bohemian enclave, where artists of all sorts (Mark Twain, Edgar Allan Poe, Henry James, Winslow Homer, to name a few) could find cheap lodging and companionship. In the 1950s it was at the center of the Beat movement; in the 1960s and '70s the area around Christopher Street became the center of a burgeoning gay rights movement (in the '80s it was a hotbed of AIDS-related activism).

Today, the high real estate prices have dulled the Village's edge, and you're more likely to see moms with strollers than long-haired poets walking these streets. And that mom might be Sarah Jessica Parker or Uma Thurman, two of the many celebs who now call the tree-shaded brownstones of the Village home sweet home. But the charms of the area are still intact, as is the illusion that you've entered another city altogether. Very few buildings in the neighborhood reach to 10-stories (most are lower than that) and small shops elbow out chain stores. It's a wonderful place to simply come and get lost in.

MIDTOWN

Chelsea & the Meatpacking District

Best for: *Art galleries, nightlife, shopping, the Highline, gay bars*

What you won't find: *Theater, Museums*

Parameters of the neighborhood: *Roughly the area west of Sixth Avenue from 14th Street to 30th Street*

Manhattan's Chelsea neighborhood is today what Soho was 10 years ago, and what Greenwich Village was 20 years ago. The major galleries have moved here, as has Greenwich Village's large gay population. This makes for a lively cultural scene with many bars and clubs (dance clubs are in abundance from 22nd and 29th streets between Tenth and Eleventh avenues). The so-called Meatpacking District, named for the slaughterhouses in the area, has also become an extremely popular nightlife destination (as well as a shopping mini-mecca for its handful of super-trendy stores). An off-shoot of Chelsea, it's NYC's adult Disneyland, filled with late-night clubs, bars, and restaurants that are unhindered by the city's zoning laws (as there are no schools or churches in this part of town). A final reason to come here: the High Line Park, a marvel of urban reclamation (see p. 159).

The Flatiron District, Union Square & Gramercy Park

Best for: Dining, historic sites, architecture, Off-Broadway theater

What you won't find: Museums, nightlife (with a few exceptions)

Parameters of the neighborhood: The Gramercy Park area is from about 16th to 23rd streets, east from Park Avenue South to about Second Avenue; the **Flatiron District** is south of 23rd Street to 14th Street, between Broadway and Sixth Avenue; **Union Square** is the hub of the district from 14th Street to 18th Street.

If you look up as you meander through these three bustling, adjoining (and overlapping) areas, you're likely to see brown street signs proclaiming LADIES MILE. It was on this stretch, mostly on Broadway and Park Avenue South, that the first wave of department stores transformed the lives of New Yorkers in the 1850s. Instead of hopping from a dry goods shop for fabric to a milliners for hats to a cobbler for shoes, women from all over the city came here to outfit themselves and their homes in stores that, wonder of wonders, had everything they needed under one roof. Notice the large plate-glass windows on many of the facades, another department store innovation. Above, the windows are much smaller and point to a second element of the "Ladies Mile": brothels. When the stores closed for the day, the establishments upstairs opened. And where there's prostitution, theater often follows. The area around Union Square was New York's first show district.

Interestingly, the same area has become another important theater district for New York's Off-Broadway playhouses in recent years. The dining scene is also hot here.

For the best strolling, head directly for the **Gramercy Park** area, named for the only privately-owned park in the city (the keys go to those apartment owners whose windows overlook the park). Around the park are a number of beautifully preserved historic homes and clubs, including the wisteria-clad home of former Mayor James Harper (4 Gramercy Park S.), the Players Club (at 16 Gramercy Park S; its members included Edwin Booth and Mark Twain), and the National Arts Club (15 Gramercy Park S., a hangout for Woodrow Wilson and Theodore Dreiser).

Times Square & Midtown West

Best for: Theater and entertainment of all sorts, the **Museum of Modern Art, Rockefeller Center, Macy's**

What you won't find: Serenity

Parameters of the neighborhood: From 34th Street to 59th Street west of Fifth Avenue to the Hudson River

Midtown West, a vast area, encompasses several famous names: Madison Square Garden, the Garment District, Rockefeller Center, the Theater District, and Times Square. It's the area people think of when they think of New York and the reason why so many visitors say with a smirk "Well, it's a nice place to visit, but I couldn't ever live there." And because they're basing their judgments on crowded, loud, pushy midtown, they're absolutely right: it's unlivable . . . which is why so few New Yorkers actually live in this area. In certain parts of Midtown there's no residential housing whatsoever, and it's only the tourists who attempt to get a good night's sleep in this bustling neighborhood.

Midtown East & Murray Hill

Best for: Great architecture, shopping (and window-shopping), historic sites, the United Nations, the Empire State Building

What you won't find: Museums, nightlife (again, with some exceptions)

Parameters of the neighborhood: East from Fifth Avenue to Third Avenue, north from 42nd Street to 57th Street

In the 1950s, Madison, Park, and Lexington Avenues started to sprout with skyscrapers and soon were rivaling the Wall Street area for office space. That's primarily what you'll find here: people in suits, looming glass towers, and lots of traffic. Among all that are some spectacular architectural sights like **Grand Central Station** (p. 125), **St. Patrick's Cathedral** (p. 128), the **Chrysler Building** (p. 123), and the **Seagram's Building.** Go closer to the East River and the area becomes largely residential with little to recommend it to visitors beyond Bloomingdales and the UN.

A tremendously popular stretch of Midtown East is Fifth Avenue as it runs from 57th Street down to the Empire State Building at 34th Street. Stroll it for some of the best window-shopping on the planet.

UPTOWN

Upper West Side

Best for: *Museums* (**like the American Museum of Natural History** *and the* **New York Historical Society**)*, Central Park, bars, kid-friendly restaurants, classical music and dance at* **Lincoln Center** *and elsewhere*

What you won't find: *Great shopping (again with some exceptions), edge*

Parameters of the neighborhood: Starts at 59th Street and encompasses everything west of Central Park.

In some ways, the Upper West Side has the most suburban vibe of any of Manhattan's neighborhoods. National chain stores line the major thoroughfares and the sidewalks swarm with strollers. It's a popular area for families thanks to its proximity to Central Park, the American Museum of Natural History, and the Children's Museum of Manhattan.

It wasn't always this way. When I was growing up on the Upper West Side, and even before that, the neighborhood had a reputation for being an intellectual hotbed, a place where highly political New Yorkers planned protests.

No more. But it's still an extremely pleasant place to visit with good, if unoriginal, shopping; a handful of topnotch museums; New York's famous art hub, Lincoln Center; and, of course, access to the glories of Central Park. And the Time Warner Center gives the neighborhood the dubious distinction of having the priciest food court in the world.

Upper East Side

Best for: *Museums, architecture, window-shopping, Central Park*

What you won't find: *Fine dining (although, I list some exceptions to that), theater, music clubs*

Parameters of the neighborhood: Starts at 59th Street and encompasses the area east of Central Park

10021 is the richest zip code in the world, and it belongs to the Upper East Side, in particular the swank swatch of pavement that runs from 61st to 80th streets. Also known as "The Gold Coast" and "Millionaires Mile," this is the stomping grounds for New York's high society: the Prada-clad women and old money men who sit on the boards of the neighborhood museums, go to a lot of cocktail parties, and endow scholarships for kicks. Their mansions and marble-face townhouses make for nifty sightseeing for those interested in architecture; and the shops along **Madison Avenue** offer a peek into the extravagant fashions adopted by the ultra-rich and the top designers who serve them.

Museums also play a key role on the Upper East Side, and there's a greater concentration of top-flight museums here than anywhere else in the country, with the exception of the Mall in Washington, D.C. You'll want to spend at least 1 day exploring **Museum** Mile—the **Metropolitan, Guggenheim, Whitney, Cooper-Hewitt,** and more are all in the area.

Harlem

Best for: *Dining, bars, clubs, historic sites*

What you won't find: *Theater, shopping, museums (except for the* **Studio Museum** *and the* **Museo del Barrio**)

Parameters of the neighborhood: Harlem proper stretches from river to river, beginning at 125th Street on the West Side, 96th Street on the East Side, and 110th Street north of Central Park. East of Fifth Avenue, **Spanish Harlem (El Barrio)** *runs between East 100th and East 125th streets.*

Perhaps the most rapidly transforming neighborhood in the city, Harlem is safer and cleaner than it's been in decades . . . but may be losing some of its intrinsic character. A largely African-American neighborhood since the 1920s—and home to some of the greatest black writers, politicians, and artists of the 20th century—the neighborhood is now drawing an increasing number of Caucasian residents, lured here by lower real-estate prices and the beauty of a brownstone-lined community. My recommendation: Visit here soon before the authentic soul and Caribbean joints disappear, the gospel churches lose their swing, and the rhythm of the streets changes its beat. There's much to see, including the Studio Museum, dozens of well-preserved Beaux Arts brownstoners, and hopping clubs.

THE OUTER BOROUGHS

Brooklyn

Best for: *Museums, parks, lovely architecture, innovative galleries, dining, great views of Manhattan*

What you won't find: *You find pretty much all the same types of attractions in Brooklyn that you will in Manhattan. It deserves a visit!*

If Brooklyn had not traded its sovereignty to become a borough of New York City in 1898, it would be the fourth largest city in the United States, just after New York City, Los Angeles, and Chicago. With 2.6 million residents (according to the last census), it certainly is the most populous borough of the city and at 71 square miles, it's also the largest. Which is all a long way of saying it's very difficult to pin down the nature of Brooklyn, as it's just too darn big to be summarized in a nutshell.

The two most affluent neighborhoods are **Brooklyn Heights,** which is right off the Brooklyn Bridge, boasting spectacular views of Manhattan; and **Park Slope,** the area surrounding Frederick Law Olmstead's *other* great work of landscape architecture (after Central Park), Prospect Park. Both are stellar strolling areas, filled with lovely Beaux Arts brownstone buildings (Brooklyn Heights was the first neighborhood in the city to be landmarked).

The borough's artists tend to live in Red Hook, Williamsburg (though many are getting priced out here), and a few hold-outs still live in DUMBO (the area "Down Under the Manhattan Bridge Overpass"). You can pop by all for afternoons of gallery hopping. **Williamsburg** has one of the largest Hasidic Jewish communities in the world. Walk the streets peopled by this sect and you may feel as if you've stepped back into an old country Shtetl (an illusion only somewhat ruined by the incongruous but ever-present cellphones).

Eastern Europe also makes an appearance in **Brighton Beach,** which has the largest ex-pat Russian community in the world. It's not the friendliest area, but fascinating to visit nonetheless, with stores selling endless rows of nesting dolls and Lenin t-shirts, and small-scale nightclubs that out-glitz and out-crass Vegas. Just up the shore from Brighton Beach is famed **Coney Island,** which is open again, despite the ravages of Hurricane Sandy. It's still an amusement park, though one with less panache than in its heyday.

Among the touristic highlights of the borough are the view from the **Brooklyn Heights** promenade; **Peter Luger,** an iconic steakhouse in Williamsburg; the shows at the **Brooklyn Academy of Music;** and in **Park Slope** a constellation of sights including the **Brooklyn Museum,** the **Brooklyn Botanical Gardens,** and **Prospect Park.**

The Bronx

Best for: *Baseball, Italian restaurants, zoos, and gardens*

What you won't find: *Museums, nightlife, other types of noteworthy food, hotels, theater*

I may be condemned for this assessment, but to my mind there are only four reasons a tourist should even think of going to the Bronx: **Yankee Stadium,** the **Bronx Zoo,** the **New York Botanical Gardens,** and the Italian restaurants and stores of **Arthur Avenue.** If you have no interest in any of these sights or facilities, you can skip this giant borough without too much regret.

Queens

Best for: *Museums, ethnic dining, affordable hotels*

What you won't find: *Theaters, great shopping, top architecture*

Archie Bunker no longer lives in Queens. In fact, the grouchy, bigoted xenophobe at the center of the famed 1970s sitcom *All in the Family* probably wouldn't recognize the borough today. In just the past 50 years it's gone from being a somewhat insulated community of Irish- and Italian-Americans to the most international community in the United States.

It's this ability by tourists to globe trot in an afternoon that makes Queens appealing, despite the dreary, industrial look of much of it. Whether you're downing samosas or shopping for saris in very Indian **Jackson Heights;** breaking plates at a Greek restaurant in Astoria; or buying miracle water and tacos at a Mexican *botanica* in Corona, there's much to taste, smell, and experience.

Museums are another big draw, and the borough now tops Brooklyn for its cultural attractions, boasting four great ones: **The Museum of the Moving Image, PS 1 Museum of Contemporary Art, Isamu Noguchi Galleries,** and **the Louis Armstrong House.**

Staten Island

Best for: *Views of Manhattan from the ferry*

What you won't find: *Notable museums, nightlife, hotels, theaters, truly great restaurants, interesting architecture*

And I'll again be blunt: Except for the fun and free ferry ride here, there's no reason a tourist should visit here. Yes, there are a handful of cultural and historic sites, but none that justify the commute.

WHERE TO STAY

Time now for a change of mood. In a book that celebrates the fun and attractions of New York, it's necessary for just a short while—the length of this chapter—to deal with a far less pleasant topic: the over-priced accommodations of New York. By and large, hotels in Gotham charge more than hotels anywhere else in the U.S. (an average of $300 per night) for rooms that often aren't nearly as spacious or full of amenities. Why? Over 52 million people visited NYC in 2013, keeping occupancy rates at over 85% for much of the year. Hotels could charge pretty much whatever they darn pleased . . . and most of them did.

3

But though I concede this unpleasant fact, I'm not discouraged by it. Bargains can still be found in all price categories of hotels. Values do—and will continue to—exist. And this chapter will introduce you to the very best of them, as well as to a few worthy splurges, for those willing to splash out.

Furthermore, the hotels in this book are properties that could only exist in the Big Apple. They will give you a more authentic experience than you could ever have by searching randomly through the Internet. And that promise—it is a promise—will in the end make up for the high cost of lodgings in New York.

PRACTICAL MATTERS: THE HOTEL SCENE
Getting the Best Deal

In the listing below, I've tried to give you an idea of the kind of deals that may be available at particular hotels. But there's no way of knowing what the offers will be when you're booking, so also consider these general tips:

o **Choose your season carefully.** Room rates can vary dramatically—by hundreds of dollars in some cases—depending on what time of year you visit. Winter, from January 4 through mid-March, is best for bargains, with summer (especially July–August) second best. Fall is the busiest and most expensive season after Christmas, but November tends to be quiet and rather affordable, as long as you're not booking a parade-route hotel on Thanksgiving weekend. All bets are off at Christmastime, New Year's and the weekend of the NYC marathon—expect to pay top dollar then.

WHAT YOU'LL really PAY

You'll notice that the rates listed in this chapter are more than a little bit odd. A typical hotel listing will state that rates start at $199 per night but can go up to $399—for the same room category. That's not a typo. Unfortunately, getting a bed in this city is a bit like playing roulette: you never know what number will come up. It's all based on occupancy rates. And in high season, that means hotels charge whatever they feel they can get away with (see more about that below).

I've calculated the rates in this chapter by looking at what discounters are offering in three different seasons and then showing you the range, from low to high. But the sad truth is: **rates can change at any time,** meaning you may find even higher rates than those listed in this guide. I've tried to list the averages, for high and low season, for these hotels, but nothing is average here. Alas, that's the nature of NYC, the city that not only never sleeps, it never stops seeking to squeeze out an extra buck. Good luck!

Bizarrely enough, when the city fills up, lesser quality hotels will often charge prices that are equal to or even higher than the luxury hotels. It makes no sense, but it happens quite often. So it's important to NEVER try and assess the quality of a hotel by the price it's asking. Instead, read the reviews carefully and compare the prices you're being quoted to make sure you're not getting taken.

o **Go uptown, downtown, or to an outer borough.** The advantages of a Midtown location are overrated, especially when saving money is your object. The subway can whisk you anywhere you want to go in minutes; even if you stay on the Upper West Side, you can be at the ferry launch for the Statue of Liberty in about a half-hour. You'll not only get the best value for your money by staying outside the Theater District, in the residential neighborhoods where real New Yorkers live, but you'll have a better overall experience: You won't constantly be fighting crowds, you'll have terrific restaurants nearby, and you'll see what life in the city is really like. Lodgings in Brooklyn and Queens offer particularly good savings.

o **Visit over a weekend.** If your trip includes a weekend, you might be able to save big. Business hotels tend to empty out, and rooms that go for $300 or more Monday through Thursday can drop dramatically, as low as $150 or less, once the execs have headed home. These deals are prevalent in the Financial District, but they're often available in tourist-saturated Midtown, too. Also, you'll find that Sunday nights are the least expensive. Check the hotel's website for weekend specials.

o **Buy a money-saving package deal.** A travel package that combines your airfare and your hotel stay for one price may just be the best bargain of all. In some cases, you'll get airfare, accommodations, transportation to and from the airport, plus extras—maybe an afternoon sightseeing tour or restaurant and shopping discount coupons—for less than the hotel alone would have cost had you booked it yourself. Most airlines and many travel agents, as well as the usual booking websites (Priceline, Travelocity, Expedia) offer good packages to New York City.

o **Shop online.** There are so many ways to save online and through apps, we've devoted an entire box to the topic. See p. 28.

o **Choose a chain.** With some exceptions, I have not listed mass-volume chain hotels in this chapter. In my opinion, they tend to lack the character and local feel that most independently-run hotels have. And it's that feel, I believe, that is so much a part of the travel experience. Still, when you're looking for a deal, they can be a good option. Most hotels—particularly such chains as Comfort Inn and Best Western—are market-sensitive. Because they hate to see rooms sit empty, they'll often negotiate good rates at the last minute and in slow seasons.

You can also pull out all the stops for discounts at a budget chain, from reward points to senior status to corporate rates. Most chain hotels let the kids stay with parents for free. Ask for every kind of discount; if you get an unhelpful reservation agent, call back. Of course, there's no guarantee.

Two chains with franchisees in Manhattan are: **Best Western** (© **800/780-7234;** www.bestwestern.com), though their rack rates for New York hotels are higher than you'd expect, and **Howard Johnson** (© **800/446-4656;** www.hojo.com; its brands in NYC include Wyndham, Night, and Tryp). There's a Best Western at South Street Seaport and at two Midtown locations, and a Howard Johnson in Soho, three in Queens and two in the Bronx. Check their websites for all the details.

At these and other franchised hotels—such as the ones run by **Apple Core Hotels** (www.applecorehotels.com), a management company that handles the **Comfort Inn Midtown,** the **Ramada Inn Eastside,** the **New York Manhattan Hotel** (p. 50), the **Hotel Times Square, La Quinta** (p. 63), along with several others—doubles can go for as little as $109. Scan the chains' websites for the best discounts.

A good source for deals is **Choice Hotels** (© **877/424-6423;** www.hotelchoice.com), which oversees Comfort Inn, Quality Hotel, and Clarion Hotel chains, all of which have Manhattan branches.

o **Avoid excess charges and hidden costs.** Use your own cellphone, pay phones, or prepaid phone cards instead of dialing direct from hotel phones, which usually incur exorbitant rates. Don't be tempted by minibar offerings: Most hotels charge through the nose for water, soda, and snacks. Finally, ask about local taxes and service charges, which can increase the cost of a room by 15% or more. If a hotel insists on charging an "energy surcharge" that wasn't mentioned at check-in, you can often make a case for getting it removed.

o **Make multiple reservations.** This strategy is only necessary in high season. But often then, as the date of the stay approaches, hotels start to play "chicken" with one another, dropping the price a bit one day to try and lure customers away from a nearby competitor. Making this strategy work takes vigilance and persistence, but since your credit card won't be charged until 24-hours before check-in, little risk is involved.

Alternative Accommodations

o **Consider private B&B accommodations.** Alas, it is now illegal to rent short-term vacation apartments in New York City. So I will not be listing the names of companies that offer that service in this book.

However, you can legally rent a room in an apartment, if the owner remains in residence. Think of it as a private B&B (though often breakfast is not included).

This type of stay is usually much cheaper than a hotel room; it allows you to meet a friendly local, and it places you in a residential neighborhood where you live like a local, rather than a visitor. Some of the companies that matchmake for these types of stays include: **Manhattan Getaways** (℗ **212/956-2010;** www. manhattangetaways.com), **Affordable New York City** (℗ **212/33-4001;** www. AffordableNewYorkCity.com), and **AirBnB.com.** Be sure to get all details in writing and an exact price for the stay, including applicable taxes and fees, before booking.

o **Stay at a guesthouse affiliated with a religious order or at a military hotel.** Around Manhattan are a number of specialty lodgings operated by the U.S. Military, various churches, and other non-profit organizations. In some cases they're open to all, in others you must be a member to stay here, but they all are clean, friendly, well-located hotels, offering private rooms (for as little as $100 per night). In the case of the religious hotels, there's no required attendance at services, though at some, unmarried couples are not allowed to share the same room. Here are four we heartily recommend; contact them well ahead of your visit as they do sell out:

The Seafarers and International House (123 E. 15th St., just off Irving Place; ℗ **212/677-4800;** www.sihnyc.org; subway: 4, 5, 6, N, R, L to Union Square). Open to all, run by the Lutheran Church.

Soldiers', Sailors', Marines' & Airmens' Club (283 Lexington Ave., between 36th and 37th sts.; ℗ **800/678-8443** or 212/683-4353; www.ssmaclub.org; subway: 6 to 33rd St.). Open to active military and veterans from the U.S. and allied nations, as well as first responders.

The House of the Redeemer (7 E. 95th St. off Fifth Ave.; ℗ **212/289-0339;** www. houseoftheredeemer.org; subway: 6 to 96th St). Open to all, run by the Episcopal Church.

The Leo House (332 W. 23rd St., between Eighth and Ninth aves.; www.leohouse-nyc.com; ℗ **800/732-2438** or 212/929-1010; subway: E, C to 23rd St). Open to all, run by the Catholic Church.

o **Look into hostels.** Open to people of all ages as well as families, the following hostels have a mix of dorm accommodations and private rooms. Rates start at $50–$60 per person at these facilities, varying by date and type of room. Here are NYC's best maintained hostels:

Hosteling International New York (891 Amsterdam Ave., at the corner of 103rd St.; ℗ **212/932-2300;** www.hinewyork.org; subway: 1 to 103rd St., or 1, 2, 3 to 96th St.)

Jazz on the Park (W. 106th St. between Manhattan Ave. and Central Park West; ℗ **212/932-1600;** www.jazzonthepark.com; subway: B, C to 103rd St.)

Price Categories
We list double rooms only. Please assume that suites will be more pricey, and those few hotels that offer single rooms will do so for less than the rate listed in this guide. **Inexpensive:** $175 and under **Moderate:** $175–$300 **Expensive:** $300 and up

TURNING TO THE internet or apps FOR A HOTEL DISCOUNT

Before going online, it's important that you know what "flavor" of discount you're seeking. Currently, there are four types of online reductions:

1. **Extreme discounts on sites where you bid for lodgings without knowing which hotel you'll get.** You'll find these on such sites as Priceline.com and Hotwire.com, and they can be real money-savers, particularly if you're booking within a week of travel (that's when the hotels get nervous and resort to deep discounts to get beds filled). As these companies use only major chains, you can rest assured that you won't be put up in a dump. For more reassurance, visit the website BetterBidding.com. On it, actual travelers spill the beans about what they bid on Priceline.com and which hotels they got. I think you'll be pleasantly surprised by the quality of many of the hotels that are offering these "secret" discounts to the opaque bidding websites.

2. **Discounts on the hotel's website.** Sometimes these can be great values, as they'll often include such nice perks as free breakfast or parking privileges. Before biting, be sure to look at the discounter sites below.

3. **Discounts on online travel agencies as Hotels.com, Quikbook.com, Expedia.com, and the like.** Some of these sites reserve these rooms in bulk and at a discount, passing along the savings to their customers. But instead of going to them directly, I'd

recommend looking at such dedicated travel search engines as **Hipmunk.com, HotelsCombined.com, Momondo.com,** and **Trivago.com.** These sites list prices from all the discount sites as well as the hotels directly, meaning you have a better chance of finding a discount.

Note: Sometimes the discounts these sites find require advance payment for a room (and draconian cancellation policies), so double check your travel dates before booking.

Another good source for discounts, especially for luxury hotels is **Tingo.com,** a site founded by TripAdvisor. Its model is a bit different than the others. Users make a pre-paid reservation through it, but if the price of the room drops between the time you make the booking and the date of arrival, the site refunds the difference in price.

4. **Try the app HotelsTonight.com.** It only works for the day on which you use it, but WOW!, does it snare great prices for procrastinators (up to 70% off in many cases). A possible strategy: make a reservation at a hotel, then on the day you're arriving try your luck with HotelsTonight. Most hotels will allow you to cancel without penalty, even on the day of arrival.

What I've just discussed involves a lot of surfing, I know, but in the hothouse world of Big Apple hotel pricing, this sort of diligence can pay off.

THE FINANCIAL DISTRICT

In this part of downtown (it's at the southernmost, bottom tip of Manhattan), you are far away from the bustle of Midtown. Busy during the day, the Financial District empties out at night, creating an almost eerie calm to the neighborhood.

Best for: Visitors doing business in the Financial District during the week, people who like things quiet (as quiet as they get in Manhattan) at night. Plus, there are some substantial savings to be found when staying at a Financial District hotel on a weekend.

Drawbacks: It's a fairly long cab/subway/bus ride to many attractions.

Moderate/Expensive

Andaz Wall Street ★★★ Hurricane Sandy's impact was felt at the Andaz, which experienced serious flooding of its concourse level, requiring a thorough re-do of its already impressive gym and spa in 2013. So expect even more state-of-the-art equipment and treatments. Other than that, the Andaz continues to feel like a wonderfully chic haven from the storms of Manhattan. Designed by David Rockwell with a comfy, loft sensibility, the rooms are larger-than-the-norm, with floor-to-ceiling windows that let in scads of light (but are soundproofed for serenity). Filled with plush yet minimalist furnishing and designed for usability (love how the full-length mirror pops into and out of the built-ins), these may be among the most livable rooms in the city. Another perk: complimentary wine and coffee 24-hours in the lobby.

75 Wall St. (at Water St.). www.andazwallstreet.com. © **212/590-1234.** 253 units. $191–$400 double. Subway: 2 or 3 to Wall St. **Amenities:** Restaurant; bar; concierge; fitness center and spa; room service, free Wi-Fi, complimentary snacks and nonalcoholic-beverage minibar; Geneva sound system; unlimited local calls.

The Wall Street Inn ★★ Gracious. That's the first word that pops to mind when one walks into this frilled little inn, a place so old-fashioned it still has a payphone in a nook of the lobby and Laura Ashley-type florals on the walls and furnishings. But the staff are cheery and helpful, the rooms decent-sized (those ending in 01 are smallest, pick the top floor for the least street noise), and the bedding quite plush. Best of all: prices plunge on weekends by a good $100 (in mid-season, you might pay just $199 on a Saturday night but $299 on a Tuesday).

9 S. William St. (at Broad St.). www.thewallstreetinn.com. © **800/747-1500** or 212/747-1500. 46 units. $179–$450 double. Rates include continental breakfast. Subway: 2 or 3 to Wall St.; 4 or 5 to Bowling Green. **Amenities:** Babysitting; concierge; well-outfitted exercise room w/sauna and steam; common guest kitchen w/microwave.

Moderate/Inexpensive

Club Quarters Wall Street ★ Your neighbors at this somewhat bland property will be the movers and shakers who work for J.P. Morgan, Oracle and other Fortune 500 companies. These corporations belong to the "club" here, which means they often pack these motel-like, but pleasant, rooms midweek. On weekends, however, prices drop sharply since so few people know about the property. That, the unusually kindly

Downtown Accommodations

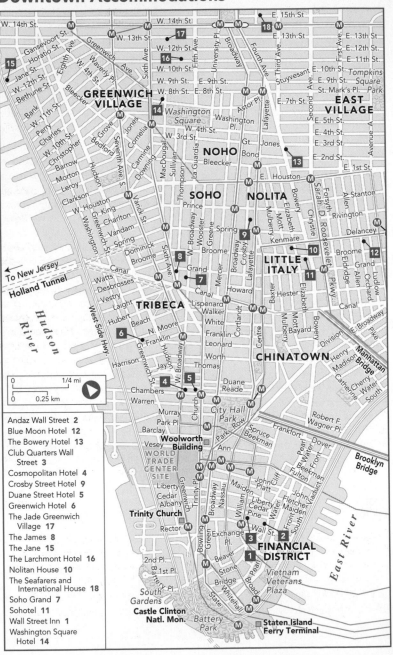

Andaz Wall Street 2
Blue Moon Hotel 12
The Bowery Hotel 13
Club Quarters Wall
 Street 3
Cosmopolitan Hotel 4
Crosby Street Hotel 9
Duane Street Hotel 5
Greenwich Hotel 6
The Jade Greenwich
 Village 17
The James 8
The Jane 15
The Larchmont Hotel 16
Nolitan House 10
The Seafarers and
 International House 18
Soho Grand 7
Sohotel 11
Wall Street Inn 1
Washington Square
 Hotel 14

staff, and its location in the heart of the canyons of Wall Street, make it a good pick for penny-pinchers.

52 William St. (at Wall St.). www.clubquarters.com. ℭ **212/269-6400.** 289 units. $150–$290 double. Subway: 2 or 3 to Wall St.; 4 or 5 to Bowling Green. **Amenities:** Restaurant; bar; small but well-outfitted exercise room.

TRIBECA, THE LOWER EAST SIDE & NOLITA

Arguably the most expensive real estate in New York, TriBeCa is a mostly residential neighborhood with excellent restaurants. Both TriBeCa and the Lower East Side offer a taste of New York neighborhood living with lots of street life.

Best for: A taste of life Downtown with a capital "D." The Lower East Side, in particular, boasts some of the city's most vibrant clubs and hippest restaurants.

Drawbacks: Both neighborhoods are a little off the beaten track in terms of sightseeing, and the LES is hard to get to via public transportation.

Expensive

The Greenwich Hotel★★   Named for the street it's on, this plush hotel could as easily be named for Greenwich, CT. It has that same sort of "old money" feel to it. By which I mean, while elegant it's not overdesigned. Walls tend to be cream colored, with just a few pieces of art on them (many created by co-owner Robert DeNiro's father). The couches are velvety and squashy, like you might find at an English manor house. Touches such as a fireplace in one suite, and a real sauna in another, tell you you've entered the upper strata of NYC hotels. Need more evidence? Room service comes from one of the best Italian restaurants in town (Locanda Verde, p. 68), and guests have their own private lounge and garden in which to eat and drink (when I was there, Heidi Klum and her four children were enjoying a meal). The basement spa, with a swimming pool topped with the beams of an ancient Japanese farmhouse, is just as understated yet, unmistakably, lux. Final touch? If you need to travel anywhere below 34th Street, the hotel's limo will sweep you there at no extra charge.

377 Greenwich St. (at Franklin St.). www.thegreenwichhotel.com. ℭ **212/941-8900.** 88 units. $525–$650 double. Subway: 1 to Chambers St. **Amenities:** Restaurant; concierge; fitness club; indoor heated pool; spa; limo service; free Wi-Fi; free in-room snacks.

Pet Policies

I've indicated in the listings in this chapter those hotels that accept pets. However, understand that these policies may have limitations, such as weight and breed restrictions; may require an extra fee, deposit and/or a signed waiver against damages; and may be revoked at any time. Always inquire when booking if you're bringing Fluffy or Spike— *never* just show up with a pet in tow.

Moderate/Expensive

Blue Moon Hotel ★ You don't have to be Jewish to stay at New York's first Kosher hotel, just a lover of history, as the owners here take the heritage of the Lower East Side seriously. Rooms are named after the famous men and women who came from the 'hood (Fanny Brice, Milton Berle), and a mezuzah graces every guestroom door (that's the Jewish talisman that's nailed to the doorframe of Jewish homes; it contains the opening words of the Old Testament). Best of all, these (often) apartment-sized rooms are filled with furniture that looks like a cousin of what would have been in use a century ago (the beds are more comfortable now, though many have old-fashioned wrought iron frames). And if you *are* Jewish, even better: the included continental breakfast comes from a local kosher bakery and the free happy hour features a surprisingly good kosher wine.

100 Orchard St. (near Delancey St.). www.bluemoon-nyc. ℂ **212/533-9080.** 45 units. $200–$350 double. Subway: F to Delancey St. **Amenities:** Free breakfast; concierge; free Wi-Fi; free wine and cheese.

Duane Street Hotel ★★ Not that it matters (ahem), but the Duane may well have the handsomest staff in Manhattan, suave young fellows with vaguely European accents and just the right amount of stubble. The rooms in this slim hotel (just 26 feet wide) are just as dashing, if petite at the lower price categories, with high ceilings and shiny black walls, off-set by sleek blond wood built-ins (all designed to maximize the space) and cool pieces of art here and there. Such niceties as rainfall showers and iPod docking stations add to the plush vibe. Among the other pluses: workable in-room desks and cookies 24-hours at reception.

130 Duane St. (at Church St.). www.duanestreethotel.com. ℂ **212/964-4600.** 45 units. $229–$414 double. Subway: A or C to Chambers St. **Amenities:** Restaurant; concierge; free passes to nearby Equinox gym; free Wi-Fi.

Nolitan Hotel ★★ "Hello There" reads the carpet in the elevators, an obvious sign—not needed—that this is one of the friendliest hotels in the city. Guests can already tell, thanks to the free, nightly happy hour in the living room-like lobby; the offers of multiple loaners to guests (before you arrive, they'll let you know that you can use their laptops, iPads, and bikes while on property); and the gracious service. Rooms, too, have a happy air to them with bright splashes of color on a blanket or chair, which contrasts nicely to the shabby-chic concrete ceilings (this was once a parking garage). Some rooms even have that rare-for-NYC amenity: a balcony. For really great views—at slightly more expense—ask for the "cityscape" rather than the "neighborhood" rooms. In 2013, the hotel added two rooms in a former storage area, a sign of how popular the place is—book early!

30 Kenmare St., (btw. Elizabeth and Mott sts.). www.nolitanhotel.com. ℂ **212/925-2555.** 55 units. $229–$355 double. Subway: 6 to Spring St. **Amenities:** Restaurant; bar; concierge; 24-room service; pets allowed; bicycle and skateboard complimentary rentals; free use of a nearby, full-service gym.

Inexpensive/Moderate

Cosmopolitan Hotel–Tribeca ★ George Washington never slept here, but the staff at the Cosmopolitan swear that Abraham Lincoln did, back when the building was

Hotel Girard. Built in the 1840s, it's always been a hotel of some sort or another, and the Lilliputian dimensions of some of the cheaper rooms reflect how much smaller people were back then. Still, it's often a great value, with simple but comfortable furnishings (think Ikea) and a crack housekeeping staff that keep everything extremely tidy (no fraying carpets or tell-tale signs of the last guest here).

95 W. Broadway (at Chambers St.). www.cosmohotel.com. © **888/895-9400** or 212/566-1900. 105 units. $120–$279 double. Subway: 1, 2, 3, A, or C to Chambers St. **Amenities:** Free Wi-Fi; room service; fitness room.

Sohotel ★   One of the oldest hotels in the city (built in 1822), Sohotel housed Union soldiers during the Civil War. They probably wouldn't recognize it today—in fact, people who visited just 5 years ago wouldn't recognize it, as the hotel has had some major improvements. Flat-screen TVs and handsome bureaus now grace rooms; walls are chic exposed brick or painted a happy shade of yellow or blue. There are some lapses still, especially in the mattress department: if you get a stony one, ask to be moved (they vary by room). Also asked for another room if you're placed in one ending in the numbers 21, 23, or 25, as these overlook a popular bar and can be noisy. But in general, the standard of service and comfort has changed for the better. *Warning:* This is not the place for people with mobility impairments, as there are steps to the lobby and many of the rooms.

341 Broome St. (near Bowery). www.sohotel.com. © **800/737-0702** or 212/566-1900. 105 units. $117–$279 double. Subway: 1, 2, 3, A, or C to Chambers St. **Amenities:** Free Wi-Fi.

SOHO

Despite numerous chain stores moving into SoHo, the area still has great charm, due to its abundance of cast-iron buildings. In terms of hotels, the neighborhood is strictly high end.

Best for: A stay in the SoHo area offers close proximity to Chinatown, designer-name shopping, and some very fine restaurants.

Drawbacks: You won't find much in the way of budget/value accommodations in the neighborhood. Also, because of the downtown arts scene, Soho has two high seasons: May and June as well as the fall months. So you'll find fewer deals here than in other areas.

Expensive

Crosby Street Hotel ★★★   As much gallery as hotel, the Crosby Street is eye-candy of the first degree. Designed by co-owner Kit Cosby, every room and every public area features quirky, often funny, and always compelling works of sculpture and painting. This includes the guestrooms, each of which has a different look from the next (mine was all done in black and white, but others are saturated with colors, perhaps taking on the ambiance of a garden, or the vibrant color palette of Morocco). Floor-to-ceiling warehouse-style windows light up the rooms and the deluxe bathrooms feature such niceties as heated towel racks and bidets. None of this comes cheap, but with an on-site movie theater, fabulous location, and a very good restaurant, the Crosby Hotel is perfect for a special-occasion stay.

79 Crosby St. (btw. Prince and Spring sts.). www.crosbystreethotel.com. ✆ **212/226-6400.** 86 units. $489–$675 double. Subway: N or R to Prince St. **Amenities:** Restaurant; bar; concierge; fitness center; room service; screening room; free Wi-Fi.

The James ★★ Welcome to the "locavore" hotel. Everything at the James is meant, in some way, to celebrate and reflect New York City, a concept that works in spades. So, the luxurious sheets on the beds are bought from a local manufacturer, as are the chocolates placed on the pillows each evening. The hallways are a gallery to New York City artists; simply train your cellphone at the barcodes embedded on the walls to learn more about each one. Best of all, this skyscraper hotel, custom built in 2010, is all glass, so the "sky lobby" and every guestroom, has spectacular, floor-to-ceiling views, bringing NYC directly into your bedroom. Other perks include a plunge pool and hip rooftop lounge called **The Jimmy,** an urban garden on the second floor for more outdoor lounging; and room service from star chef David Burke, whose restaurant is on the first floor.

27 Grand St. (at Thompson St). www.jameshotels.com. ✆ **888/526-3778.** 114 units. $279–$540 double. Subway: 1 to Canal St. **Amenities:** Restaurant; bar; concierge; rooftop pool; fitness center with complimentary training sessions; pet friendly; room service; free Wi-Fi.

Moderate/Expensive

Soho Grand ★★ Very few hotels actually deserve the honorific but in this case the hotel's not only "grand," but grand in a wonderfully "New York" way. You enter from one of the chicest streets in the city (West Broadway) to a space that's at once post-industrial (lots of exposed brick) and utterly magnificent, with soaring ceilings, massive drapes, and gargantuan stuffed peacocks that hang in gilded cages over the lounge. (Silly, but it works.) Rooms (which start at a decent-for-NYC 230 square feet), have a subtle "50 Shades of Gray"-vibe to them, thanks to the leather backboards and silky linens on the beds, contrasted with the hard edges of the brass tables. If you're looking for a sexy, weekend getaway, you've found it. Don't book through the hotel, though; you'll get better prices through Hotels.com, Expedia.com or the app Hotels-Tonight (and I got that bit of intel directly from one of the hotel's staff).

310 W. Broadway (btw. Canal and Grand sts.). www.sohogrand.com. ✆ **212/389-1000.** 353 units. $241–$432 double. Subway: 6, N, R, Q to Canal St. **Amenities:** Restaurant; bar; nightclub; concierge; fitness center; room service.

THE VILLAGE

Greenwich Village, despite the influx of big name stores, still has that romantic appeal, with its winding, narrow streets, brownstones, and intimate dining spots.

Best for: People who love to explore classic/historic old neighborhoods, close to shops, restaurants, bars, and clubs.

Drawbacks: Can be noisy and crowded, particularly on weekends. While it's got its residential streets, Downtown is where New York (and the surrounding area) goes to party.

Expensive

The Bowery Hotel ★★★ The "wow" factor is high at the Bowery Hotel, which channels the kind of grand mansions E.M. Forster would have described (think

PLENTY OF room AT THE INN

Don't assume that all NYC hotels are in skyscrapers. This is a diverse city, and that diversity can be found in its accommodations, too. If you want an alternative to the quintessential huge Gotham hotel, a taste of urban hominess, try the following options.

Breakfast prepared by culinary students of the New School is one of the highlights of the **Inn on 23rd Street ★**. Each of the inn's 14 rooms is distinctly decorated by the personable owners, Annette and Barry Fisherman, with items they've collected from their travels over the years. See p. 39 for a detailed review.

The first home of the Gay Men's Health Crisis, an 1850 brownstone in the heart of Chelsea, is now the quirky **Colonial House Inn,** 318 W. 22nd St. (www.colonialhouseinn.com; ✆ **212/243-9669**). This 20-room four-story walk-up caters to a largely GLBT clientele, but everybody is welcome. Some rooms have shared bathrooms; deluxe rooms have private bathrooms, and some have working fireplaces. The roof deck is a popular meeting place for guests and non-guests alike.

On the residential, Upper West Side is the very special **Inn New York City ★★★** (p. 58), where there are just four swank self-contained units so comfortable you will be hard pressed to leave and see much of the city.

For another genuine New York brownstone experience, head to Harlem. It's anything but a flophouse, but that's what they call **Harlem Flophouse,** 242 W. 123rd St., between Adam Clayton Powell and Frederick Douglass boulevards (www.harlemflophouse.com; ✆ **347/632-1960**). Owner René Calvo has restored the historic row house to Harlem Renaissance splendor, when the "flophouse" was frequented by top musicians and artists of that era. If you visit in the summer, you just might get invited to one of Calvo's impromptu barbecues.

In a lovely area of Brooklyn, the **Sofia Inn** (p. 63) offers up two family-friendly, floor-wide suites, and four very affordable rooms that share bathrooms. Near subways and the Brooklyn Museum, it's an ideal way to experience life in this vibrant borough. A second choice, as the commute into Manhattan is longer, and it's not near any tourist sights, is the friendly and affordable **Honey's B&B** (p. 63).

Finally, consider three inns with very similar names—the **Chelsea Lodge ★★** (p. 39), the **Chelsea Pines Inn ★★** (p. 38), and the **Chelsea Inn** (p. 39)—but very different characters. The Lodge has charm aplenty, but no private bathrooms; the Pines is run by a charismatic owner and is the most service-heavy of the three; and the "Inn" is the choice for budgeteers, as prices here are often amongst the cheapest in Manhattan.

ultra-luxurious colonial outposts). The lobby—which you should visit for a drink, even if you don't stay here—is decorated with fine pieces of woodwork and furniture salvaged (I was told) from European churches and historic homes; the tile floors and walls, too, speak of long journeys from abroad (Morocco, most likely). But though the hotel looks old, it was actually built in 2007 by New York University as a dorm (they changed their minds and sold the building off). Oddly, no two guestrooms are alike (you'd think NYU would have wanted more consistency), but all are light-bathed and comfy, with more antique furnishings, fine linens and a teddy bear (dressed as one of the bellmen), gracing each bed.

335 Bowery (at 3rd St.). www.theboweryhotel.com. ✆ **212/505-9100.** 135 units. $345–$505 double. Subway: 6 to Bleecker St. **Amenities:** Restaurant; bar; concierge; room service; gym; free Wi-Fi.

Moderate/Expensive

The Jade Greenwich Village ★
If hotels were movie stars, this one would be Carol Lombard. It has that 1930s glamour and swagger, from the ornate red headboards on the beds (same design but in blue in the suites) to the sleek art deco lamps and heavy curtains. And the real dial telephones on the bedside tables are a hoot. On the ground floor is a hidden, speak-easy-like bar/restaurant; the hotel also has a gym and outdoor terrace. Though it only opened in spring of 2013, it already is quite popular (the terrific Village location doesn't hurt). That being said, the rooms are too small for the high season prices they charge. Only book here if you can get a decent rate.

52 W. 13th St. (btw. Fifth and Sixth aves.). www.thejadenyc.com. ✆ **800/222-0418** or 212/777-9515. 160 units; $221–$515 double. Subway: B to 14th St. **Amenities:** Restaurant; bar; exercise room.

Washington Square Hotel ★
This hotel has always had a top location, right off graceful Washington Square Park, but today has a decor to match, filled with Art Deco touches and paintings, murals, and photos that pay homage to the many stars who stayed here over the years. Built in 1904, it served as a second home for many top vaudeville and Broadway performers until the '50s, when it devolved into a rather seedy apartment hotel housing a number of struggling artists, actors, and musicians, including Joan Baez, Bob Dylan, Barbra Streisand, Bill Cosby, and Phyllis Diller. Legend has it that the Mamas and the Papas wrote "California Dreamin'" on a gray winter day at the Washington Square. The rooms, though small, are smartly designed with cushy duvets, richly jeweled-colored walls, and space-saving features (such as wall-mounted TVs) that make the rooms appear *slightly* bigger than they actually are.

103 Waverly Place (btw. Fifth and Sixth aves.). www.wshotel.com. ✆ **800/222-0418** or 212/777-9515. 160 units; $215–$312 double. Rates include continental breakfast. Subway: A, B, C, D, E, F to 4th St. (use 3rd St. exit). **Amenities:** Restaurant and lounge; exercise room.

Inexpensive

The Jane ★★
In 1912, when the survivors of the Titanic were brought by the SS Carpathian back to New York, many stayed that first night at this hotel. It seems appropriate therefore that most of the Jane's rooms have the look of a ship's cabin (or perhaps a railway sleeping car)—highly compact with a shelf above the bed for luggage. Let me go a bit further in explaining what I mean by "compact": these may well be the smallest rooms in NYC (which says a lot)—when I was standing in one recently, I spread out my arms and came within about 5 inches of touching both walls at once. So this ain't the place for claustrophobes. Rooms for two, in the lower category, have bunk beds, making the space seem even smaller. As you might expect, the cheaper rooms all share bathrooms; larger, pricier rooms have private facilities. That being said, these dollhouse size rooms have every luxury they can cram in: the walls are paneled with burnished anigre wood, a marble counter at the

window doubles as a tiny desk and boasts an iPod docking station, and a flat-screen TV is attached to the wall at the foot of the bed. Two bars—one on the roof and one in the massive lounge area in the lobby—are true scenester haunts, and the public areas are really fun, looking like they were lifted from a movie about opium dens in the "Gay '90s."

114 Jane St. (at West St.). www.thejanenyc.com. © **212/924-6700.** 170 units. $125–$145 double. Subway: A, C, E to 14th St. **Amenities:** Restaurant; 2 bars; free loaner bikes; free Wi-Fi.

Larchmont Hotel ★★   Location, location, location. Those are the key elements that the Larchmont offers in spades, as it's situated on one of the prettiest tree-lined streets in the Village, a block of historic brownstones just a short stroll from top dining, shopping, and the subway. What the Larchmont doesn't have (because the hotel is housed in a historic Beaux Arts-era brownstone) are private bathrooms and showers for the guest rooms—it simply doesn't have the plumbing to support multiple loos. Instead, travelers share two toilets and two showers per floor (with either six or seven other rooms). Should this keep you from choosing this hotel for your stay? I hope not, because other than the fact that you have to pad down the hallway to use the facilities, this is a charming, extremely well-maintained hotel in which the owners strive to keep the period feel throughout, filling the rooms with rattan furniture, bookshelves brimming with hardcover books, and good firm beds. There are also some very high-class amenities here, such as portable sacks of really nice soaps and shampoos and cotton robes and slippers.

27 W. 11th St. (btw. Fifth and Sixth aves.). www.larchmonthotel.com. © **212/989-9333.** 62 units, all with shared bathroom. $90–$125 single; $119–$149 double. Rates include continental breakfast. Children 12 and under stay free in parent's room. Subway: A, B, C, D, E, F to W. 4th St. (use 8th St. exit). **Amenities:** Common kitchenette.

CHELSEA

Now the center of contemporary art in Manhattan, Chelsea has also surpassed the West Village in housing the largest and most prominent gay community in the city. You'll find some good nightlife in Chelsea, and it's just a short walk to the shopping of Herald Square, to Union Square, and Madison Square Garden.

Best for: People who want to be close to the action, but not in the center of it; a good range of accommodations from high-end to moderate.

Drawbacks: Can be noisy at night along the main drags (especially the avenues and along 23rd Street).

Expensive

Dream Downtown ★★★   Remember the Woody Allen movie "Sleeper"? You'll feel like you've awakened into that film when you arise in the morning in your all white and groovy room, with its massive round window (upon which a silvery curtain floats), the walls cut out like an origami project. Oddly, the design for the hotel (which has more of a modern Vegas-aspect in the lobby) is by Hendel and Company, the same folks who did the sombre 9/11 Memorial. When it first opened, this high-design drew a lot of celebrities. Today, you're more likely to share the outdoor pool (complete with rentable cabanas), the party bar on the rooftop, and massive, state-of-the-art gym, with corporate execs (a large sign at the check-in counter permanently welcomes Google staffers; their corporate headquarters is next door). Still, if you want to feel like a celeb, ignore the scruffy, programmer-types who are your fellow guests, and indulge.

355 W. 16th St. (off Ninth Ave.). www.dreamhotels.com. ℰ **877/753-7326** or 646/625-4847. 315 units. $243–$509 double, though the discounter Otel.com often shaves that top price by $200, even in high season. Subway: A, E, C to 14th St, L to Eighth Ave. **Amenities:** Restaurant; bar; outdoor pool; large gym; roof terrace with bar.

Eventi ★★   I must start this review with a warning; when I visited in 2013, a large hole in the ground, ready for construction of another (competing) hotel, sat next to this property. So by the time you read this, there may be some major construction noise to contend with for those who choose to stay here. But . . . that could lead to discounts, which would be an overall win, as this is quite a nice property, with spacious, handsome guest rooms (can't beat Kimpton's signature bed, Frette linens, and floor-to-ceiling windows), nightly wine reception, a good-sized gym, and on-site spa. Last year, the hotel got rid of its business center and instead lends any guest who asks a laptop computer, iPad, Kindle, you name it. Guests can even print documents from their rooms on these devices, which may be why the hotel is so popular among business travelers. As for the neighborhood, it's central if a bit industrial. But subways and your own two feet can whisk you to more interesting 'hoods in minutes.

851 Sixth Ave. (btw. 29th and 30th sts.). www.eventihotel.com. ℰ **212/564-4567.** 292 units. $331–$471 double. Subway: B, D, F, M, N, R, Q to 34th Street. **Amenities:** Restaurant; food court; concierge; fitness center; room service; spa; pets welcome; free Wi-Fi.

Moderate/Expensive

Chelsea Pines Inn ★★★   The most welcoming hotel in the Chelsea area (and one of the friendliest in Manhattan) is owned and operated by Jay Lesiger, a native Brooklynite who seems bent on dispelling the myth that New Yorkers are cold and unfriendly. Jay bends over backwards to make sure guests enjoy their visit; along with personally baking a different loaf of bread for each morning's breakfast (it's served amidst an ample spread of bagels, fruits, and cereals), he and his staff publish a daily newsletter for guests covering walking tours, concerts, and other events happening that day. Jay also serves as concierge and is happy to make dinner reservations (he's worked out a 10% discount at some of the best local restaurants), book limousines, and get theater tickets, for which he takes no commission whatsoever (in fact, he scours the Web for cheaper seats for his guests). He and his partner opened the guesthouse in 1985 when it was a rundown boarding house. To hide the scarred walls (since renovated), Jay covered them with his large collection of movie posters, and the tradition stuck: Now each room is named after a different star and filled with movie memorabilia. Rooms are cozy and pretty, the beds topped with 300-thread-count sheets. I'd recommend a room on the second or third floor, where the ceilings are higher. Single rooms are available for a lesser amount than the doubles. *One final note:* Though 70% of the guests at Chelsea Pines are gay, everyone is made to feel comfortable here, and I highly recommend this hotel for people of all orientations. It's a genuinely special place.

317 W. 14th St. (btw. Eighth and Ninth aves.). www.chelseapinesinn.com. ℰ **212/929-1023.** 22 units. $219–$319 double. Subway: A, C, E to 14th St, L to Eighth Ave. **Amenities:** Continental breakfast; concierge; free Wi-Fi.

Inn on 23rd Street ★   A genuine B&B, of only 13 rooms, each far more spacious than New York-bound travelers expect, the Inn on 23rd isn't as pretty as its competing Inn New York City on the Upper West Side (p. 58), but it isn't nearly as pricey, either. Instead, the rooms are quaint, each with a theme—the canopy room has a four-poster bed, Ken's Cabin has a Vermonty-look to it, you get the picture. A generous breakfast is included in the library (which is filled with guidebooks, yay!); in the evenings, guests gather here to partake of the reasonably priced honor bar and tinkle the keys of an upright piano. And because it's so small, staff and guests seem to develop far more of a rapport than usual. When I last visited, I overheard the front desk clerk having a lively discussion with a guest on line at TKTS, who was trying to pick which play to see. They chatted like old friends, and he made no attempt to rush her off the phone. Now that's service!

131 W. 23rd St. (btw. Sixth and Seventh aves.). www.innon23rd.com. ℂ **877/387-2323** or 212/463-0330. 13 units. $199–$319 double, including continental breakfast; best discounts at Agoda.com. Extra person $50. Children 11 and under stay free in parent's room. Subway: F or 1 to 23rd St. **Amenities:** Restaurant; complimentary computer use; cozy library w/stereo and VCR; free Wi-Fi and local and long-distance calls.

Inexpensive

Chelsea Inn ★   Straddling the border between two great neighborhoods, the Chelsea Inn's prices are low because many rooms share a bathroom (never more than two rooms to a toilet, and you'll have a shower and sink in your room). It has a lived-in ambience, thanks to a decor of mismatched antique bedsteads, old wooden armoires, gracefully swooping curtains, and patchwork quilts on the firm beds—kind of like what you'd find in the home of an elderly aunt. A nice touch: All rooms have small fridges and coffeemakers.

46 W. 17th St., (near Fifth Ave.). www.chelseainn.com. ℂ **800/640-6469** or 212/645-8989. $71–$169 double. Subway: Q, N, R, L, 4, 5, 6, L to Union Square. **Amenities:** Free Wi-Fi.

Chelsea Lodge ★★   What do you get when you cross a traditional Greek Revival town house with a Midwestern hunting and fishing cabin? The result might be very close to what you find at this refreshingly quirky, original inn (think a décor of duck decoys, family portraits, and gingham wallpaper). The only downside here is that, with the exception of four suite/apartments, guest rooms have only showers and sinks, with guests sharing toilets, one for every four rooms. But that seems like a small inconvenience for lodgings this adorable and friendly. Rooms come equipped with nice quilt-covered beds, useable desks, and flat-screen cable TVs.

318 W. 20th St. (btw. Eighth and Ninth aves.). www.chelsealodge.com. ℂ **800/373-1116** or 212/243-4499. 22 units, all with semiprivate bathroom. $99–$169 single; $109–$179 double. Subway: 1 to 18th St.; C or E to 23rd St. **Amenities:** Free Wi-Fi; breakfast included.

UNION SQUARE, FLATIRON DISTRICT & GRAMERCY PARK

Farmer's markets, topnotch restaurants, an active street life and pockets of charming brownstones and historic buildings—what's there not to like about this tripartite district? I think it's probably the best place in the city to base yourself, partially because

Midtown Accommodations

Affinia Dumont **20**
Americana Inn **22**
Ameritania Hotel **39**
Andaz Fifth Avenue **25**
Bryant Park Hotel **24**
The Carlton Arms **10**
The Casablanca Hotel **48**
The Chatwal **31**
Chelsea Inn **3**
Chelsea Lodge **6**
Chelsea Pines Inn **4**
Dream Downtown **5**
Hotel Elysees **34**
Eventi Hotel **13**
414 Hotel **45**
Gansevoort Park Hotel **18**
Gershwin Hotel **12**
Gramercy Park Hotel **9**
Hotel Grand Union **19**
Herald Square Hotel **14**
Hotel 17 **1**
Hyatt Union Square **2**
Inn on 23rd Street **8**
King and Grove **17**
Leo House **7**
Library Hotel **26**
Langham Place **21**
The Mayfair Hotel **43**
The Milford NYC **7**
The Michelangelo **40**
New York Manhattan Hotel **15**
The Nomad **11**
Novotel **40**
The Out Hotel **51**
Le Parker Meridien **37**
The Park Savoy **36**
The Plaza Hotel **35**
The Pod Hotel **28, 33**
Radisson Martinique **14**
The Refinery Hotel **23**
Roommate Grace Hotel **47**
The Royalton Hotel **29**
Salisbury Hotel **38**
Skyline Hotel **42**
Sofitel New York **30**
St. Giles—The Tuscany **27**
Travel Inn **50**
Waldorf Astoria **32**
Washington Jefferson Hotel **41**
Hotel Wolcott **15**
Yotel **49**

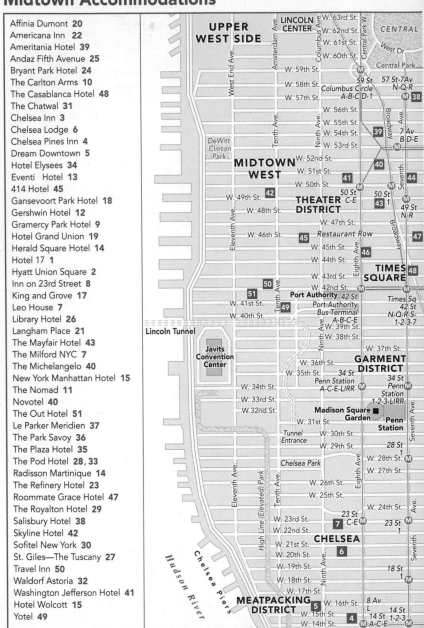

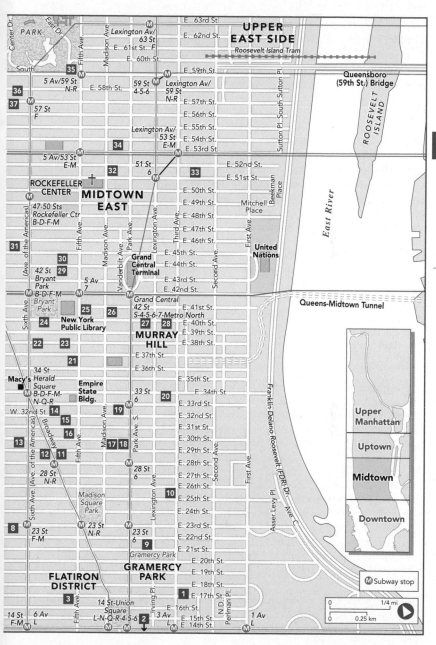

CENTER Dr.

PARK

East Dr.

South

Fifth Ave.

Lexington Ave.

Madison Ave.

E. 63rd St.

Lexington Av/
63 St

E. 62nd St.

**UPPER
EAST SIDE**

Roosevelt Island Tram

E. 61st St. F

E. 60th St.

E. 59th St.

**Queensboro
(59th St.) Bridge**

35

5 Av/59 St
N-R

E. 58th St.

59 St
4-5-6

Lexington Av/
59 St
N-R

E. 57th St.

36

37

57 St
F

E. 56th St.

E. 55th St.

Lexington Av/
53 St
E-M

E. 54th St.

34

E. 53rd St.

E. 52nd St.

5 Av/53 St
E-M

32

51 St
6

33

E. 51st St.

**ROCKEFELLER
CENTER**

E. 50th St.

**MIDTOWN
EAST**

E. 49th St.

Mitchell
Place

47-50 Sts
Rockefeller Ctr
B-D-F-M

E. 48th St.

E. 47th St.

31

E. 46th St.

**United
Nations**

30

Grand
Central
Terminal

E. 45th St.

29

42 St
Bryant
Park
B-D-F-M

E. 44th St.

5 Av
7

E. 43rd St.

Bryant
Park

E. 42nd St.

Grand Central
42 St
S-4-5-6-7-Metro North

25

26

Queens-Midtown Tunnel

24

**New York
Public Library**

27

28

E. 40th St.

22

23

**MURRAY
HILL**

E. 39th St.

E. 38th St.

21

E. 37th St.

34 St
Herald
Square
B-D-F-M-
N-Q-R

E. 36th St.

Macy's

E. 35th St.

**Empire
State
Bldg.**

E. 34th St

33 St
6

20

W. 32nd St.

14

E. 33rd St.

15

E. 32nd St.

19

E. 31st St.

16

E. 30th St.

13

E. 29th St.

12

11

17

18

E. 28th St.

28 St
N-R

28 St
6

E. 27th St.

E. 26th St.

10

E. 25th St.

**Madison
Square
Park**

E. 24th St.

8

23 St
F-M

23 St
N-R

23 St
6

E. 23rd St.

E. 22nd St.

9

E. 21st St.

Gramercy Park

**GRAMERCY
PARK**

E. 20th St.

**FLATIRON
DISTRICT**

E. 19th St.

E. 18th St.

3

1

E. 17th St.

14 St-Union
Square
L-N-Q-R-4-5-6

E. 16th St.

2

14 St
F-M

6 Av
L

E. 15th St.

E. 14th St.

East River

ROOSEVELT ISLAND

Sutton Pl. South Sutton Pl.

First Ave.

Beekman Place

Second Ave.

Third Ave.

Lexington Ave.

Park Ave.

Vanderbilt Ave.

Madison Ave.

Fifth Ave.

(Ave. of the Americas)

Sixth Ave.

Broadway

Fifth Ave.

Park Ave. S.

Irving Pl.

N.D. Perlman Pl.

Asser Levy Pl.

Franklin-Delano-Roosevelt (FDR) Dr.

Ave. C.

1 Av
L

3 Av
L

**Upper
Manhattan**

Uptown

Midtown

Downtown

Ⓜ **Subway stop**

0   1/4 mi

0   0.25 km

Union Square is one of the most useful hubs in the subway system, hosting a crosstown train (the L), several that go from east to west (the N, Q, and R) and the green line that runs up the east side (4, 5, 6).

Best for: People who like a centrally located neighborhood that's not dominated by skyscrapers, but still has great lodging, shopping, theater, and dining options, and easy subway connections.

Drawbacks: Not the cheapest neighborhood in Manhattan, plus no museums or other tourist sights are here.

Expensive

Gramercy Park Hotel ★★★   One of the most coveted status symbols in NYC is a key to Gramercy Park (only those apartments overlooking the city's only private park get one). Stay here, though and you can join the elite, in more ways than just park access. Few hotels in the city, or anywhere for that matter, are as truly luxurious or as riotously artistic. The public spaces of this 1925-built gem are *de facto* galleries, where the art changes every other month and features such heavy hitters as Damien Hirst and Andy Warhol. The rooms are aglow with the colors of a Tiffany lamp and filled with fine photography plus an exquisite mix of Edwardian and modern furnishings—an embroidered chair here, a velvet headboard there, DVD players hidden in mahogany English drinking cabinets. One of the best Italian restaurants in the city, Danny Meyer's **Maialino** (p. 80) not only has residence in the lobby but is responsible for the 24-hour room service. A true original, and sometimes it even discounts (go to such sites as Trivago or Momondo for price cuts).

2 Lexington Ave. (at 21st St.). www.gramercyparkhotel.com. ℂ **212/920-3300.** 185 units. $367–$519 double. Subway: 6 to 23rd St. **Amenities:** 2 Restaurants; 2 bars; concierge; fitness center and spa; room service; rooftop lounge; key to Gramercy Park.

The NoMad ★★★   Imagine if Gustave Klimt and Edward Gorey were to collaborate on the design of a hotel, and you'll have a good sense of the whimsical elegance of The NoMad. (In actuality it was designed by Jacques Garcia, a well-known Parisian architect). Klimt-like touches abound in the lobby, with its elaborate painted panels and movie-set like spaces (such as the spiffy, two-story library that serves as an ante-room to the bar area and the wondrous, massive skylight that hovers over the dining room). Gorey's territory, the guestrooms, look like a humorous, if elegant, take on an English nobleman's abode. Huge fabric faux-dressing screens serve as the barrier between bedroom and bathroom; a dozen paintings hang, gallery style, on the white walls; and fine pieces of wooden furniture are paired (in some rooms) with a free-standing, old fashioned bathtub that sits right in front of the large windows. It's quite a sight. *Some tips:* Be sure to ask for a room on the second or third floor, as the ceilings are highest there. And consider eating-in one night: the 24-hour room service is provided by the NoMad Restaurant in the lobby, one of the finest fine dining places in the city (see p. 80).

1170 Broadway (at 28th St.). www.thenomadhotel.com. ℂ **212/769-1500.** 168 units. $269–$475 double. Subway: L, N, Q, R, 4, 5, 6 to Union Square. **Amenities:** Restaurant; bar; concierge; gym; room service.

A surreal STAY IN THE ARTFUL APPLE

The Carlton Arms ★★   This is not a place for everyone. If you get worried when you notice that your room is listing a bit to the right, if you expect a maid to change your sheets daily, if you prefer a hotel with more than two phone lines (yes, you'll sometimes get a busy signal when you call), then this is not the hotel for you. But if you're the type who wants to try something really different, and who finds the idea of being cocooned in art interesting, then choose this 160-year-old hotel with the soul of William Blake in all of its wacky, joyous excess.

Over the years, the Carlton has invited artists to paint murals and create unusual environments in their guest rooms, which many have done with wild glee. There's the Egyptian Hallway, with mummy portraits of staff members; the Japanese Room, with its elaborate dragons and Buddhas; and the Goth Room, where "she-male" portraits leer down at the occupants. Even the now famous Banksy added murals to the stairwell. It's a real looker, and some of the artfully-painted rooms reach museum level in their artistry.

The Carlton Arms is also now the cheapest in this 'hood, with double rooms with private facilities going for a low $150 year round and singles for $120. Share a bathroom and you'll save $30–$40 a night. Affordable triples and quads are also available.

160 E. 25th St. (at Third Ave.). www.carltonarms. com. ℂ **212/679-0680.** 40 units. $120–$150 double. Subway: N, R, or 6 to 28th St. **Amenities:** Free-Wi-Fi.

Moderate/Expensive

The Gansevoort Park Hotel ★   Bringing the Meatpacking District hipster vibe to this tamer neighborhood, the custom-built Gansevoort Park (it opened in 2010) is as notable for its rooms, as for the constant party that takes place in front of the open fireplace in its glam lobby. The rooms are big, averaging 475 square feet; suites are a humongous (1,500 square feet) with large closets, deep soaking tubs, and featherbeds on top of the mattress for just that extra-bit of cushioning. And with an indoor/outdoor rooftop bar and plunge pool, plus an Exhale spa and gym, the hotel has amenities that most others can't match. Top perk: the chauffeur-driven Paneramas Porsche that's available to guests on a first-come, first-served basis.

420 Park Ave. S (at 29th St.). www.gansevoortpark.com. ℂ **888/830-9889.** 249 units. $272–$464 double. Subway: 6 to 28th St. **Amenities:** Restaurant; 2 bars; concierge; gym; indoor/outdoor pool; room service; Exhale Spa; Cutler salon; LaCoste boutique; pet friendly; free Wi-Fi.

Hyatt Union Square ★★   I have a feeling that quite soon this hotel will move fully into the "expensive" category. It certainly has enough bells and whistles to do so. But as one of the newest additions to the scene (it opened in spring 2013), it's still finding an audience, which means that many nights, rooms here go for just $249. That's an excellent price for these chic charmers, which feature furnishings as curvaceous and sexy as Marilyn Monroe (even the very usable in-room desks are curved), cloud-like bedding, handsome hardwood floors, and such amenities as Geneva sound-systems and rainfall showers. The hotel itself is jammed with wacky, fun art works, all chosen by trendy interior designer Paul Vega, and features a rooftop bar.

134 Fourth Ave. (at 13th St.). www.unionsquarehyatt.com. © **212/253-1234.** 178 units. $249–$439 double. Subway: 4, 5, 6, L to Union Square. **Amenities:** Restaurant; bar; concierge; complimentary access to nearby gym; room service; rooftop garden; free Wi-Fi.

Moderate

King and Grove ★ You know you've spent too much time researching New York City Hotels when a rate of $249–$259—one that seems to stay steady, low season to high—makes your heart go pitter pat. That price is the most impressive thing about this hotel, frankly, though you won't regret staying here. Newly opened in 2013, the rooms have a bland efficiency to them (read: smallish, quality beds, usable desks, standard decor), though the lobby is chic enough to meet a client in, and has a small bar. As for the location: it's within easy walking distance of the Empire State Building and a whole bunch of subway lines.

29 E. 29th St. (off Madison Ave.). www.kingandgrove.com. © **800/804-4480** or 212/689-1900. 276 units. $249–$259 double. Subway: 6 to 28th St. **Amenities:** Concierge; lobby bar; 24-hour gym.

Moderate/Inexpensive

Gershwin Hotel ★ From the outside, the Gershwin looks like an extension of the Museum of Sex next door, with huge Plexiglas and metal appendages thrusting upward in a most provocative manner from this 100-year-old Beaux Arts building. They are just the first trumpetings of a hotel infatuated with pop art; not only are numerous walls covered with silk screens and paintings, but many of the guests are artists and musicians (everyone who plays at Joe's Pub stays here), and there's even a resident artist program to help struggling would-be-Warhols. What the Carlton Arms (p. 43) is to Dalí-esque experiential art, the Gershwin is to those who find beauty in a can of Campbell's Soup. The hotel has a number of different types of guest rooms, including ones big enough for families. At the lowest end of the price scale, are the standard doubles: simple but quite pleasant, with shiny wood floors, quality beds, white walls, and pops of color in the wall art and fixtures. Go up in price and you get more art and more artful furnishings (think groovier West Elm). The hotel hosts a number of events from film screenings to concerts.

7 E. 27th St. (btw. Fifth and Madison aves.). www.gershwinhotel.com. © **212/545-8000.** 150 units. $130–$230 standard double. Extra person $20. Subway: N, R, or 6 to 28th St. **Amenities:** Bar; coffee bar; babysitting; free Wi-Fi.

Inexpensive

Hotel 17 ★ Fans of Charles Dickens will feel right at home at this very old-fashioned, spotless if somewhat cheerless hotel (think "Bleak House"). The rooms are done in Edwardian fashion, the beds tend to squeak, and most rooms share a bathroom with others. But when all is said and done, this is a *very* well-located, affordable place to stay in a city that has few such options. Along with doubles are single and triple rooms. And the crowd who stay here—mostly young European backpackers—seem to be having a fine time, despite the dismal décor. The hotel's sister property, **Hotel 30,** offers the same sort of pricing and furnishings.

Union Square, Flatiron District & Gramercy Park

WHERE TO STAY

225 E. 17th St. (off Third Ave.). www.hotel17.com. ☏ **212/475-2845.** 150 units. $130–$150 standard double with shared bathroom. Subway: 4, 5, 6, N, Q, R, L to Union Square. **Amenities:** Free Wi-Fi.

TIMES SQUARE & MIDTOWN WEST

Times Square might be the heart of Manhattan, but it's also the city's most congested neighborhood (if you can really call it a neighborhood). Corporate Midtown West is centrally located, but as a result, high in demand for both business and leisure travelers. Hotels here are almost always fill up fast, thus prices tend to be substantially higher than most other areas.

Best for: People who want to be in the center of "the city that never sleeps"; steps from Broadway theaters, and both high-end and affordable restaurants.

Drawbacks: Staying here puts you among tourists, rather than locals and keeps you from experiencing more of the "real" New York. It's also the most frenetic, exhausting, loud neighborhood in the city (so not great for sleeping).

Expensive

Bryant Park Hotel ★★ "Everything in the room is for sale," the bellman told me, as we entered the room. And my first thought was "that's a smart side business. I bet they make a lot of money that way." I, for one, would love to have the nubby, putty-colored couch, or the Scandinavian-chic, lacquered black bed—they give the room such élan. The entire bedroom, in fact, was unexpectedly attractive, with blond wood floors, scads of air and light, and a vibe that was distinctly Californian. A surprising aesthetic choice, as the hotel is in the landmark Radiator Building, a 1924 skyscraper that, because of its black brick façade, spiky towers, and gold trim, has a distinctly Goth look (fit for a vampire). But not once you're inside. And evil-doers would never approve of all the freebies this hotel is giving away, which include free valet parking on weekends and a free happy hour at the bar each night from 5pm to 6pm. The gym is also unusually nice. And you can't beat those Bryant Park views!

40 W. 40th St. (btw. Fifth and Sixth aves.). www.bryantparkhotel.com.☏ **212/642-2200** or 212/861-0100. 128 units. $333–$399 double. Subway: B, D, F, or M to 42nd St. **Amenities:** Restaurant; bar; concierge; fitness center; room service; screening room; free Wi-Fi.

The Chatwal ★★ What a surprise it is to walk off 44th Street into the Great Gatsby-esque splendor of the Chatwal! Built as a theater in 1905 by architect Stanford White (a movie about his life plays on continuous loop in the elevators), it was converted to a church in the 1960s and most recently into a hotel. That last transformation took a full 9 years, as the owner wanted to get every lux detail right, from the burnished, art deco wooden fittings of the lobby to the round caps and white gloves of the bellmen. The rooms, though small for this price point, are swanky, too, with all leather desks, superior beds and suede walls (it takes an hour to clean each room between guests, as every inch of the walls must be brushed down to remove handprints). Bathrooms contain TVs hidden behind mirrors and Japanese toilets (like bidets but much more, er, interactive). Butler service is part of the inclusions, as are a topnotch spa and gym.

130 W. 44th St. (btw. Sixth and Seventh aves.). www.chatwalny.com. ℂ **212/764-6200.** 76 units. $565–$735 double. Subway: 1, 2, 3, 7, N, R, Q, S to 42nd St.–Times Square. **Amenities:** Restaurant; bar; complimentary butler service; concierge; fitness club including lap pool; room service; spa; free Wi-Fi.

Le Parker Meridien ★★   Sometimes, in your search for a hotel, the out-of-room extras are more important than the rooms themselves. Take the Parker Meridien, which boasts a superb location (just two blocks from Central Park in one direction, the stores of Fifth Avenue in the other), and a host of nifty amenities. Not only does the hotel feature a 17,000-square-foot fitness center (with basketball and racquetball courts, a spa and a rooftop pool), it also is the site of two of the most unique restaurants in Midtown (Norma's, p. 89, and Burger Joint, p. 89), plus a spectacularly beautiful espresso bar called **Knave.** (It's worthwhile just popping in to see the space, which looks like something out of a wing of a palace in St. Petersburg, Russia.) As for the rooms: They're more than respectable, if nowhere near as creative as the rest of the hotel, featuring beds with feather-top mattresses, workable desks with fancy Aeron chairs, a good amount of elbow room, and comfy armchairs. The hotel is a favorite among families, for their large suites, that rooftop pool, and the cartoons that play in the elevators.

119 W. 56th St. (btw. Sixth and Seventh aves.). www.parkermeridien.com. ℂ **800/543-4300** for reservations, or 212/245-5000. 726 units. $297–$500 double. Subway: F, N, Q, or R to 57th St. Pets accepted for a charge. **Amenities:** 2 restaurants; espresso/cocktail bar; concierge (2 w/Clefs d'Or distinction); fitness center; spa and rooftop pool; room service; sun deck.

Sofitel New York ★★   You'll feel like you're sleeping in a Fortune 500 company board room here. And I mean that in the very best way. The walls and furnishings are covered with the most burnished of woods, the rooms are huge, and the art is of a quality that's usually guarded by hidden security cameras (and not placed in private rooms). Beds, as you might expect are covered with the finest of linens and very sleepable. Bathrooms are downright splendid, with separate showers and soaking tubs. This hotel has every amenity and service you could want, from a workout room that would please Arnold Schwarzenegger, to a polished, unflappable staff (many from France).

45 W. 44th St. (btw. Fifth and Sixth aves.). www.sofitel.com. ℂ **212/354-8844.** 398 units. $399–$648 double. 1 child stays free in parent's room. Subway: B, D, F, or M to 42nd St. Pets accepted. **Amenities:** Restaurant; bar; concierge; exercise room; room service; free Wi-Fi.

Moderate/Expensive

Casablanca Hotel ★★   Yes, this hotel is an act of homage to that famous movie. So the breakfast room, which doubles as a wine-and-cheese lounge in the evenings (and has free treats around all day) is called **Rick's Café.** Some nights there's free piano music ("Play it again, Sam!"), and in winter, guests gather round the fire. Rooms (small, but what else is new in New York?) are equipped with rattan furniture, ceiling fans and wooden blinds for that 1940s hideaway-in-Morocco atmosphere. The building offers two outdoor areas, a rooftop deck and a second

Times Square & Midtown West

WHERE TO STAY

floor courtyard, so that you can enjoy the sunshine without having to deal with the madding crowds of Times Square (which is just down the block). Did I mention that most of the staff seems to have as sweet a temperament as Ingrid Bergman (translation: service is topnotch). The Casablanca is deservedly popular, so get your reservations early.

147 W. 43rd St. (just east of Broadway). www.casablancahotel.com. © **888/922-7225** or 212/869-1212. 48 units. $249–$499 double. Rates include continental breakfast, all-day cappuccino, wine and cheese reception every evening. Subway: N, R, 1, 2, or 3 to 42nd St./Times Square. **Amenities:** Concierge; free access to New York Sports Club; room service; video library, free Wi-Fi.

The Michelangelo ★★ Walking into the marble-clad lobby of The Michelangelo is a bit like hopping the pond to Europe. It has the same swellegant ambiance as the "Grand Dames" of Milan and Paris do, not surprising as The Michelangelo is owned by the Star group (which operates some 20 hotels in Italy). And while the lobby has always been grand, it's only in recent years that the guest rooms have caught up. Today, they're done in soothing creams, tans, and browns, with raw silk draperies, deep whirlpool tubs, and carpeting so thick, you sink down a good half-inch as you walk. A continental breakfast is included in the nightly rate, and though there's no on-site restaurant, 24-hour room service is provided; and light snacks are available at the lobby bar.

152 W. 51st St. (btw. Sixth and Seventh aves.). www.michelangelohotel.com. © **800/237-0990** or 212/765-0505. 179 units. $269–$499 double. Subway: N or R to 49th St. **Amenities:** Lounge; concierge; fitness center; room service.

Novotel New York ★ In fall of 2013, the Novotel completed an $85 million renovation that transformed its lobby into a set for "Star Trek." Okay, not really, but your first vision of the hotel, of pulsing, purple halls that look like the entrance to a Disney ride, is a, er, stunner. Rooms, which are now called "Next Rooms" (they'll soon be standard across the chain), are almost as whiz-bang, with a TV entertainment system that you can control from your cellphone; truly soundproofed windows (you can't hear the city at all); and a lighted frame on the backboard of the bed that gives the room an eerie glow. Other than that, they're not all that odd, but quite comfortable and spacious, with excellent views of the city, good desk space, and even better beds. Families can easily share the rooms with two double beds. The breakfast room has one of the best views of Times Square in town.

226 W. 52nd St. (at Broadway). www.novotel.com. © **212/315-0100.** 480 units. $253–$374 double. 2 children 16 and under eat for free (with adults) and stay free in parent's room. Subway: B, D, or E to Seventh Ave. Pets accepted. **Amenities:** Restaurant; bar; concierge; huge fitness room; room service.

The Out Hotel ★ Billing itself as the "First Straight Friendly" hotel in New York City, the Out proudly waves the rainbow flag. It's known among non-tourists for one of the best gay night clubs in town (the 14,000 square foot XL), and a spa with a steam room that seems perpetually filled with eligible bachelors from around the world. Its only problem may be that it's been a bit too successful on the nightlife front: rooms near the disco are too loud for sleeping (so make sure you ask for another location). But when you fall into your bed after all that dancing, it will be a cushy one, in an adequately sized, contemporary-looking room. Unless, that is, you choose one of the

Out's sleep share rooms, where you get to bunk (in a bunk bed) with three others (strangers or perhaps new friends) for $79 to $99 per night.

510 W. 42nd St. (near Tenth Ave.). http://theoutnyc.com. © **212/947-2999.** 101 units. $259–$369 double. Subway: A, C, E to 42nd St. **Amenities:** Restaurant; fitness center; spa; nightclub; bar; garden; sun deck.

The Refinery ★★ This sophisticated hotel opened in the summer of 2013, bringing a dash of style to what is otherwise a drab, garment center street. It does that, interestingly, by paying homage to its manufacturing roots (the installation behind the front desk is actually made of old millinery tools, appropriate since this 1912 building was once a hat factory). Rooms come in a range of sizes (starting at 250 square feet), but feel bigger than they are thanks to the 12-feet-high ceilings and large windows. Original, abstract art work, oak hardwood floors, and custom furniture up the design ante. Bathrooms feature marble mosaic floors, polished brass fixtures, and rainfall showers. All in all, a very nice addition to the NYC hotel scene.

69 W. 38th St. (btw. Fifth and Sixth aves.). www.refineryhotelnewyork.com. © **646/664-0310.** 197 units. $230–$443 double. Subway: N, Q, R, B, D to 34th St. **Amenities:** Restaurant; bar; oversized gym; pool; free Wi-Fi.

Royalton Hotel ★★ "Back in 1898, when the building was first built, rooms had views," Adrien, the friendly receptionist, chuckled when I noted that I was looking out my window at a brick wall. "But then buildings grew up all around the place." Ah well, views, schmooze! I certainly didn't mind the lack of cityscape as there was more than enough to catch my interest in these chic, nautically-themed rooms, the first created by famed interior designer Philip Starck for a hotel. The heads of the beds are notched into the walls, for a cozy, almost four-poster effect; and some of the standard rooms have super-cool round bathtubs, tiled in tiny mirrors. A nice touch: loaner iPads in each room, with free Wi-Fi. Even if you don't stay here, stop by for a cocktail: Happy hour in the block long train of lounges here is quite the scene.

44 W. 44th St. (btw. Fifth and Sixth aves.). www.royaltonhotel.com. © **800/697-1781** or 212/869-4400. 169 units. $249–$499 double. Subway: B, D, F, or M to 42nd St.–Bryant Park. **Amenities:** Restaurant; 2 bars; concierge; fitness room; room service.

The Salisbury Hotel ★ A church-owned hotel, the Salisbury often seems to take a, well, more charitable view of pricing than do its brethren. At times, when most every property nearby is charging $249, it's often possible to get a $179 room here. Alas, the Salisbury HAS discovered high season, and during those periods, prices can jump to $339 (but they rarely seem to go higher than that; use a discounter site to get the best rates). Built by Calvary Baptist next door, the décor is what you'd expect in a church-sponsored place: a bit bland and not recently refreshed but spotlessly clean. What's *un*expected here is the size of the rooms—massive (the hotel was originally designed as an apartment building)—and the fact that a number of units come with kitchenettes (minifridges, microwaves, toaster ovens) at no additional cost. All of that, combined with the (sometimes) lower prices makes this an excellent choice for families. Rooms with two double beds will comfortably house a family of four, and the location is unbeatable.

123 W. 57th St. (btw. Sixth and Seventh aves.). www.nycsalisbury.com. © **888/NYC-5757** or 212/246-1300. 201 units. $179–$339 double. Subway: B, D, F, or M to 42nd St. Pets accepted. **Amenities:** Kitchenettes (in most rooms).

Moderate

414 Hotel ★★   Charm is a pricey amenity in the world of NYC hotels, which is why I was so pleased to stumble upon Hotel 414. Set in two small apartment buildings connected by a lovely little courtyard, it's decorated with what can only be called "élan"—the walls are bathed in chic colors, furnishings are cheeky (a chest of drawers that looks like a wooden file cabinet, suede checkerboard headboards, elongated vases with flowers) and rooms, while on the small side, never feel cramped. Breakfast is included in the daily rate and guests have access to a shared kitchen (with fridge, microwave, and two burners). To top it all off, the staff are genuinely gracious. The only downside: There is sometimes noise from guests walking above, so if you're a light sleeper ask for a room on a top floor (no elevator, alas).

414 W. 46th St. (btw. Ninth and Tenth aves.). www.hotel414.com. (℃) **866/414-HOTEL** (414-4683) or 212/399-0006. 22 units. $185–$265 double. Subway: A, C, E, or 7 to 42nd St. **Amenities:** Complimentary continental breakfast; complimentary coffee; juice; and tea; concierge; free Wi-Fi.

Room Mate Grace Hotel ★   The lobby here is the sexiest in Midtown and the rooms among the oddest. But let's start with the pluses: A purple-lit pool is the centerpiece of the ground-floor, and right off it a bar, so that drinkers can watch their compatriots frolic, and those in the pool can swim up for a tipple. It's a fun, party scene most nights. (The hotel also features a steam room, sauna, small gym and free continental breakfast.) Now, ahem, onto the rooms which have some problems. First off, those too near to the pool/bar area can be noisy; and while the configuration of the rooms is very different from one to the next, a large number of them mount the beds on high, often wide platforms, requiring the agility of a gymnast to climb into for the night. That being said, many of the rooms are just fine, and some feature multiple beds and bunk beds, perfect for families. In short: This is a good choice for party people, and folks who want to be right off Times Square.

125 W. 45th St. (btw. Sixth Ave. and Broadway). www.room-matehotels.com. (℃) **212/354-2323.** 139 units. $179–$329 double. Subway: B, D, F, or M to 47th–50th sts./Rockefeller Center. **Amenities:** Bar; complimentary Spanish-inspired breakfast; gym; pool; sauna; steam room; free Wi-Fi; minifridge; free local calls.

Washington Jefferson Hotel ★   Before World War II, this hotel was two: the Washington and the Jefferson. Each was a home-away-from-home for the performers who worked in the area, and today the WJ still retains that, well, homey feel thanks to the helpful, happy-seeming staff and the simple, but stylish décor (think soft grays with touches of deep red, platform beds with cushioned headboards and slate-tiled bathrooms). Rooms vary in size and some can be quite small, so ask for a switch if you're unhappy.

318 W. 51st St. (btw. Eighth and Ninth aves.). www.wjhotel.com. (℃) **888/567-7550** or 212/246-7550. 135 units. $140–$335 double. Subway: C or E to 50th St. **Amenities:** Restaurant; exercise room; room service; free Wi-Fi.

Inexpensive/Moderate

Ameritania ★★   In a city where each hotel room looks like the next (trust me, I've visited almost all of them), it's refreshing to come to a hotel with its own aesthetics, in a price range that's not outrageous. Guest rooms are unusually stylish, with handsome works of art on the walls, mod clocks, and textured wallpapers. They come in all shapes and sizes, so ask to switch if you're not happy with the one you get. Included in the room price is a large breakfast, and while Wi-Fi incurs an extra fee, let's just say that if you ask some of the staff members in an unobtrusive way, they'll share the password with you. (You didn't hear that from me, though).

230 W. 54th St. (right off Broadway). www.ameritanianyc.com. ✆ **212/247-5000.** 249 units. $167–$263 double. Subway: 1 to 50th St. **Amenities:** Gym; free continental breakfast; lounge/bar.

Mayfair Hotel ★ Just west of Times Square, on a block that also houses the Majestic Theater and Eugene O'Neill Theater (and the crowds that descend on them eight times a week), the Mayfair Hotel bills itself a "European-style, boutique hotel," which I've found to be the code phrase for "Our rooms are very, very small, but they sure do look pretty." That's certainly the case here, with rooms that are oddly shaped, usually opening onto a tiny alcove area with a doorway to the bathroom, behind which is wedged a full, queen, or king-size bed and a small desk. Pretty comes into the equation with the Wedgwood china–like bedspreads and curtains, white with either baby blue or pink scenes of peasants at play. As with many Theater District hotels, rates rise sharply on the weekends. Penny-pinching couples can rent single rooms to share but this is only recommended for very loving twosomes (it's a tight fit). Free Internet access, computers in some rooms.

242 W. 49th St. (btw. Broadway and Eighth Ave.). www.mayfairnewyork.com; ✆ **800/556-0300** or 212/586-0300. 78 units. $163–$231 double. Subway: N, Q, R to 49th St. **Amenities:** Free Wi-Fi.

Milford NYC ★ Will wonders never cease? The weary, old Milford Plaza Hotel has not only gotten a new name, it's been flipped. And that doesn't mean the staff has gone nuts. Highgate Hotels stepped in and gave it a thorough makeover. Today, when you check in, no longer does a tiny room with chipped and aged furniture await you. Now, your tiny room (well, they couldn't move walls) has a jaunty look, with a fresh white duvet on the beds, two curtains in front of the window (one for daytime and one for night), and a cheery tangerine-colored wall. Bathroom tiling and fixtures are also bright and new as of the summer of 2013. Alas, prices seem to be rising, too, though it still is possible, on some nights, to catch 40 winks here for just $131.

700 Eighth Ave. (btw. 44th and 45th sts.). www.milfordplaza.com. ✆ **888/352-3650** or 212/869-3600. 1300 units. $131–$250 double. Subway: A, C, or E to 42nd St./Port Authority. **Amenities:** Restaurant; fitness center.

New York Manhattan Hotel ★ Just like the city, this place is so nice they named it twice. A Red Roof Inn before 2012, it was originally converted from an office building, meaning rooms come in all shapes and sizes. So a very small standard room might cost the same as a much larger one (ask to switch rooms if you're not pleased with the first one your get). That being said, even the smaller rooms have such a smart design, they feel adequately large. Such perks as a free continental breakfast, free Wi-Fi and free calls within the U.S., an oversized gym (with multiple treadmills and elliptical machines, so there should be no waiting), concierge and central location also make NYMA a particularly good value, considering the price (which ranges from $179–$279 most nights).

Times Square & Midtown West

WHERE TO STAY

6 W. 32nd St. (btw. Broadway and Fifth Ave.). http://applecorehotels.com/the-new-york-manhattan-hotel. ☏ **800/755-3194** or 212/643-7100. 171 units. $109–$329 double. Children 12 and under stay free in parent's room. Subway: B, D, F, N, R, or M to 34th St. **Amenities:** Breakfast room; wine-and-beer lounge; continental breakfast included; concierge; exercise room; free Wi-Fi.

Radisson Martinique ★   Here's proof that you'll find scintillating Gotham history in the darndest of places. What looks like a faceless Radisson if you just glance at the building's awning, is actually the oldest continually operating hotel in the city. Once known as the Hotel Martinique, it was designed by Henry Hardenberg, the architect behind the much, much pricier Plaza Hotel, and opened in 1898. The Professional Golf Association of America was born in its ballroom, and when the Empire State Building started its construction, champagne was (illegally) tippled here to mark the event. A Beaux Arts pep is still evident in the façade, with the beautifully tiled lobby floors and the spectacular curved staircase to the left of the lobby as you enter. Happily, rooms are larger than most in the city (most, see below) as they were once meant to house the city's elite. Alas, they're no longer decorated with the pizzazz they would have been during the heyday of the hotel. Still, they're comfy, clean, with "sleep number" beds and all the usual amenities. *Tips:* Rooms are available for single travelers and are significantly cheaper than the doubles (ask; they have full-sized beds so are potentially usable by very intimate couples). Also: request rooms above the fifth floor to get away from the cigarette smoke emanating from the fourth floor (the building's only smoking floor).

49 W. 32nd St. (near Broadway). www.radisson.com. ☏ **212/736-3800.** 200 units. $125–$350 double. Children 14 and under stay free in parent's room. Subway: A, C, E to 50th St. **Amenities:** Restaurant; fitness center.

Skyline Hotel ★   Really a motel, set in an area of Manhattan that could be best described as "Siberia," the Skyline does its best to offset its dreary, far west location with a cluster of amenities that can only be replicated at one other hotel in the city. First off, the Skyline has that rarest of all luxuries: an indoor swimming pool, and a nice one at that, on the roof. Guests can store cars or vans for a mere $10 per day in the hotel's basement parking lot. And the rooms, enormous by New York standards (particularly the luxury rooms, which are only 10% more than normal), are bright and comfortable, and come with such nice extras as Nintendo games and fridges. In the front wing (slightly smaller rooms), rates start at $139 a night, but can soar to $400 (usually they hover in the mid-200s and I wouldn't pay more than that).

725 Tenth Ave. (at 49th St.). www.skylinehotelny.com. ☏ **800/433-1982** or 212/586-3400. 232 units. $139–$237 standard. Extra person $20. Children 14 and under stay free in parent's room. Subway: A, C, E to 50th St. **Amenities:** Restaurant; fitness center; Internet access in lobby; indoor pool.

Yotel ★   "Airport" is the theme at this ultra-modern hotel, appropriate since Yotel was first developed in the airports of Europe as a way to give weary travelers a place to rest between flights in small, but serviceable "cabins." Rooms are still called "cabins" and they're still teeny-tiny (170 square feet for the smallest ones), but so well-designed they actually feel spacious (floor-to-ceiling windows helps with that allusion). When you enter, your bed is pulled up into couch shape; push a button when you want to sleep and, like a larger version of a business class seat, it unfolds to accommodate you. The street level is staffed by a "ground crew" who help guests self-check

FAMILY-FRIENDLY hotels

Lugging the kids to New York City can be a daunting experience. Finding a hotel that makes that experience (whether in the accommodations or in the amenities) a bit less overwhelming can be a huge help. Here are some of the city's best accommodations for families:

Affinia Dumont (Midtown east; p. 56) Real kitchens in which to cook for picky kids, plus rooms of a size that allows all the family members to spread out.

Gershwin Hotel (Flatiron District; p. 44) High space-to-dollar ratio with the Family Room, a two-room suite.

Hotel Beacon (Upper West Side; p. 58) In-room kitchenette, on-site laundromat, and spacious rooms in a kid-friendly neighborhood—what more do you want?

Le Parker Meridien (Midtown West; p. 46) Cartoons playing in the elevators, a great swimming pool, a kid-friendly burger joint in the lobby, and spacious rooms and suites.

The Lowell (Upper East Side; p. 61) Total *luxe*, but with the feel of a residential dwelling. Most units are equipped with a kitchenette or full kitchen.

Novotel New York (Midtown West; p. 47) Kids 16 and under stay free in their parent's room and eat free at the hotel's Café Nicole.

Pod 39 (Midtown West; p. 57) Bunk bed rooms plus ping pong and pool tables in the lobby. Can you say kiddie heaven (and at an affordable rate)?

Skyline Hotel and **Travel Inn** (Midtown West; p. 51 and p. 52) Inexpensive ($10) to free parking at the Skyline and Travel Inn, respectively, oversize rooms, and swimming pools (a rarity in affordable hotels).

in at kiosks (hmmm . . . where did they get that idea?). And like some more upscale airports today, the on-site restaurant is helmed by a celebrity chef (Richard Sandoval of Pampano, p. 91), there's a gym on-site, and even a large outdoor terrace with bar. Families should check out the bunk-bed rooms.

570 Tenth Ave. (at 41st St.). www.yotel.com. (C) **877-90YOTEL** or 646/449-7700. 669 units. $169–$297 premium cabin. Subway: A, C, E, 7 to 42nd St. **Amenities:** Restaurant; bar; fitness room; workstations; outdoor lounge; indoor private lounges; free Wi-Fi.

Travel Inn ★ The Travel Inn is a dead ringer for the Skyline (p. 51), but with a few important differences. Like the Skyline, it has a pool, a gym, and parking facilities, but it one-ups its rival with the size of its pool (a summer-only facility about twice as large as its rival's), its gym (also a hair bigger), and the fact that it gives guests free parking—a very, very rare perk in this parking-poor city. Rooms are renovated each year and are therefore immaculate, with good firm mattresses and a standard motel look, but they're markedly smaller than Skyline's though the prices are similar. Locale? Though it's as far west as the Skyline, in this area of town the Off-Broadway theaters crawl down 42nd Street all the way to Tenth Avenue, so it feels less remote.

515 W. 42nd St. (just west of Tenth Ave.). www.thetravelinnhotel.com. © **888/HOTEL58** (468-3558), 800/869-4630, or 212/695-7171. 160 units. $105–$250 double. Extra person $10. Children 15 and under stay free in parent's room. Subway: A, C, or E to 42nd St./Port Authority. **Amenities:** Coffee shop; fitness center; terrific outdoor pool w/deck chairs and lifeguard in season; room service.

Hotel Wolcott ★   The digs here are a real mixed bag. Some rooms have nice period touches such as high ceilings with intricate plaster designs (the building was erected in 1904), others are swathed in dreary, mud-colored wall papers, made even more dingy looking by light-trapping, wall-facing windows. Though the rooms vary wildly in size, those in the same category are priced identically, so you could end up paying a premium for a closet-sized room or very little for a very nice one. So be pro-active when you check in; I recommend the place because often, it's the best value in town for hotel rooms with private bathrooms. And the lobby is one of the most impressive of any budget hotel, with its giant columns and fake Louis XIV plasterwork all installed by the architect who designed Grant's tomb.

4 W. 31st St. (off Fifth Ave.). www.wolcott.com. © **212/268-2900.** 175 units. $114–$248 double. Subway: 6 to 34th St. **Amenities:** Continental breakfast included.

Inexpensive

Americana Inn ★   Hard-core budgeteers—but those who value their sleep—would do well to consider the Americana, though it is another bathless wonder. But here just three to four rooms share a bathroom with shower (rooms do come with sinks) and some of those rooms will be very low-cost singles. Families may want to look into the rooms that have three twin beds. As for décor, think standard, motel-like furniture but with mattresses that are better than you usually get at this price point. To ensure that you make the most of them, ask for a room in the back, away from the street noise. The other nice extra here is the kitchenette on each floor available for guest use (along with coffeemakers).

69 W. 38th St. (at Sixth Ave.). www.theamericanainn.com. © **888/HOTEL-58** (468-3558) or 212/840-6700. 50 units, all with shared bathroom. $102–$199 double. Extra person $20. Subway: B, D, F, or M to 34th St. **Amenities:** Common kitchen.

Herald Square Hotel ★   What an emotional rollercoaster the Herald Square puts its guests on. The outside is promising, a lovely Beaux Arts facade complete with gold-leaf cherub, but once you enter you're confronted with that most ominous of hotel sights: a bullet-proof, glass-encased check-in desk. Turns out that's merely a holdover from the bad old days when this was a welfare hotel, but what a terrible first impression it makes. Of course, first impressions aren't everything, and the solicitous staff and spiffy rooms should soon dispel any lingering worries. In the most expensive rooms, the mattresses have comfy pillowtops, the lighting is via crystal-laden chandelier, the floor is a shiny hardwood, and a fancy dream-maker clock radio/iPod station wakes you in the mornings. Although the smaller, cheaper rooms are nowhere near as *au courant* in their appearance or amenities (bye-bye dream-maker, though the mattresses are fine), they're white-glove clean and pleasantly decorated with brass beds, white duvets, and framed *Life* magazine covers (the building was erected in 1894 to house the magazine's offices and staff). The best discounts on rooms here tend to come from Booking.com.

19 W. 31st St. (btw. Fifth Ave. and Broadway). www.heraldsquarehotel.com. ℰ **800/727-1888** or 212/279-4017. 100 units. $169–$219 double. Subway: N, Q, R, B, D to 34th St.–Herald Square. **Amenities:** Complimentary tea and coffee in lobby; guest laundry facilities; free Wi-Fi.

Park Savoy Hotel ★ Try and ignore the fact that this little hotel just about defines the saying "Well, it ain't the Savoy." For a hotel this well-located (just one block from Central Park), I'm willing to overlook beds that are a bit rocky (though not lumpy), scuff marks on the walls and chipped furniture. Yes, the hotel needs refreshing, but the staff keep what it has very clean. And it's near impossible to do better than the prices here in Manhattan, which include a coupon for breakfast at the pizzeria next door (no joke, they make eggs and waffles apparently).

158 W. 58th St. (btw. Sixth and Seventh aves.). http://parksavoy.com. ℰ **212/245-5755.** 50 units. $129–$167 double. Subway: N, Q, R, to 57th St. **Amenities:** Breakfast coupon.

MIDTOWN EAST & MURRAY HILL

This is "Mad Men" territory, where the barons of advertising and big business reside. As a result, you'll find some of the grandest hotels—and also the most expensive.

Best for: People who like to stay in a more residential area, with a wide variety of (more high-end) accommodations.

Drawbacks: There's not a lot of variety in the dining options (particularly in the budget category), and a lot of the city's attractions are found more to the West side or further uptown.

Expensive

Andaz Fifth Avenue ★★ How's this for luxury: They'll even clean your feet for you at the Andaz in Fifth Avenue. No, there are no handmaidens on call, but in each massive, slate-faced shower is a ledge seat, along with knee-height spigot and bowl, so that you can sit and soak your tootsies at the end of a long day of pavement pounding. That spigot is one of three shower heads (rainbow above, handheld in the middle) in this swank bathroom. Other spiffy touches include panels on either side of the bed that control every single light in the oversized room, blackout curtains (along with regular ones), wonderfully high ceilings, and a complimentary snack and beverage bar (excluding alcohol) that sits in all-glass cases that look like they were lifted from Saks Fifth Avenue. The piece de resistance? Splendid views of the Public Library, which is right across the street.

485 Fifth Ave. (at 41st St.). www.andaz5thavenue.com. ℰ **212/601-1234.** 194 units. $352–$476 double. Subway: B, D, F, M to 42nd Street. **Amenities:** Restaurant; bar; concierge; oversized fitness center; room service; free Wi-Fi.

The Plaza Hotel ★★★ Everything is as you would expect it to be at the glamorous, glorious Plaza Hotel. Rooms are simply dripping with gold leaf, crystal chandeliers and crown molding. The furnishings are French Empire, including pieces with fine inlaid woods. And though half the building is now private apartments, the Fairmont Chain has taken over the other half and is keeping standards high. A new, state-of-the-art gym was installed in the basement in early 2013; and a spa inhabits the 4th floor. And in some ways, the Plaza is more fun than ever, thanks to a wonderfully gourmet food court/restaurant in the basement (see p. 81), which coexists alongside the classic Palm Court (still the best place in New York to go for high tea). *Some tips:* Only eight rooms now have a Central Park view in the hotel (those went to the apartment units), so ask yourself if having that is important to you. As well, Fairmont loyalty members get free Wi-Fi, so join the club (also free), before checking in. Is there a more ideal place for a honeymoon? I can't think of many.

768 Fifth Ave. (at Central Park South). www.theplazany.com. (C) **888/850-0909** or 212/759-3000. 282 units. $538–$666 double. Subway: N, R to Fifth Ave. **Amenities:** 3 restaurants; 2 bars/lounges; food court; fitness room; spa; butler service for suites.

Langham Place ★★ Half hotel, half apartment building, and formerly known as The Setai, this ultra-exclusive skyscraper property is expert at coddling its guests. What that means is free shoe shines when they arrive (can't have dusty tootsies in a place this fancy), a town car available at all hours to whisk them around town, complimentary access to the mini-bar, and rooms that feel like they're the dimension of a squash court (the smallest start at 700 feet). Bathrooms feature soaking tubs and TVs hidden behind the mirrors. Not enough? On-site is a celeb-helmed restaurant (Ai Fiori from Michael White), a massive spa and gym, and the Julian Farel salon. Those who ante up for suites, get even more luxury, including, full and state-of-the-art kitchens (in the larger ones), espresso machines, and even more room. While the immediate area of the hotel is rather grungy, it's just a few short blocks from Bryant Park and the Empire State Building.

400 Fifth Ave. (btw. 36th and 37th sts.). www.langhamplacehotels.com. (C) **212/695-4005.** 214 units. $535–$885 double. Subway: B, D, F, M, N, R, Q to 34th St. **Amenities:** Restaurant; bar; fitness center; personal assistants; 24-hr. room service; spa; salon; complimentary pressing service upon arrival; free Wi-Fi.

Waldorf Astoria and the Waldorf Towers ★★ Though it's still an Art Deco masterwork, the Waldorf no longer has quite the cachet of, say, the Plaza. It's a numbers game: The Waldorf simply has many, many more rooms to fill, so it often plays "Let's Make A Deal" with guests. For example, as I write this, a would-be visitor can upgrade from a standard room to a suite for just $150 and that upgrade will entitle them to a 50-minute massage at the Guerlain spa (a $200 value). I was assured there's no end in sight for this promotion. So what else do you get if you stay here? A lot of eye-candy architecture and décor. The rooms are all generously proportioned (even the standard queen rooms), and feature molded ceilings, fine antique furnishings (like bureaus of inlaid wood and marble tops) and attractive, large bathrooms. Those who stay in the Waldorf Towers (suites only) get butler service and an even higher level of opulence in the furnishings. And just walking through the lobby here, with its elaborate tiles, murals, and iconic central clock, is a thrill. (In 2013, the Lexington Avenue lobby was renovated to bring it up to the standards set by the fabulous lobby on Park Avenue).

301 Park Ave. (btw. 49th and 50th sts.). www.waldorfastoria.com. (C) **800/WALDORF** (925-3673), 800/774-1500, or 212/355-3000. 1,245 units (180 in the Towers). Waldorf Astoria $259–$585 double;

Waldorf Towers $299–$437 double. Extra person $35. Children 17 and under stay free in parent's room. The discounters Otel.com seems to have the best rates here. Subway: 6 to 51st St. **Amenities:** 4 restaurants; 4 bars; concierge and theater desk; executive-level rooms; 3,000-sq.-ft. fitness center and excellent spa; room service.

Moderate/Expensive

Affinia Dumont ★★   Many hotels claim they have kitchenettes but the Affinia truly delivers (great news for families). Each of their suites—and this is an all-suite hotel—features a kitchen that would make many native New Yorkers jealous, with a four-burner stove, full-size fridge, microwave, and full complement of flatware and cookware. The large on-site gym/spa is the Affinia's other lure (the hotel will even provide you with a "fit kit" if you wish to work out in your room). Rooms themselves are very livable, with huge desks, armchairs, multiple beds (with multiple pillow options, through the pillow menu) and lots of closet space. Again, an excellent choice if you're going to be sharing the room among several generations or just like to be able to stretch out.

150 E. 34th St. (btw. Third and Lexington aves.). www.affinia.com. (C) **212/481-7600.** 241 units. $213–$371 for a studio suite (the smallest unit here, it's big enough for four). Subway: 6 to 33rd St. **Amenities:** Restaurant; concierge; health club and spa; room service; grocery-shopping service; full kitchens in all units.

Hotel Elysée ★★★   You would expect to find a hotel like this on a side-street in the Marais in Paris. It has that sort of gentility. But no, this little, brick, 1926 gem sits where it always has, as glass skyscrapers have sprouted all around it. This is the famed hotel that was once a haunt for such artists as Tennessee Williams, Maria Callas, and Vladimir Horowitz (the piano he donated still sits in the Piano Suite). In it is the Monkey Bar, with its iconic murals still in place. Unchanged, too (though refreshed), are the gracious, Gallic furnishings in the rooms, which include heavy embroidered curtains draping the windows, fine mahogany dressers, and unexpected touches, like a chinoiserie vase here, a fine marble-based lamp there. Rooms will vary greatly one to the next: some have fireplaces, others have kitchens or solariums, and some (the cheapest ones) are just good-sized, elegant places to sleep. A generous breakfast (fruits, bagels, pastries) is included in the room rates, as are wine and cheese every night between 5 and 8pm.

60 E. 54th St. (btw. Park and Madison aves.). www.elyseehotel.com. (C) **800/535-9278** or 212/753-1066. 103 units. $249–$549 double. Rates include continental breakfast, all day refreshments and nightly wine-and-cheese reception. Subway: E or M to Fifth Ave. **Amenities:** Restaurant; bar; concierge; free access to nearby gym; room service; free Wi-Fi.

The Library Hotel ★★   You gotta love a place that pays homage to the Dewey Decimal System. Here at the Library (it's located one block from the New York Public Library), each room is named for a different category of literature from art to children's readers to erotic tomes (and if you pick the Erotic Books room, you'll spot a healthy dose of Anais Nin on the shelves). That being said, the rooms décor doesn't vary (it's done in distinguished woods, with marble countertops, and high thread-count bedding), though room size does. Petite rooms are just 200 square feet with full-size beds, the deluxe are 250 square feet, and the junior suites are 350 square feet. But even if you choose a tiny room, you'll have more than enough places to spread out thanks to The Library's public spaces, which include a reading room where weekday wine and cheese and a complimentary daily breakfast are served (snacks are both available and free there 24 hours), a writer's den with a fireplace and flat-screen TV, and a rooftop terrace with bar. All in all, a very civilized base in Gotham.

299 Madison Ave. (at 41st St.). www.libraryhotel.com. © **877/793-7323** or 212/983-4500. 60 units. $249–$399 double. Subway: 4, 5, 6, 7, or S to 42nd St./Grand Central. **Amenities:** Restaurant; roof garden lounge; continental breakfast buffet, all-day snacks, wine and cheese nightly included; free access to nearby health club; room service; huge book library and video library of American Film Institute's Top 100 films; free Wi-Fi.

St. Giles—The Tuscany ★★   Sexy and big: that's always a good combination, right? And that about sums up the experience of staying at this off-shoot of the St. Giles Hotel (which finished up a massive, multi-million dollar renovation in late summer of 2013). The rooms are among the largest I've seen in NYC (especially at this price point), and so are the soaking tubs in the oversized bathrooms. Sexy comes into play with the black and red color scheme (sounds tawdry, but it works) and the use of velvet and leather on the armchairs and headboards (again, it should be a bordello look but it isn't). Once you leave your room, there's a free (and generous) continental breakfast awaiting you in the lobby; and a more-than-decent gym so that you, too, can look sexy.

130 E. 39th St. (off Park Ave.). www.stgilesnewyork.com. © **212/686-1600.** 124 units. $209–$399 double. Subway: 4, 5, 6, S to Grand Central. **Amenities:** Restaurant; bar; fitness club; room service; free Wi-Fi.

Inexpensive/Moderate

Hotel Grand Union ★   An older property that's nonetheless well preserved, each medium-sized room done up in dignified blues, grays, and plums, with a fridge, desk, small closet area, and tidy bathroom. Though the rooms don't get much sunlight and the beds don't have much give, they'll be fine for those who, well, like to sleep late on extra-firm mattresses (and save big doing so). My only complaint would be the fluorescent lighting, but at these prices that seems like a quibble. The hotel also has decently priced quads for families. No room service, but the diner right next door keeps long hours.

34 E. 32nd St. (btw. Madison and Park aves.). www.hotelgrandunion.com. © **212/683-5890.** 95 units. $129–$273 single or double. Subway: 6 to 33rd St. **Amenities:** Coffee shop; free Wi-Fi.

The Pod Hotel ★★ **and The Pod 39** ★★   Both the original Pod (on 51st Street) and its off-shoot on 39th Street, offer high style, and even high jinx, at low, low prices. As you might have guessed from the name, most of the rooms are pretty small—combining and enlarging them would have forced the owners to raise prices—and some at the original one (on 51st Street) do share a bathroom. But even these negatives don't detract too much. The designer has done a bang-up job of making savvy use of the space, building dressers into the bases of the beds, for example, attaching small TVs at each level of the bunk beds (yes, some doubles have bunk beds) and covering the beds with sofa-like covers in primary colors, so that they can be used as couches during the day. All this in rooms that have a smart, Scandinavian look, with clean-lined light-wood and brushed metal furnishings, fine modern prints on the walls, and such non-budget touches as flat-screen TVs, free Wi-Fi, CD players, and iPod recharging stations in each room. In addition, both properties go out of their way to make stays fun for their guests, with rooftop bars, bustling on-site restaurants, and lobbies that double as lounges (the downtown one offers a ping pong and pool table for guests). Though most of the guests are in their 20s and 30s, people of all ages will enjoy staying at these cheery and affordable hotels (including families; a number of rooms are perfect for them).

230 E. 51st St. (off Third Ave.). www.thepodhotel.com. *©* **800/742-5945** or 212/355-0300. 348 units. $125–$199 double. Subway: 6 to 50th St. or 145 E. 39th St. (off Lexington Ave.) *©* **855/ POD-5700** or 212/865-5700. 360 units. Subway: 4, 5, 6, S to Grand Central Station. **Amenities:** Restaurants; roof bars; free Wi-Fi.

3 | UPPER WEST SIDE

Families and chain stores are the chief residents of the Upper West Side, though it also has some significant sights (including Lincoln Center, Central Park, and the Museum of Natural History).

Best for: Visitors who want a more residential neighborhood, not as congested and noisy as Midtown, and who are comfortable on the bus or subway; rooms are often larger and a better value than in Midtown.

Drawbacks: Midtown attractions are a bus/subway/taxi ride away, and downtown ones even more so.

Expensive

Inn New York City ★★★ What a find! This is the type of sweet inn you'd expect to stay at in Vermont (in fact, there's a "Vermont" room) but here it is on a quiet side street of the Upper West Side, offering grace, charm, stained glass, and a slew of amenities that most native New Yorkers don't have (like the massive Jacuzzi tubs in the spa suite; and a washer dryer in another unit). Each suite has a large bedroom, lovely Victorian furnishings, and a full—and cookable—kitchen. And though this may sound like a honeymoon place (and it certainly does get lots of those), one unit is perfect for families, as it has a sofa bed in the living room and pocket doors giving each room privacy. Unlike any other place in the city; book well in advance as it does sell out. Free Wi-Fi and free snacks are part of the deal.

266 W. 71st St. (btw. Amsterdam and West End aves.). www.innnewyorkcity.com. *©* **212/580-1900.** 4 units. $645 double. Subway: 1, 2, 3 to 72nd St. **Amenities:** Full kitchens, stocked with free supplies and wine; free Wi-Fi; free access to the nearby Reebok Sports Club.

Moderate/Expensive

Hotel Beacon ★★ Comfort comes well before style at the Beacon and that's just fine. I'm not saying the rooms are ugly; with their olive green and white furnishings, newly refurbished in 2013, they're actually kind of handsome in a "college town parent's hotel" sort of way. But what gives the Beacon two stars are its creature comforts: each room comes with a fully usable kitchenette and is a generous 340 square feet or more, not including a good-sized bathroom and roomy closet. And because most of the standard rooms come with two double beds, they're ideal for families. Up one level, but still affordable, are big one- and two-bedroom suites each with a pullout sofa

Uptown Accommodations

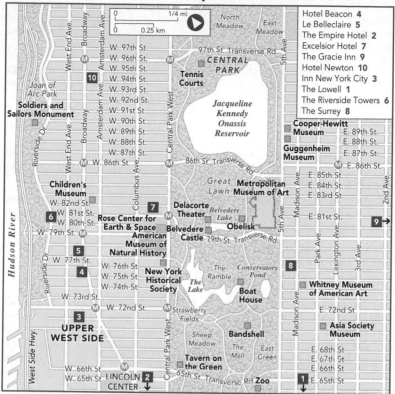

Hotel Beacon **4**
Le Belleclaire **5**
The Empire Hotel **2**
Excelsior Hotel **7**
The Gracie Inn **9**
Hotel Newton **10**
Inn New York City **3**
The Lowell **1**
The Riverside Towers **6**
The Surrey **8**

(families of five and six, take note). The two-bedroom suites have a second bathroom and are almost big enough for the Duggar family!

2130 Broadway (at 75th St.). www.beaconhotel.com. © **800/572-4969** or 212/787-1100. 265 units. $224–$325 double. Extra person $15. Children 12 and under stay free in parent's room. Subway: 1, 2, or 3 to 72nd St. **Amenities:** Gym; free Wi-Fi.

Moderate

The Empire ★★ The Empire Hotel's large, neon sign has been a neighborhood landmark for over 50 year now, but it wasn't until a 2005 renovation that anyone would actually want to stay here. Now, it's as swank as its surroundings (it's right across the street from Lincoln Center), and even the smallest rooms have a feeling of luxury to them, with Rothko-like paintings on the wall, handsome leather and dark wood furnishings, and very cushy beds. Because of the hotel's 10-foot ceilings, even the smaller rooms feel spacious (though they're only 205 square feet). This is also that rare NYC hotel to have a rooftop pool (it's small, but usable) and a fun suntanning deck with cabanas. The only disappointment? The lillliputian bathrooms (though they do have rainfall shower heads).

44 W. 63rd St. (btw. Broadway and Columbus Ave.). www.empirehotelnyc.com. ℂ**212/265-7400.** 420 units. $176–$299 double. Subway: 1 to 66th St.; A, B, C, D, or 1 to 59th St./Columbus Circle. **Amenities:** Restaurant; 2 bars; concierge; fitness center and spa; rooftop pool; free Wi-Fi.

Excelsior Hotel ★ It's the Excelsior's stupendous location, down the block from Central Park and across the street from the Museum of Natural History, that keeps it in this guide. Other than that plus—and it's a major one, to be sure—this is your standard bus-tour hotel (when I was last there, signs for Cosmos Tours were all over the lobby). So the rooms have the kind of art and furnishings that one expects in a mass-volume tourism joint. Not that they're uncomfortable— actually the rooms are roomy and feature quality bedding. But they're the sort of digs that one forgets what they look like the minute you go out the door. Rooms with a park view will be pricier, rooms overlooking the courtyard are a bit dark, but very quiet.

45 W. 81st St. (btw. Columbus Ave. and Central Park West). www.excelsiorhotelny.com. ℂ**212/362-9200.** 198 units. $182–$364 double. Extra person $20. Children 12 and under stay free in parent's room. Subway: B or C to 81st St./Museum of Natural History. **Amenities:** Restaurant; breakfast room with 2 open-air decks and daily breakfast buffet; concierge; exercise room.

Inexpensive

Le Belleclaire ★ Recently remodeled—the lobby now looks like an odd cross between a bordello and a sidewalk café—the rooms here also have an overtly sensual air to them, with poofy red leather backboards and deep red drapes. Some might find it sexy, others a little silly, but what's indisputable is that the prices are good for the location and one cannot find fault with the place's upkeep (it's spotless). Rates are even better if you're willing to accept a room with shared bathroom. These rooms are the same size (relatively small), have in-room sinks and share hall bathrooms at a ratio of three to one. The family suite offers two attached, semiprivate bedrooms with a bathroom, a minifridge, and a big walk-in closet.

250 W. 77th St. (at Broadway). www.hotelbelleclaire.com. ℂ **800/643-5553** or 212/362-7700. 189 units, 39 with shared bathroom. $89–$269 double with shared bathroom; $169–$369 double with private bathroom. Subway: 1 to 79th St. **Amenities:** Gym; lobby coffee bar; free Wi-Fi.

Hotel Newton ★ Everything is literally "coming up roses," thanks to a peachy color scheme, flat-screen TVs and handsome red wood furnishings that have given guest rooms a much plusher look than they used to have. Along with more expensive "superior" rooms and suites, two rooms per floor share a bathroom; these go for about $100 to $160 depending on the date (*hint:* ask for a third floor shared bathroom as there's only one room on that floor without a private bathroom, meaning you get it to yourself). The suites are good sized, and the choice for families who need extra room to spread out (they have sofa beds).

2528 Broadway (btw. 94th and 95th sts.). www.thehotelnewton.com. ℂ**888/HOTEL58** (468-3558) or 212/678-6500. 180 units. $100–$175 double with shared bathroom or single room with private bathroom; $135–$225 double with private bathroom. Extra person $25. Children 14 and under stay free in parent's room. Subway: 1, 2, or 3 to 96th St. **Amenities:** Room service.

The Riverside Towers ★ The floor coverings are industrial rugs, the rooms cramped and old, the mattresses covered with plastic (below the sheets), the sinks are chipped, and woe betide you if you get a room near the elevator because it emits a whine that would startle a dog in heat. So why even bother to write about the Riverside Towers as an option? Because New York City is so crazy expensive, and commuting from New Jersey is such a vacation-buster, that some travelers will put up with this hotel's (many) deficiencies for the ability to stay in a lovely, Manhattan neighborhood at a reasonable price (and all rooms have private bathrooms). Are you among those who don't mind indoor camping? If you are, the Riverside Towers may be your cup of tea. *Note:* When I last visited there was no Wi-Fi in the rooms, though the management says that's coming soon.

80 Riverside Dr. (at 80th St.). www.riversidetowerhotel.com. ℂ **888/724-3136** or 212/877-5200. 110 units. $129 double rooms year-round. Subway: 1 to 86th St. **Amenities:** Café on main floor.

UPPER EAST SIDE

Beautiful townhouses, world-class museums and the shops of Madison Avenue define the Upper East Side. It's a tony, quiet area to use as a base.

Best for: Visitors who like an upscale residential neighborhood, close to Central Park and Museum Mile, with luxury shopping and some fine dining.

Drawbacks: It's not the best-served by public transportation and can be one of the more expensive areas of town.

Expensive

The Lowell ★★★ The Lowell is the only hotel in New York City that puts actual wood-burning fireplaces in some of its rooms. That may seem like an odd fact to point out first, but it sums up, for me, the very special ambiance of the place, which somehow manages to be quite homey despite being outrageously elegant. Rooms and suites are divided into two categories. The "traditional" ones have a chicly cluttered look, with antique rugs and bookshelves brimming with books. The contemporary rooms are just as lovely, but with bigger bathrooms, a dusty pastel color palette (of browns, gray-blues, tans and greens), and slightly more modern couches and chairs. All feature exquisite works of art on the walls (a Chinese watercolor in one, a French print in another) and lovely pieces of porcelain here and there. The location is also swell, just one block from Central Park on a quiet, brownstone-lined street.

28 E. 63rd St. (btw. Madison and Park aves.). www.lowellhotel.com. ℂ **212/838-1400.** 70 units. $620–$700 double. Subway: F to Lexington Ave.–63rd St. Pets under 15 lbs. accepted. **Amenities:** 2 restaurants; tearoom; babysitting; concierge; well-outfitted fitness room; room service; video library; free Wi-Fi.

The Surrey ★★ In 2009, the Beaux Arts Surrey was literally gutted and re-built at a cost of $60 million. In the process it was transformed, well, into the sort of hotel that one usually sees downtown rather than uptown. By which I mean: it now has edge. On the walls are contemporary artworks by such big names as Chuck Close, Richard Serra, and Jenny Holzer; and the décor, instead of consisting of tastefully tassled couches and velvet chairs (like so many other Upper East Side hotels), is proudly contemporary. That's not to say rooms aren't comfortable: they are—in the extreme. Spacious, well-appointed and wow, each has a Duxiana mattresses, an amenity that alone costs about $15,000 per room. The one disappointment here: the walls could be thicker (they're not always fully soundproof). Even if you don't end up staying, drop by for a drink at the comely rooftop garden bar; a treatment at the state-of-the-art Cornelia Spa; or a meal at Café Boulud. (It supplies the room service here.)

20 E. 76th St. (btw. Fifth and Madison aves.). www.thesurrey.com. © **212/288-3700.** 189 units. $482–$597 salon. Subway: 6 to 77th St. Pet-friendly. **Amenities:** Restaurant; 2 bars; Les Clefs d'Or concierge; fitness center and spa; room service; rooftop garden.

Moderate

The Gracie Inn ★ Remember your first apartment? That's what the Gracie Inn looks like. The furniture screams "hand me down," as do the prints on the walls, but that's where the negatives end. Because this is, on most weeks, a great value, with rooms that are dust-free and a breakfast that is delivered free to your door each morning, at the hour you request. Not that you need the staff to supply breakfast: each room and suite has a full and useable kitchen, complete with flatware, plates, pots, and pans. The two-bedroom suites can easily hold a family. As for its location, the Gracie is in a tidy residential neighborhood and not too far from the crosstown bus (though it's a hike to get to the subway).

502 E. 81st St. (near York Ave.). www.gracieinnhotel.com. © **212/628-1700.** 13 units. $189–$214 studio suite. Subway: 6 to 77th St. **Amenities:** Useable kitchens in each room; free Wi-Fi.

BROOKLYN & QUEENS

The properties listed here offer substantial savings compared to what you would pay across the river. Some are in vibrant neighborhoods, others in areas that are just beginning the gentrification process, but all are safe and more convenient to the sights of Manhattan than a New Jersey hotel would be.

Best for: Visitors who are planning on outer borough as well as Manhattan activities; people comfortable with public transportation; foodies who want to be close to some of New York City's most interesting restaurants.

Drawbacks: You'll be taking a cab/subway/bus ride to Manhattan and its various attractions, activities, and restaurants. With that in mind, I've ONLY listed hotels that will be less expensive than their Manhattan equivalents.

Condor Hotel ★★ It's startling to find a hotel this contemporary and well, chic, in the heart of Hasidic Williamsburg, Brooklyn (there's a yeshiva just down the street). The Condor pays homage to its location with mezuzah's (tiny parchments of Hebrew prayers in decorated cases affixed to the doorposts of Jewish homes) on its door frames, but other than that it's its own, well, bird: a sexy, stylish place to stay with generously proportioned rooms, all done up in handsome teals and browns and some including terraces. Nightly rates include continental breakfast, plus cookies and lemonade 24 hours at the front desk. The little garden out back is a delightful place to decompress when the weather's good. I just wish it were less of a walk to the nearest subway (it's about a third of a mile to the Flushing stop).

56 Franklin Ave. (near Flushing Ave.), Brooklyn. www.condorny.com. © **347/587-2484.** 80 units. $109–$219 double. Subway: G to Flushing or J or M to Lorimer St. **Amenities:** Free Wi-Fi; breakfast included; garden; concierge.

Country Inn and Suites ★ Just one and half blocks from a subway stop that's one stop from Manhattan—that's the main attraction of this cookie cutter chain motel. Oh, and the prices are excellent, the rooms are clean and big, and a continental breakfast is part of the deal here. As for the neighborhood, it's on its way up, so though it can look industrial, it's very safe.

40–34 Crescent St. (near 41st Ave.), Queens. www.countryinns.com. © **800/830-5222** or 718/729-2111. 48 units. $87–$125 double. Subway: N, Q to 39th Ave. **Amenities:** Free Wi-Fi; included breakfast; garden; concierge.

Honey's B&B ★★ One doesn't expect to be staying in a Victorian house with a yard when visiting the Big Apple. But Brooklyn has many neighborhoods where the green outpaces the asphalt, and this is one (though it's only a 3-minute walk to the subway and just 30 minutes from there into Manhattan). Owned by an outgoing couple, the Berger's home is cheerfully furnished with pretty plates from around the world, and a large living room and porch for guests to lounge in. Rooms share a bathroom (one for every two) and feature such niceties as pillowtop mattresses, homemade quilts on the beds, bay windows, original wood paneling, and stained glass (in places). Guests have kitchen privileges, too.

770 Westminster Rd. (btw. Avenue H and Glenwood Rd.). www.honeysbedandbreakfast.com. © **917/873-9493.** 4 units. $105–$125 per night double or single. Subway: Q to Avenue H. **Amenities:** Free Wi-Fi; breakfast included; use of the kitchen.

La Quinta Inn ★ Free parking, a friendly staff, and a commute that's just two-subway stops into Manhattan—so what's wrong with staying in Queens? Okay, the elevated subway that passes right by the front of the hotel can be disruptive to sleep patterns. But those who choose a room in the back—MAKE SURE you get a room in the back—won't hear it at all. Other than that odd requirement, this is like any other La Quinta on the planet, by which I mean bland in décor but comfortable and tidy.

37–18 Queens Blvd. (at 37th St.), Queens. www.lq.com. © **718/729-8775.** 45 units. $140–$165 double. Subway: 7 to 40th St. **Amenities:** Free Wi-Fi; breakfast included; free local calls; fitness room.

Sofia Inn ★★ You'll understand why so many people want to live in Prospect Heights after visiting this handsome little inn. First lure is the quiet, tree-shaded street which, despite its serenity, is within easy walking distance of a slew of fab boutiques and restaurants, as well as the Brooklyn Museum, Prospect Park, the Botanical Gardens, and subways into Manhattan (about a 20–25 minute ride). Next, is the style of the place, which is oh-so-Brooklyn. Owner Billy Tashman a former public school math teacher (he's a very sweet guy) salvaged massive, school science posters from the 1950s (on such topics as "Symbiosis" and "Evolution"); these give each room a quirky charm, which is further enhanced by the antique chandeliers, carved wooden bed frames and lovely armchairs he and his designer bought, mostly from Craig's List. The final appealing element: the price. There's no way you could get a full apartment in Manhattan, with kitchen, for under $200 a night (as you will with the two suites here). Rooms that share bathrooms (two guestrooms per loo) are also reasonable in cost. All in all, a real find.

288 Park Place (off Vanderbuilt Ave.), Brooklyn. www.brooklynbedandbreakfast.net. © **917/865-7428.** 6 units. $95–$135 double. Extra person $25. Subway: 2, 3 to Grand Army Plaza. **Amenities:** Free Wi-Fi; kitchens in some rooms.

Union Hotel ★   Set on a funky (but very safe) street near the Historic Boerum Hill area, this colonial-looking brick hotel features cheery contemporary rooms at excellent prices. So what that you won't be able to walk around your bed once you've laid your suitcase next to it? The bed is a highly comfortable one, and you're getting digs with private bathroom at prices some places charge for rooms with shared facilities. The included breakfast consists of a coupon to a nearby diner. And it's just two short blocks from a subway that will zoom you into Manhattan.

611 Degraw St. (btw. Third and Fourth aves.), Brooklyn. www.unionhotelbrooklyn.com. © **917/865-7428.** 40 units. $108–$147 double. Subway: R to Union St. **Amenities:** Free Wi-Fi; breakfast included.

WHERE TO EAT

ts competitors are Hong Kong and Paris, Brussels and San Francisco, and Rome and New Orleans. But I'll argue hard that none of these other great restaurant cities has quite the same number of serious, satisfying eateries as New York, nor its amazing variety of cuisines in every price range . . . and quirk. Would you believe restaurants that serve only mac 'n' cheese or peanut butter concoctions—and flourish doing so?

How did the surprising volume and variety of NYC restaurants come about?

o New York has a larger and more varied immigrant population than any of the other foremost restaurant cities—and that means ethnic specialties of every sort;
o New York has an unprecedented number of topnotch cooking schools, the offices of international magazines devoted to the art of cooking, and the headquarters of the Food Channel;
o The pace of life here is more hectic and pressured than in other famous restaurant cities, creating a vast population with "no time to cook."

Mix all these reasons together, sauté them over the bright flame of the city's celebrity, and you have a mecca for foodies, a place where people obsess over the gratification of their taste buds without anyone thinking it's odd. In China, one way of saying "hello" is to ask, "Have you eaten?" In Gotham, we say, "Where have you eaten—and do you need a reservation?"

PRACTICAL INFORMATION

Sad but true, sometimes a restaurant that's crowded one week will be closed by the next. So though I've done my best to only recommend the ones I think have staying power, I don't have psychic abilities. Do call in advance to make sure the place you're intending to dine is still in business. It likely will be, but better safe . . . .

Reservations

Reservations are always a good idea in New York, and a necessity for popular restaurants. Call *far* ahead for any special meal you don't want to miss. Most top places start taking reservations 30 days in advance. If you're booking a holiday dinner, call even earlier, or head to **OpenTable.com,** a reservations site that handles more than 200 NYC restaurants, as soon as you decide on the date of your dinner.

But if you didn't call well ahead, don't despair. Often, early or late hours—between 5:30 and 6:30pm or after 9pm—are available, especially on weeknights. And most restaurants have bar seating, for which one needs no reservations. Or go for lunch, which is usually much easier to book without advance notice. If you're staying at a hotel with a concierge, don't be afraid to use him or her—a well-connected concierge can often get you into hot spots.

Tipping

Tipping is easy in New York. The way to do it: Double the 8.75% sales tax and *voilà*, happy waitstaff. Don't forget to tip: waiters make less than minimum wage and are taxed on what the government expects them to make in tips. So when you stiff the waiter, he not only loses that extra bit of income, he still has to pay taxes on it.

Leave $1 per item, no matter how small, for the checkroom attendant. You don't need to tip the host who escorts you to your table.

FINANCIAL DISTRICT & TRIBECA

Expensive

Brushstroke ★★★ JAPANESE   There are three ways to dine at Brushstroke, all of them pretty, well, splendid. Those with advance planning skills and a dash of luck, call many months ahead for the chance to sit at the sushi bar in front of master chef Eiji Ichimura and try his *omakase* or tasting menu ($150). Ichimura is one of the few people in the U.S. to practice the Edo-mae style of sushi making, which substitutes fish cured in salt, soy sauce or vinegar for fresh fish, with spectacular results.

But even if you don't get a reservation with that master, you can try the tasting menus devised by the *other* on-site eating guru, owner David Bouley. He's been working with the Japanese Culinary Institute to create the *kaiseki* experience here, which means a meal created from many exquisite small plates. When we were there recently that included such delicacies as summer vegetables and squash blossoms in a vinegar gelee, soft-shell crabs with fresh uni (sea urchin), and tender sashimi (from Ichimura). Even the wasabi was the tastiest I've ever tried (my husband finished the entire little pile *after* he was done with his sashimi). The service is almost kabuki-like in its formality (I've never had a waiter walk me to the bathroom before, open the door, and say gravely "Enjoy," before). But that, too, is part of the fun. *Tip:* If you don't want to spend the $135 for the full tasting menu, try version number three of the meal: take the tasting menu instead ($85). It allows you to choose different items off the kaiseki menu. By varying your choices and sharing, you can *almost* re-create the pricier experience. There's also a tasting menu for vegetarians ($85).

30 Hudson St. (btw. Duane and Reade sts.). ℭ **212/791-3771.** www.davidbouley.com. Kaiseke menu $135; Omakase menu $150; Vegetarian or regular tasting menu $85. Mon–Sat 5:30pm–midnight. Subway: 1 to Franklin St.

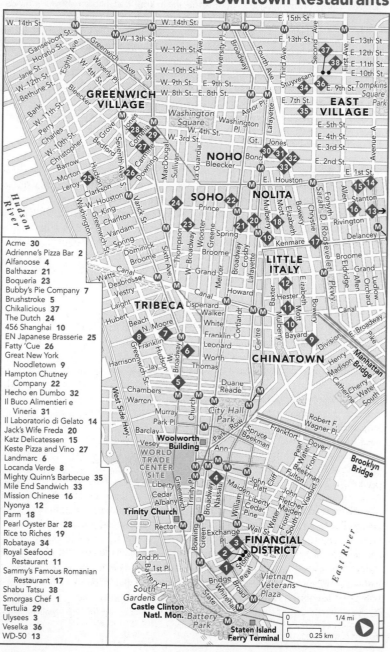

Acme **30**
Adrienne's Pizza Bar **2**
Alfanoose **4**
Balthazar **21**
Boqueria **23**
Bubby's Pie Company **7**
Brushstroke **5**
Chikalicious **37**
The Dutch **24**
456 Shanghai **10**
EN Japanese Brasserie **25**
Fatty 'Cue **26**
Great New York
Noodletown **9**
Hampton Chutney
Company **22**
Hecho en Dumbo **32**
Il Buco Alimentieri e
Vineria **31**
Il Laboratorio di Gelato **14**
Jack's Wife Freda **20**
Katz Delicatessen **15**
Keste Pizza and Vino **27**
Landmarc **6**
Locanda Verde **8**
Mighty Quinn's Barbecue **35**
Mile End Sandwich **33**
Mission Chinese **16**
Nyonya **12**
Parm **18**
Pearl Oyster Bar **28**
Rice to Riches **19**
Robataya **34**
Royal Seafood
Restaurant **11**
Sammy's Famous Romanian
Restaurant **17**
Shabu Tatsu **38**
Smorgas Chef **1**
Tertulia **29**
Ulysees **3**
Veselka **36**
WD-50 **13**

Locanda Verde ★★★ ITALIAN I have a single girlfriend who comes here whenever she's feeling blue. She claims the sheep's milk ricotta crostini is a picker-upper like no other. But the real reason may be she always gets picked up here. Darkly lit, with plush leather booths, a handsome art deco-ish décor and a bar populated by eligible bachelors, Locanda Verde completes the neat trick of making Grandma's cooking seem as sexy as George Clooney. That's due to chef Andrew Carmellini (also of the **Dutch,** p. 72) who must have had quite the talented ancestors if the recipe for "My Grandmother's Ravioli" was actually passed down to him. Fabulous food and that handsome décor make this the perfect date place.

377 Greenwich St. (at N. Moore St.). ℂ **212/925-3797.** www.locandaverdenyc.com. Reservations highly recommended. Main courses $17–$28. Mon–Fri 11:30am–3pm; daily 5:30–11pm; Sat–Sun 10am–3pm. Subway: 1 to Franklin St.

Moderate

Bubby's Pie Company ★ AMERICAN The quintessential TriBeCa restaurant—though it looks like a cross between a roadside diner and your great aunt's parlor—this is the place where celebs go for their mac-and-cheese fix. Join 'em: the homey American classics are topnotch here, whether you order the crunchy buttermilk fried chicken or head here for a breakfast of fluffy sour-cream pancakes. Kids love this place, not only for the child-friendly menu, but for the endless supply of crayons and paper doled out by the staff, and the bookshelf in the back, brimming with children's books.

120 Hudson St. (at N. Moore St.). ℂ **212/219-0666.** www.bubbys.com. Main courses $8–$20 breakfast, brunch, and lunch; $17–$25 dinner. Mon–Thurs 8am–11pm; Fri 8am–midnight; Sat 9am–4:30pm and 6pm–midnight; Sun 9am–10pm. Subway: 1 to Franklin St.

Landmarc ★ FRENCH/ITALIAN/MEDITERRANEAN A happy, little bistro where meats are cooked over an open fire, children are more than welcome, and the service is downright sweet. Head here if you want a really good meal without pretension (a rarity in New York City), and you enjoy a glass of vino that won't break the bank (the restaurant has an excellent selection for both glasses and bottles, with an unusual number of affordable ones). Landmarc now has an uptown location, too, at the Time Warner Center, but it doesn't have the charisma of the original.

179 W. Broadway (btw. Leonard and Worth sts.). ℂ **212/343-3883.** www.landmarc-restaurant.com. Main courses $15–$34. Mon–Fri noon–2am; Sat–Sun 9am–4pm and 5:30pm–2am. Subway: 1 to Franklin St.

Inexpensive

Alfanoose ★ MIDDLE EASTERN The best place to eat in the vicinity of the 9/11 Memorial. The name means "magic lantern" and if you peer closely at the shelves, scattered here and there are a couple that look like they can be rubbed. They provide the only decoration in this spartan Middle Eastern restaurant, which is jam-packed with local office workers at lunchtime. Most come for the falafel, which are fried to order. Yes, that does slow the service, but the results are worth it.

8 Maiden Lane (near Broadway). ℂ **212/528-4669.** www.alfanoose.com. Main courses $6–$13; Mon–Sat 11:30am–9:30pm. Subway: 4, 5 to Fulton St.

history written in STONE STREET

Just off Hanover Square is the oldest street in Manhattan (it's thought to be the only one still in the place the Dutch put it). It's lined by 15 lovely Greek Revival industrial buildings (all built right after the great fire of 1835), and happens to be a splendid place to dine, especially when the weather's nice. That's when the cute-as-kittens restaurants that now fill these historic structures place tables right on the cobblestone street, which is closed to traffic to allow for some of the most picturesque al fresco dining in Manhattan. The best of them are:

Smorgas Chef ★★ SCANDINAVIAN   A sunny yellow and sea-blue Scandinavian restaurant that exposes its customers to all the greatest hits of the region: Norwegian smoked salmon (on top of eggs, chives, and bread), salty herring from Denmark, and, yes, Swedish meatballs as light as beach balls and carrying a nice smattering of lingonberry sauce.

53 Stone St. ℭ **212/422-3500.** www.smorgas chef.com. Main courses $12–$24. Daily 11am–4:30pm and 5–11pm. Subway: 2, 3 to Wall Street, R, Q to Whitehall.

Ulysees ★ IRISH/GREEK   Ulysees bills itself as a Greco-Gaelic pub, if you can imagine that, which anchors the street on its north end. More Irish than Greek (though there are tributes to the Greek hero on some of the walls), it's huge but divided adroitly into intimate "snugs" and furnished with several tons of County Clare shale (forming oh-so-Irish country walls). What's not-so-Irish about this place is the food, which is much better than I've had in the pubs of Eire, especially the lunchtime carvery, where you can get a heaping plateful of meat and veggies.

58 Stone St. ℭ **212/482-0400.** www.ulysees nyc.com. Main courses $9–$26. Daily 11am–4am. Subway: 2, 3 to Wall Street, R, Q to Whitehall.

Adriennes Pizza Bar ★ PIZZA   Square instead of round, and thin-crusted, this isn't your usual pizza joint and that's just fine. The sauce is well spiced and the cheese high quality.

54 Stone St. ℭ **212/248-3838.** www.ulysees nyc.com. Main courses $8–$15. Daily 11am–4am. Subway: 2, 3 to Wall Street, R, Q to Whitehall.

CHINATOWN

Inexpensive

456 Shanghai ★★ CHINESE   Few foods are as fun to eat—or as dangerous to one's attire—as soup dumplings (aka juicy buns). Pucker-topped dumplings filled with broth, and either pork or pork with crabmeat, they explode in your mouth—or down your shirt when you bite into them. But the flavor, enhanced by a vinegared soy sauce with slivered ginger, is so luscious, most diners don't mind the mess. And the best place in Manhattan for them is this bustling eatery, which draws a mostly local crowd. Other Shanghai specialties are worth trying, too, like sautéed eels with chives or the scallion pancakes wrapped around hoisin beef and coated with fried egg.

69 Mott St. (btw. Canal and Bayard sts.). ℭ **212/964-0003.** Entrees $7–$16. Daily 11am–10pm. Subway: N or R to Canal St.

Great New York Noodletown ★★ CHINESE It ain't much to look at: The lighting's too bright and the seats are crowded together, but there are few finer dining experiences to be had in this restaurant-crammed city. In fact, in the years I've been coming here, I've seen chefs from far pricier places, still in their chef's whites, dining here after their shifts were over. I couldn't see what they ordered, but I always go for the sautéed pea shoots, a delicate, very green taste sensation; the salt-baked squid, the seafood equivalent of potato chips, they're that light and crunchy; some slices off one of the ducks that hang in macabre style in the window; and the heat-packing Singapore chow fun ($5.95), an al dente, spicy mix of thin, long pasta, diced vegetables, and pork. No reservations accepted.

28½ Bowery (at Bayard St.). © **212/349-0923.** Main courses $4–$15. No credit cards. Daily 9am–3am. Subway: N, R, or 6 to Canal St.

Nyonya ★ MALAYSIAN The menu is a good 10 pages long at Nyonya, reflecting the broad mélange of influences that go into Malaysian cuisine. From India, there are rich curries, such as *roti canai*, light-as-air fried bread that you use to scoop up a bright yellow, chunky curry sauce. Another appetizer, the oyster omelet with chili sauce speaks of China in its flavor profile, and delightful texture. As do the crabs with dried shrimp and chilis. Wash it all down with excellent house-made juices (my daughters' fave is the green apple/kiwi concoction). Don't come if you're in a hurry or want a romantic atmosphere: the décor is non-existent and there's always a line to get in.

194 Grand St. (btw. Mulberry and Mott sts.). © **212/334-3669.** www.ilovenyonya.com. Appetizers $2–$8; noodle soups $4–$6; main dishes $6–$23. No credit cards. Sun–Thurs 11am–11:30pm; Fri–Sat 11am–midnight. Subway: 6 to Spring St.

Royal Seafood Restaurant ★★ DIM SUM The classic Chinatown meal is the dim sum brunch or lunch. Dim sum, for those who've never tried it, is a meal made up of many small dishes, primarily different sorts of dumplings and buns, a tradition that started in the tea houses that lined China's Silk Road many centuries ago (scholars believe the custom began shortly after A.D. 300, when the long-held notion that tea should not be accompanied by food fell out of favor). And the top place for dim sum in Chinatown today is this cacophonous, always-jammed restaurant, where the clientele is often entirely Chinese, and the dishes range from the expected to the un: boiled snails, tripe stews, eggplant with shrimp paste. Since many of the servers don't speak English, you'll have to point at what interests you. If you make a mistake (hard to do, as it's all tasty), it's no big deal, as most dishes cost just a few bucks.

103–105 Mott St. (just off Canal). © **212/334-3669.** Daily 8am–10:30pm. Meal $6–$12 per person on average. Subway: N, R, or 6 to Canal St.

LOWER EAST SIDE

Expensive

WD-50 ★★★ MOLECULAR GASTRONOMY Every bite tastes different. That's the greatest compliment I can give the food at WD-50 and part of what makes eating here such darn fun. After the waitress rattles off the list of the, oh, 10-20 ingredients that make up whatever dish you're having, you start to strategize. Should I mix that little bit of shrimp, with the red sauce or the yogurt concoction? Will that bit of sweetbread taste better with the dehydrated lychee nut? Should I scoop up that daisy green or pine needle or bit of chamomile powder now or later? You start to collaborate with the long-haired genius chef who's behind the madness here, Wylie Dufresne (you've likely seen him on Top Chef), and the little miracle is: whatever combination you try, it ends up being extraordinarily tasty. Which may be what makes Dufresne's molecular gastronomy different than others in the genre. The meal isn't about food appearing from a puff of smoke or melting down in front of your eyes. Instead, the chef takes odd ingredients—lots and lots of them—and weaves them into cohesive, yet surprising, dishes. A note for penny pinchers: though the tasting menus here are pricey (see below), if you're willing to sit at the bar, you can order two dishes off of either menu, for "just" $50. Another perk to sitting at the bar: the friendly bartender will often top of your wine glass at no extra charge.

50 Clinton St. (btw. Stanton and Rivington sts.). © **212/477-2900.** Tasting menu $155 or $90; meals at the bar from $50. Daily 6–10pm. Subway: F or J to Delancey/Essex St.

Sammy's Famous Romanian Restaurant ★★ ROUMANIAN At some point in their lives, nearly every New Yorker makes his or her way to Sammy's, a nightly bar mitzvah masquerading as a steak joint. Set in a basement on the Lower East Side, its decor is gloriously tacky: business cards stuck all over the ceiling, balloons at the tables, and photos of patrons cramming the walls. Completing the ambience is an aged fellow at an electric keyboard who regales the crowd with Yiddish songs, selections from *Fiddler on the Roof,* and the hoariest Jewish jokes you've ever heard. Diners dance in the aisle, and sometimes members of the crowd take to the microphone to sing as well (especially if they've ordered the house special drink: a bottle of vodka encased in a block of ice). The crusty, gruff waiters will try to push you into ordering too much food: Resist them. There's no reason whatsoever to order the prix fixe menu; and the steaks are a foot long and overhang the plate, so order one for every two people with just one side of fried potatoes. You have to start with a helping of the chopped liver, a heart attack in a bowl, which the waiter mixes tableside, combining the liver with fried onions, plain onions, and literally a cup and a half of schmaltz (for the uninitiated that's liquefied chicken fat). One order of the liver is enough for four people. Bring a group as there are few better places in the city for a blowout party.

157 Chrystie St. (at Delancey St.). © **212/673-0330.** Main dishes average $35. Mon–Thurs 4–10pm; Fri–Sat 4–11pm; Sun 3–9pm. Subway: F to Delancey St., B, D, Q to Grand St.

Inexpensive

Katz's Delicatessen ★ DELICATESSEN One of the city's longest-running success stories, Katz has been in business since 1888. You may feel a sense of déjà vu as you enter, as this is where Meg Ryan, ahem, made a scene in *When Harry Met Sally,* and it looks just as it did in the flick: a cavernous, loud space with linoleum-topped tables; celebrity photos and testimonials plastering the walls; and curtains of hanging salami in the window. Though its menu is varied and long, only the uninitiated bypass the corned beef sandwich ($12)—the best in the city—a towering stack of meat cured for as long as 30 days, which gives it a richness and depth that you simply don't find with commercially prepared corned beef (which is "pressure injected" to cure in a mere 36 hours).

205 E. Houston St. (at Ludlow St.). ℂ **212/254-2246.** http://katzsdelicatessen.com. Reservations not accepted. Sandwiches $5–$16. Mon–Wed 8am–10:45pm; Thurs 8am–2:45am; Fri–Sun 24 hr. (open Fri 8am and close Sun 10:45pm). Subway: F to Second Ave.

Mission Chinese ★★★ CHINESE/FUSION   An import from San Francisco, few restaurants have opened with as much buzz as Mission Chinese did in 2013. It was all justified. The food, a wacky fusion of Chinese techniques with ingredients from all corners of the culinary world (Kung Pao pastrami, anyone?), is revelatory, delicious and inexpensive. And the "Maine clam shack during Chinese New Years' décor is unlike anything you'll find in New York. Don't be put off by the grungy appearance of the front counter, or the crowd of rowdies drinking from the keg as you enter. Join them! Mission provides free beer to make the wait for a table a little more, well, palatable. (Some reservations are taken, but you have to get online at 10am exactly a week to the day before you want to visit to nab one; most of the seats are for walk-in guests).

154 Orchard St. (btw. Rivington and Stanton sts). ℂ **212/529-8800.** www.missionchinesefood. com/ny. Shareable entrees are $12–$18. Daily noon–3pm and 5:30pm–midnight. Subway: F to Second Ave.

SOHO & NOLITA

For a quick, non-sit down bite in these areas, I highly recommend **Hampton Chutney Company** (68 Prince St. near Broadway; ℂ **212/226-9996;** daily 11am–9pm) which serves *dosas,* southern Indian pancakes, rolled up with all sorts of fillings, both Indian and not. Nearby, **Jack's Wife Freda** (224 Lafayette St., near Spring St.; ℂ **212/510-8550;** Mon–Sat 10am–midnight, Sun 10am–10pm) serves hearty Israeli food in a cramped but cheery café, where the service is speedy.

Expensive

Balthazar ★★ FRENCH   Walt Disney's imagineers couldn't do a better job than restaurateur Keith McNally has of re-creating the perfect Parisian brasserie. But not only does Balthazar look picture-perfect with its zinc bar, smoked mirrors, soaring ceiling and serious, vest-wearing waiters, the food hits the mark as well. Open for breakfast, brunch, lunch, and dinner, it's the place to come for delectable pastries, perfectly executed French classics (like *steak au poivre* or *moules frites*), and tiptop cocktails. The whole concept should feel phony, but instead the effect is charming.

80 Spring St. (btw. Broadway and Crosby St.). ℂ **212/965-1414.** www.balthazarny.com. Main courses $19–$36. Mon–Fri 11:30am–3pm; Sat–Sun 10am–3pm; Sun–Wed 5:30pm–midnight; Thurs–Sat 5:30pm–1am. Subway: C or E to Spring St.

The Dutch ★★ AMERICAN   Forget herring. The Dutch doesn't serve food from the Netherlands. Instead, it references the fare that would have been popular in *Olde* NYC. And by that I mean the gay '90s version, not New Amsterdam. So the pies are a specialty and there are oysters galore, plus juicy steaks, grilled pork chops, baked beans, turnips, and other classic east coast ingredients. But often these staples are updated, as are the pasta dishes, with Asian or Latin touches, by the talented chef Andrew Carmellini (also of **Locanda Verde,** p. 68). Though it's a large restaurant, with several rooms, reservations are a must as it fills up nightly with locals, here to celebrate special occasions . . . or just life. It's that kind of place.

131 Sullivan St. (at Prince St.). ℂ **212/677-6200.** www.thedutchnyc.com. Reservations highly recommended. Main courses $19–$36. Mon–Fri 11:30am–3pm; Sat–Sun 10am–3pm; Sun–Wed 5:30pm–midnight; Thurs–Sat 5:30pm–1am. Subway: C or E to Spring St.

Moderate

Boqueria ★★ SPANISH/TAPAS   The music thumps, the seats are all high stools (though with backs, so you're comfortable), and the din of happy voices around you make you feel like you're at a bar rather than a restaurant. Then the food arrives and it's clear: you're definitely at a fine-dining establishment, and one that's at the top of its game. Traditional tapas are superb (such as the creamy croquettes and perfectly crisped *patatas bravas*) while the creative tapas are downright exhilarating (who would ever have guessed that raw scallops with yogurt, hazelnuts, and pomegranate seeds would be such a sublime combo?). The paella, artisanal cheese and meat plates, and sangria are topnotch, too. One suggestion: bring a group so that you can try as many of these small plates as possible, without over-ordering.

171 Spring St. (btw. Thompson and W. Broadway). ℂ **212/343-4255.** www.boquerianyc.com. Reservations for groups of 6 or more. Tapas $5–$14; *raciones* (main courses) $19–$29. Daily noon–midnight. Subway: C, E to Spring St. Also at 53 W. 19th St. (btw. 5th and 6th aves.). ℂ **212/255-4160.** Subway: F, M to 23rd St.

Inexpensive

Parm ★ ITALIAN   There's Italian food and then there's Italian American food. And for decades the latter version was looked down on as being, well, a bit déclassé. No more. This proudly old fashioned red sauce joint does such a superb job with the "canon" of Italian American staples—chicken parmigiana, sausage and peppers, baked ziti—that you come away feeling like you've experienced the most cutting-edge meal possible. And all in a cute, checkered-tablecloth restaurant that will bring you back, in spirit, to 1950s New York.

248 Mulberry St. (btw. Prince and Spring sts.). ℂ **212/993-7189.** www.parmnyc.com. Main dishes $9–$17. Sun–Wed 11am–11pm; Thurs–Sat 11am–midnight. Subway: B, D, F, M, 6 to Spring St. or N, R to Prince St.

THE EAST VILLAGE & NOHO

Beside the restaurants listed below, I highly recommend **Mile End Sandwich** ★★ (53 Bond St. off Bowery; ℂ **212/529-2990;** daily 10am–6pm) which brings Montreal-style deli to the Big Apple (read more on p. 90). Also of note is the new **Il Buco Alimentari e Vineria** ★★ (53 Great Jones St. off Bowery; ℂ **212/837-2622;** www.ilbucovinieri.com; Mon–Thurs 7am–3pm and 6–11pm, Fri 7am–3pm and 6pm–1am, Sat 11am–3pm and 5:30pm–1am, Sun 11am–3pm, 5:30–10pm), which features excellent Italian wines paired with equally as noteworthy small plates and pasta platters. And for those who like to do their own cooking there's **Shabu Tatsu** ★ (216 E. 10th St. off Second Ave.; ℂ **212/477-2972;** Sun–Thurs 5–11pm, Fri–Sat 5am–1:30am) where diners dip meats, noodles, and vegetables into a pot of boiling water before immersing them in scrumptious dipping sauces. Kids LOVE this place.

Moderate

Acme ★★ SCANDINAVIAN   Foie gras and langoustine—the ultimate surf and turf? It is when they're plated together at Acme, one of the two Manhattan restaurants being helmed by leaders of the new Nordic cuisine movement (see p. 101 for the other). In recent years, chefs in Stockholm and Copenhagen have been melding traditional ingredients with contemporary cooking techniques to rave reviews. Bringing that food to NYC is chef Mads Refslund, of Copenhagen's acclaimed Noma restaurant. And he's doing it in a rather low-key fashion. While the food is adventurous (carrots roasted in pine needles and served under a sheet of thin lardo, for example), the décor is decidedly downscale; Refslund simply took over a long running BBQ joint and kept it looking very much the same. The crowd, though, is different, and the models and media-types certainly spiff up the place. You will, too, when you visit (as you should, if you enjoy truly unusual culinary experiences).

9 Great Jones (at Lafayette St.). ✆ **212/203-2121.** www.acmenyc.com. Main courses $20–$32. Sun–Wed 6–11pm; Fri 6pm–midnight; Sat 11am–3pm and 6pm–midnight; Sun 11am–3pm and 6–11pm. Subway: 6 to Bleeker St.

Robataya ★★★ JAPANESE   This is where we take out of town guests because it is, quite literally, dinner and a show. Ask for space in the front room when you make your reservations, so you can sit at the squared bar, in the center of which two Japanese chefs kneel. In front of them is a grill, onto which, with gestures that are as delicate as a ballerina, they flip seafood, meats, and vegetables, gathering the ingredients they need with a 10-foot-long paddle. That paddle is later used to serve you your dishes, hot off the grill. It's a bit difficult to describe the experience adequately, but trust me, it's one you'll remember. Kids love this place, too, not just for the experience but for the food, which is scrumptious but straightforward (there aren't a lot of sauces or spices used in most cases).

231 E. 9th St. (btw. Second and Third aves.). ✆ **212/777-7773.** www.robataya-ny.com. Main courses $7–$35. Wed–Thurs noon–2:30pm and 6–10:45pm; Fri noon–2:30pm and 6–11:45pm; Sat 6–11:45pm; Sun–Tues 6–10:45pm. Subway: 6 to Astor Place.

Inexpensive

Hecho en Dumbo ★★ MEXICAN   The Manhattan "child" of a very popular Brooklyn joint (the Dumbo in the title refers to the "Down Under Manhattan Bridge Overpass" neighborhood it is in), Hecho is the slow food version of Mexican fare. All of the ingredients are organic, many are locally sourced, and all breads, salsas and even cheeses are made in house, a fact that elevates even the simplest quesadilla. But you don't come here for simple fare; the food is more complex and original than that, incorporating such ingredients as roasted bone marrow or huitlacoche mushrooms into the tacos. All of this yummy, healthy stuff is served in an airy, industrial-chic space right on the Bowery.

354 Bowery (at Great Jones St.). ✆ **212/937-4245.** www.hechoendumbo.com. Main courses $14–$20. Sun–Thurs 5:30–11:30pm; Fri–Sat 5:30pm–midnight; Sat–Sun 11:30am–4pm. Subway: 6 to Bleeker St.

Mighty Quinn's Barbecue ★★ BARBECUE   Meet Texalina BBQ: that's Texas spices (and some of the dishes here are fiery) with that Carolina vinegar-taste. It's a mighty fine combination, so good that owner Hugh Magnum was able to parlay his popularity as a vendor at an outdoor Brooklyn market into this indoor, Manhattan restaurant. Though you'd never know you were in NYC if you were somehow transported here blindfolded. The décor is pure Southern roadhouse and the BBQ isn't simply "good for NYC," it would hold its own against any 'cue down south. Best on the menu: the meltingly tender brisket, which is slow cooked for 22 hours, before hitting your cardboard plate. *Warning:* there's always a line out the door, so be prepared to wait.

103 Second Ave. (at 6th St.). $\textcircled{C}$ **212/677-3733.** www.mightyquinnsbbq.com; Main courses $6–$9. Sun–Thurs 11:30am–11pm; Fri–Sat 11:30am–midnight. Subway: 6 to Astor Place.

Veselka ★ UKRANIAN A popular spot for East Village hipsters, Goth guys and gals, families, businesspeople, and anybody who's ever had a deep need for cold borscht at 3am in the morning When Veselka debuted in 1954, the area was awash in Ukrainian diners, but most have since gone belly-up (or have upgraded to the point of assimilation), leaving this crowded, tall-windowed eatery the standard-bearer for pierogis, kielbasa, and other Eastern European fare.

144 Second Ave. (at 9th St.) $\textcircled{C}$ **212/228-9682.** No website. Main courses $8–$13. Daily 24 hr. Subway: 6 to Astor Place.

GREENWICH VILLAGE

Expensive

EN Japanese Brasserie ★★★ JAPANESE EN has something very few other restaurants in New York have: elbow room. Set in a space as large and high ceilinged as an old-fashioned train station, the restaurant has a serenity that most lack. That's not why you come here, of course. It's for the food, creative *Izakaya* cuisine (meaning Japanese small plates) that is exquisite and hearty by turns. On the delicate side is the house-made tofu, creamy as a cloud and sided with a tart vinagered soy sauce that adds just the right bit of oomph. On the hearty side are toothsome noodles in duck broth, fabulously ungreasy fried chicken, and plates of root vegetables in rich sesame sauce. But that's just the beginning of the menu, which serves Japanese food of a complexity one rarely gets outside of Japan itself. It also has one of the widest selections of fine sakes and *shochus* (a vodka-like liquor) in the city.

435 Hudson St. (at Leroy St.). $\textcircled{C}$ **212/647-9196.** www.enjb.com. Main courses $15–$35; *kaiseki* $65–$90 per person. Mon–Thurs noon–2:30pm and 5:30–11:30pm; Fri–Sat noon–2:30pm and 5:30pm–midnight; Sun 5:30–11pm. Subway: 1 to Christopher Street.

Tertulia ★★★ SPANISH/TAPAS An Irish guy from Vermont, Seamus Mullen, runs this place, yet in atmosphere and food Tertulia is the quintessential Iberian taberna. No, on second thought, the food and festive atmosphere here may be even *better* than what you'd find in recession-plagued Spain today. Food first, which is cooked (mostly) in a roaring, wood-fired oven (copied from one Mullen saw in a small Basque town, near Bilbao); try to get a seat near the stove, as it's mesmerizing to watch the chefs work it, creating food that's perfectly charred and just a touch smoky. I highly recommend the tasting menu, but if you don't want to shell out for that, build a meal

SWEETS FOR THE sweet

Dessert is given a place of honor on the NY restaurant scene, with venues ranging from beloved bakeries to all-dessert restaurants. Here are some of the best:

Chikalicious ★★★ A dessert-only restaurant, it's owned by a diminutive pastry chef named Chika Tillman (hence the name) who presides from behind the central counter in this glossy, all-white restaurant (it reminds me a bit of the "Milk Bar" in the movie A Clockwork Orange). All customers get a three-course tasting menu for $15. And what desserts they are! Ms. Tillman, who has baked at some of the top restaurants in the city, has a rich imagination when it comes to food, and though the pairings she makes seem weird—molten chocolate tart with red peppercorn ice-cream (studded with little bits of pepper) and red wine sauce is one—they're right on. Better than that, actually; if desserts can be revelatory, these are.

203 E. 10th St., right off Second Ave. ℂ 212/995-9511. www.chikalicious.com. Wed–Sun 3–10:45pm. Subway: 6 to Astor Place

Il Laboratorio di Gelato ★★ John F. Snyder, founder of Ciao Bella, plays the "mad scientist," whipping up new flavors in the back while his mother (often) serves customers. Double-scoop cups or cones start at $3.50, and are concocted from wacky, fun ingredients. Try the sour cream, cucumber, or cheddar cheese gelato.

188 Ludlow St. (at E. Houston). ℂ 212/343-9922. Cash only. Mon–Thurs 7:30am–10pm; Fri 7:30am–midnight; Sat 10am–midnight; Sun 10am–10pm. Subway: F to Delancey St., or J, M, Z to Essex St.

Insomnia Cookies ★ Large, soft, cookies, in 12 flavors (including snickerdoodle and chocolate chunk) and heated to just the right temperature are sold here, along with non-alcoholic beverages. And as you might have guessed, the joint stays open late.

405 Amsterdam Ave. (at 8th St). ℂ 212/343-9922. www.insomniacookies.com. Daily 11am–3am. Subway: 1, 2, 3 to 86th St. Other locations on Upper East Side and the Village.

Rice to Riches ★★★ A delightful one-trick pony, it serves only rice pudding. This isn't the rice pudding your mom made, however; it's tarted up with all sorts of exotic flavorings and unfortunately cutesy names such as "Sex, drugs and rocky road" and "Surrender to Mango." I have yet to discover a flavor that wasn't absolutely ambrosial.

37 Spring St. (btw. Mott and Mulberry sts.). ℂ 212/274-0008. www.ricetoriches.com. Sun–Thurs 11am–11pm; Fri and Sat 11am–1am. Subway: N, R to Prince St.

Venieros ★ A beloved Italian bakery, in business since 1894, with an attached café for those who'd like an aperitivo or café with their cannoli.

342 E. 11th St. (at First Ave.). ℂ 212/674-7070. www.venierospasty.com. Sun–Thurs 8am–midnight; Fri and Sat 8am–1am. Subway: N, R to Prince St.

around tapas (the *tosta matrimonio*, which "marries" black and white anchovies with sheep's mild cheese, is a knock-out) and the chef's crunchy yet succulent chicken paella. Bring a party with you if you can. Tertulia only accepts reservations for parties of four or more, so it's a good way to avoid the line outside.

359 6th Ave (at Washington St.). ℂ 646/559-9909. www.tertulianyc.com. Tapas $5–$23. Mon–Fri 11:30am–3pm; Sun–Thurs 5:30–11:30pm; Fri–Sat 5:30pm–midnight; Sat–Sun 11:30am–3:30pm. Subway: A, B, C, D, E, F to West 4th.

Moderate

Fatty 'Cue ★ BBQ/MALAYSIAN   It's now a proven fact: there are few finer toppings for a pulled-pork sandwich than a slaw made from papaya, carrots, and ginger. And though that may sound like heresy to classic, American BBQ fans, I became a convert to fusion-barbecue after a few meals at this smoked-wood spin-off from the Fatty Crab crowd (p. 94). Along with pulled pork, Fatty Cue features such other standards as ribs and brisket, all with a lively Asian touch and a side of strong, creative-cocktails, in a setting handsome enough to bring a date to.

50 Carmine St. (btw. Bleecker and Bedford). ℰ **212/929-5050.** www.fattycue.com. Main courses $13–$26; *kaiseki* $65–$90 per person. Mon–Wed noon–11pm; Thurs–Fri noon–midnight; Sat 11am–midnight; Sun 11am–11pm. Subway: 1 to Houston St.

Pearl Oyster Bar ★★ SEAFOOD   The Big Apple equivalent of your favorite Maine clam shack, Pearl's serves the best lobster roll in the city (big chunks of lobster meat, just enough mayo, sided by a nice pile of shoestring fries) and can't be beaten on its clam roll, either. But even the seafood that doesn't come in a bun is darn tasty, from the buckets of steamers to excellent pan roasted and grilled fish of all sorts. If you want to get in quickly (they don't take reservations), you may have to hunker down at the marble-topped bar up front, though tables do turn over relatively fast, and Cornelia Street is a lovely place to linger.

18 Cornelia St. (near Bleecker St.). ℰ **212/691-8211.** www.pearloysterbar.com. Main courses $15–$30 (lobster and oysters at market price). Mon–Fri noon–2:30pm and 6pm–11:30pm; Sat 6pm–11:30pm. Subway: A, B, C, D, E to 8th St.

Inexpensive

Keste Pizza and Vino ★★★ PIZZA   Used to be that John's Times Square (p. 89) was the one restaurant on the block that saw lines out the door. Alas, foodies are fickle, and now this upstart, which serves Neapolitan-style pizzas created by an actual Neapolitan (Roberto Caporuscio), has all the glory (and the waits to get in). Deservedly so, I must say. Topped by house-made mozzarella, with a perfectly balanced sauce and a whole raft of ingredients to play with (Keste offers 40 options), this is, hands down, the best pizza I've had in the U.S. and may be a very close second to what I gorged on in Naples. Full pies only are sold, but they're so delish, even single diners are able to put them away. Keste means "this is it" in the Neapolitan dialect, by the way.

271 Bleecker St. (near Cornelia St.). ℰ **212/243-1500.** www.kestepizzeria.com. Pies $9–$20. Mon–Thurs noon–3:30pm and 5–11pm; Fri–Sat noon–11:30pm; Sun noon–10:30pm. Subway: 1 to Christopher St.

CHELSEA

In addition to the choices below, there are some excellent casual eateries both on the High Line (p. 159)—in this case, some are simple food stands—and within Chelsea Market (p. 175). For a meal on the run or a picnic outdoors, they're great fun.

Expensive

Scarpetta ★★★ ITALIAN   The word "scarpetta" means "little shoe" in colloquial Italian. But it's not the type of shoe one puts on one's foot. Instead the "shoe" referred to are the bits of bread people use, after they've finished their plate of pasta, to scoop up every last bit of sauce from the plate. It's therefore an apt name for this restaurant, helmed by celebrity chef Scott Conant (you may recognize him from "Chopped" and "Top Chef"), as you're going to want to get every morsel off these plates. In fact, picking them up and licking them is a temptation, though the restaurant is a fancy one. Conant is cooking Italian food here, but doing it in an unusually flavor-packed manner. He's not afraid to use rich ingredients—like ravioli stuffed with duck and foie gras or agnoletti containing brisket and bone marrow—and it pays off. But even when the dish is slightly less fat laden—like the tuna *suschi* (raw tuna wrapped around preserved truffles and pickled vegetables) or the seared divers scallops with morels and spring peas—somehow he manages to make every, single taste bud sing. My only beef with the place: It's too darn loud. But that's the case in many NYC restaurants nowadays.

355 W. 14th St. (at Ninth Ave.). *℃* **212/691-0555.** www.scarpettanyc.com. Main courses $25–$45. Mon–Thurs 5:30–11pm; Fri–Sat 5:30pm–midnight; Sun 5:30–10:30pm. Subway: A, C, E, or L to 14th St.–8th Ave.

4

Moderate

The Tipsy Parson ★ AMERICAN REGIONAL   And that parson would be drinking a fine bourbon, because most everyone is, at this Southern-themed restaurant, where brown liquors fill the well-mixed cocktails, and patrons pop deviled eggs like they were M&Ms. Fried green tomato po'boys, shrimp and grits, spoon-bread, are other specialties. As for the atmosphere, it's darn cute, with bric-a-brac lining the walls and a pressed tin ceiling.

156 Ninth Ave. (btw. 20th and 21st St.). *℃* **212620-4545.** www.tipsyparson.com. Main courses $24–$30. Mon–Thurs 11:30am–11pm; Fri 11:30am–midnight; Sat 10am–3:30pm and 5:30pm–midnight; Sun 10am–3:30pm and 5:30–10pm. Subway: C, E to 23rd St.

Inexpensive

Co. ★★ PIZZA   Yes, this is a chic pizza joint, with a sleek, woodsy look, but don't hold that against the place. The pies are first class (and you can order only pies no slices, from traditional tomato and cheese ones to delicious creations with leeks and sausage or shitake mushrooms with a carmelized onion-walnut puree). Co.'s salads, cheese plates and soups are darn impressive, too, as is the wine list.

230 Ninth Ave. (btw. 24th and 25th sts.). *℃* **212/243-1105.** www.co-pane.com. Pizzas $9–20. Mon 5–11pm; Tues–Sat 11:30am–11pm; Sun 11am–11pm. Subway: C, E to 23rd St.

Coppelia ★★ LATIN AMERICAN   The sign outside reads DINER but the Caribbean colors inside (down to the teal faux shutters on the walls), the long marble bar, and the salsa and samba soundtrack let you know this ain't your usual NYC greasy spoon. As does the menu, which ranges across the Caribbean and Latin America, offering up perfect renditions of such regional stars as *lomo saltado* (a toothsome tomato and ginger beef stir-fry from Peru), Cuban roast pork with crispy chicharons and Brazilian sweet-corn empenadas. Open 24-hours, Coppelia also offers breakfast items, day and night, and these, too, have a Latin-flair (like the *Pan Francese*, a take on French toast which is topped with creamy *dulce de leche*). A fun place, night or day.

207 W. 14th St. (near Seventh Ave.). *℃* **212/858-5001.** www.ybandco.com. Main courses $7–$18. Daily 24 hr. Subway: 1, 2, 3 to 14th St.

THE prime cut: STEAKS! STEAKS!

Though NYC is no longer famous for its cheesecakes, or even its deli fare (with some exceptions), for red meat, it still reigns supreme. The city is brimming with topnotch steak joints, perfect for those on expense accounts, a little daunting for the rest of us. Still, if you're in the mood for a perfectly aged rib eye, with a side of creamed spinach and crisped potatoes, one of the following places will do you right:

Peter Luger Steakhouse ★★★
See p. 102. The original and still in many ways, the best, though because of its Brooklyn-locale it's not as convenient as some of the ones listed below. I'd argue that the commute's worth it.

Sparks ★★ 210 E. 46th St. near Third Ave. (℃ 212/687-4855, www. sparkssteakhouse.com), reputedly used to be a mafia favorite. With its "ye olde steakhouse" décor, crammed into a low-ceilinged modern building, it still has that *cosa nostra* air, part of the fun of coming here. The other part (along with the perfect hollandaise sauce and aged meats) are the wise-cracking waitstaff, with their thick outer-borough accents. They typify the type of service that used to be *de rigueur* in NYC, but alas, rarely exists anymore. Take a look at the wall of cigars before you head out; you can't legally smoke them in here, but they're apparently still big sellers.

Strip House ★ 15 W. 44th St. off Fifth Ave. (℃ 212/336-5454; www. striphouse.com) and 15 E. 12th St. near University Place (℃ 212/328-0000), merges steaks with strippers, placing photos of noted ecdysiasts from the 40s and 50s on the walls in an all-red, leather and wood interior, that's sexy and fun. And the beef? It's like buttah.

Ben & Jack's Steakhouse ★★
Opened by two former Peter Luger staffers, this steakhouse has two locations in Manhattan: 219 E. 44th St., between Second and Third aves. (℃ 212/682-5678; www.benand jackssteakhouse.com) and 255 Fifth Ave., between 28th and 29th sts. (℃ 212/532-7600). They learned their trade well.

Quality Meats ★ 57 W. 58th St., between Fifth and Sixth avenues (℃ 212/371-7777; www.qualitymeat snyc.com). Set in a stunning, bi-level space designed by the famous team of AvroKO, the quality of the food matches the quality of the design. It has some nontraditional steakhouse menu items such as pan-roasted lamb T-bones with figs and mint, and a flat-iron steak with blackberries.

Prime and Beyond ★★ a Korean-helmed steakhouse at 90 E. 10th St., near Third Ave. (℃ 212/505-0033; http://primeandbeyond.com) is proving that scallion salad is just as tasty a condiment on steaks as A-1. They're very proud of their aging facilities (meats are aged an unusually long 7 to 9 weeks for intense flavor); ask, and they'll take you on a tour while your food cooks.

La Nacional ★ SPANISH/TAPAS Welcome to the oldest Spanish restaurant in New York City, the quintessential hole in the wall, but one with a storied past: it was at this one-time social club that Gabriel Garcia Marquez spent his NY time, among his fellow ex-pats. Today, you'll find as many locals as Spaniards, but that's okay, because the tapas are authentic, the Spanish wines unusual, and spirits still run high here. You can eat in the more serene dining room in front, or sit in the back if you want to catch a soccer game on the TV that seems to always be on.

239 W. 14th St. (btw. Seventh and Eighth aves.). © **212/243-9308.** www.lanacionaltapas.com. Main courses $16–$18; tapas $7–$9. Sun–Wed noon–10pm; Thurs–Sat noon–11pm. Subway: A, C, E, 1, 2, or 3 to 14th St.

UNION SQUARE, FLATIRON DISTRICT & GRAMERCY PARK

Expensive

Maialino ★★★ ITALIAN   Though the press releases at its opening identified this restaurant as being inspired by the *trattorias* of Rome, I'd be more specific than that. To me, Maialino takes its cues from the Roman neighborhood of Testaccio, which was, for many years, the slaughterhouse area of that city, and is known for its hearty, expert preparations of all the cuts of meat we in the U.S. discard. So, when you come to Maialino and you see the menu item "pig face salad," know that you will get a plate of food that looks just like what it was in life (and is spectacularly delicious). Salami plates, a tortellini stuffed with liver and dishes of spicy tripe also shine. But you don't have to be an adventurous eater to enjoy the fare here; even such standards as *spaghetti a la carbonara* or *spaghettini alle vongole* are done in a way that's a cut above the usual. And the beyond-lovely wait staff make every meal here feel like a special event. A truly delightful place to dine.

2 Lexington Ave (at 21st St., in the Gramercy Park Hotel). © **212/675-7223.** www.maialinonyc. com. Main courses $17–$45. Mon–Thurs 7:30–10am, noon–2pm, 5:30–10;30pm; Fri 7:30–10am, noon–2pm, 5:30–11pm; Sat 10am–2:30pm and 5:30–11pm; Sun 10am–2:30pm and 5:30–10:30pm. Subway: 6 to 23rd St.

The NoMad ★★★ AMERICAN   Forgive them for the cutesy spelling, the name is the only part of this restaurant that isn't sophisticated in the extreme. Set in the Nomad Hotel (p. 42) and "chef-ed" by rising star Daniel Humm, it's a primo date restaurant, with a sexy, *Belle Epoque* design; "kiss me now" cocktails, including one made with absinthe; and food that is wonderfully colorful as well as scrumptious. The menu changes constantly, but when I was last there, the spring garlic veloute was swoon-worthy, and the poached lobster was just as luxurious as it should have been. The only thing I don't like about the NoMad is how maddening it is to try and get a reservation here (call weeks in advance); and how uncomfortable the bar seating is, if you decide to dine here that way. Ah well, no place is perfect, I suppose.

Inside the Nomad Hotel, 1170 Broadway at 28th St. © **212/796-1500.** www.thenomadhotel.com. Main courses $20–$37. Mon–Thurs 7–10am, noon–2pm, 5:30–10:30pm; Fri 7–10am, noon–2pm, 5:30–11pm; Sat 7–10am, 11am–2:30pm, 5:30–11pm; Sun 7–10am, 11am–3pm, 5:30–10pm. Subway: N, R to 28th St.

Moderate

Maysville ★★ AMERICAN REGIONAL   Named for the birthplace of Kentucky bourbon, the bar is a big part of the experience at Maysville. It stretches the length of

FOODIE food courts

Don't come expecting to find any of the regulars you see at your local mall food court (sorry Aunt Annie) at the spaces below. In New York City, food courts are the places where celebrity chefs ply their wares, usually mixing together booths that sell ingredients, with full-blown, sit-down restaurants.

That's certainly the case at the upscale **Plaza Food Hall by Todd English** in the Plaza Hotel (www.theplazafoodhall.com). In this 5,400-square-foot eating emporium, you can dine on oysters flown in from all corners of the globe, exquisite tarts, sushi, freshly grilled steaks or fish, you name it. It's all very posh, though ultimately, a bit squashed, too, with diners sitting on stools at cramped stations around a large room.

I prefer the famed **Eataly** at 200 Fifth Ave., between 23rd and 24th sts.

((✆ **212/229-2560**; www.eatalyny.com), as much a tourist sight today as a market. Encompassing a full city block, this enterprise was founded by Mario Batali (Babbo, Del Posto) along with Joe and mother Lydia Bastianich and it's a food court like no other—a true taste bud nirvana. Here you will find 12 different "eateries," including one for vegetarians, one that concentrates on pastas, and an outdoors, top floor Italian beer garden, Birreria. with retractable roof. Along with the eateries, you can browse various Italian foodstuffs like salami and cheese, fresh and dry pasta, meat, seafood, vegetables, wine, coffee, and much more. And get this: those with kitchens can use the "vegetable butcher here." You pick out whatever vegetable you need, and the on-site "butcher" cuts it to your specifications, making stewing a snap.

the restaurant, its bartenders hopping to and fro to churn out brown cocktail after brown cocktail (they're terrific, by the way, especially the Manhattans). But the appeal of Maysville isn't strictly alcoholic; there's real artistry in the food here, too. Chef Kyle Knall takes such classics as grits, fries them in cubes, and tops them with sliver thin pieces of pork as an appetizer. The result is a wonderful mélange of creamy, crunchy and salty, unlike anything I've ever tasted before. He smokes an entire trout and then serves it as part of a perfectly dressed salad, the fish and the greens playing off one another in a seriously savory fashion. Other highlights of the menu include the nettle *agnoletti* and duck breast with a hunk of almost-frozen foie gras (it gives the dish an ice-cream like appeal). So why two stars instead of three? That goes back to the bar, which attracts such a large, noisy crowd that patrons have to shout to be heard in other parts of this handsome high-ceilinged restaurant. A shame, since in other ways, this place is terrific.

17 W. 26th St. (near Broadway). ✆ **646-490-8240.** www.maysvillenyc.com. Main courses $10–$17. Mon–Thurs 11:30am–3pm and 5:30–11pm; Fri 11:30am–3pm and 5:30pm–midnight; Sat 11am–3pm and 5:30pm–midnight; Sun 11am–3pm and 5:30–11pm. Subway: N, R to 28th St.

Momofuku Ssam Bar ★★★ ASIAN It's hard to decide which of the Momofukus—the name means "lucky peach," and it's become a small chain here in the city—is best. All of them (and they include Momofuku Noodle and Momofuku Ko) are casual restaurants (think long counters and shared tables) with decidedly elegant, Asian food. Ko, which is a tasting menu only place, is near impossible to get into,

Midtown Restaurants

Aquavit **44**
Bar Americain **36**
La Bernardin **35**
Ben and Jacks **20**
The Breslin **12**
Burger Joint **40**
Carnegie Deli **37**
Cho Dang Gool **15**
Chola **45**
Chop't **26**
City Sandwich **30**
Co. **14**
Coppelia **4**
Danji **32**
Eataly **9**
Gyu Kaku **28**
Ippudo **3**
John Dory Oyster Bar **12**
John's Times Square **27**
Keen's Steakhouse **18**
La Nacional **5**
Maialino **7**
Marea **39**
Marseilles **29**
Maysville **10**
The Modern **41**
Molyvos **38**
Momofuku Ssam Bar **1**
The NoMad **11**
Norma's **40**
Oyster Bar and Restaurant **23**
Pam Real Thai **31**
Pampano **22**
Plaza Food Hall by Todd
   English **43**
Pure Food and Wine **2**
Quality Meats **42**
Salvation Taco **17**
Sapporo **34**
Scarpetta **6**
Sparks **21**
Shake Shack **8**
Strip House **24**
Sushi Yasuda **19**
Tipsy Parson **13**
Toloache **35**
Xian Famous Foods **25**
Zengo **16**

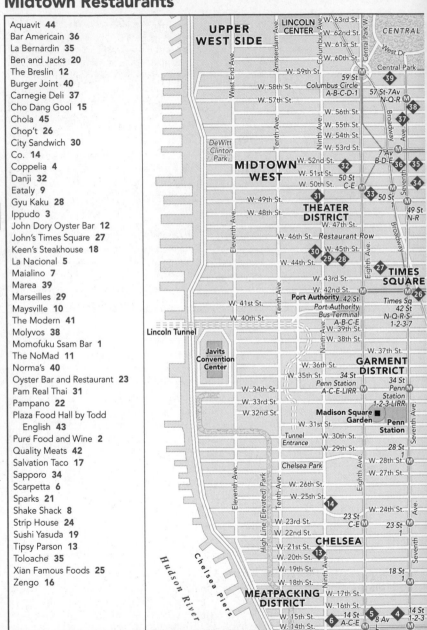

4

WHERE TO EAT | Union Square, Flatiron District & Gramercy Park

PARK

East River

East Dr

PARK

Fifth Ave.

Madison Ave.

Lexington Av/
63rd St. F

M

E. 63rd St.

E. 62nd St.

E. 61st St. F

E. 60th St.

UPPER
EAST SIDE

Roosevelt Island Tram

5 Av/59 St
N-R

South

43

E. 59th St.

59 St
4-5-6

M

Lexington Av/
59 St
N-R

45

Queensboro
(59th St.) Bridge

E. 58th St.

42

E. 57th St.

40

57 St
F

44

E. 56th St.

Lexington Av/
55 St
E-M

E. 55th St.

E. 54th St.

41

5 Av/53 St
E-M

E. 53rd St.

Lexington Av/
53 St
E-M

M

51 St
6

E. 52nd St.

ROOSEVELT ISLAND

ROCKEFELLER
CENTER

MIDTOWN
EAST

E. 51st St.

Park Ave.

Madison Ave.

Lexington Ave.

Third Ave.

E. 50th St.

22

E. 49th St.

Mitchell
Place

Beekman
Place

47-50 Sts
Rockefeller Ctr
B-D-F-M

Fifth Ave.

E. 48th St.

E. 47th St.

21

E. 46th St.

25

24

42 St
Bryant
Park
B-D-F-M

5 Av
7

M

Vanderbilt Ave.

Grand
Central
Terminal

23

E. 45th St.

E. 44th St.

20

E. 43rd St.

E. 42nd St.

19

Second Ave.

First Ave.

United
Nations

East River

Sixth Ave.
(Ave. of the Americas)

Bryant
Park

New York
Public Library

M

Grand Central
42 St
S-4-5-6-7-Metro North

E. 41st St.

Queens-Midtown Tunnel

17

18

E. 40th St.

E. 39th St.

MURRAY
HILL

E. 38th St.

E. 37th St.

E. 36th St.

16

15

34 St
Herald
Square
B-D-F-M-
N-Q-R

Macy's

Empire
State
Bldg.

E. 35th St.

E. 34th St.

Franklin-Delano-Roosevelt (FDR) Dr.

Ave. C

W. 32nd St.

Fifth Ave.

Madison Ave.

Park Ave. S.

33 St
6

E. 33rd St.

E. 32nd St.

E. 31st St.

E. 30th St.

12

E. 29th St.

Broadway

Sixth Ave.
(Ave. of the Americas)

M

28 St
N-R

11

M

28 St
6

Second Ave.

First Ave.

E. 28th St.

E. 27th St.

10

Madison
Square
Park

E. 26th St.

E. 25th St.

8

E. 24th St.

9

M

23 St
F-M

M

23 St
N-R

M

23 St
6

E. 23rd St.

E. 22nd St.

7

Gramercy Park

E. 21st St.

E. 20th St.

Asser Levy Pl.

FLATIRON
DISTRICT

Union
Square

GRAMERCY
PARK

E. 19th St.

E. 18th St.

14 St
F-M
L

6 Av
L

14 St-Union
Square
L-N-Q-R-4-5-6

Fifth Ave.

M

Irving Pl.

2

3 Av

E. 17th St.

E. 16th St.

3

L

E. 15th St.

E. 14th St.

1

N.D. Perlman Pl.

1 Av
L

M

M Subway stop

Upper
Manhattan

Uptown

Midtown

Downtown

0   1/4 mi
0   0.25 km

THE hole TRUTH: NEW YORK'S BEST BAGELS

Not many things are more "New York" than a bagel, and New Yorkers are loyal to their favorite bagel stores. In fact, discussions about who makes the best bagel can lead to heated arguments. Following are the top contenders:

Absolute Bagels. 2708 Broadway, between 107th and 108th sts. (**℃ 212/932-2052**). A new player on the scene, their egg bagels, hot out of the oven, melt in your mouth, and their whitefish salad is perfectly smoky, not overpowering.

Ess-A-Bagel. 359 First Ave., at 21st St. (**℃ 212/260-2252;** www.ess-a-bagel. com). When it comes to size, Ess-a-Bagel's are the best of the biggest; plump, chewy, and *oh* so satisfying. Also

at 831 Third Ave., between 50th and 51st sts. (**℃ 212/980-1010**).

Kossar's Bialys. 367 Grand St., at Essex St. (**℃ 877/4-BIALYS** [424-2597]; www.kossarsbialys.com). We know about their bialys, but don't forget about their bagels. Also hand rolled, the result is a slightly crunchy exterior with a tender, moist middle. Sure, you came for the bialys, but you will leave with both.

Murray's Bagels. 500 Sixth Ave., between 12th and 13th sts. (**℃ 212/462-2830**), and 242 Eighth Ave., at 23rd St. (**℃ 646/638-1335;** www.mbchelsea.com). There's nothing like a soft, warm bagel to begin your day, and Murray's does them beautifully. Their smoked fish goes perfectly on their bagels.

so it drops off the list; and the noodle bar, while good, has been upstaged by Ippudo (p. 85). So that leaves Momofuku Ssam, where chef/owner/culinary savant David Chang pays homage to pork, in many, many forms. There's the delightful Asian-style burrito in the name of the restaurant, the artisanal ham plate, and the pork steak (which comes with blue cheese, beets, and shisito peppers, yet works amazingly well). The *piece de resistance:* a whole pork butt for 6 to 10 people (this must be ordered in advance). Beyond pig, Chang is a master with vegetables and fish and . . . well, everything he serves. Alas, this place doesn't take reservations, but it's always worth the wait.

207 Second Ave (at 13th St.). ℃ **212/777-7773.** www.momofuku.com. Main courses $10–$17. Daily 11:30am–3:30pm, Sun–Thurs 5pm–midnight, Fri–Sat 5pm–1am. Subway: N, Q, R, L, 4, 5, 6 to Union Square.

Pure Food and Wine ★★VEGETARIAN   At this elegant restaurant—with one of the nicest garden dining areas in the city—the food is not just vegetarian, it's vegan and raw. So the "cheeses" are made from fermented nuts, the "pasta" in the lasagna is thin sheets of zucchini, and the breads are made from sprouted grains. Sounds weird, I know, but the meal proceeds a bit like a magic show, as you try each substitution and realize "wow, this works." I'm a dedicated carnivore, but I don't miss meat when I come here. Instead I realize that I've rarely tasted tomatoes as, well, tomatoey as those in the lasagna here; or "cheeses" as creamy. An experience.

54 Irving Place (btw. 16th and 17th sts.) ℃ **212/477-1010.** www.purefoodandwine.com. Main courses $22–$27. Daily noon–4pm and 5:30–11pm. Subway: N, Q, R, L, 4, 5, 6 to Union Square.

Union Square, Flatiron District & Gramercy Park

WHERE TO EAT

Inexpensive

Ippudo NY ★★★ JAPANESE   Ever see that Japanese film, *Tampopo*? The one about the couple who spent their time tramping from one ramen place to another, searching for the perfect noodle? I didn't realize I, too, was on that quest until I tried Ippudo, and understood, for the first time, just how life-changing sublime ramen could be. That will sound hyperbolic until you try the silky soups here, made from the finest Berkshire pork and filled with toothsome noodles. The only shortcomings? I'm not the only one who feels this way, so the waits to get in average an hour and a half (go at lunch). It also is not the place for quiet conversation, as a full-throated Japanese greeting is hurled at each guest who enters.

65 Fourth Ave. (at 9th St.). © **212/388-0088.** www.ippudony.com. Reservations not accepted. Main courses $14–$17. Mon–Thurs 11am–3:30pm and 5–11:30pm; Fri–Sat 11am–3:30pm and 5pm–12:30am; Sun 11am–10:30pm. Subway: 4, 5, 6, L, N, Q, R to Union Square.

Shake Shack ★★★ BURGERS   The successful, NYC chain's only actual "shack," this was the original, set in lovely Madison Square Park and still attracting hordes of diners. When the weather's good (there's no indoor seating here), there are few more delightful places to dine in Manhattan. And though many will argue, I think they serve the best burger in Manhattan: always juicy, high quality meat, with the perfect bun-to-patty ratio. The shakes are pretty orgasmic, too. If you have kids, grab a burger, some fries, a shake, and then head to the nearby playground for dinner.

In Madison Square Park (near 23rd St. and Madison Ave.). © **212/889-6600.** www.shakeshack. com. Burgers $4–$7. Daily 11am–11pm. Subway: 6, N, R to 23rd St. A number of other locations, including one right across from the Museum of Natural History, dot the city.

TIMES SQUARE & MIDTOWN WEST

People often find themselves eating on the fly in Midtown. To do so healthfully, head to **Chop't** (1460 Broadway, near 42nd. St; © **212/354-3284;** www.chopt.com; Mon–Sat 10:30am–10pm, Sun 10:30am–7pm) a local chain that serves super-fresh, made-to-order salads, with all sorts of fine and fancy toppings. For an extraordinary sandwich, I recommend **City Sandwich** (649 Ninth Ave. near 45th St; © **646/684-3943;** Mon–Fri 9am–10pm, Sat–Sun 10am–10pm) in Hell's Kitchen, which serves Portuguese fare—salt cod, blood sausage, roasted eggplant or less exotic ingredients—all between two slices of excellent Portuguese bread. At lunch, the line for this place can snake down the block, but the staff is quick, so add yourself to the back.

For a more elegant, sit-down meal, beyond the selections below, you might consider **The Modern** (at the Museum of Modern Art, 9 West 53rd St. between Fifth and Sixth aves.; © **212/331-1220;** www.themodernnyc.com; daily 11:30am–2:30pm and 5–10:30pm); that temple of seafood helmed by celeb-chef Eric Ripert, or the super-expensive **Le Bernardin** (155 W. 51st St., near Seventh Ave.; © **212/554-1515;** www. le-bernardin.com; Mon–Thurs noon–2:30pm and 5:15–10:30pm, Fri noon–2:30pm and 5:15–11pm, Sat 5:15–11pm).

Expensive

Bar Americain ★ REGIONAL AMERICAN Every wonder how celeb Chef Bobby Flay wins all those "take downs"? The mystery is solved at his swank, Midtown restaurant, a fine choice for dinner before or after a show. Flay takes southern standards, like shrimp with grits, and puts his own spin on them, making the grits oh-so-buttery and flecking the dish with bits of bacon. He also borrows from other cuisines, giving the traditional French onion soup an all-American treatment, with Vidalia onions, a biscuit-lid and a heap of cheddar cheese melted on top. Steaks, grilled fish and sinful desserts also appear on the extensive menu, and the setting just screams "big night out in the big city."

162 W. 52nd St. (near Seventh Ave.). © **212/265-9700.** www.baramericain.com. Main courses $27–$42. Mon 11:45am–2:30pm and 5–10pm; Tues–Thurs 11:45am–2:30pm and 5–11pm; Fri 11:45am–2:30pm and 5–11:30pm; Sat 11:30am–2:30pm and 5–11:30pm; Sun 11:30am–2:30pm and 5–10pm. Subway: N, Q, R to 49th St.

Keens Steakhouse ★ STEAK For a taste of Olde New York—and some of the best chops in the city (lamb chops, mutton chops, short ribs)—head to this iconic restaurant, established in 1885 and still going strong. The portions are humongous, so don't be afraid to share. And spend some time simply wandering around this museum-like eatery with its collection of ceramic pipes on the ceiling (some of the regulars who had their own pipes here included Albert Einstein and Babe Ruth), its working fireplaces, memorabilia-laden walls, and plush leather banquettes. You go here as much for the experience as the food.

72 W. 36th St. (at Sixth Ave.). © **212/947-3636.** www.keens.com. Main courses $26–$45. Mon–Fri 11:45am–10:30pm; Sat 5–10:30pm; Sun 5–9pm. Subway: B, D, F, N, Q, R, or M to 34th St./Herald Square.

Marea ★★★ ITALIAN/SEAFOOD The *New York Times* critic wrote, when awarding Marea its 3 stars, that trying the restaurant's *ricci* (sea urchin roe with lardo and sea salt on toast) was like "kissing an extremely attractive person for the first time—a bolt of surprise and pleasure combined." The metaphor holds for the entire experience of dining here, I'd say. There are few restaurants anywhere as attractive (or as comfortable to dine in, thanks to their tremendously cushy leather chairs); and the pleasure quotient here is high. A lot of the credit should go to chef Michael White who has an extraordinary talent coaxing every last bit of flavor from a fish, whether he's serving it raw (crudo) with some delightful sauce; or simply grilled, again with a fab sauce. He also knows his way around noodles, creating inventive dishes (such as tiny gnocchi with ruby red shrimp, chilies, and rosemary). And keep your eyes peeled, as this place is a celebrity magnet.

240 Central Park South (near Columbus Circle). © **212/582-5100.** www.marea-nyc.com. Main courses $31–$49. Mon–Thurs noon–2:30pm and 5:30–11pm; Fri noon–2:30pm and 5–11:30pm; Sat 11:30am–2:30pm and 5–11:30pm; Sun 11:30am–2:30pm and 5–10:30pm. Subway: N, Q, R to 57th St.

Molyvos ★ GREEK Within easy walking distance of both Carnegie Hall (p. 204) and City Center (p. 204), Molyvos has long been the go-to place for a quick, but elegant, meal before a show. Deservedly so. Though it's one of the grandfathers in this always-changing neighborhood, it has kept its standards high, meaning that its mezes (appetizers, such as cold spreads or grilled octopus) are among the tops in town, its spanakopita (spinach pie) is light as a cloud and bursting with flavor, and its *moussaka* (a sort of lasagna with ground lamb), will make you feel like you're tasting the dish for the first time. Service can be brusque, but they know how to time the meal so that you get to the curtain on time.

871 Seventh Ave. (btw. 55th and 56th sts.). © **212/582-7500.** www.molyvos.com. Main courses $17–$29 at lunch (most less than $20); $23–$36 at dinner. Mon–Thurs noon–11:30pm; Fri–Sat noon–midnight; Sun noon–11pm. Subway: N or R to 57th St.; B, D, or E to Seventh Ave.

Moderate

Cho Dang Gool ★★★ KOREAN   I knew immediately I was in the right place the first time I walked into Cho Dang Gool. It wasn't its looks, which are pleasant but unmemorable: wooden tables, tan walls, a few Korean musical instruments hung here and there as decoration. Nor was it the smells issuing from the kitchen or the look of the food going by. No, it was the realization, as I entered, that not a word of English was being spoken. The restaurant was jammed, and every guest was of Korean origin. As soon as I tasted the food I knew why: this was by far and away the best Korean food I'd ever had, each dish better than the last, from the home-made tofu (some crafted from black sesame seeds, some from white), to the piping hot and savory *bulgogi* (a beef and rice stew) to the parade of small plates, which included fried seaweed as addictive as crack. The *piece de resistance* was the kimchee, a dish that I sometimes find overpowering. Here it was just fiery enough, with a citrus zing that was downright refreshing. My only worry in sending you here, dear reader, is that it will spoil you for all other Korean restaurants. Yes, it's that good.

55 W. 35th St. (off Avenue of the Americas) © **212/695-8222.** www.chodanggolNY.com. Shareable casseroles and entrees $21–$42. Daily 24 hr. Subway: N, Q, R to 34th St.

Danji ★★ MODERN KOREAN   The hipster counterpoint to Cho Dang Gool (see above), Danji reinvents Korean classics in odd, but very tasty ways. That might mean a kimchee, bacon, and spam paella (weird, but delish) or tofu infused with ginger before being flash-fried. The young chef here, Hooni Kim, got his chops cooking for such master chefs as Daniel Boulud. At this point, he's starting small, so his little restaurant, while serving superb food and looking chic, isn't the most comfortable. To amortize the space, most everyone has to perch on high stools, elbow to elbow, as they dine. And he keeps it hopping with a "no reservations" policy, which means you just might miss the curtain if you try to dine here before a show. But if you're into experiencing exciting, new food combinations, it's hard to do better than Danji.

346 W. 52nd St. (btw. Eighth and Ninth aves.). © **212/586-2880.** www.danjinyc.com. Tapa style dishes $7–$22. Mon–Fri noon-2:30pm and 5:15pm–midnight; Sat 5:15pm–1am. Subway: C, E to 50th St.

Gyu Kaku ★ JAPANESE   Think of Gyu Kaku as a do-it-yourself Benihana. In front of you is a grill, you're served meats, vegetables and/or fish (your choice) and you get to cook it yourself—no fancy knife skills required. Kids love the experience, as it's interactive, but adults do, too, because the quality of the ingredients is high and the dipping sauces are phenomenal. A fun night out.

321 W. 44th St. (btw. Eighth and Ninth aves.). © **646/692-9115.** www.gyu-kaku.com. Main courses $10–$25. Mon–Thurs 11:30am–11pm; Fri–Sat 11:30am–midnight; Sun 11:30am–10pm. Subway: A, C, E to 42nd St.

THE pizza CAPITAL OF THE UNITED STATES

No city in the U.S. has better pizza than New York. And in recent years, with the emergence of many new, authentic Neopolitan places, it's gotten even better. Here I've separated the old-school New York pizzerias from the new kids on the block. You won't go wrong with any of the choices below.

OLD SCHOOL

DiFara Pizza ★★ 1424 Avenue J, Brooklyn, at E. 15th Street (© **718/258-1367;** subway: Q to Avenue J/16th St.). DiFara's lives up to its reputation for having the best traditional NY pizza in the city (worth a commute from Manhattan), thanks to the zeal of owner Dominic DeMarco, who, for over 40 years, has made every pizza himself. That means service can be slow (expect to wait an hour for a pie, maybe a bit less for a slice). But it's worth it!

John's Times Square ★ See p. 89. Full pies only, with brick oven goodness.

Lombardi's 32 Spring St., between Mulberry and Mott streets (© **212/941-7994;** www.firstpizza.com; subway: 6 to Spring St.). Claiming to be New York's first "licensed" pizzeria, Lombardi's opened in 1905 and still uses a generations-old Neapolitan family pizza recipe. The coal oven kicks out perfectly cooked pies, topped with ingredients such as pancetta, homemade sausage, and even fresh-shucked clams. Garden seating during warm weather.

Totonno's Pizzeria Napolitano 1524 Neptune Ave., between West 15th and West 16th streets, Coney Island, Brooklyn (© **718/372-8606;** subway: D to Stillwell Ave./Coney Island). This unassuming little pizzeria has been at the same spot since 1924, and it makes pizzas almost exactly as it did 80 years ago—thin crust, fresh sauce, mozzarella, and that's about it.

NEW SCHOOL

Co. ★ See p. 78. A more upscale experience than your average pizzeria, with topnotch pizzas, and exceptional salads, to boot.

Keste Pizzeria & Vino ★★★ 271 Bleecker St., near Seventh Avenue South (© **212/243-1500;** www.keste pizzeria.com). A member of the *Associazione Pizzaiuoli Napoletani* (the Association of Neapolitan Pizza), Keste maintains strict ingredient and cooking guidelines. How does the pizza taste? At Keste it's so fresh, so authentically Neopolitan, that many have abandoned the nearby slice joints, including Johns (see left), in its favor.

Trattoria Zero Otto Nove ★★ 2357 Arthur Ave., at 186th Street, the Bronx (© **718/220-1027;** www. roberto089.com). Taking its name from the Salerno, Italy, area code, you'll think you're in Salerno when you bite into one of Roberto Paciullo's Neapolitan pizzas. The mozzarella is made at nearby Casa de Mozzarella, the tomatoes are San Marzano, the pies cooked in a wood-burning brick oven, the basil from the Arthur Avenue Market across the street—the result: pure pizza perfection. And the good news for people who can't make the trip up to the Bronx is that the pizzeria has opened a branch at 16 W. 21st St. in Manhattan.

Marseille ★ FRENCH   New York has a number of places that attempt, with varying degrees of success, to look and taste like they were airlifted, intact, from France. Marseilles is one of the few that does just that. The food is classic Mediterranean fare, very much like what you'd get in the restaurant's namesake city (the bouilla-baisse is particularly fine), and the setting is adorable, with wonderfully cozy booths, intricate tiling and the kind of big round lamps you'll see in France. A good choice for a pre- or post-theater meal; go for the $38 prix fixe if you have a big appetite.

630 Ninth Ave. (btw. 44th and 45th St.). © **212/333-2323**. www.marseillenyc.com. Main courses $18–$28. Mon–Wed 11:30am–3pm and 5–11pm; Thurs–Fri 11:30am–3pm and 5pm–midnight; Sat 11am–3pm and 5pm–midnight; Sun 11am–3pm and 5–11pm. Subway: A, C, E to 42nd St.

Norma's ★ AMERICAN   The schtick here are what I'd call "stunt breakfasts," dishes so huge and overloaded with ingredients, they'd make a trucker faint. I'm not saying these humongous concoctions—like chocolate waffles with peanut butter and toffee crunch filling or omelets stuffed with lobster and asparagus—aren't delicious. They are. But don't expect to have room for lunch, or even dinner, after your meal. Which is good, since the prices are pretty darn high for breakfast. An over-the-top experience.

In Le Parker Meridien hotel, 118 W. 57th St. (btw. Sixth and Seventh aves.). © **212/708-7460**. www.normasnyc.com. Main courses $8–$28. Mon–Fri 6:30am–3pm; Sat–Sun 7am–3pm. Subway: B, N, Q, or R to 57th St.

Toloache ★★ MEXICAN   You'll notice that there aren't very many Mexican res-taurants in this book. That's not an oversight; Mexican food simply isn't done as well in New York City as it is in, well, states that are closer to Mexico. But Toloache is an exception, a restaurant that's at once very authentic (hey, they've got crickets on the menu!) and terrifically creative. That means tacos with succulent brisket or ceviche with lobster, strawberry, avocado, truffles, and red onions. They're also expert at get-ting you to the theater on time; service is brisk but friendly. Be sure to make a reserva-tion, as they book up well in advance.

251 W. 50th (at Eighth Ave.) © **212/581-1818**. www.toloachenyc.com. Main courses $10–$28. Sun–Mon 11:30am–10pm; Tues–Thurs 11:30am–11pm; Fri–Sat 11:30am–midnight. Subway: B, N, Q, or R to 57th St. Also at 166 E. 82nd St. (near Lexington Ave.). © **212/861-4505**. Subway: 4, 5, 6 to 86th St.

Inexpensive

Burger Joint ★ AMERICAN   A greasy spoon among silver spoons, the Burger Joint is hidden behind a curtain in the lobby of the ultra-swank Parker Meridien Hotel. Pull back that curtain and you enter a hidden diner that looks like it was yanked off some side street in Detroit. But it serves up the juiciest, most perfectly charred burgers ($5.50) in the western half of Midtown. Order them with "the works" (red onions, let-tuce, tomato, pickles, mustard, and mayo) for not a cent extra.

In Le Parker Meridien hotel, 118 W. 57th St. (btw. Sixth and Seventh aves.). © **212/245-5000**. Burgers $8. Sun–Thurs 11am–11:30pm; Sat–Sun 11am–midnight. Subway: B, N, Q, R to 57th St.

John's Times Square ★ PIZZA   About a half-block west of Broadway, John's has the top pizza in the area, served in a soaring, elegant space that was once a church (you can still see the lovely stained glass windows in places). But come hungry! John's serves only large full pies big enough for two—no slices—and they are potently, toma-toey, charred, thin-crusted circles of delight. You can also order salads and pastas, but it's the pizza that's exceptional.

THE NEW YORK deli NEWS

Alas, New York delicatessens are a dying breed. Few are left and few are worth going to anymore. With the following exceptions:

Barney Greengrass, the Sturgeon King 541 Amsterdam Ave., between 86th and 87th streets on the Upper West Side (✆ **212/724-4707**). This unassuming, daytime-only deli has become legendary for its high-quality salmon (sable, gravlax, Nova Scotia, kippered, lox, pastrami—you choose), whitefish, and sturgeon.

Carnegie Deli 854 Seventh Ave., at 55th Street (✆ **800/334-5606** or 212/757-2245; www.carnegiedeli.com). It's worth subjecting yourself to surly service, tourist-targeted overpricing, and elbow-to-elbow seating for some of the best pastrami in town. But do share: no one person can down one of the

meat Cadillacs they call sandwiches here.

Katz's Delicatessen ★ 205 E. Houston St., at Ludlow Street (✆ **212/254-2246**). It's rightly famous for its corned beef and remains fabulously old-world despite its hipster-hot Lower East Side location For more on Katz's, see p. 71.

Mile End Sandwiches ★★ 53 Bond St. at Bowery (✆ **212/529-2990;** www.mileenddeli.com) Mea culpa! But I prefer the Montreal-style deli sandwiches at this spiffy, white tiled little take-out place, to any of the delis above. Portions are reasonable, and the deli meats—pastrami, salami, corned beef (all cured in Brooklyn)—are first rate. Some sandwiches are topped with unusual items, such as fried capers or poached eggs, that enhance their flavors immensely.

260 W. 44th St. (btw. Broadway and Eighth aves.). ✆ **212/391-7560.** Pies $14–$21. Daily 11:30am–11:30pm. Subway: 1, 2, 3, N, Q, R, S to 42nd St.

Pam Real Thai ★ THAI   Here the name doesn't lie: it's owned by a chef named Pam and what's on offer is *real* Thai food (a rarity in New York, where sugar too often substitutes for spice). Be careful with your reply when they ask if you want your dinner spicy, because they mean business: The fiery fare will drain your sinuses (in fact, there's a constant symphony of patrons blowing their noses and clearing their throats). But even the most combustible dishes are tremendously flavorful, loaded with fresh vegetables, sweet coconut milk, and complex spices. While this isn't a place for a special occasion dinner—the decor's too plain for that—the service is speedy enough for you to eat here before the theater, and get to your seats in time.

404 W. 49th St. (at Ninth Ave.). ✆ **212/333-7500.** www.pamrealthaifood.com. Main courses $8–$14. Daily 11:30am–10:30pm. Subway: A, C, E to 50th St.

Sapporo ★ JAPANESE   Sumo-sized portions of tasty and authentic ramen noodles are the lure here and quite a lure they are. This place is always crowded, yet in this most-touristy area of town, you rarely encounter visitors. They'd have trouble squeezing past the legions of office workers, many originally from Japan, who make this place their unofficial canteen. My favorite soup: the *tantan-men,* which is topped with a spicy sesame paste.

152 W. 49th St. (btw. Sixth and Seventh aves.). © **212/869-8972.** Reservations not accepted. Main courses $7–$11. No credit cards. Mon–Sat 11am–11pm; Sun 11am–10pm. Subway: N or R to 49th St.

Xian Famous Foods ★ CHINESE   If this restaurant were a laboratory—and it looks very much like one, with its sterile white tiled walls and stools for chairs (casually pulled up to counters built into the wall)—the scientists working here would be studying just how much spice the human tongue can take before it literally implodes. Yes, this is a restaurant for chili heads, and its menu doesn't lie: "spicy and tingly beef with hand-ripped noodles," the house specialty ($6), will make your entire body heat up. This is truly authentic Sichuan food, family recipes of a caliber rarely tasted in the U.S. For those who can't take the heat, there are less fiery choices that are nearly as delish. Brave the line to get in: it moves quickly.

24 W. 45th St. (btw. Fifth Ave. and Avenue of the Americas). Reservations not accepted. Main courses $6–$8. Daily 11am–9pm. Other branches around the city. Subway: 4, 5, 6 or S to Grand Central or B, D, F, M to Rockefeller Center.

MIDTOWN EAST & MURRAY HILL

Also consider Chef Richard Sandoval's (Pampano, see below) other New York venture, the sprawling **Zengo at** 622 Third Ave, at 40th Street (© **212/808-8110;** www.richard-sandoval.com/zengony), where classic Latin dishes are fused with Asian (think Mexican sushi). If you just want a drink, 400-plus tequilas are on tap in the restaurant's lower lounge, La Biblioteca De Tequila.

Expensive

Aquavit ★★ SCANDINAVIAN   When Aquavit opened in 1987, the concept behind it seemed like a radical one: a cuisine no one in New York knew (Scandinavian), served in a setting far more elegant than obscure ethnic foods usually enjoyed. Of course, today, chef Marcus Samuelsson is world famous (as the winner of Top Chef Masters) and Nordic cuisine is sweeping the city (p. 74 and p. 101). In fact, it's done in a far more wacky and creative manner other places than here. But that doesn't mean Aquavit has lost its ability to please. Quite the contrary. The food here consists of classic continental and Scandinavian fare, perfectly done, whether you go for the light-as-light Swedish meatballs with ligonberries, expertly grilled fish dishes, or the excellent, imported herring. How you dine here is up to you. At the front is a less formal (and cheaper) café. For those who wish to splash out, there's the swank dining room in the rear.

65 E. 55th St. (btw. Park and Madison aves.). © **212/307-7311.** www.aquavit.org. Café main courses $9–$32; main dining room fixed-price meal $45 lunch, $89 dinner. Mon–Fri noon–2:30pm; Sun–Thurs 5:30–10:30pm; Fri–Sat 5:15–10:45pm. Subway: E or F to Fifth Ave.

Pampano ★★ MEXICAN/SEAFOOD   Set in a handsome townhouse, this is where you go when your date wants Mexican that's a bit more refined than the taco truck. The food is a creative retread of Mexican classics (tacos, enchiladas, tamales) by chef Richard Sandoval. If it's on the menu, pick the corn soup as a starter: it tastes like summer, its sweetness balanced by a crisp ribbon of *huitlacoche* (black fungus) vinaigrette that the chef squiggles across the soup (it's so colorful it looks a bit like a late Matisse collage). Seafood is also a specialty, and done every which way, from moist paellas to shrimp tamales in a delish tomato-almond-pipian preparation. Don't skip dessert, a very grown-up treat here, with not-too-sweet chocolate flan acting as an exclamation point on a terrific meal.

209 E. 49th St. (at Third Ave.). ℂ **212/751-4545.** www.modernmexican.com. Main courses $23–$30. Mon–Fri 11:30am–2:30pm; Mon–Wed 5–10pm; Thurs–Sat 5–11pm; Sun 5–9:30pm. Subway: E or M to Lexington Ave./53rd St.; 6 to 51st St.

Sushi Yasuda ★★★ JAPANESE   Pure Japanese sushi, as it's been made for centuries (that is, no mayonnaise, or other fusion touches), cut, dabbed with soy sauce, and patted into shape by master chefs. That's the zen formula here, and it works so well that the *New York Times* has twice awarded this little restaurant three stars. My advice: sit at the sushi bar, so that you can consult with the small army of white-coated sushi ninjas about which of the 60-fish on offer you should try. And go for the nigiri sushi rather than rolls: with fish this meltingly tender, you don't want it buried in a lot of rice.

204 E. 43rd St. (btw. Second and Third aves.). ℂ **212/972-2001.** www.sushiyasuda.com. Sushi $5–$11 per piece. Mon–Fri noon–2:15pm, Mon–Sat 6–10:15pm. Subway: 4, 5, 6, 7, S to 42nd St.–Grand Central.

Inexpensive/Moderate

Chola ★★ INDIAN   Normally, I'd be suspicious of a restaurant that attempted to serve foods from pretty much every region of the vast country of India. But somehow Chola makes it work, whether sending out perfectly crisp yet supple *dosas* (a form of Southern Indian pancake, often wrapped around other ingredients); chicken tikka masala that's both moist and flavorful; and the Calcutta dish of lamb and okra cooked in a sweet and sour sauce (another knockout). The lunch buffet is especially recommended; beyond the buffet table, waiters walk around with a number of freshly cooked specialties, at no extra charge.

225 E. 58th St. (btw. Second and Third aves.). ℂ **212/688-4619.** wwwfineindiandining.com. Main courses $14–$23; lunch buffet $16. Mon–Fri noon–3pm; Sat–Sun 11am–3pm; daily 5–11pm. Subway: 4, 5, 6, N, or R to 59th St.

Oyster Bar and Restaurant ★   Opened in 1913, this Gilded Age holdover in Grand Central Station has changed very little in nearly a century, and the architecture—a series of swooping, tiled vaults that always remind me of the grand crypts of some European cathedrals—still impresses. Don't bother going to the restaurant side; you want to be able to see the handwritten menu above the shelling station (on the right as you enter), where the best choices will be laid out. There will be fresh oysters and clams, flown in from all parts of North America; shellfish pan-roasts and stews; and, of course, chowders of all kinds (from $4.75). Ignore the paper menu entirely (for some reason, everything that comes out of the kitchen is overcooked and tepidly sauced); confine yourself to the list of foods that is prepared right at the bar, and you'll have a real, old-fashioned feast.

Lower level, Grand Central Station (42nd St. btw. Vanderbilt and Lexington aves.). ℂ **212/490-6650.** www.oysterbarny.com. Average meal $15-$30. Mon–Fri noon–3pm; Sat–Sun 11am–3pm; daily 5–11pm. Subway: 4, 5, 6, N, or R to 59th St.

FAMILY-friendly RESTAURANTS

While it's always smart to call ahead to make sure a restaurant has kids' menus and highchairs, you can count on the following to be especially accommodating. And what kid doesn't love pizza? See the sidebar "The Pizza Capital of the United States," on p. 88, for suggestions.

Here are some other options for the entire family:

Bubby's ★ (p. 68). With shelves of children's books and toys and a menu that features pies and American classics, this place couldn't be more family-friendly.

Gyu Kaku ★ (p. 87). At this Times Square area Japanese BBQ joint the food is simple enough for even the most picky kid to like, and all kids enjoying cooking it themselves (though with hot grills set in the tables, this is only recommended for kids over the age of 6).

Landmarc ★★ (p. 68). The kids' menu features pigs in a blanket, PB and Nutella, and green eggs and ham pesto, not to mention cotton candy for dessert. For the grown-ups, more sophisticated fare and fine wines. A win-win place for families.

Norma's ★ (p. 89). Half-a-dozen types of pancakes (many with ice cream) make breakfast the most fun meal of the day. An over-the-top exercise in gluttony . . . but fun.

Robataya ★★★ (p. 74).This is my daughters' favorite restaurants. They love the ritual of watching a kneeling chef cook dinner, love the food, and love heading to the Japanese toilet here.

Serendipity 3 ★ (p. 99). Kids will love this whimsical restaurant and ice-cream shop, which serves up a huge menu of American favorites, followed up by colossal ice-cream treats.

WHERE TO EAT | Upper West Side

UPPER WEST SIDE

The Time Warner Center (at 10 Columbus Circle) holds some of the most celebrated—and pricey—restaurants in the nation. Those willing to spend close to $1,000 for a meal with alcohol can do so (and will likely enjoy it) at both **Per Se** (✆ **212/823-9335;** www.perseny.com; Mon–Thurs 5:30–10pm, Fri–Sun 11:30am–1:30pm and 5:30–10pm) and the Japanese restaurant **Masa** (✆ **212/823-9800;** www.masanyc.com; Tues–Fri noon–1pm and 6–9pm, Mon and Sat 6–9pm). Reserve a month to the day of your intended meal.

Expensive

A Voce Columbus Circle ★★ ITALIAN   As with every restaurant in the Time Warner Center, you go partially for the grand views of Central Park, as seen through the massive floor to ceiling windows. But at A Voce, the food is just as majestic, the chefs pairing odd-ball items with simple ones to stunning effect. When I went recently, I started with the creamiest mushroom salad I've ever tasted (made appropriately enough with trumpet royal mushrooms) and then sprang for a decadent plate of capal-letti (garlic and parsley filled purses of pasta) with red-wine braised snails and bread-crumbs. These were, apparently, the foods of the Italian region of Umbria: the restaurant changes its geographic focus with the seasons. What doesn't change is the

93

excellence of the food, and that extends to the house-made gelatos, sorbets, and granites (Italian ices) offered for dessert.

10 Columbus Circle, 3rd Floor. ℰ **212/823-2523.** www.avocerestaurant.com. Main courses $28–$38; pastas $18–$25. Mon–Sat 11:30am–2:30pm; Mon–Thurs 5–10pm; Fri–Sat 5–10:30pm; brunch Sun 11am–3pm. Subway: A, B, C, D, 1 to 59th St./Columbus Circle.

Telepan ★★ AMERICAN "Eat your vegetables" could be the motto at this cleanly modern townhouse restaurant on the Upper West Side. Not only does a large painting of asparagus greet diners, but the sides here usually carry as much weight as whatever protein is supposed to be the main event of the dish. That's the case when the dish isn't wholly vegetarian (and many of the best dishes here are, like the pea pancakes with pea agnoletti). Chef Telepan (he's the owner, too) has a way with things that grow in the ground, so consider what's in the small print when you order, though I doubt you'll be disappointed with anything you get here. Consistent quality and welcoming service have made the restaurant a long-running favorite in the neighborhood.

72 W. 69th St. (at Columbus Ave.). ℰ **212/580-4300.** www.telepan-ny.com. Main courses $29–$36. Wed–Fri 11:30am–2:30pm; Mon–Thurs 5–11pm; Fri–Sat 5–11:30pm; Sun 5–10:30pm; brunch Sat–Sun 11am–2:30pm. Subway: B or C to 72nd St.

Moderate

Fatty Crab ★ MALAYSIAN I'm always tempted to call Fatty Crab "messy" crab; its signature dish, a bowl of crabs in a pungent, spicy orange sauce, may well be one of the hardest dishes in Manhattan to eat. Hard shelled crabs with most of the meat hidden away in the hard to get nooks and crannies of the shell, the dish is tasty but time consuming, and will leave your hands with an *eau de crustacean* perfume for a good two days after you dine here. Since it's also the most expensive item on the menu by far, I recommend some of the other dishes more highly: the Lincoln Log-like construction of papaya slices with sugar, salt, and spice; fatty duck, a dish which rivals Peking duck in the crisp snap of the skin and the spice-infused tenderness of the meat; or the steamed pork buns ($9), which are served with *kicap cair,* a type of gooey soy sauce that's the Malaysian equivalent of ketchup (you'll understand why it's so popular there after you taste it).

2170 Broadway (btw. 76th and 77th sts.). ℰ **212/496-CRAB** (496-2722). www.fattycrab.com. Main courses $7–$22. Daily 5pm–midnight; brunch Sat–Sun 11am–4pm. Subway: 1, 2, or 3 to 72nd St. Also at 643 Hudson St. (btw. Gansevoort and Horatio sts.). ℰ **212/352-3590.** Mon–Wed noon–midnight; Thurs–Fri noon–2am; Sat–Sun 11am–midnight. Subway: A, C, E, or L to 14th St.

Fishtag ★★ SEAFOOD Forgive Fishtag for having the most complicated menu in Manhattan, with appetizers mixed willy-nilly with entrees, and certain dishes, for no apparent reason, on another sheet of paper altogether. The waiter will explain, you'll say "huh," and then you'll sit back in this cozy, brownstone restaurant, and order what will likely be one of the most satisfying meals you have in the city. That's because Fishtag not only sources wonderfully fresh ingredients, it pairs them in creative ways. A platter of cheese or smoked fish, for example, will come with three or four lovely jams and sauces, so that you can build your own taste sensations. Branzino isn't just grilled, but stuffed with headcheese for an over-the-top rich dish. Smoked octopus, another highlight, is served with a puree of hearts of palm, dates, and olives. Or you

APRIL bloomfield: TRAILBLAZER

Read through this chapter, and you'll see me mention a battalion of chefs, all of whom have made their names cooking up a storm in the Big Apple. I'm chagrined to say there's not a woman among them (which I hope says more about the world of NYC cooking than any sort of myopia on my part). But their ranks have been breached in the last decade by a chef who, arguably, serves cuisine that's more testosterone-laden than any of the guys'. April Bloomfield is her name, and heavy, fatty, absolutely scrumptious fare is her game. I find that I can't go to her restaurants too often because the scale scolds me the next morning. But when I do, boy, do I enjoy the experience.

Being from the U.K., her first venture in New York was a British gastropub, called the **Spotted Pig ★★** 314 W. 11th St., at Greenwich Street (℮ **212/620-0393;** www.thespottedpig. com). It was the first of its kind in the city, a triumphant announcement to us Yanks that British food didn't have to be, well, awful. Like the gastropubs of London, which have taken classic fare and settings and made them cool, she served items like crispy pigs ear salad and squid with roasted fennel to great acclaim.

Her next successful outing was **The Breslin ★★★** 16 W. 29th St., off the lobby of the Ace Hotel (℮ **646/214-5780;** www.thebreslin. com), which went even further with the Brit grub, serving up such iconic dishes as Scotch Eggs, beef and stilton pie, blood sausage, and even pigs foot for two (romance is not dead on the NYC dining scene). Once again, huge cheers and huge crowds.

Then Ms. Bloomfield took a new direction, two actually. First she opened a fish restaurant the **John Dory Oyster Bar ★★** 1196 Broadway at 29th Street in the Ace Hotel (℮ **212/792-9000;** www.the johndory.com), which serves the heartiest fish dishes I've ever tasted (most are fab). And then she turned her attention to Mexican food, with **Salvation Taco ★★** inside the Pod 39 Hotel, 145 E. 39th St. between Lexington and Third Avenue (℮ **212/865-5800;** www.salvationtaco. com). I should note, though, that though she's serving tacos and other classic south of the border dishes, she gets creative with them: those tacos are as likely to be filled with Moroccan lamb or crispy sweetbreads, as they are with shredded pork. Bottom line: another winner for Ms. Bloomfield.

I, for one, can't wait to see what she tries next.

can have any fish on the menu simply grilled with just a touch of lemon. Geek chef Michael Psilkas, also of Kefi (p. 96), understands the appeal of simple preparations. 222 W. 79th St. (btw. Broadway and Amsterdam). ℮ **212/362-7470.** www.fishtagrestaurant.com. Main courses $10–$26. Sun–Thurs 5–10pm; Fri–Sat 5–11pm; Sat–Sun noon–3pm. Subway: 1 to 79th St.

Inexpensive

Celeste ★ ITALIAN The spirit of the city of Naples is being channeled at this quirky, little restaurant—for all the good and the bad that implies. Starting with the possible negatives, it's a cacophonous place, made even louder by the cheerful insults the waiters sling at one another as they rush around the room. Reservations aren't accepted so there's always a wait. Tables are so close together you're going to feel as if you need elbow pads to dine safely. But all that may well recede into the background when you get your first taste of the food, so authentic, so fresh, and so darn toothsome it's almost as if they teleported it direct from the Boot.

502 Amsterdam (near 84th St.). *C* **212/874-4550.** Main courses $9–$15. Mon–Thurs 5–11pm; Fri–Sat 5–11:30pm; Sun 5–10pm. Subway: 1 to 86th St.

Flor de Mayo ★ CUBAN/CHINESE   When Cubans of Chinese heritage came to the city after the Cuban revolution, they brought this hybrid "Chino-Latino" cuisine with them. It's an interesting concept, but the Latino side of the menu is far better than the Chinese here—whether you order the chopped beef with yellow rice, the excellent avocado salad, or Dominican chicken with rice ($7.50). Solid food and wonderfully affordable.

2651 Broadway (btw. 100th and 101st sts.). *C* **212/663-5520** or 212/595-2525. Main courses $5–$19 (most under $10). Daily noon–midnight. Subway: 1 to 103rd St. Also at 484 Amsterdam Ave. (btw. 83rd and 84th sts.). *C* **212/787-3388.** Subway: 1 to 86th St.

Kefi ★★ GREEK   A water main break in spring of 2013 sidelined what has to be one of the most popular restaurants on the Upper West Side. It should be re-opened by the time you read this book, though I can't say for certain that the décor will be the same (white with blue highlights in the last iteration—a classic Greek look). But the rustic menu won't be tampered with, I'm sure. There'd be riots if they did! Among the many highlights of the menu are their classic spreads, their moist *souvlaki,* and their many fresh fish dishes. Here's hoping all the repair work doesn't cause this always affordable place to have to raise its prices!

505 Columbus Ave. (at 84th St.). *C* **212/873-0200.** www.kefirestaurant.com. Main courses $10–$20. Tues–Fri noon–2:30pm; Sun–Thurs 5–10pm; Fri–Sat 5–11:30pm; Sat–Sun noon–4pm. Subway: B or C to 86th St.

Salumeria Rossi Parmacotto ★★ ITALIAN   Ignore the odd, dungeon-like décor, with its bizarre plaster map of Italy (it spreads across the ceiling of the room like a white, bumpy stain). Oh, and try to forgive the fact that you'll be bumping elbows with your neighbor as you shovel pasta into your mouth. The food here is so lovingly well-made, all sins are forgiven by the end of the meal. That goes for the perfectly spiced cured meats (of which there are many; get a sampler plate), the pepolino pasta with a carrot and celery based tomato sauce (it's simmered for 7 hours to concentrate the flavors), the short ribs (that also get the long cooking treatment, having been braised for 4 hours until they fall apart at the touch of your fork), the wine, the bread, you name it. In a neighborhood that's short on good restaurants, this one is a standout.

283 Amsterdam Ave. (at 73rd St.). *C* **212/877-4800.** www.salumeriarosi.com. Main courses $12–$17. Mon–Fri noon–10pm; Sat–Sun 11am–11pm. Subway: 1, 2, 3 to 72nd St.

Sookk ★ THAI   This tiny but stylish restaurant has a very, very specific focus: the foods that are sold by the street vendors of Yaowarat Road in the city of Bangkok. That's the city's Chinatown, so though the food is Thai in origin it incorporates Chinese (and sometimes Indian) elements as well, for an intriguing blend of flavors.

You might find yourself noshing on turnip cakes (a staple street food) topped with a stew of mussels and vegetables; or cinnamon duck in a clay pot with dates. Yes, you can get pad thai, but why would you when the choices here are so much more interesting?

2686 Broadway (at 103rd St.). © **212/870-0354.** No website. Main courses $10–$13. Daily 11am–11pm. Subway: 1 to 103rd St.

UPPER EAST SIDE

Expensive

Daniel ★★★ FRENCH   Restaurants, as we all know, are more than just places to get fed. We use them to celebrate the milestones in our lives. Though some may disagree, I can't think of a better place for this important type of meal than Daniel (I celebrated my first wedding anniversary there, so I'm partial). The look is right: a Versailles-opulent setting, with neo-classical architecture and towering vases fresh flowers everywhere you look. So is the service, formal but unusually kindly; these waiters know that people are here for event eating and do their darndest to keep things festive and happy for guests. And then there's the food, which is inventive yet classic and often revelatory. So a butter poached abalone will come with a beurre blanc infused with sake; a trio of veal will include the cheek and the sweetbreads and be sided by carmelized artichoke. Bizarrely, with the prix fixe at "just" $116, for three courses, it ends up often being less expensive than other restaurants of lesser quality.

20 E. 76th St. (btw. Madison and Fifth aves.). © **212/772-2600.** www.danielnyc.com. Main courses $25–$43. Daily 5:45–11pm, Tues–Sat noon–2:30pm (no lunch Sat July–Aug). Subway: 6 to 77th St.

The Mark Restaurant ★★ CONTEMPORARY AMERICAN   Chef/restaurateur Jean-Georges Vongerichten is a master of *umami.* That's the Japanese word for the mouth-feel you get with foods that are creamy or rich. Somehow the food at The Mark not only tastes good, it also feels good on your tongue. In fact, life itself feels good at this graceful restaurant in the lobby of the Mark Hotel. Tables are set at a civilized distance from one another, the seating is super comfortable, the lighting flattering and the waitstaff gracious and informative. Maybe that's why you'll often see celebrities here; I caught a glimpse of Martha Stewart on my last visit. As for the food, it's up to the chef's usual standards (high) with a menu that covers such American classics as pea soup, Caesar salad, and chicken with a parmesan crust. For those traveling with kids (or preferring the foods that usually star on the kids menu), there are upscale versions of burgers and pizza.

In the Mark hotel, 25 E. 77th St. (at Madison Ave.). © **212/606-3030.** www.themarkrestaurantnyc.com. Main courses: $21–$48. Mon–Fri 11:30am–2:30pm; Sat–Sun 11:30am–3pm; Mon–Sun 5:30–11pm. Subway: 6 to 77th St.

Moderate

Café Sbarsky ★ AUSTRIAN   Right on Museum Mile and set in a wood-paneled mansion designed by Carrere and Hastings (architects of the New York Public

Uptown & Harlem Restaurants

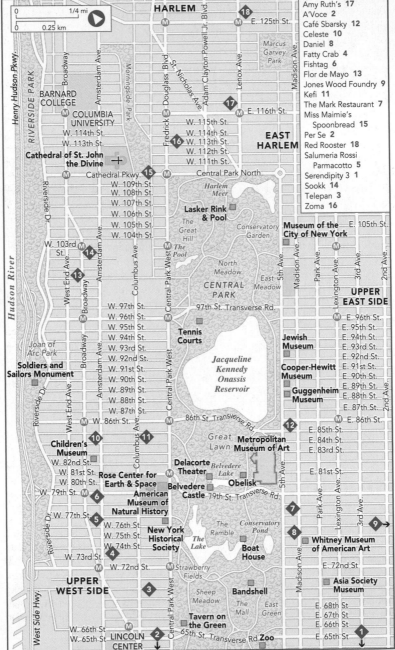

Amy Ruth's **17**
A'Voce **2**
Café Sbarsky **12**
Celeste **10**
Daniel **8**
Fatty Crab **4**
Fishtag **6**
Flor de Mayo **13**
Jones Wood Foundry **9**
Kefi **11**
The Mark Restaurant **7**
Miss Maimie's
  Spoonbread **15**
Per Se **2**
Red Rooster **18**
Salumeria Rossi
  Parmacotto **5**
Serendipity 3 **1**
Sookk **14**
Telepan **3**
Zoma **16**

Library at 42nd Street)—there are few places as pleasant for breakfast, lunch, or tea in the city. The restaurant is actually part of the Neue Galerie, a museum of Austrian and German art (p. 137), so this transplanted Viennese café serves all the heavy Teutonic specialties of that city from bratwurst to creamy spaetzle with vegetables, along with an assortment of lighter salads and sandwiches. These are all fine, but you really come here for the delicious pastries and Viennese coffee so strong it will grow hair on your tongue.

Inside the Neue Museum, 1048 Fifth Ave (at 86th St.). ✆ **212/288-0665.** www.theneuegalerie. org. Main courses $10–$29. Thurs–Sun 9am–9pm; Mon and Wed 9am–6pm. Subway: 4, 5, 6 to 86th St.

Jones Wood Foundry ★★★ BRITISH   If this restaurant were in my neighborhood, I'd eat here at least once a month, and I can't say that about any other Upper East Side joint. The Foundry (and I have no idea why it has that name) reminds us that British food can be quite tasty and British people exceptionally cool (think David Bowie rather than David Blair). An extra-long bar greets diners as they enter, followed by a warren of little rooms filled with Brit-a-brac, and a sweet little garden. Sit at the bar so you can flirt with the David Beckham-handsome bartenders as you dine; they have a nice habit of complimenting those people who pick the most British of the selections (like the perfect steak and kidney pie, the crispy scotch eggs and kedgeree, a happy fried bread dish with smoked haddock and saffron rice).

401 E. 76th St. (near First Ave.). ✆ **212/249-2700.** www.joneswoodfoundry.com. Main courses: $17–$26. Daily 11am–4pm and 6–11pm. Subway: 6 to 77th St.

Inexpensive

Serendipity 3 ★ AMERICAN   A good ol'-fashioned ice cream parlor complete with Tiffany-style lamps and a toy shop that you have to pass to get in and out (quite a feat when you have sugar-crazed kids in tow). The dish to order here (one tureen of it will easily satisfy two or three) is the deservedly famous Frozen Hot Chocolate, a slushy, utterly satisfying chocolate soup. You can get an idea of the magical effects of that treat if you rent the slightly treacly John Cusack comedy *Serendipity* (filmed here).

225 E. 60th St. (btw. Second and Third aves.). ✆ **212/838-3531.** www.serendipity3.com. Main courses $9–$23; sweets and sundaes $6–$20 (most under $10). Sun–Thurs 11:30am–midnight; Fri 11:30am–1am; Sat 11:30am–2am. Subway: N or R to Lexington Ave.; 4, 5, or 6 to 59th St.

HARLEM

Moderate

Red Rooster ★ AMERICAN/SOUTHERN   A destination restaurant, Red Rooster is the only reason many well-heeled New Yorkers ever come to Harlem. Three words why: Chef Marcus Samuelsson (also of Aquavit, p. 91 he won "Top Chef: Masters" in 2012). So is it "all that"? I'm on the fence. Yes, it has a wonderful atmosphere (it's one of the few truly multiracial social scenes in the city), a hopping bar, live music in the basement and a handsome décor. Most of the appetizers—which like the rest of the menu range from Southern classics to African fare to Scandinavian cuisine—are delish. But when it comes to the pricier main dishes I'm inevitably disappointed, especially in the signature yard bird (fried chicken, very dry); and Helga's meatballs (too heavy). Since I once lived in the neighborhood for 6 months, I ate there half a dozen times, and eventually started making my meals entirely of appetizers. If you do the same, I think you'll enjoy the place immensely.

310 Lenox Ave. (btw. 125th and 126th sts.) ℂ **212/792-9001**. www.redroosterharlem.com. Main courses $18–$29. Daily 11:30am–3pm and 5:30–10:30pm. Subway: 2, 3 to 125th St.

Inexpensive

Amy Ruth's ★ AMERICAN REGIONAL   Amy Ruth's was named for the grandmother of owner Carl Redding, and he'll readily admit that it's her recipes that he uses in the dining room. But part of what makes the food so good here is the freshness of the ingredients: very green veggies, perfect sweet potatoes, and the honey for the honey-fried chicken that comes from beehives on the roof. You'll also enjoy dining here if you know anything about New York politics, as this is the unofficial clubhouse for Harlem's political elite, many of whom have dishes named for them on the menu. It's not unusual to see Congressman Charles Rangel when you're eating the tasty meatloaf platter named for him, or Al Sharpton when you're munching on "his" waffles and chicken platter.

113 W. 116th St. ℂ **212/280-8779**. http://amyruthsrestaurant.com. Main courses $8–$15. Sun–Thurs 7:30–11pm; Fri–Sat 24 hr. Subway: 2, 3, B, C to 116th St.

Miss Mamie's Spoonbread ★ AMERICAN REGIONAL   Another Harlem restaurant named for a relative, this one pays homage to owner Norma Jean Darden's mother, who passed down to Darden the recipes featured on the menu. It feels like a family affair as well, with old black-and-white photographs of relatives staring down at you from the walls, and homey touches, such as wicker chairs and the little, white picket fence surrounding the sidewalk dining area. The food continues the theme, with many recipes that could be served up at a family reunion: exceedingly tender BBQ ribs, big slabs of slightly spicy corn bread, greaseless fried chicken and shrimp, and delectable smothered pork chops. The only missteps here occur when you leave the South—the jerk chicken is numbingly spicy. Other than that, the food is first rate. By the way, if Darden's name sounds familiar, it's because she penned, along with her sister, the best-selling cookbook "Spoonbread and Strawberry Wine."

366 W. 110th St. (btw. Columbus and Manhattan aves.). ℂ **212/865-6744**. Main courses $9–$16. Mon–Sat noon–midnight. Subway: B, C to Cathedral Pkwy.

Zoma ★★ ETHIOPIAN   For those who've never tried it, Ethiopian food is a true culinary adventure. Long-simmering stews of lamb or chicken, beef tartars (called *keftas*) and grilled beef dishes (*tibs*) are dusted with a slow-burning spice mix called *berbere*, giving many dishes an eye-opening wallop. Onion, ginger, and cinnamon, important supporting characters, lend sweetness and depth of flavor. And because the Orthodox Ethiopian religious calendar requires numerous days be set aside for meat-free fasts, lentils, collard greens, potatoes, and other vegetables are the focus of a number of dishes, making this an excellent cuisine for vegetarians. Most fun of all, Ethiopian cuisine banishes the fork. Instead, your dishes are served on a pizza-sized round of *injera,* a winningly sour, spongy bread, that diners use to scoop up their meals. Yup, you get to eat with your hands! Though some might disagree, I'd say that Zoma serves the best Ethiopian in NYC, in a spare but elegant room. Worth the trip to Harlem!

2084 Frederick Douglas Blvd. (at 113th St.) ℂ **212/662-0620.** Main courses $13–$20. Mon–Fri 5–11pm. Subway: B, C to Cathedral Pkwy.

THE OUTER BOROUGHS

Brooklyn

Pizza is big in Brooklyn. You can skip Grimaldis (overrated) in favor of the 1924-established and little-changed **Totonno's** at 1524 Neptune Ave., between West 15th and West 16th streets in Coney Island (ℂ **718/372-8606);** or **Forcella** in Williamsburg, at 485 Lorimer St. (ℂ **718/388-8820;** www.forcellaeatery.com). Totonno's was damaged in Hurricane Sandy, but is back up and running today. For more information on all of the above, see "The Pizza Capital of the United States" on p. 88.

EXPENSIVE

Aska ★★★ SCANDINAVIAN   The dish felt like a dare. "Fried pigs blood with [unpronounceable Scandinavian] berry," the waiter said, placing a small slab of wood with a fried ball in front of me. And then he gave me a second look and a grin, as if to say, "So, are you really going to eat that?" I did, without hesitation, as I did later with crispy pike skin with crème fraiche and vinegar powder; a scallop "chip" (dehydrated with a dill puree); a serving of pork neck with birch tree oil; and the other oddities that make up the tasting menu at New York's premiere "New Nordic" restaurant. That's the cuisine that's been adding luster (and stars from big name reviewers) to the Scandinavian restaurant scene. Here its main promulgator is a young chef named Fredrik Berseleus, who promises on his website that all the produce he serves is handpicked by his staff. It certainly tastes that way, just as the other items on the menu taste like the sea, or the essence of cream, or meat at its, well, meatiest—at once very familiar flavors but done in totally unexpected ways. Can you tell I love the place? And I say that despite the fact that eating here made me feel mighty old. At 40-something, I was a good decade older than the other patrons (and certainly the least tattooed person in the joint). But I never felt out of place, thanks to the marvelously friendly service and the overall "let's put on a restaurant"-ambiance to the place (which is in an odd-ball setting, with an art studio above, concrete floors, and a scattering of plain wooden tables). *One warning:* the bar's a la carte menu is bar food only and nothing like what you'll get at the restaurant itself, so spring for the tasting menu.

In Kinfolk Studios, 90 Wythe Ave. (at N. 11th St), Brooklyn. ℂ **718/388-2969.** www.askanyc.com. Tasting menu Sun and Tues–Thurs $65, Fri–Sat $115. Tues–Sun 6–10pm. Subway: L to Bedford.

Chef's Table at Brooklyn Fare ★★★ GOURMET AMERICAN   A far more upscale, but just as, well, weird, culinary experience as at Aska (see above) awaits those who get one of the few coveted reservations at the Chef's Table at Brooklyn Fare. Seating (for just 18) is in a gleaming, steel kitchen at a D-shaped counter. The intensely focused chef Cesar Ramirez and his acolytes, er, sous chefs, perform their magic at the front of the room, moving like precisely choreographed cooking ninjas around the massive stove (really, they're an eerily focused group; in the course of the 2½ hour meal, not a plate clinked, a pot rattled or, it seemed, a chef spoke a word). I can't tell you what I ate because it's forbidden to photograph the food, or even take notes here (I got caught trying). I remember, however, hearing the names of fish I had never encountered before ("blue nosed"-this, and "shark grin" that) during the 14-or-so course extravaganza. We were also plied with caviar, gold leaf, foie gras, and many other pricey delicacies, which, I suppose justified the $225 tasting menu cost (that price includes tip, but not alcohol). All in all, it was an unusual, only-in-New-York type of experience that I'd love to do again . . . especially, if someone else foots the bill.

200 Schemerhorn St. (btw. Bond and Hoyt sts.). *📞* **718/243-0050,** call 1 month to the day before you want to dine. www.brooklynfare.com/pages/chefstable. Tasting menu $225. Subway: A, C, G to Hoyt–Schemerhorn).

Peter Luger Steakhouse ★★★ STEAK   Grumpy waiters? Check. Saw dust on the floor? But of course! Beef so tender you can use a butter knife on it? Well, that's why people are still coming to this steakhouse set in a barren stretch of Williamsburg, Brooklyn. It's still hard to beat a meal here, and that goes for everything from the beef to the lamb chops to the legendary creamed spinach. If you love steak, then book a table and hop a cab to Williamsburg. Two important notes: credit cards aren't accepted, so be sure to bring wads of cash. And you'll need to reserve well in advance to get a table.

178 Broadway (at Driggs Ave.), Williamsburg, Brooklyn. *📞* **718/387-7400.** www.peterluger.com. Main courses (steaks) $35–$45. Mon–Thurs 11:45am–9:45pm; Fri–Sat 11:45am–10:45pm; Sun 12:45–9:45pm. Subway: J, M, or Z to Marcy Ave.

MODERATE

Talde ★★ ASIAN FUSION   On first glance, Talde looks like so many other Brooklyn restaurants: pressed tin ceiling, large marble bar at the front, decorative carved wooden trim everywhere. But when you look a bit closer, you realize that Buddha is carved into the wood, along with other Asian symbols. And the menu contains all sorts of unlikely marriages, like pretzel-crusted pork dumplings (spectacular!) and yuzu guacamole (which turns out to be avocado and yuzu mashed together and slathered, finger-food style, over cakes of crispy rice). Other stars of the menu include a creamy tom kha soup with lobster, a pad thai with bacon and oysters, and the *hola hola* dessert—shaved ice with a changing mix of toppings (when we were there, it was fresh berries, Captain Crunch, and balls of tapioca, which sounds odd but tasted fabulous). My one complaint: the waiters push customers to order more than they need (portions are larger than they say).

369 Seventh Ave. (at 11th. St.), Brooklyn. *📞* **347/916-0031.** www.taldebrooklyn.com. Main courses (steaks) $10–$22. Mon–Thurs 11:45am–9:45pm; Mon–Fri 5pm–midnight; Sat–Sun noon–3pm and 5pm–midnight. Subway: F to Seventh Ave.

INEXPENSIVE

Frankie's Spuntino 457 ★★ ITALIAN   "How do you like your meatballs?" the waitress innocently asked the guy sitting at the table next to me. "They're pissing me off," he growled. "They're better than my grandmother's." Then he stabbed his fork into one of the three tennis ball-sized orbs in front of him, and silently ate on. I did the same, because, like most everyone who eats here, I had come specifically for the balls, doused in a richly tomatoey sauce with pine nuts, and so good, they don't need spaghetti. But meatballs are not the end-all of the menu, which does extremely well by other classic Italian-American dishes (like the sausage and peppers), as well as by the items that wouldn't be considered part of this cuisine (like a luscious kale crostini, with a generous helping of siracha aioli). All is served up by a friendly staff, in a cozy, brick-walled, pressed-tin ceiling joint with few pretensions and even less elbow room. Two notes: choose seats in the garden out back when the weather's nice; it has a much less crowded feeling than the interior of the restaurant. And if you're a light eater, know that they will serve a one-meatball portion, even though it's not on the menu.

457 Court St. (btw. 4th Place and Luquer St.). ℂ **718/403-0033.** www.frankiesspuntino.com. No reservations. Main courses $9–$18. Sun–Thurs 11am–11pm; Fri–Sat 11am–midnight. Subway: F or G to Carroll St. Also at 570 Hudson St. (btw. Perry and W. 11th sts.) ℂ **212/924-0818.** Sun–Thurs 11am–midnight; Fri–Sat 11am–1am. Subway: F or M to Delancey St.

Zizi Limona ★★ MIDDLE EASTERN   The food is just marvelous at Zizi Limone, drawn from the family recipes of chef Nir Mesika (of Moroccan heritage, he grew up in Israel) as well, one gathers, from his fertile imagination. He takes such classic dishes as *shakshuka* (an Israeli tomato stew with a fried egg on top) and elevates it with strips of perfectly medium-rare skirt steak; or slowly roasts ox tail for 5 or 6 hours before encasing it in a filo dough shell and serving it with two delicious dipping sauces. Even such classics as a lamb kebab sandwich taste special here, as they're topped with a fabulous hummus and served in fresh-from-the-oven pita breads. Don't you dare skip dessert: Mesika's grandfather was a baker for the king of Morocco, and he turns out pastries that are as light as a dream. A final reason to head here? It gets you into the heart of artsy Willliamsburg, Brooklyn, a delightful place for a stroll.

129 Havemeyer St. (btw. 1st and Grand St.). ℂ **347/763-1463.** http://zizilimona.com. Main courses $9–$17. Daily 11am–3pm and 5–11pm. Subway: L to Bedford of J to Marcy Ave.

Queens
MODERATE

M. Wells Dinette ★★ AMERICAN   In 2011, M. Wells Dinette was the best-reviewed new restaurant in all of New York City. But that wasn't enough to keep it from losing its lease and abruptly closing that summer. It has re-emerged as the in-house restaurant for the Museum of Modern Art's Queen's outpost. "P.S. 1," with all its moxie intact, though its hours (sadly) are cut to jibe with the museum's schedule (see below). Still, there are few finer lunch places in the city, especially if your tastes run to creatively elegant concoctions liked fluke crudo on a bed of smoked sour cream with gooseberries and jalapeno; or pillowy ricotta gnocci with a cheese foam, a red sauce and huge, juicy chunks of lobster. Those were just two of the dishes on offer when I last visited; Quebecois chef Hugue Dufour changes the menu daily (desserts are mighty fine, too). Taking its cue from the fact that the museum was a working public school until the mid-60s, the restaurant is designed to look like a classroom, down to the little nooks in some of the "dining desks" that hold colored pens and pads of graph paper. Flipping through the notebook in my "desk" I came across a cartoon of a goggle-eyed diner with the words "Stop staring at me, weirdo, and keep eating." That's sage advice here. *One note:* While I recommend visiting the museum, you don't have to do so to dine here.

Inside PS 1, 22–25 Jackson Ave. (at 46th St.). ✆ **718/768-1800.** www.momaps1.org/about/mwells. Main courses $12–$25. Thurs–Mon noon–6pm. Subway: E, M, 7 to Court Square or G to 21st St.

INEXPENSIVE

Sripraphai Thai Restaurant ★★★ THAI   Throw everything you think you know about Thai food out the window. Because here you get the real stuff: baby corn that actually has a flavor, oddities like dried catfish (crispy, salty and addictive), and dishes that perfectly balance sweet with sour, salty with spicy. On that last note: Take it seriously when they ask you how hot you want your meal. I left the restaurant after my last visit and almost walked into a telephone pole, I was so lightheaded from the powerful spices I'd just eaten. Among the many recommended dishes are the green duck curry with pineapple, the ground pork with lime and peanuts, and the duck salad (they do duck extremely well here). Expect a wait, as the restaurant doesn't take reservations and it's always jammed. By the way, the name is pronounced see-PRA-pie.

64–13 39th Ave. (near 64th St.). ✆ **718/899-9599.** www.sripraphairestaurant.com. No reservations. Main courses $8–$17, most in the $9–$10 range. Thurs–Tues 11:30am–9:30pm. Subway: R to 165th St. or 7 to Flushing/Main St.

Taverna Kyclades ★★ GREEK/SEAFOOD   Nobody will be smashing plates, but other than that, eating here is a Zorba-rific experience, thanks to the all-Greek waitstaff and the seafood, simply prepared, that tastes like it jumped out of the bluest of oceans and right onto your plate. Start with a tasting of spreads (they're topnotch), make your way next to the grilled octopus (Taverna's signature dish), and end with some sort of fresh fish (your choice) sided by their famous lemon potatoes. The only downer here? The Taverna is the most popular restaurant in the Greek section of Queens and doesn't take reservations, so come early or be prepared to wait.

3307 Ditmars Blvd. (at 33rd St.). ✆ **718/545-8666.** www.tavernakyclades.com. No reservations. Main courses $13–$21, more for larger, shareable whole fish. Mon–Thurs noon–11pm; Fri–Sat noon–11:30pm, Sun noon–10:30pm. Subway: N, Q to Astoria/Ditmars.

RESTAURANTS BY CUISINE

AMERICAN

Bubby's Pie Company ★ p. 68
Burger Joint ★ p. 89
Chef's Table at Brooklyn Fare ★★★
   p. 101
Chopt ★ p. 85
City Sandwich ★ p. 85
Shake Shack ★★★ p. 85
The Dutch ★★ p. 72
Telepan ★★ p. 94
M. Wells Dinette ★★ p. 103
The Mark ★★ p. 97

The NoMad ★★★ p. 80
The Modern ★★ p. 85
Norma ★ p 89
Per Se ★★★ p. 93

AMERICAN REGIONAL

Amy Ruth's ★ p. 100
Bar Americain ★ p. 86
Maysville ★★ p. 80
Miss Mamies Spoonbread ★ p. 100
Red Rooster ★ p. 99
The Tipsy Parson ★ p. 78

WHERE TO EAT   Restaurants by Cuisine

ASIAN FUSION
Momofuku Ssam Bar ★★★ p. 81
Talde ★★ p. 102

AUSTRIAN
Café Sbarsky ★ p. 97

BARBECUE
Fatty 'Cue ★ p. 77
Mighty Quinns ★★ p. 74

BRITISH
Jones Wood Foundry ★★★ p. 99
Spotted Pig ★★ p. 95
The Breslin ★★★ p. 95

CHINESE
456 Shanghai ★★ p. 69
Great NY Noodletown ★★ p. 70
Mission Chinese ★★★ p. 72
Royal Seafood Restaurant ★★ p. 70
Xian Famous Foods ★ p. 91

DELICATESSEN
Katz' Delicatessen ★ p. 71
Mile End ★★ p. 90
Deli Round-up p. 90

ETHIOPIAN
Zoma ★★ p. 100

FRENCH
Balthazar ★★ p. 72
Daniel ★★★ p. 97
Marseilles ★ p. 88

GREEK
Kefi ★★ p. 96
Molyvos ★ p. 86
Taverna Kyclades ★★ p. 104

INDIAN
Chola ★★ p. 92

ITALIAN
A Voce Columbus ★★ p. 93
Celeste ★ p. 95
Il Buco Alimentari e Vineria ★★ p. 73
Frankie's Spuntino 457 ★★ p. 102
Locanda Verde ★★★ p. 68
Maialino ★★★ p. 80
Marea ★★★ p. 86
Parm ★ p. 73
Salumeria Rossi Parmacotto ★★ p. 96
Scarpetta ★★ p. 77

IRISH
Ulysees ★ p. 69

JAPANESE
Brushstroke ★★★ p. 66
EN Japanese Brasserie ★★★ p. 75
Ippudo ★★★ p. 85
Masa ★★ p. 93
Robataya ★★★ p. 74
Sapporo ★ p. 90
Sushi Yasuda ★★★ p. 92

KOREAN
Cho Dang Gool ★★★ p. 87
Danji ★★ p. 87

LATIN AMERICAN
Coppelia ★★ p. 80
Flor de Mayo ★ p. 96

MALAYSIAN
Nyonya ★ p. 70
Fatty Crab ★ p. 94

MEDITERRANEAN
Landmarc ★ p. 68

MEXICAN
Hecho en Dumbo ★★ p. 74
Pampano ★★ p. 91
Salvation Tacos ★★ p. 95
Toloache ★★ p. 89
Zengo ★ p.91

MIDDLE EASTERN
Alfanoose ★ p. 68
Zizi Limone ★★ p. 103

MOLECULAR GASTRONOMY
WD-50 ★★★ p. 70

PIZZA
Adrienne's Pizza Bar ★ p. 69
Co. ★★ 78
John's Times Square ★ p. 89
Keste ★★★ p. 77
Pizzaria round-up p. 88

ROMANIAN
Sammy's Famous Romanian ★★ p. 71

SEAFOOD
Fishtag ★★ p. 94
John Dory Oyster Bar ★★ p. 95

4

WHERE TO EAT | Restaurants by Cuisine

Le Bernardin ★★★ p. 85
Oyster Bar and Restaurant ★ p. 92
Pearl's Oyster Bar ★★ p. 77

SCANDINAVIAN

Acme ★★ p. 74
Aska ★★★ p. 101
Acquavit ★★ p. 91
Smorgas Chef ★★ 69

SPANISH

Bocqueria ★★ p. 73
La Nacional ★ p. 79
Tertulia ★★★ p. 75

STEAK

Keen's Steakhouse ★ p. 86
Luger Steakhouse ★★★ p. 102
Steakhouse round-up p. 79

THAI

Pam Real Thai ★ p. 90
Sook ★ p. 96
Sripraphai ★★★ p. 104

UKRAINIAN

Veselka ★ p. 75

VEGETARIAN

Pure Food and Wine ★★ p. 84

EXPLORING NEW YORK CITY

Ask New Yorkers about their feelings for their city, and they will often respond, "There's just one New York." By that they mean: one city so full of museums (more than 40 major ones); historical sites; world-famous institutions; parks; zoos; universities; lectures; concerts and recitals; theaters for opera, musicals, drama, and dance; architectural highlights; and kooky galleries. It's diversions are limitless, and you will never be bored. If you had the speed and stamina of a Usain Bolt, you would still be hard pressed to cover all of the attractions in several months of touring.

Because your own time is more limited than that, I'm confining my coverage to two categories of sights in this chapter: First, the city's "iconic" attractions, by which I mean the places universally associated with Gotham—the headliners that make the city so massively popular. These include the major museums (the Metropolitan Museum of Art and the Guggenheim, just to name two); the great historical and architectural sites (including Grand Central Station and the Brooklyn Bridge); and, in a category all its own, New York's most sobering site: the 9/11 Memorial.

Second are the less famous attractions that, if they were magically transported to almost any other city in America, would instantly become that city's top cultural draw and bring it acclaim, prestige, and millions of dollars in tourist revenue (no, I do not exaggerate). These attractions—such as the Tenement Museum, the Museum of the Moving Image, The Frick Collection—while lesser known, can add immensely to a New York City visit. And therefore it's important occasionally to step off the tourist treadmill (Empire State, Times Square, Statue of Liberty) and try one of the so-called secondary sights. If you have the time, visit at least one of the places you might never have heard of before picking up this book.

How do you plan (and time) a satisfying itinerary? I've given you a slew of suggestions in chapter 2 of this book. Now on to the individual sights, which are grouped by area, to make for easier touring.

NEW YORK CITY'S ICONIC SIGHTS

- Brooklyn Bridge (See below)
- Central Park (p. 152)
- Ellis Island (p. 109)
- Empire State Building (p. 124)
- Grand Central Station (p. 125)
- Guggenheim Museum (p.134)
- New York Public Library (p. 127)

- 9/11 Memorial (p. 112)
- Rockefeller Center (p. 131)
- Statue of Liberty (p. 115)
- Times Square (p. 132)
- The United Nations (p. 128)
- Wall Street (p. 118)

OTHER TOP ATTRACTIONS

- American Museum of Natural History (p. 138)
- The Bronx Zoo (p. 145)
- The Brooklyn Museum (p.146)
- The Cathedral of St. John the Divine (p. 140)
- The Cloisters (p.144)
- Coney Island (p.147)
- Cooper Hewitt National Design Museum (p. 133)
- The Frick Collection (p. 133)

- The Intrepid Sea, Air and Space Museum (p. 129)
- The Morgan Library (p. 127)
- Museum of Modern Art (p. 130)
- Museum of the Moving Image (p. 149)
- New-York Historical Society (p. 141)
- NYC Police Museum (p. 114)
- Staten Island Ferry (p. 115)
- The Tenement Museum (p. 119)
- The Whitney Museum (p. 137)

DOWNTOWN
Financial District/New York Harbor

Brooklyn Bridge ★★★ ICON/ARCHITECTURE   New York has a grand Gothic cathedral in St. Patrick's, but for many New Yorkers, the city's true cathedral, the point at which earth and water join and thrust upwards towards the heavens, is the Brooklyn Bridge.

To fully appreciate its dazzle, you must **walk the bridge.** Start on the Manhattan side and walk first to one of the great Gothic towers that hold up the bridge's cables. It took 7 years and massive heartbreak to build these two structures. When architect and immigrant John A. Roebling was surveying the area in 1869 (just 2 weeks after the project had been approved), a ferry accidentally rammed into the place where he was standing, crushing his foot. He died of lockjaw 3 weeks later. His son Washington took over and created a method of sending pneumatic caissons, basically large pressurized pine boxes into which compressed air was pumped to keep the water out, down to the river bed. This allowed six workers at a time to descend and lay the foundation for these towers. Because they didn't have a good understanding of the effects of underwater pressure on the human body (known to scuba divers as "the bends"), many were killed or injured in the caissons, including Washington Roebling. In 1872 he had to be carried out of the chamber, partially paralyzed. He remained an

CityPass is New York's best sightseeing deal. Pay one price ($106, or $79 for kids 6–17) for admission to six major attractions:

o The American Museum of Natural History (including the Space Show)
o The Guggenheim Museum *or* Top of the Rock
o The Empire State Building
o The Museum of Modern Art
o The Metropolitan Museum of Art
o The Statue of Liberty and Ellis Island, *or* a 2-hour Circle Line harbor cruise.

Individual tickets would cost more than twice as much (though I should point out that the "Met" (Metropolitan Museum of Art) and Museum of Natural History charge only "suggested" admission fees, so that you can actually pay less).

More important, CityPass is not a coupon book. It contains actual tickets, so you can bypass lengthy lines. This can save you hours, as sights such as the Empire State Building often have ticket lines of an hour or more.

CityPass is good for 9 days from the first time you use it. It's sold at all participating attractions and online at **www.citypass.com/city/ny**. To avoid online service and shipping fees, you may buy the pass at your first attraction (start at an attraction that's likely to have the shortest admission line, such as the Guggenheim). However, if you begin your sightseeing on a weekend or during holidays, when lines are longest, online purchase may be worthwhile.

invalid for the rest of his life, and his wife Martha took over directing the job, learning advanced mathematics in the process. Washington watched the progress of the bridge through binoculars from his apartment, and when the bridge was competed after 13 years, Grover Cleveland (then president), the governor, and the mayor all came to his home to personally thank him for his efforts.

Walk to the center of the bridge and take in the spectacular views of both Brooklyn and Manhattan. When the bridge was built, its span—1,595 feet—was the longest leap across an open space of any on Earth, and the first bridge to connect Manhattan with any of the lands that surrounded it. Take a look up at the cables; these, too, were an innovation, the first steel cables to be used on a bridge (before then cables were iron). It took 2 years to string the cables back and forth before work could begin building the suspension bridge. The cables each contain 5,434 wires and weigh 870 tons. Take a moment at the Brooklyn side to read the plaque on the construction of the bridge.

When you depart the bridge, consider taking a stroll in brownstone-heavy Brooklyn Heights, the first neighborhood in the city to be landmarked. You can catch the A train at Cadman Plaza/High Street back to Manhattan.

Subway: A, C to High St.; 4, 5, 6 to Brooklyn Bridge–City Hall.

Ellis Island ★★★ HISTORIC SITE   The epicenter of the largest migration in human history, Ellis Island was in near-continuous use from 1892 to 1954 as the point-of-entry processing center for the majority of immigrants (including my grandmother) who settled in the U.S. during those years. Over 12 million people passed through its halls, sometimes as many as 12,000 in a single day.

Downtown Attractions

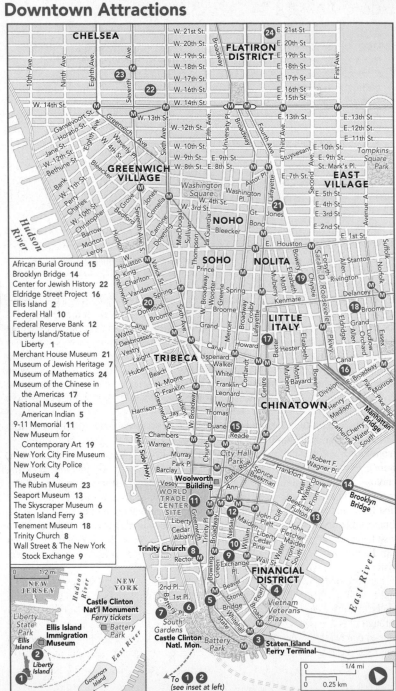

African Burial Ground **15**
Brooklyn Bridge **14**
Center for Jewish History **22**
Eldridge Street Project **16**
Ellis Island **2**
Federal Hall **10**
Federal Reserve Bank **12**
Liberty Island/Statue of Liberty **1**
Merchant House Museum **21**
Museum of Jewish Heritage **7**
Museum of Mathematics **24**
Museum of the Chinese in the Americas **17**
National Museum of the American Indian **5**
9-11 Memorial **11**
New Museum for Contemporary Art **19**
New York City Fire Museum **13**
New York City Police Museum **4**
The Rubin Museum **23**
Seaport Museum **13**
The Skyscraper Museum **6**
Staten Island Ferry **3**
Tenement Museum **18**
Trinity Church **8**
Wall Street & The New York Stock Exchange **9**

colonial-era SACRED GROUND

African Burial Ground ★ Some 15,000 African slaves were buried in a Manhattan graveyard in the 17th and 18th centuries, but their final resting places were lost to memory until 1991 when construction workers stumbled upon human remains during renovations of a federal building. The site is now considered one of the most important archeological finds in the United States. In 2006, a handsome, symbol-laden National Monument (operated by the National Parks Service) was dedicated by poet Maya Angelou and Mayor Michael Bloomberg. A visit to the **African Burial Ground,** and the small museum that's attached, should take no more than half an hour, but it's a worthy pilgrimage, uncovering, as it does, a part of American history that is too often brushed to the side.

At the corner of Duane and Elk sts. ℂ **212/637-2019.** www.nps.gov/afbg. Free admission. Daily 9am–5pm.

The stories of these immigrants—what they were escaping, what they found once here, and what they experienced in their short time in the purgatory that was Ellis Island—is movingly told here in a number of ways. First off there's a short film but I think you'll find it much more enlightening (and fun) to follow the path that the immigrants themselves took, seeing the tale unfold room by room.

Start in the second-floor **Grand Hall** (officially titled the **"Registry Hall"**), awe-inspiring with its massive white tile-vaulted ceiling (created by the same firm that did the ceiling in Grand Central Station's Oyster Bar) and larger than any church or temple these immigrants likely would have attended in their home villages.

Behind the Grand Hall is a warren of small rooms where immigrants were tested for mental competency, literacy, and communicable diseases. How these tests were done—and the fear they inspired—is chronicled in historical photos, wall text, and most poignantly at listening stations, where immigrants share their memories of their time on the island.

The top floor of the museum chronicles the history of the processing facility itself. These exhibits can be skipped if you're short on time, but don't miss the **"Treasures from Home"** exhibit, also on this floor, which features 2,000 of the possessions that were brought through Ellis. Somehow seeing the china dolls, the precious wedding photos, the native costumes, and the letters home, brings the immigrant experience more vividly to life than any other part of the museum. If you have time, return to the first floor, and browse through the **"Peopling of America"** exhibit that discusses the ethnic make-up of the U.S. today. In all, you should allot a minimum of 2 hours for a visit here; there's a cafeteria on-site should you need a break, along with the **"American Family History Center,"** where American visitors can track their genealogical history.

I am one of the 40% of all Americans who had a relative come through Ellis Island, and I find it difficult to tour this museum without tearing up at some point. I have no doubt that even those visitors without this direct a connection will find the journey through Ellis to be one of the most moving experiences of their New York visit. (*Note:* Due to damage from Hurricane Sandy, Ellis Island was closed at the time this edition was being researched. Be sure to check that it's re-opened before scheduling a visit).

Touring tip: Ferries run daily to Ellis Island and Liberty Island from Battery Park and Liberty State Park at frequent intervals; see the **Statue of Liberty** (p. 115) for details.

In New York Harbor. ℭ **212/363-3200** (general info) or 877/LADY-TIX (523-9849; ticket/ferry info). www.nps.gov/elis/index.htm, www.ellisisland.org, or www.statuecruises.com. Free admission (ferry ticket charge adults $17, seniors $14, children 4–12 $9). Daily 9am–5pm. For subway and ferry details, see the Statue of Liberty listing on p. 115 (ferry trip includes stops at both sights).

Federal Reserve Bank ★★ Although you won't see the currency being printed—that function was moved from this site to New Jersey in 1992—you will likely see more lucre than you ever will again in your lifetime when you descend 80 feet down to the basement of this financial fortress, where a gold vault right out of *Mission Impossible* is housed. Down here, behind a door that's a good 5 feet thick, the Fed keeps $100,000 billion worth of gold bars, a full 25% of all the gold reserves in the world, and far more than is housed in Fort Knox. Ninety-five percent of the gold stored here belongs to foreign nations, who use this facility, embedded in the bedrock of Manhattan and guarded by a small army of marksmen (they have their own on-site firing range for practice), because it's considered the safest place in the world for this type of storage. I wish I could give you more details, but the security here is so span-dex-tight that my reporter's notebook was confiscated at the door.

The gold is supplemented by precious coins (one worth $7 million), in an exhibit in the lobby by the Numismatic Society in partnership with the Fed. Also featured are brief videotapes detailing the work of the Fed, and an interactive exhibit explaining what the massive, semi-governmental agency does (it's an interesting topic). The entire tour takes a bit less than an hour.

33 Liberty St. (at the corner of Nassau). ℭ **212/720-5000.** www.ny.frb.org. Free admission. Mon–Fri 9:30am, 10:30am, 11:30am, 1:30pm, and 2:30pm; reservations required 5 days in advance. Subway: 2, 3, 4, 5, A, C, J to Fulton St.

9/11 Memorial ★★★ HISTORIC SITE/MUSEUM   Ten years and a day after the two hijacked planes brought down the twin towers of the World Trade Center, and close to 3,000 people were killed, a memorial to that fateful day finally opened to the public. Since its opening, it has become the most-visited attraction in New York City.

The centerpiece within the 8-acre **Memorial Plaza** are the two reflecting pools and waterfalls, located in the 1-acre footprints of the individual towers. Each reflecting pool is surrounded by a brass parapet where the names of the victims of both the 9/11 and February 1993 bombings are engraved and arranged in an order as to where they worked, close to their co-workers or friends, or wherever their families thought they could best be located.

Despite the cacophony of construction work that surrounds the Memorial (the Freedom Tower; the skyscraper to replace the Twin Towers, is still under construction, as are other adjacent buildings), the experience is a moving one and a reminder of not only the horror of that tragic day, but of the valor of those who gave their lives to save others.

Also under construction is the **National September 11 Memorial Museum,** which was originally scheduled to open September 11, 2012; when it will be completed is still a question mark.

Admission to the area is free, but to visit, you must make a $2 **online reservation** at **www.911memorial.org/visitor-passes**. Same-day visits are available at the Memorial's Preview Site: 20 Vesey St. (at Church St.) beginning at 9:00am, the NYC & Co. kiosk at City Hall, and the NY Water Taxi booth at the South Street Seaport (limited to four passes per person on a first-come, first-served basis). Security, as you can imagine, is tight. You and your bags will be scanned/searched. For more information visit the Memorial's website: **www.911memorial.org**.

Entrance at Albany and Greenwich sts. www.911memorial.org. Free admission, $2 per booking fee. Mar 18–Sept 22 10am–8pm daily, 10am–6pm otherwise. Subway: A, C, J, Z, 2, 3, 4, or 5 to Fulton St., 2, 3 to Park Place, E to World Trade Center, R to Rector St.

Museum of Chinese in America ★ MUSEUM   The story of the Chinese immigrant experience in the U.S. is wholly different from that of any other ethnic group that came here. Arguably, these Chinese-Americans, and the African Americans who came here as slaves, had it worst, and the tales of what they endured—thanks to the limited work they were allowed to do and the "Chinese Exclusion Act," a federal law barring further Chinese immigration (that separated countless families) give this museum true power. For a preview, take a look at Maya Lin's video tour of the museum (she's the museum's designer and creator of the Vietnam Veteran's Memorial in Washington, D.C.) which is found at **www.mocanyc.org/visit**.

215 Centre St. ℭ **212/619-4785**. www.mocanyc.org. Admission $7 adults, $4 students and seniors, free on Thurs and for children 11 and under. Mon and Fri 11am–5pm; Thurs 11am–9pm; Sat–Sun 10am–5pm. Subway: 6, N, R, Q, J, M to Canal St.

Museum of Jewish Heritage—A Living Memorial to the Holocaust ★ MUSEUM   It can be an emotionally draining experiences to visit the Museum of Jewish Heritage, which deals in explicit fashion with the Holocaust. To be fair, the museum is not in any way a showcase of horrors; its curators have been very careful to create a rounded picture of what life was like before, during, and after World War II. But be aware, before you decide to come, that you may need to skip other sightseeing after you leave here to recover a bit.

Your tour will begin in the older section of the museum—an elegant six-sided building by architect Kevin Roche, meant to evoke both the Star of David and the six million Jews who were murdered during the Holocaust. The first floor covers life before the war with a sensitively constructed exhibit detailing the various aspects of daily existence. The second floor is dedicated to the war years, and as might be expected, many of the images shown are quite graphic and disturbing. (People with children under 12 would be well-advised to skip this floor by taking the elevator directly from the first floor up to the third.) In addition to photos, objects, and text, the museum is a repository for videos from Steven Spielberg's Shoah Foundation's Visual History project, and these vivid accounts of life in the camps and ghettos are the highlight of the museum.

The final floor discusses the *Diaspora,* with exhibitions on Jewish life in the United States, Israel, and Europe. There are also changing exhibits, and programs of lectures and music. For those looking for a very in-depth experience, there is a self-guided headphone tour (an additional $5) narrated by Meryl Streep and Itzhak Perlman. On site, too: a kosher café.

36 Battery Place (at 1st Place), Battery Park City. © **646/437-4200.** www.mjhnyc.org. Admission $12 adults, $10 seniors, $7 students, free for children 11 and under and for everyone Wed 4–8pm. Sun–Tues and Thurs 10am–5:45pm; Wed 10am–8pm; Fri and eves of Jewish holidays 10am–3pm (10am–5pm Fri during daylight saving time). Subway: 4, 5 to Bowling Green.

National Museum of the American Indian, George Gustav Heye Center ★ MUSEUM A branch of the Smithsonian Institution, this museum is notable primarily for the touring exhibits it hosts (and to be truthful, while some have been impressive others have been duds). Housed in the magnificent Customs House, designed by architect Cass Gilbert (see the first walking tour in chapter 7), the museum offers a robust program of performances, lectures, and courses on Native American topics each year.

1 Bowling Green (btw. State and Whitehall sts.). © **212/514-3700.** www.nmai.si.edu. Free admission. 10am–5:30pm (Thurs until 8pm). Closed on Christmas. Subway: 4, 5 to Bowling Green; R to Whitehall; 1 to South Ferry.

New York City Police Museum ★★ MUSEUM This little museum packs a surprisingly emotional wallop, mostly because it deals with the events of 9/11 in an intricate, thoughtful manner. The museum was being created at the time of the attacks; it opened just 6 months later, and many of the exhibits conclude with a bit of information that will "pull you" directly back into that harrowing time.

Start your visit on the top floor at the 9/11 exhibit (on the right as you enter), which profiles the actions of two officers who died on that day. Video of the attack accompanies this exhibit, so if you're traveling with small children you may wish to skip this room. Next to the 9/11 room is a space for changing exhibits, and then on the left end is the sobering "Hall of Heroes," dedicated to the 700-plus officers over the years who have lost their lives in the line of duty.

The second floor is largely devoted to illustrating how officers do their jobs today. The New York City Police Department (NYPD) has 38,000 officers plus 20,000 civilian employees, making it the largest police force in the world. How the NYPD's various units interact and the highly specialized nature of their jobs is explored in a series of interactive, videotaped interview/montages. These are fascinating, in-depth depictions, far more interesting and inspiring than any TV drama (in fact, I recently left thinking, for the first time in my life, that perhaps I should consider a career change to law enforcement—you may feel the same way).

The ground floor covers the different methods of transportation and communication that the force has used over the years and can be glossed over fairly quickly; you'll want to spend the majority of your time here upstairs.

100 Old Slip (btw. Water and South sts.). © **212/480-3100.** www.nycpolicemuseum.org. Admission $8 adults; $5 seniors, students, and children; free for children 2 and under. Mon–Sat 10am–5pm; Sun noon–5pm. Subway: 2, 3 to Wall St. **Note:** Because of damage from Hurricane Sandy, the museum was closed at press time. Check to see that it has re-opened before visiting.

Seaport Museum New York ★ MUSEUM/HISTORIC SITE What will you see here? A massive collection of, well, sailing stuff—20,000 pieces of scrimshaw, models, maritime paintings, and other ephemera. So landlubbers may find it a bit of a yawn. Better are the daily tours of the three humongous historic sailing vessels the museum has moored off Pier 16; the 1895 schooner cruises that often take place at sunset. To be fair, the museum often goes "off message" with worthy exhibits on topics tangentially related to the Seaport (like the history of early NYC or the poet Walt Whitman). The Seaport Museum also sponsors daily walking tours, concerts, and lectures. The area surrounding the seaport I find equally as uninspiring, a sad case of an historic area (dating back to the 17th century) transformed into a tawdry mall.

At Water and South sts.; museum visitor center is at 12 Fulton St. (?) **212/748-8725** or 212/ SEA-PORT (732-7678, for events). www.seany.org. Museum admission $15 adults; $12 students, seniors, and children; free for children 1 and under. Museum Apr–Dec Tues–Sun 10am–6pm; Jan–Mar Thurs–Sun 10am–5pm; ships open noon–4pm. Subway: 2, 3, 4, 5 to Fulton St. (walk east, or downslope, on Fulton St. to Water St.). **Note:** Due to continuing clean up efforts after Hurricane Sandy, hours may be curtailed, and the entry way may be in a different spot than usual.

Skyscraper Museum ★ MUSEUM   Don't dimiss this small museum: it's far more interesting than one would expect. An architecturally innovative space in and of itself (notice how the shiny metals, ascending ramp, and mirrored surfaces gives the smallish room its own skyscraper aspect), the museum explores not only the structural feats behind these soaring structures, but also the economic forces that shaped them and their sociological impact.

39 Battery Place (Little West St. and 1st Place). (?) **212/968-1961.** www.skyscraper.org. Admission $5 adults; $2.50 seniors and students. Wed–Sun noon–6pm. Subway: 4, 5 to Bowling Green.

Staten Island Ferry ★★ ICON/TRANSPORTATION   Most visitors—and even some New Yorkers—don't know that the **Staten Island Ferry** makes its own daily excursion within Polaroid distance of the Statue of Liberty, Ellis Island, and Governor's Island. And riders pay absolutely nothing for the great views. You simply board the ship (be sure to wait for one of the older orange-and-green boats, because the newer ones don't have decks for viewing) and, as with the Circle Line (p. 161), sit on the right side (stay at the back of the ferry for the best view of the Manhattan skyline). It's a joke in New York that this is the best "cheap date" in the city, so don't be shy about toting along a bottle of wine, some bread, and cheese. But be sure to dress warmly: In winter the outdoor decks can be frigid. One-way, the trip takes approximately a half-hour, after which you'll need to disembark and take the next ferry back.

Departs from the Whitehall Ferry Terminal at the southern tip of Manhattan. (?) **718/727-2508.** http://home2.nyc.gov/html/dot/html/ferrybus/statfery.shtml#info. Free-of-charge. 24 hr.; every 15 min. during rush hour, every half-hour or hour during nights and weekends. Subway: N, R to Whitehall St.; 4, 5 to Bowling Green; 1 to South Ferry (ride in one of the 1st 5 cars).

Statue of Liberty ★★★ ICON/MONUMENT   The great harbor of New York and the grand lady who guards it are, after Ground Zero and the Empire State Building, the city's top must-visit attractions. You'll follow in the footsteps of the millions of immigrants and visitors who came here before you, their way lighted by the torch and the promise inscribed on the statue's base: that the "teeming masses yearning to breathe free" would find succor, freedom from persecution, and economic opportunity in this new land.

You will have a fine view of Lady Liberty from the shores of Battery Park, but if you have the time, it's worth it to board a ferry out to Liberty Island and take the

THE STATUE OF LIBERTY—in brief

The French connection: Dreamed up at a dinner party of French intellectuals in 1865, the statue was first proposed as a hundredth birthday present from France to the U.S. (and as a not-so-subtle jab at France's then-authoritarian Second Empire). Fundraising woes kept it from being completed in time for that anniversary, but in 1881, after over a decade of begging for money (a lottery finally did the trick), sculptor Auguste Bartholdi was able to finish the massive work.

The battle for the base: Though the statue was completed in 1881, it took another 2 years for the Americans to keep their half of the bargain and create a pedestal for it. Newspaperman Joseph Pulitzer finally stepped in, and in a series of angry editorials condemning the wealthy for not contributing, he finally convinced thousands of lower-income Americans to send in what they could to get the job done. Thanks to

their dimes and nickels, the pedestal was finally built (designed by Richard Morris Hunt); and the statue was dedicated on October 28, 1886.

Crafting the Lady: *Repousse*, a technique of hammering and shaping thin strips of copper, was used to create Lady Liberty. Though the statue is massive at over 151 feet from base to torch, the "skin" of the piece is just $\frac{3}{32}$ of an inch thick. It is thought that the ancient Colossus of Rhodes was built using this method.

A key to the symbolism: Every piece of the statue has meaning. The seven rays in the crown represent the seven seas of the world, and the 25 windows there give a nod to the 25 gemstones found on earth. On the tablet Liberty is holding are inscribed the Roman numerals for July 4th, 1776. And though it's difficult to see, Liberty is breaking shackles with her right foot.

official ranger tour of the monument. The tour includes a small museum on the history of the statue, the chance to stand just feet from the original torch, which had to be replaced in the mid-1980s due to severe water damage. Limited numbers of visitors conclude the tour with a thrilling, exhausting climb up a circular stairway to the crown of the statue (go to the website for more than that). On the way up, you'll view the intricate metal work that French engineer Gustave Eiffel (of the Eiffel Tower) created to anchor the statue; it acts like a spring, allowing the "skin" of the structure to adjust to different temperatures and sway up to 3 inches in 50-mph winds.

If you do want to take the tour—and I recommend it—it's extremely important to order timed tickets in advance, either by phone or through the website (see below). Some 3,000 visitors take the tour each day, but on certain days, in summer and around the holidays in particular, nearly 15,000 show up and have to be turned away. This, and the 9/11 Memorial are the two major New York sites that you really do have to plan ahead for, as often capacity doesn't keep up with demand.

Those without tickets to the monument can take a ranger-led tour of the island, but the better option may be to simply stay on the ferry, which slows down as it approaches the statue, giving those onboard a good view of Lady Liberty in all of her surprisingly delicate beauty. Spend the time you'll save to go on to Ellis Island (see above),

Liberty's sister monument, with no entrance quotas. I think Ellis is ultimately the more rewarding of the two.

On Liberty Island in New York Harbor. ℂ **212/363-3200** (general info), or 877/523-9849 (ticket/ferry info). www.nps.gov/stli or www.statuecruises.com. Free admission; ferry ticket to Statue of Liberty and Ellis Island $12 adults, $10 seniors 62 and older, $5 children 4–12. Daily 9:30am–5pm (last ferry departs around 2pm); extended hours in summer. Subway: 4, 5 to Bowling Green; 1 to South Ferry. Walk south through Battery Park to Castle Clinton, the fort housing the ferry ticket booth.

Trinity Church ★ CHURCH/HISTORIC SITE   This is actually the third Trinity Church to stand on this site. The first version was destroyed in the fire set by fleeing colonists in 1776 to thwart British occupiers (it ended up razing one-third of the structures in Manhattan). The second was poorly constructed, and its roof collapsed in a heavy snowstorm. But the third was a keeper and is considered by many to be one of the best, if not *the* best, Gothic Revival buildings in the United States.

Designed by Richard Upjohn, the religious structure can be seen as the stone and mortar embodiment of a theological movement that was sweeping the Anglican Church at that time, one that attempted to invigorate the Church by harkening back to its Catholic roots. Specifically, it paid heed to the idea that the Church needed a strong hierarchy to survive. So instead of creating a boxy, continuous space, like so many churches of the period (and like St. Paul's further down Broadway), Upjohn used self-consciously medieval features designed to underscore the sacred nature of the clergy's space, including a chancel. Normally, in a Gothic cathedral, the chancel (which is the area behind the altar, reserved for the clergy and choir) is marked off by railings, but that idea was quite controversial in Democratic New York, so Upjohn created a subtle solution, raising this area a few feet above the ground, to give the feeling of an exalted place, without prominent barriers in place. Other Gothic features include the towering 280-foot spire, which was the tallest structure in the city until the piers of the Brooklyn Bridge were built; the flying buttresses; and the lovely stained glass windows. The doors were modeled after Ghiberti's famous bronze doors for the Baptistery of Florence and were designed by noted American architect Richard Morris Hunt, though the sculptures on them were done by Austrian immigrant Karl Bitter. You can see the latter's self-portrait in the knoblike head sticking out of the lower right hand corner of the door; above him is Richard Upjohn and above that Richard Morris Hunt (who also designed the base of the Statue of Liberty).

Don't miss touring the graveyard, which holds the remains of many Revolutionary War–era New Yorkers. Among the notables are Captain James Ludlow, who uttered the famous command, "Don't give up the ship," in the War of 1812; he's buried in the tomb that looks like a ship, on the southern side of the church, surrounded by a fence made from captured British cannons. Behind Lawrence and to the right a bit is the most famous tomb here, that of Alexander Hamilton; beside Hamilton is the grave of steamboat designer Robert Fulton.

The church runs a brief **tour** daily at 2pm (a second Sunday tour follows the 11:15am Eucharist); groups of five or more should call ℂ **212/602-0872** to reserve. There's a small museum at the end of the left aisle displaying documents (including the 1697 church charter from King William III), photographs, replicas of the Hamilton-Burr duel pistols, and other items.

At Broadway and Wall St. © **212/602-0800** or 212/602-0872 for tour information. www.trinitywall street.org. Free admission and free tours at 2pm daily. Museum Mon–Fri 9am–5:30pm (closed during the 12:05pm service); Sat–Sun 9am–3:45pm. Subway: 4, 5 to Wall St.

Wall Street & the New York Stock Exchange ★ ICON   This is the most famous (some would say infamous) financial institution in the world, the New York Stock Exchange. The building's towering columns, crowded ornamental pediment, and huge flag trumpet louder than any opening bell that this is a place of incomparable might and prestige (interestingly, it's a much more imposing building than the government's plainer Federal Hall across the street). In front of the Stock Exchange is a scraggly buttonwood tree, meant to invoke the buttonwood that New York's first traders stood under in 1792 when they met to begin brokering the Revolutionary War debt—the first stock market in America.

One odd fact about the Stock Exchange: Though it's associated in the popular imagination with Wall Street, its facade actually fronts Broad Street, not Wall.

Unfortunately, the NYSE is no longer open to the public for tours, but you can grab a cup of coffee and drink it in nearby Zuccoti Park, the place where the OWS (Occupy Wall Street) movement was founded.

11 Wall St. © **212/656-3000.** www.nyse.com. Subway: J, Z to Broad St.; 2, 3, 4, 5 to Wall St.

Lower East Side

Eldridge Street Project ★   An 1887 synagogue, the oldest house of worship in the city for Eastern European Jews, the Eldridge Street Project has the kind of grandeur that one normally associates with the cathedrals of Europe. There's a poignancy to the place as well, as the building was abandoned for 40 years before restoration began in the 1990s, and it's crumbling picturesquely away in places. An hourly "From Bottom to Top" tour covers the history of the synagogue and the issues involved in its restoration.

12 Eldridge St. (btw. Canal and Division sts.). www.eldridgestreet.org. Admission $10 adults, $8 seniors and students, $6 children 5–18, free to all on Mon. Sun–Thurs 10am–5pm, Fri 10am–3pm; closed on all national and Jewish holidays. Subway: B, D to Grand St.; F to W. Broadway.

Merchant's House Museum ★ MUSEUM   New York City has never been very good at preserving its past (perhaps we have too little room . . . or patience), but on East 4th Street this precious sliver of history has survived utterly intact. In fact, this is the *only* Victorian-era structure in New York City preserved both inside and out. A handsome Greek Revival town house, it was once the home of the Tredwell family, who furnished it in the highest style of the day, all mohair couches, crystal chandeliers, and deep red curtains. These furnishings, the clothing of the 10-person family, their cookware, and anything else you might want to see, are all on display, thanks to the efforts in 1936 of a preservationist (before there really was such a thing) named George Chapman. A lovely garden and frequent ghost sightings add to the home's appeal.

29 E. 4th St. (btw. Lafayette and Bowery). © **212/777-1089.** www.merchantshouse.org. Admission $10 adult, $5 seniors and students, free member and children 11 under. Thurs–Mon noon–5pm. Subway: 6 to Astor Place; N, R to 8th St.; F, B to Broadway/Lafayette

New Museum of Contemporary Art ★ MUSEUM   Perhaps the greatest sign of New York City's ever increasing prosperity is the fact that now, even the gritty, grimy Bowery (birthplace of the term "bowery bums" for the homeless people who used to swarm its cheap bars and bunk in its missions) now has a museum. And a bright and shiny one at that, a massive steel and glass tower. As with much of the art of the moment, the exhibits range from the sublime to the silly (I was stopped dead in my tracks at a recent exhibit by a cardboard box and a big plastic bag among all the sculptures—was it art, or the container the art came in? I knew the answer intellectually, but my heart kept crying out: recycle that bag and box, and do something useful with it!). Wall text is hard to find, so buttonhole one of the gallery guides wearing big "ask me" buttons; sometimes their explanations will be more interesting than the art itself.

235 Bowery (at Prince St.). ℂ **212/219-1222.** www.newmuseum.org. Admission $12 adult, $10 senior, $8 student, free 18 and under. Thurs 11am–9pm; Wed and Fri–Sun 11am–6pm. Subway: 6 to Spring St; N, R to Prince St.

The Tenement Museum ★★★ MUSEUM   At first glance, this museum looks like just one of many brownstone building on this Lower East Side block . . . and that's exactly the point. The first-ever National Trust for Historic Preservation site that was *not* the home of someone rich or famous, it was preserved to tell the story of the immigrants who once lived in this building (97 Orchard St.) and in the surrounding buildings. Those stories are rich and varied: this five-story tenement housed some 10,000 people from 25 countries between 1863 and 1935. A visit here makes an excellent follow-up to an Ellis Island trip.

Visits to the museum are by **hour-long guided tour only,** and visitors have a choice of four programs, each of which illuminates the lives of different sorts of tenants, from garment workers who did piece work in their apartment to a family who survived not one but two depressions. Best for children is the weekend-only program: "Confino Family Apartment," which is less tour than interactive experience in which a costumed character, teenaged Victoria Confino, instructs new immigrants (the people on the tour) in a candid, revealing, and totally improvised manner on how to get along in New York. (It sounds hokey, I know, but to my mind, it's the most vivid of tours.) Many of the other tours are only offered to those over the age of 12; check before booking.

The museum also periodically offers walking tours of the neighborhood, culinary experiences, and rotating exhibits.

Tours are limited in number and sell out quickly, so it pays to buy tickets in advance, which you can do online or by calling ℂ **866/606-7232.**

108 Orchard St. (btw. Delancey and Broome sts.). ℂ **212/431-0233.** www.tenement.org. All tours $25 adults, $20 seniors and students. There are 6 different tours leaving at various hours daily 10am–6pm (the schedule is complicated and varies by month, so check the website or call). Subway: F to Delancey St.; J, M to Essex St.

Center for Jewish History ★ CULTURAL CENTER/MUSEUM   Persons interested in tracing their Jewish ancestry can visit the Center for Jewish History, which is the largest repository of Jewish records, artifacts, books, and letters in the world—100 million archived documents in all—and has a state-of-the-art genealogical library open to all. Three to four temporary exhibits, drawn usually from these vast archives, are housed in three large, on-site galleries. Cultural programs are held in the small auditorium three or four times a week.

15 W. 16th St. (btw. Fifth and Sixth aves.). ℂ **212/294-8301.** www.cjh.org. Admission to Yeshiva University Museum $8 adults, $6 seniors and students, free for children 4 and under; free to all

Mon, Wed 5–8pm, and Fri. Free admission to all other facilities. Yeshiva University Museum Sun, Tues, and Thurs 11am–5pm; Mon 3:30–8pm; Wed 11am–8pm; Fri 11am–2:30pm. Reading Room and Genealogy Institute Mon 9:30am–7:30pm; Tues–Thurs 9:30am–5pm; Fri 9:30am–1:30pm; Sun 11am–4pm. All other exhibition galleries Sun 11am–5pm; Mon and Wed 9:30am–8pm; Fri 9am–3pm; Sun 11am–5pm. Subway: L, N, R, 4, 5, 6 to 14th St./Union Square; F, M to 14th St.

Rubin Museum of Art ★★ MUSEUM   Travelers who need a break from the bustle and stresses of New York can escape to the Rubin, a serene, contemplative museum of art from the Himalayas. Secular in origin—the museum was founded by an American millionaire and his wife who fell in love with the art of this region—its effect is nonetheless tremendously spiritual, as the paintings, drawings, sculptures, and artifacts shown are all religious items, many used by traveling monks to teach Buddhism or to help worshippers deepen their meditation (that's why so many of the works are done on fabric—they're meant to be rolled up and carried). Many tell the stories of the various Buddhas, portraying meditating men with halos, snarling demons, teachers, and commoners in the deepest blues, ruby reds, emerald greens, and dazzling golds. For sheer beauty, the 1,500 works housed in this museum are hard to top.

Set on the site of the former Barney's Department Store (the Rubins chose it because the central circular stairway looked like a "mandala," a never-ending circle surrounded by a square, which is the Tantric Buddhist diagram of the cosmos), the museum also hosts an impressive array of lectures, performances, film screenings, and more. Its children and teen programs are particularly well done. The only disappointment here are the audio guides ($3), which are poorly done. Don't waste your time with them; instead, ask questions of the knowledgeable guides, wearing big red ASK ME buttons, on each floor.

150 W. 17th St. ✆ **212/620-5000.** www.rmanyc.org. Admission $10 adults; $5 seniors, artists, and neighbors; $2 students (with ID); free for children 12 and under; and free to all Fri 6–10pm. Mon and Thurs 11am–5pm; Wed 11am–7pm; Fri 11am–10pm; Sat–Sun 11am–6pm; closed Christmas and Thanksgiving. Subway: A, C, or E to 14th St.; 1 to 18th St.; 2, 3 to 14th St.

MIDTOWN

Flatiron District

Flatiron Building ★★ ARCHITECTURE   You'll probably know the Flatiron Building even before you see it thanks to the famous photos of the building taken by Alfred Stieglitz, who snapped it numerous times, calling the Fuller Building (its original name) "a picture of new America still in the making." Many consider it the first skyscraper in New York; it certainly was one of the first to use a steel frame, the classic skyscraper structure. Its unusual triangular shape was architect Daniel Burnham's solution to a space problem: The building rests on the bow-tie intersection where Broadway and Fifth Avenue cross each other. In order to produce a decent amount of rentable space, he built it to a towering 375 feet on every sliver of land he had available to him. The apex is just 6 feet across at its narrowest point. When it was first erected in 1902, crowds used to gather in Madison Square Park across the street to wait for it to fall down! Later men were drawn here by the urban

Midtown Attractions

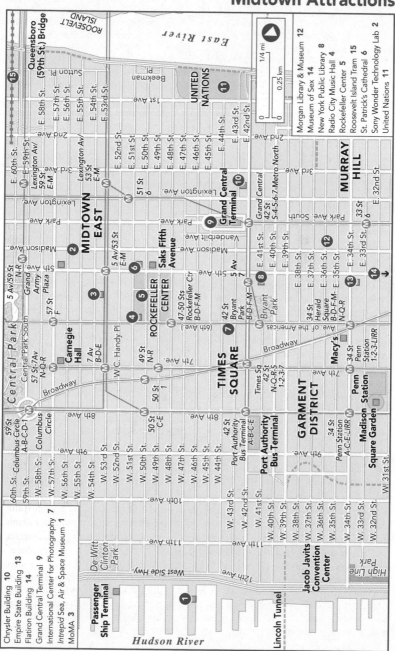

Chrysler Building **10**
Empire State Building **13**
Flatiron Building **14**
Grand Central Terminal **9**
International Center for Photography **7**
Intrepid Sea, Air & Space Museum **1**
MoMA **3**

Morgan Library & Museum **12**
Museum of Sex **14**
New York Public Library **8**
Radio City Music Hall **4**
Rockefeller Center **5**
Roosevelt Island Tram **15**
St. Patrick's Cathedral **6**
Sony Wonder Technology Lab **2**
United Nations **11**

CHELSEA CALLING: MEET THE new art district

More than 250 galleries are now on the blocks spanning 20th to 29th streets between Tenth and Eleventh avenues in West Chelsea, effectively making the Big Apple the planet's premiere marketplace for contemporary art. Gallery after gallery has taken over the former warehouse and industrial spaces of this dusty old 'hood, creating an eminently walkable arts district. You can have a perfectly lovely time simply getting lost in the area and wandering blindly from one space to the next, although you can hit a lot of clunky exhibitions (just as with any collection of new art, some are better than others)—but so what? If you want to take this course of action, start on 24th Street, which has the largest assortment of "name" galleries. A better tack might be to catch a tour of the area (see below) or to concentrate on the following 10 galleries, which have made their reputations with consistently thought-provoking shows.

Note: The standard schedule for all Chelsea galleries is Sept–May Tues–Sat 10am–6pm; and June–Aug Mon–Fri 10am–6pm. Your best subway option is to take either the C or E lines to 23rd St.

303 Gallery 525 W. 22nd St. (© **212/255-1121;** www.303gallery.com). The Whitney biennial has this gallery on speed dial, having picked up works by several of the young to mid-career, cutting-edge photographers and painters who present shows here. For a good look at the artists the gallery represents, visit the website first.

Paula Cooper 534 W. 21st St. and 521 W. 21st St. (© **212/255-1105;** www.paulacoopergallery.com). Cooper used to be one of the biggest names in art, the dealer that everyone wanted. Though she's slipped in the last decade and lost some of her big-name clients, she still has the exquisite taste she's always had, and exhibits a number of prominent artists, including: Jennifer Bartlett, Donald Judd, Sol LeWitt, and Andres Serrano.

Gagosian 555 W. 24th St. (© **212/741-1111;** www.gagosian.com). A massive, important family of galleries (one uptown, one in Los Angeles, another in London), it presents blockbuster shows of works from such major 20th- and 21st-century figures as Roy Lichtenstein, Helen Frankenthaler, Nan Goldin, and Cindy Sherman.

Barbara Gladstone Gallery 515 W. 24th St. (© **212/206-9300;** www.gladstonegallery.com). Come here to see the artists who have emerged as big honchos in the last decade or so such as Matthew Barney and Richard Prince. Gladstone tends to feature conceptual, often highly political. art—most prominently photography and videos, but also sculpture and paintings.

Yossi Milo 525 W. 25th St. (© **212/404-0370;** www.yossimilogallery.com). One of my personal favorites, Milo works almost exclusively with photographers and has a terrific eye for the next big thing. He also runs a very friendly gallery, and he and his staff are always happy to talk with interested patrons. Because

myth that the building's shape caused strange wind patterns that were effective in blowing up women's skirts. The cops who dispersed these groups of gaping men on 23rd Street would call out "23 skidoo!," and so a slang term was born. One of the most beloved buildings in the city, it has been compared by many to a mighty ship sailing up Fifth Avenue.

175 Fifth Ave. (at 23rd St.). Subway: N, R to 23rd St.

he represents photographers, some of them selling multiple editions of their work, you just may be able to afford to buy something here.

Pace Gallery 534 and 510 W. 25th St. (℗ **212/929-7000;** www.pacegallery. com). Another "Blue Chip" gallery, with two outposts in Chelsea (see above). one in Midtown (32 E. 57th St.), one in London and one in Beijing. Pace has been a powerhouse since the 1960s, when it was founded in Boston. Shows in 2013 featured the works of such biggies as Maya Lin, James Turrell, and an Alexander Calder retrospective.

Andrea Rosen 525 and 544 W. 24th St. (℗ **212/627-6000;** www.andrearosen gallery.com). The Rosen gallery is a terrific place to see emerging artists, especially those who are "installation happy" and like to create entire environments for their viewers. It seems that each time I come here I'm stepping into some new type of utopia (or dystopia); the experience can be chilling and exciting.

Sonnabend Gallery 536 W. 22nd St. (℗ **212/627-1018;** www.sonnabendgallery.com). Maybe I've just hit it right, but I find that the Sonnabend has something that's missing from so many galleries: a sense of humor. Most of the work I've seen here has been purposefully funny—odd *Star Wars* sculptures, videos of Germans singing along to Madonna songs, clocks shaped like ships—and after all of the "serious art" at other places, coming into this playful atmosphere is a delight.

Sonnabend is one of the more established galleries, founded by the former wife of famed dealer Leo Castelli.

David Zwirner 525 W. 19th St. (℗ **212/727-7020;** www.davidzwirner. com). This is not the place for people with delicate sensibilities, but if you don't mind seeing art that's really on the edge, you'll often find something here that will get your adrenaline pumping. Zwirner was profiled in the *New York Times* in March 2013, which praised his "idiosyncratic roster, with great oddballs like R. Crumb and Raymond Pettibon alongside institutional darlings like Stan Douglas and Francis Alÿs."

A gallery tour: Allowing an expert to lead you through this ever-shifting maze of art is a good idea. And New York's foremost expert in the Chelsea Gallery scene—he visits 50 to 70 shows a week just to keep current—is Raphael Risemburg of **NY Gallery Tours** ★ (℗ **212/946-1548;** www.nygallerytours. com). Risemburg, a former professor at Keane College in New Jersey, has a droll, friendly manner and leads his tours in Socratic fashion: He'll tell you what he thinks of the art at the four to five galleries you cover on your tour, and then ask your opinion on the unanswered questions it poses. His open tours are offered almost every Saturday ($20), and he also leads private tours for $300 (though you can bring along multiple people on those).

East Side

Chrysler Building ★★★ ARCHITECTURE   In the Chrysler Building we see the roaring twenties version of what Alan Greenspan called "irrational exuberance"— a last burst of corporate headquarter building before stocks succumbed to the thudding crash of 1929. Throughout the previous decade, real estate speculators had been throwing up building after building, adding almost 100 skyscrapers of 20 stories or more, and utterly transforming the skyline of the city. Automaker Walter P. Chrysler commissioned architect William Van Alen to top them all, instructing him that he wanted a building "higher than the Eiffel Tower," the tallest in the world at that time. What Chrysler would soon learn was that the gentlemen behind the Bank of America had the same ambition, and they had hired Van Alen's former partner (and sworn enemy) H. Craig Severance to build them the tallest building on the planet down on Wall Street. Soon the race was on, as each architect returned continually to the drafting board, adding 10 more stories of penthouses here, a lantern there, a 50-foot flagpole. In the fall of 1929, Severance was sure he had won, so he completed the Bank of America building at 927 feet. Van Alen then unveiled the *coup de grâce* that he had been hiding in an elevator shaft—a silver spike to crown his building, making it, at 1,046 feet, an unbeatable 117 feet higher than his rival's.

Not only taller, the Chrysler was the more striking of the two buildings, its scalloped spire set like a jaunty jester's cap atop a sleek tower. Take a look at the sharp stainless steel eagles that jut out just below the roof; the "gargoyles" below those on the 61st floor are actually modeled after the hood ornament of the 1929 Chrysler Plymouth.

The Chrysler remains one of the most impressive Art Deco buildings ever constructed, but it wasn't the tallest for long. Less than a year after it was completed, the Empire State Building assumed that mantle and held it until the World Trade Center came along.

405 Lexington Ave. (at 42nd St.). Subway: S, 4, 5, 6, 7 to 42nd St./Grand Central.

Empire State Building ★★★ ARCHITECTURE There's no better introduction to New York than a visit to the Empire State Building. The apex of the New York skyline, both literally (at 102 stories and 1,454 ft.) and figuratively, the view from its Observation Deck is at once instructive and exhilarating. From your bird's-eye perch, you orient yourself geographically and see, with a clarity not possible on the ground, the miracle of Manhattan, that runt of an island that couldn't get much wider or longer, and so did what no other city before it had done and expanded to the skies, becoming a dense, pulsating city of boxy towers set on a painfully narrow strip of land.

Look first to the **south,** where the Financial District's powerful skyscrapers loom over the field of lower, mostly residential housing that stands between it and Midtown. Beyond the Financial District, in the harbor, are the Statue of Liberty to the right and the Brooklyn Bridge (the most graceful of the three bridges you'll see in this direction). **Right below** you will be the triangular Flatiron building, one of the most thrillingly odd in Manhattan (it was Frank Lloyd Wright's favorite building). Just to the side of it are the glittering gold roof of the Metropolitan Life Tower and the World Life Insurance Towers, once centers of New York's high society and now just part of the landscape. Drift to the **north side** of the building and you will be among a riot of skyscrapers, thrown up in a manner that seems wildly chaotic from this vantage point. This strip of Midtown contains more office space per acre than any other area in the world. Peer through the curtain of buildings to catch a glimpse of Central Park, looking like a modest lawn from this great height.

The Empire State Building—in Brief

- Opened in 1931 after just 14 months of construction (total cost: $25 million)
- Tallest building in the world from 1931 to 1970, when the World Trade Center took the title. It is now the seventh tallest building on the planet.
- The oddly shaped spire at the top was meant to be a landing port for blimps, but high winds kept dirigibles from ever being able to anchor here.
- In 1945, a plane accidentally crashed into the building, killing 17 people.
- Every Valentine's Day, 14 couples are married for free on the Observation Deck.

The Empire State Building keeps longer hours than any other tourist attraction in the city, opening at 9am and closing at 2am to accommodate the close-to-four-million visitors who troop through yearly. As you may have heard, the lines here can be epic. Some ways to "game the line" include:

- Arrive promptly at 8am or during the dinner hour, which are relatively uncrowded times.
- Plan to visit on a Tuesday or Wednesday, the least popular days of the week. You'll encounter the biggest crowds on Saturday and Sunday, followed closely by Monday and Friday.
- Bite the bullet and buy an "Express Ticket" (pricey, but possibly worth it), which will allow you to jump to the head of all of the lines and get to the top in 20 minutes flat.
- Purchase and print out a ticket from the Empire State Building website, which will allow you to skip the ticket line (though *not* the lines for security or the elevators). Purchase of the **City Pass** (p. 109) brings the same perks. The **New York Pass** is not quite as good a deal, because you'll have to wait in the ticket line to change your voucher into a ticket.
- If it's the view you're seeking and not just the experience of being at the Empire State Building, consider Top of the Rock (p. 132) which has instituted timed tickets and therefore never has a wait.

350 Fifth Ave. (at 34th St.). © **212/736-3100**. www.esbnyc.com. 86th Floor Observatory admission $25 adults, $22 seniors, $19 children 6–12, free for children 5 and under. Express Pass $48 (all ages); 86th and 102nd floor combination pass: $42 adults; $36 children 6–12; $39 seniors. Express pass $64.50. Daily 8am–2am (last elevator at 1:15am). Subway: B, D, F, N, Q, R, M to 34th St.; 6 to 33rd St.

Grand Central Station ★★ ARCHITECTURE   In ancient Roman times, the entrances to great cities were framed with monumental arches, meant to awe all who passed through. When Grand Central Station was being built at the turn of the last century, it was recognized that our railroad terminals were our grand gateways, the first view a traveler would have of the metropolis. So the architects of both Grand Central and the late great Pennsylvania Station (the original, torn down in the 1960s) conspired to create as much pomp and stateliness as possible, filling these spaces with the symbols and architecture of imperial Rome. On Grand

A PARK & a ride

On October 24, 2012 a small miracle occurred: **Franklin D. Roosevelt Four Freedoms Park** on Roosevelt Island finally opened. An austerely beautiful tribute to the four-term president, it was designed by star architect Louis Kahn shortly before his death in 1974. It took the intervening 38 years for the project finally to come to fruition (mostly due to the efforts of Kahn's son, who created a documentary about his father's vision which helped raise the millions necessary to build the monument). The park offers wonderful views of the Manhattan skyline, as well as a serene break from the bustle of NYC. But perhaps one its greatest lures is the amusement park-like ride one takes to the island aboard the **Roosevelt Island Tram (℃ 212/832-4555;** www.rioc.com/transportation.htm). This is the aerial vehicle you have probably seen in countless movies, most recently *Spider-Man*. It originates at 59th Street and Second Avenue, costs $2.75 each way, and takes about 5 minutes to traverse the East River to Roosevelt Island, where there are a series of apartment complexes (part of the fun is peering into the apartments as you swoop by). The tram operates daily from 6am until 2am and until 3:30am on weekends.

Central's facade, 10 colossal Doric fluted pillars tower over Park Avenue; above them a massive statue of Mercury, the god of travel, spreads his arms in welcome as Hercules and Minerva, gods of strength and wisdom, lounge at his feet. (The face of the clock below the sculpture is the largest piece of Tiffany glass in the world.)

The station's interior is no less impressive, its concourse soaring the equivalent of nine stories to a vaulted ceiling on which the signs of the zodiac are created from 59 fiber-optic lights and 2,500 painted stars. The side walls feature massive windows that throw shafts of light onto the acre-long Indiana marble floor. Not that the station needed them: One of its innovations was the use of electric lights, so you'll see bare bulbs sprinkled throughout the station and on the massive chandeliers that overhang the concourse. Two hundred buildings were demolished to make way for the station, which opened on February 2, 1913, bearing a price tag of $80 million.

As you walk through, take in all of the trendy shops housed in the arteries of the main concourse; the dining concourse below, with the famed **Oyster Bar** at its heart (p. 92); and the **Campbell Apartments**, former office of a finance tycoon and now a fab bar (p. 219). If you're traveling with children, take them to the "whispering gallery" right outside the Oyster Bar. Stand on one side of the arch there and have your child stand on the other, and then whisper to each other back and forth; a trick of acoustics allows sound to travel from one side of the vault to the other.

Walking tours of the station are offered daily at 12:30; go to the information window on the Grand Concourse to join. If you'd like to do an **audio tour,** those, too, are available from 9am to 6pm at that same window.

42nd St. at Park Ave. ℃ **212/532-4900.** www.grandcentralterminal.com. Subway: S, 4, 5, 6, or 7 to 42nd St./Grand Central.

The Morgan Library & Museum ★★ LIBRARY/MUSEUM Famed Canadian scientist George Mercer Dawson once wrote that a great library contained "the diary of the human race." With that definition, very few libraries come as close to greatnesss as the Morgan, which contains examples of the written word from the beginning of recorded time—pictorial Mesopotamian cylinder seals (4th millennium B.C., a precursor to writing) to papyrus rolls from ancient Egypt, Greece, and Rome to brilliantly colorful medieval illuminated manuscripts. Its crowning jewels are three editions of the Gutenberg Bible, the first book to be created using moveable type. (This is the only collection in the world to boast three; scholars come from across the globe to study them, as each is unique). Also in the collection today are manuscripts by Mark Twain, Jane Austen, Charles Dickens, the Bronte sisters, Galileo, Bob Dylan, Alexander Calder and James Joyce. One of the 25 known surviving copies of the Declaration of Independence is another highlight, along with a First Folio of Shakespeare. (The fragility of these treasures means that they cannot be constantly on display, but you'll usually see one of the Gutenbergs when you visit, along with other exquisite books.)

The Morgan in the name of the library was 19th century billionaire J. Pierpont Morgan (1837–1913), and he collected more than just books. But many of his greatest artistic acquisitions were donated to the Wadsworth Atheneum (in Hartford) and the Metropolitan Museum after Morgan's death.

When you visit, be sure to put aside at least an hour and a half to take in the ever-rotating special exhibitions, along with the exquisite architecture. The original library, a marble villa in High Renaissance style, was designed by Charles Follen McKim (of the famous firm of McKim, Meade and White). An expansion by lauded architect Renzo Piano, completed in 2006, added massive steel and glass pavilions, doubling the size of the facilities without diluting their Italianate flair. Along with a gift store, a terrific café and restaurant were added (so you may want to combine your visit with lunch).

225 Madison Ave. (btw. 36th and 37th sts.). © **212/685-0008.** www.themorgan.org. $15 adults, $10 seniors and students, free for children 11 and under; free for all Fri 7–9pm. Tues–Thurs 10:30am–5pm; Fri 10:30am–9pm; Sat 10am–6pm; Sun 11am–6pm. Subway: 6 to 33rd St.

Museum of Sex ★ MUSEUM Though it tries hard to avoid a carnival atmosphere, with voluminous and often soporific wall text, this museum still has a major "wink, wink, giggle, giggle" quotient. If you're interested in the subject from an anthropological perspective, you may be disappointed. For the rest of us, including all of the folks who seemed to be out on dates (or perhaps they met there?), the museum is good, dirty fun. *Warning:* Due to the graphic nature of its exhibits, this museum is not for everyone.

233 Fifth Ave. (at 27th St.). © **212/689-6337.** www.museumofsex.com. Admission adults $17, $15 students and seniors. At press time, there was a $3 coupon available on its website. No one 17 and under admitted. Sun–Thurs 10am–8pm; Fri and Sat 10am–9pm. Subway: N, R, 6 to 28th St.

New York Public Library ★★ LIBRARY/LANDMARK Many art historians consider this to be the finest Beaux Arts building in the United States. It certainly is one of the grandest, completed in 1911 at a cost of over $9 million and built by the famous firm of Carrere and Hastings. The exterior takes its inspiration from the twin palaces on the north side of the Place de la Concorde in Paris and is done in the same French Renaissance style, a perfect harmony of columns, pediments, and statuary. Famous stone lions guard the entrance and are said to roar whenever a virgin passes by. Want to use the library? Well, you will be "reading between the lions" (sorry, I couldn't resist).

The library itself holds thousands of volumes, many of which are housed underground below what is now Bryant Park. A "no-browsing" facility, it uses an ancient dumbwaiter system for retrieval of books in which the tomes are stacked into a small elevator and sent up when requests are made. Along with books, **Gottesman Exhibition Hall** (first floor) often houses interesting exhibits on literary and New York history. Don't skip the Lionel Pincus and Princess Firyal room, which houses one of the most extensive collection of maps in the world (and is magnificent after a $5 million renovation).

Entrance is always free, and the palatial interior, with its expanses of marble and carved oak ceilings, is worth a look-see. For a more formal tour, time your visit to occur at 11am or 2pm, Monday through Saturday, on 2pm on Sunday, when guides lead visitors through the building.

Fifth Ave. at 42nd St. © **917/275-6975** (exhibits and events) or 212/930-0800 (general number). www.nypl.org. Free admission to all exhibitions. Mon and Thurs–Sat 10am–6pm; Tues–Wed 10am–8pm; Sun 1–5pm. Subway: 1, 2, 3 to 42nd St./Broadway; B, D, F, M to 42nd St./6th Ave.; S, 4, 5, 6 to Grand Central/42nd St.; 7 to Fifth Ave.

St. Patrick's Cathedral ★ CATHEDRAL   The largest Roman Catholic cathedral in the United States, St. Pat's is also the seat of the Archdiocese of New York. Designed by James Renwick, begun in 1859, and consecrated in 1879, St. Patrick's wasn't completed until 1906. Strangely, Irish Catholics picked one of the city's WASPiest neighborhoods for St. Patrick's. The vast cathedral seats a congregation of 2,200; if you don't want to come for Mass, you can pop in between services to get a look at the impressive interior. The St. Michael and St. Louis altar came from Tiffany & Co. (also located here on Fifth Ave.).

Fifth Ave. (btw. 50th and 51st sts.). © **212/753-2261.** www.saintpatrickscathedral.org. Free admission. Daily 6:30am–8:45pm. Mass Mon–Fri 7, 7:30, and 8am, noon, and 12:30, 1, and 5:30pm; Sat 8am, noon, and 5:30pm; Sun 7, 8, 9, and 10:15am, noon, 1, 4 (in Spanish), and 5:30pm; holy days 7, 7:30, 8, 8:30, and 11:30am, noon, and 12:30, 1, 5:30, and 6:30pm. Subway: B, D, F, M to 47th–50th sts./Rockefeller Center.

United Nations ★★ ARCHITECTURE/GOVERNMENT BUILDING   It's this seven-block stretch of international territory that makes New York City the capital of the world. No really. It's become fashionable of late in some political circles to denigrate the U.N. Though some reform is obviously necessary, a tour here will remind you of just how much the United Nations has done since its inception. It was founded, after all, with the express purpose of ensuring that there would never be another world war, and it has accomplished that, no small task. Perhaps more importantly, a visit here will remind you of how much potential the U.N. still has for effecting meaningful progress in numerous fields, from the elimination of disease and poverty to the resolution of ethnic conflicts.

Those who take the hour-long tour will visit not only the **General Assembly** (where Khrushchev once famously pounded his shoe in anger) and the **Security**

Council, but the less well-known **Economic and Social Council Room** that oversees the work of UNICEF, the World Health Organization, and 28 other U.N. programs of development (little-known fact: it's thanks to recommendations by the WHO that most countries have expiration dates stamped on milk). It's in this room that officials are working to create standardized tests for avian flu, vaccinate the world's children against polio, and promote the cause of world literacy. The Nobel Peace Prize won by the U.N. Peacekeeping forces in 2001 is displayed just outside the council room, along with an enlightening exhibit on the important work these troops are still doing throughout the world.

If you don't want to pay $16 for the tour, you can still visit, taking in the lobby of the General Assembly building, with its free, changing exhibits (photojournalism mostly), meditation room, and the memorial stained glass window Marc Chagall created for former Secretary General Dag Hammarskjöld in 1964 (to the right of the entrance). An international gift shop with trinkets from across the globe and the U.N. post office are in the basement. The sculpture garden is no longer open to the public, nor is the gallery at the Security Council when it's in session, but ordinary Joes can once again dine side by side with diplomats in the Delegates' Dining Room (call in advance for a reservation; men are required to wear jackets). My father was actually married at the U.N., so I can vouch for the food, which is quite good, especially if you hit it when a nation is sponsoring a celebratory buffet of its specialties.

At First Ave. and 46th St. ✆ **212/963-8687.** www.un.org/tours. Guided tours $16 adults, $11 seniors 60 and over and students 13 and over, $9 children 5–12. Children 4 and under not permitted. Weekday tours at 9:45am and 4:45pm. Guided tours might be canceled with short notice when heads of state and government are meeting. U.N. open weekdays 9:45am–4:45pm, weekends 10am–4:15pm. Subway: S, 4, 5, 6, 7 to 42nd St./Grand Central.

Times Square/West Side

International Center of Photography ★ MUSEUM Founded in 1974 by Cornell Capa, brother of eminent war photographer Robert Capa, ICP's focus is on photojournalism primarily, though art photography is occasionally featured. A handsome white box of a museum, it offers exhibits of probing, investigative photography that will illuminate some destination, social ill, or recent conflict. I only wish that the entrance fee was a bit lower, as you can easily see the three or so exhibits (the normal maximum at any one time) in 45 minutes or less. Still, those interested in photography or current events should enjoy this intelligent, small museum.

1133 Sixth Ave. (at 43rd St.). ✆ **212/857-0000.** www.icp.org. Admission $14 adults, $10 seniors and students, free for children 11 and under. Tues–Thurs and Sat–Sun 10am–6pm; Fri 10am–8pm. Subway: B, D, F, M to 42nd St.

Intrepid Sea, Air & Space Museum ★★ MUSEUM/HISTORIC SITE How's this for an all star line-up? Not only does the Intrepid Sea, Air and Space Museum now display the Space Shuttle *Intrepid,* it's got the world's only tourable nuclear submarine, the famed **Concorde** jet, nearly two-dozen grounded jets, a Revolutionary War-era submarine, and it itself is a World War II–era aircraft carrier. Whew! Even those who profess no interest in aviation or military history find themselves wowed by the breadth and depth of this collection. You'll likely have to devote a good 3 hours or more to see it all, so arrive early if you can.

You'll want to begin your visit at the **USS *Growler*** submarine, built in 1958 and so narrow that only small groups can enter at a time (which keeps the lines here long). You'll be taken on a brief, thrillingly claustrophobic tour introduced by a short video. Children under the age of 6 are not admitted.

Next, make your way to the Concorde, the oversized luxury lawn dart that, after flying half-empty for a number of years, was finally taken out of commission in 2003. (The jet isn't in the classic bent-nosed pose; that was only used for take-offs and landings.) This ultra-deluxe flying bus carried a mere 100 passengers at a time, most of them paying $6,000 each way for the privilege of crossing the Atlantic faster than the speed of sound (it went from 0 to 165mph in just 2½ seconds). Take a close look at places A and B, the seats reserved for Queen Elizabeth II and Prince Philip of England.

Visiting the pavilion of the **space shuttle *Enterprise*** costs an extra $7, but most will find it worth the outlay.

Then turn your attention to the **"Fighting I,"** the main focus of your visit, a 40,000 ton aircraft carrier that had one of the greatest survival stories of World War II. Though it was hit by five kamikaze planes (two of them in a single day) during its tours of duty, it continued to serve (the Japanese called it "The Ghost Ship" because it couldn't be sunk). Go directly to the Information Center on the hangar deck to inquire if there's a tour starting anytime soon. You can wander through the ship on your own, but you'll get more out of the experience with the hour-long guided tour, led by highly informed docents, most with military backgrounds.

Pier 86 (W. 46th St. at Twelfth Ave.). © **877/957-7447** or 212/245-0072. www.intrepidmuseum.org. Admission $22 adults; $18 seniors and students; $17 children 7–17; $15 veterans; $10 children 3–6; free for active military, retired U.S. military, and children 2 and under. Nov–Mar Tues–Sun 10am–5pm; Apr–Oct Mon–Fri 10am–5pm; Sat–Sun 10am–6pm. Closed Christmas and Thanksgiving. Subway: A, C, E to 42nd St./Port Authority. Bus: M42 Crosstown.

Museum of Modern Art ★★ ART MUSEUM

MOMA, as it's nicknamed, doesn't want for masterpieces. This is where you'll find seminal works by Picasso, Van Gogh, Brancusi, Dali, and Matisse among others. Its riches, however, aren't apparent on first glance. Oddly, the museum hides most of its masterworks waaaay up on the fifth floor, a ploy, I think, to get patrons to first look at the more contemporary, and often less celebrated, pieces that are housed in the lower galleries. Foil the curators by heading upstairs first and seeing the museum in "reverse order," to ensure you have enough time to meander in front of the works that make the museum great. And pick up and study the museum's gallery map; while the architecture of MOMA is justly renowned, it can be sometimes tricky to navigate from one area to the next.

And don't just spend your time indoors. The **Abby Aldrich Rockefeller Sculpture Garden,** which was enlarged during the 2004 renovation, is one of the most delightful spots in the city.

Note: MoMA has installed a museumwide Wi-Fi network so that visitors can access audio tours and commentary on their wireless devices; this includes specialized versions for children, teens, and the visually impaired.

11 W. 53rd St. (btw. Fifth and Sixth aves.). © **212/708-9400.** www.moma.org. Admission $25 adults, $18 seniors, $14 students, children 16 and under free if accompanied by an adult. All enter free on Fri between 4pm and 8pm. Sat–Mon and Wed–Thurs 10:30am–5:30pm; Fri 10:30am–8pm. Subway: E, M to Fifth Ave.; B, D, F to 47th–50th sts./Rockefeller Center.

MOMA'S mona lisas

Though there are many masterworks in the museums, be sure you give yourself enough time for the following three highlights:

o Vincent Van Gogh's **Starry Night,** which has an even more vivid impact when viewed in person, the thickness of the brush strokes making it as much sculpture as painting. Created a year before his suicide, when Van Gogh was in an insane asylum, the painting is filled with premonitions of what was to come, the foreground taken up with a soaring cypress tree, symbol of death.

o Pablo Picasso's **Desmoiselles d'Avignon,** a massive brothel scene in which Picasso experimented with a number of art styles—look closely and you'll see that one of the women's heads looks like an African mask, another profile is taken from Egyptian art, the woman in the middle assumes a classical Venus-like pose, and a leg of one of the figures devolves into cubist abstraction. Reportedly, Picasso painted the work when he was suffering from syphilis, which may be why the women appear so threatening.

o Salvador Dali's **Persistence of Memory,** in which watches melt and a long-nosed figure (some say it was a self portrait of Dali, others think it represents an unborn baby) lies prostate on the ground. You may be surprised at how small this seminal work is.

Rockefeller Center ★★ ARCHITECTURE   Gotham's splendid "city within a city" was built in the 1930s at the height of the Depression. Thanks to the jobs it gave construction workers, it was the second largest employer in the city after the federal Works Progress Association (or WPA) at the time. And it remains a marvel of elegance and aspiration, a several-blocks-wide collection of 19 buildings that, despite their mass, create a space that is airy and light, a welcoming haven for both tourists and residents. No matter how many times I come here, I still get goose bumps on the walk from Fifth Avenue through the gardened central path—called "The Channel," as it runs between the French and the British buildings.

Follow this channel-like route down to the **ice-skating rink** (the first commercial one in the world), and the golden statue of **Prometheus,** or "Leaping Louie" as wits have called him over the years, his prone position under the soaring vertical of the RCA building making him look like he just jumped. The rink is open Oct to early April, (Mon–Thurs 9am–10:30pm, Fri–Sat 8:30am–midnight, Sun 8:30am–10pm).

There's much to see at the Rock. Directly behind the statue is where the yearly 70-plus-foot Christmas tree is set on November 20th each year, a plaque marking the space. Take a left and walk towards 49th Street to the small side street with the glassed-in TV studio on the corner. This is where NBC's **Today Show** is taped, the small street the area where sign-waving crowds gather every weekday morning, as early as 5:00am, to attempt to get their faces on TV. (When the show has musical performances, guests play on a stage in this narrow alley—it looks much bigger on TV, doesn't it?)

Stroll next to Fifth Avenue between 50th and 51st streets, where *Prometheus*'s brother, mighty **Atlas,** the finest piece of art in the complex (by artist Lee Lawrie), hoists a giant globe on his shoulders, muscles rippling. From the back, *Atlas* looks a bit like a Christ figure, especially superimposed on St. Patrick's Cathedral across the street. Go into the lobby behind *Atlas* for a peek at one of the most magnificent public spaces in the city, the walls bedecked with a rare, swirling Greek marble; the gold "curtains" at the side creating an ever-changing dance of shadows on the ceiling.

Although I don't recommend the Rockefeller City tour (it doesn't go anywhere you can't yourself, and the guides are a dull lot), the **NBC Studio Tour** (𝒸 **212/664-7174;** www.shopnbc.com; $24 adults, $21 seniors and children ages 6–16; under 6 not admitted; Mon–Thurs 8:30am–5:30pm, Fri-Sat 8:30am–6:30pm, Sun 9:15am–4:30pm; subway: B, D, F to Rockefeller Center) will be of interest to *Saturday Night Live* and *NBC Nightly News* fans—both studios are usually visited. Other than that, it's a relentless commercial for NBC.

Better is a trip to **Top of the Rock** ★★ (30 Rockefeller Plaza; 𝒸 **212/698-2000;** www.topoftherocknyc.com; $27 adults, $25 seniors, $17 children 6–12; daily 8am–11pm; subway: B, D, F to Rockefeller Center), the 70th-floor Observation Deck at Rockefeller Center. While not as high as the one in the Empire State Building, it's gives the latter a run for its money with its own striking views (you have a much better vista of Central Park from here, a grand bumpy green blanket, laid at your feet) and its use of timed tickets, which eliminate the painful waits that can sour the experience at its rival. The Rock re-creates very closely the cruise-ship-themed look of the deck from the 1930s, when it was first constructed.

Finally, **Radio City Music Hall** (1260 Avenue of the Americas at 50th St.; 𝒸 **212/247-4777;** www.radiocity.com; $50–$300 show tickets, tour daily 11am–3pm $23.70 adults, $18.75 seniors and children 12 and under; subway: B, D, F to Rockefeller Center) remains the kitschy, thrilling delight it's always been: the Christmas Show is a marvels of excess, with hundreds of people and hooved animals on the stage at one time; orchestras magically rising from the pit; and best of all, the Rockette chorus line, that superhuman all-leg dancing machine.

Those who don't want to shell out for a show, or who visit when the theater is dark, can take the tour, which is well worth it, to see the exquisite Art Deco features of this sensational pleasure hall and get a picture taken with a Rockette.

Btw. 48th and 50th sts., from Fifth to Sixth aves. 𝒸 **212/247-4777** (tour info). www.radiocity.com. Subway: B, D, F, M to 47th–50th sts./Rockefeller Center.

Times Square ★ ICON   Adam Gopnik wrote about Times Square in *The New Yorker,* "No other part of New York has had such a melodramatic sensitivity to the changes in the city's history, with an image for every decade." Think for a moment and those visions of Times Square should start flooding your mind: snazzy clubs and peroxide blond chorus girls in the 1920s and '30s, sailors kissing girls at the end of World War II, the wisecracking small-time hoods of *Guys and Dolls* in the '50s, and, of course, the bleak urban decay of the '60s and '70s when, as Gopnik put it, "everything fell apart and Hell wafted up through the manhole covers."

Times Square is back on the upswing now, the porn shops banished and crime held (mostly) at bay. To get the full effect of today's Square, it's imperative you visit at night. It's then that the rainbow glitter of the flashing lights from the dozens of billboards, giant TV screens, electronic news crawls, and headlights of cars whizzing by wash over the Square, sweeping all of the litter and crowds into the background. The effect is like watching fireworks.

(This tradition of massive "spectaculars" is codified into law. In the 1980s, ordinances were passed requiring that new buildings abutting the Square have 16,000 square feet of light shows on their facades, with "moving elements" that are sufficiently bright). One of the best views is from the massive stairs atop the TKTS booth at 46th Street. You may also enjoy resting for a bit at one of the tables and chairs set up on the now-pedestrian-only sides of the square.

Beyond this theater of the streets is the legitimate theater, and Times Square still has more playhouses per acre than any other area in North America. For dawn theater, peer into the sidewalk-level television studios of *Good Morning America* (44th and Broadway).

Subway: 1, 2, 3, 7, N, Q, R, S to Times Square; A, C, E to 42nd St./Port Authority.

UPTOWN

Upper East Side

Cooper-Hewitt National Design Museum ★★ MUSEUM Architect Mies Van der Rohe famously said, "God is in the details." That could be the motto for the Cooper-Hewitt, which has made a name for itself by taking simple subjects in the world of design—say wallpapers or super-strong textiles—and dissecting them to the point not of exasperation, but of fascination. The textiles exhibit, for example, showcased what looked like crocheted bags that were actually used in reconstructive heart surgery; and entire fabric-covered kayaks that weigh less than 20 pounds. Because the Cooper-Hewitt, which is a branch of the Smithsonian, is the only design museum in the nation to cover both contemporary and traditional design, its exhibits have a breadth and depth that's quite unusual.

The museum was undergoing a massive renovation as this book went to press, with a planned re-opening late in 2014. Be sure to check the website for current details on hours and costs.

2 E. 91st St. (at Fifth Ave.). © **212/849-8400.** www.cooperhewitt.org.

The Frick Collection ★★★ MUSEUM/HISTORIC HOME Arguably the best small museum in the nation, the Frick provides a deeply satisfying experience on a number of levels. There's the highbrow fun of seeing some of the world's greatest masterpieces; the lowbrow kick of getting a firsthand peek at the home of one of the super-rich and famous; and the somewhat macabre thrill, akin to a séance in a way, of communing with someone long dead through his choices in art. In the end, the Frick Collection is as much about Henry Clay Frick and the world he created as it is about the art itself.

And that's a good thing, as Frick (1849–1919) was a fascinating figure, an entrepreneur in the steel and coke industries with only 3 years of formal schooling, who became a self-made millionaire by the time he was 30. On his death, he bequeathed his enormous art collection and the grandly colonnaded neoclassical mansion that housed it (built by Carrere and Hastings, architects of the N.Y. Public Library) to the formation of a public museum for the purpose of "encouraging and developing the study of the fine arts" in the United States.

It's not a large museum, but in each of the 16 galleries there are wonders to behold, paintings and sculptures from nearly every great artist in the Western Canon. Because Frick wanted viewers to have their own experiences of the art, there is very little wall text posted, nor is the art arranged in any "instructive" manner—different periods of art are mixed together, as are artists of various nationalities. Unlike the Barnes Collection in Philadelphia, Frick gave his trustees the right to change the arrangement of the works, and acquire new ones; a full third of what you'll see was purchased after Frick passed away.

But most of the great pieces are from Frick's era and they are a testament to his astute taste as a collector. This is a man who not only collected Rembrandts (a trifecta of them!) but chose none but the most intriguing works, such as the painter's portrait of fur merchant Nicholas Ruts, Rembrandt's first commissioned portrait and the one that launched his career.

Masterpieces by Vermeer (three of the meager 36 that still exist today), Renoir, Degas, Velazquez, El Greco (his *St. Jerome,* of which the Metropolitan Museum's version is a copy*)* and more, are also on view. The most famous painting in the collection, Holbein's portrait of Sir Thomas More, hangs next to the mantle in the Living Hall, though in an ironic move, Frick also hung Holbein's portrait of Thomas Cromwell— More's longtime political rival, who was also executed by Henry VIII—on the other side of that mantle, so that the two can stare each other down through eternity.

An erudite **audio tour,** free with admission, serves as a pleasant companion for a walk through the museum. Every hour on the half-hour, a short but interesting **movie** on the life of Frick is screened. And if you have the foresight, visit the Frick website to learn if a classical music concert will be taking place during your time in New York—the collection has a history of hosting some of the best up-and-coming talents.

1 E. 70th St. (at Fifth Ave.). ✆ **212/288-0700.** www.frick.org. Admission $18 adults, $15 seniors, $10 students. Children 9 and under not admitted. Tues–Sat 10am–6pm; Sun 11am–5pm. Closed all major holidays. Subway: 6 to 68th St./Hunter College.

Solomon R. Guggenheim Museum ★★ ART MUSEUM/ARCHITECTURE

New York is the city of the rectangle, of the sharp right angle. Our streets form a severe grid, our buildings are boxy and regular. Until you get to the Guggenheim, that is. Frank Lloyd Wright's delirious spiral of a museum sits among the towers of Fifth Avenue like a steroidal peacock among guinea hens. Architectural critic Herbert Muschamp described the look best when he wrote, "What else but a building brought back from a dream would be windowless, have walls and floors that tilt and twist, begin on the top floor, and spiral in towards the center like an enigma."

Visiting the center of this 1959 masterpiece and trudging up the ramps of curving halls transforms the standard museum experience into a profound journey (and sometimes a battle against vertigo), no matter what artworks are on display. Early critics dismissed the museum (*Newsweek*'s insipid review was headlined "Museum or cupcake?"), but I think today even the most jaded visitor will feel the power of the place, the symbolic weight of infinite circle upon circle upon circle.

Beyond the architecture, the museum is popular thanks to its curators' abilities to formulate blockbuster retrospectives on top contemporary artists (like James Turrel) and topics that combine art with history and in some cases sociology—shows on Aztec culture, motorcycles, and Brazilian art, to mention just a few that created headlines in past years.

Aside from the architecture and changing exhibits, the Guggenheim is known for its concentration of artworks by Kandinsky (150 in all), Brancusi, Picasso, Miró, and Mondrian, among other modernists. These pieces are always on display in the second-floor Tannheuser Collection room.

And to answer the question that nobody ever voices aloud: No, there haven't been any suicide jumps from over the low-slung rails, nor has anyone ever accidentally fallen to their death.

1071 Fifth Ave. (at 89th St.). ℂ 212/423-3500. www.guggenheim.org. Admission $22.75 adults, $18.75 seniors and students, free for children 11 and under; pay-what-you-wish Sat 5:45–7:45pm. Sun–Wed and Fri 10am–5:45pm; Sat 10am–7:45pm. Subway: 4, 5, 6 to 86th St.

The Jewish Museum ★★ MUSEUM The "modest" goal of this intriguing museum is to explore 4,000 years of Jewish culture through art. Surprisingly, it succeeds much of the time. Its two-floor permanent exhibition (which starts on the fourth floor) gently guides viewers from the biblical era, and the many clashes of the day over such issues as animal sacrifice and the role of the Temple (Jesus wasn't the only one up in arms over that), through the *Diaspora,* when the Israelites, forced out of their home by successive conquerors, became "wandering Jews," spreading to every part of the known world. The modern section brings the exhibition up to today, with only the briefest of mentions of the Holocaust (if that's what interests you, you'll be better served by the Jewish Heritage Museum downtown; p. 113).

The story is told through a mixed marriage, so to speak, of nearly 800 exquisite artifacts and works of art, and by a variety of story-telling devices, including a free audio tour (narrated by Leonard Nimoy among others), interactive computer programs, videos, television clips, and wall texts. What finally emerges is a portrait of a people who have not only managed to survive against the steepest of odds, but have become magnificently diverse in the process. In fact, the second half of the exhibit could be seen as a survey of world art styles as seen through Jewish eyes, making the museum of interest to a wide audience.

The fourth floor also houses a nifty playroom for kids. On the first and second floors are galleries for changing exhibits, which have housed blockbuster shows on William Steig and Chagall in the past. There's also a so-so kosher café and two handsome gift shops.

1109 Fifth Ave. (at 92nd St.). ℂ 212/423-3200. www.thejewishmuseum.org. Admission $12 adults, $10 seniors, $7.50 students, free for children 11 and under; free for all Sat. Sun–Tues and Sat 11am–5:45pm; Thurs 11am–8pm. Subway: 4, 5, 6 to 86th St.; 6 to 96th St.

Metropolitan Museum of Art ★★★ ART MUSEUM The giant among New York museums both figuratively and literally: at 1.6 million square feet, it's not just the biggest museum in the city, it's the largest one in this hemisphere. And I'd argue it competes in stature with the Louvre in Paris, the Prado in Madrid, the Uffizi in Florence, and the British Museum in London.

On view are masterworks from nearly all the world's cultures—from Egyptian mummies to ancient Greek statuary to Islamic carvings to Renaissance paintings to Native American masks to 20th-century decorative arts. Obviously, there's no way to see it all in one, two, or even five visits. So you must choose carefully among the 18 curatorial departments and decide what interests you most.

One way to do so is by taking one of the hour-long scholarly **"Highlight"** tours—free with admission and offered five times a day—led by volunteer docents. These enthusiastic art lovers are a treasure in and of themselves, highly trained and well-spoken. They'll run you all over the museum, pointing out and expounding upon the various gems of the collection, offering a quick taste of the museum's highlights so that you can come back yourself and feast upon what really interests you.

If I *had* to pick the top five highlights, I'd select:

o **The European paintings collection** on the second floor (newly expanded in 2013 from 450 works to 700) with such jewels as Velazquez's truer-than-life portrait of Juan de Pareja (the slave whom the painter respected enough—you can see it in the painting—to set free); El Greco's brooding landscape of Toledo; 20 Rembrandts; five light-kissed Vermeers; a roomful of Van Goghs; and works by Manet, Monet, de Goya, Breughel, Van Eyck, and every other master you read about in your college art-history course.

o **The period rooms,** which re-create dozens of important chambers, including Louis XIV's state bedroom in Versailles; and the stunning Cubiculum from Boscoreale, a perfectly preserved, brilliantly colorful room from a villa a mile from Pompeii that was buried by the eruption of Mount Vesuvius in A.D. 79. Whenever I visit these rooms I'm always reminded of the terrific children's novel *From the Mixed Up Files of Mrs. Basil E. Frankwiler,* in which the protagonists slept each night in a historic bed. Share it with your tweens and they'll be dying to come here.

o **The American Collection,** the most comprehensive in the world, features master-works by Sargent, Homer, Tiffany, Leutze (his sentimental but rippingly fun *Washington Crossing the Delaware*), and many more.

o **The Egyptian Collection** includes some pieces discovered by the Met's own teams of archaeologists, such as the miniature figures found in a tomb in Thebes that show in intricate detail what daily life for a wealthy Egyptian was like. There are also elaborate statuary; mummy cases; jewelry; wall paintings; and the Temple of Dendur, an actual temple to the goddess Isis (c. 15 B.C.) that was saved from the rising waters of the Nile after the construction of the Aswan Dam.

o The hidden **Hall of Art from Japan,** with its famed Iris Screens (on many Metropolitan Museum products), is also home to architectural-looking suits of armor, delicate woodcuts, and dazzling kimonos. To my mind, this one of the most ravishingly beautiful sections of the museum.

Along with all the art, the Met has half a dozen cafés and restaurants; wonderful gift shops and bookstores; and tremendously engaging art and culture programs for children of all ages (mostly on the weekends; visit the website for info).

Fifth Ave. at 82nd St. (✆ **212/535-7710.** www.metmuseum.org. Suggested admission $25 adults, $17 seniors, $12 students, free for children 11 and under. Sun–Thurs 10am–5:30pm; Fri–Sat 10am–9pm. Subway: 4, 5, 6 to 86th St.

Cocktails & Art: Evenings at the Met

On Friday and Saturday evenings, the Met remains open late not only for art viewing but also for cocktails on the roof and in the Great Hall Balcony Bar (4–8:30pm). Indoors, classical music from a string ensemble accompanies the tippling. A slate of after-hours programs (gallery talks, walking tours, family programs) changes by the week; call for the current schedule. The restaurant at Petrie Court Café and Wine Bar stays open until 10:30pm (last reservation at 8:30pm), and dinner is usually accompanied by piano music.

Museum of the City of New York ★ MUSEUM Just what it sounds like, this museum chronicles the life of the Big Apple. Its heartbeat is a masterful 25-minute video on New York history that recounts the tale of the city's growth from tiny Dutch colony to world capital. Along with rooms from historic homes, displays of children's toys, and a razzle-dazzle overview of New York theater, the museum mounts numerous temporary exhibits. If you're choosing between this one and the NY Historical Society, however, go with the latter (it has more to offer).

1220 Fifth Ave. (at 103rd St.). ℂ **212/534-1672.** www.mcny.org. Suggested admission $10 adults, $6 seniors and students, $20 families, free children 12 and under. Tues–Sun 10am–5pm. Closed Thanksgiving, Christmas, and New Year's. Subway: 6 to 103rd St.

Neue Galerie New York ★ ART MUSEUM/ARCHITECTURE Most notable for its jewel-toned paintings by Gustave Klimt, its "Didn't I sit on that in the '70s?" Bauhaus furniture, and its collection of drawings by such Teutonic masters as Dix, Schiele, and Klimt, the Neue Galerie offers a swift but effective overview of German and Austrian arts and design. Because some of these drawings are a bit racy, children under the age of 12 are not admitted, and those 16 and younger must be accompanied by an adult. Also on-site: a Viennese café (p. 97), a theater for lectures and films, and a pricey gift shop.

1048 Fifth Ave. (at 86th St.). ℂ **212/628-6200.** www.neuegalerie.org. Admission $20 adults, $10 seniors and students. Children 11 and under not admitted, children 12–16 must be accompanied by an adult. Thurs–Mon 11am–6pm. Free admission from 6–8pm the first Friday of the month. Subway: 4, 5, 6 to 86th St.

Whitney Museum of American Art ★★ ART MUSEUM "The Whitney"— you utter those two words with respect. Artists coming up in the world dream of having their work displayed at this museum. Art aficionados consider the curatorial work done here to be the most intellectually rigorous, risky, and exciting of any in the city. And over the years, a number of artists discovered by this institution—Alexander Calder, Edward Hopper, Georgia O'Keeffe, and others—have gone on to create works that then entered the canon of world art. Yet if you ask the average tourist about the museum, most won't even know it exists.

Which is a tremendous shame, because this institution, the only major museum in New York devoted to collecting *only* American fine art, consistently puts on astonishing shows and every 2 years the Whitney pushes the envelope even further, hosting its famed **Biennial** (a show of the best American art of the past 2 years). Curators scour the country for artists in every medium—sculpture, painting, video, installations, you name it—mixing the work of established artists with that of newcomers (whose careers are made by being picked).

Along with these changing exhibits (which usually take up two-thirds of the space), the Whitney showcases its fine permanent collection of American works. Here you'll find the many mournful works by Edward Hopper (who always insisted—in vain—that his paintings were not meant to have emotional content); the desert-scoured paintings of Georgia O'Keeffe; the intricate, undulating sculptures of Louise Nevelson; and my favorite, Calder's famed *Circus*, a one-ring wonder with tiny circus figures made of wire, fabric, cork, and thread, accompanied by a video of the artist gleefully making the sculpture "perform." Calder's magical mobiles, a type of sculpture that didn't exist until he dreamt it up (marrying sculpture with movement for the first time), are another highlight.

Note: The Whitney is currently in the process of relocating to a new 200,000 square foot space in the Meatpacking District. The new Whitney is scheduled to open to the public in 2015.

945 Madison Ave. (at 75th St.). © **212/570-3600.** www.whitney.org. Admission $20 adults, $16 seniors, free full-time students and ages 19–25, free for children 18 and under; pay-what-you-wish Fri 6–9pm. Wed–Thurs and Sat–Sun 11am–6pm; Fri 1–9pm. Subway: 6 to 77th St.

Upper West Side

American Folk Art Museum ★ ART MUSEUM Self-taught artists are the focus here and their stories (told in wonderful detail by the wall text) illuminate the art in invigorating ways. You'll see works from the 18th century to the present; and the breadth and variety of the art is quite stunning. Most popular objects are likely the quilts, though I prefer the sculptures. The book-and-gift shop is terrific, filled with one-of-a-kind pieces.

2 Lincoln Square (Columbus Ave. at 66th St.). © **212/595-9533.** www.folkartmuseum.org. Free admission. Tues–Sat noon–7:30pm; Sun noon–6pm. Subway: 1 to 66th St.

American Museum of Natural History ★★★ MUSEUM/PLANETARIUM Since 1869, this institution has served as both the country's preeminent private scientific research facility and its top museum for paleontology, zoology, anthropology and, in recent years, astronomy. It's this constant flow of energy and insight between the research side and the curatorial side that has kept the museum fiercely vital, fresh, and unique. Just a few years ago, for example, scientists concluded that dinosaurs had not dragged their tails as had long been thought but waved them in the air as they walked. The curators responded, painstakingly dismantling the Museum's famed dino skeletons and reassembling them with tails erect. Then, in a brilliant

Be an Early Bird

New York is the city that never sleeps, and you shouldn't either—at least not too much. Get an early start on your day. Check hours of operation for museums and attractions and be there as soon as they open to avoid the crowds. It's no fun waiting on lines or peering over throngs of people to view exhibits. So, remember: The early bird gets the worm, and the uncrowded attraction!

Timing your visit: Because the museum is so popular with school groups, it's difficult to predict when the museum will be crowded. In general, attendance is in inverse proportion to the weather: When it's lovely outside, the crowds will be sparse within. When it's blustery or rainy . . . watch out. Weekdays tend to be less crowded than weekends.

An overview tour: First-time visitors should consider taking one of the guided introductory tours that begin at 15 minutes past the hour throughout the day. Led by highly knowledgeable and well-spoken volunteer guides (they take classes for 6 months), tours vary by guide and will often hit different highlights of the museum.

Especially for kids: Families with children will want to visit the **Discovery Room,** an educational center where kids can pretend to dig up dinosaur bones, do a scavenger hunt, work with microscopes, and more. Timed tickets are given for admission here, so be sure to grab one early in the day before they run out.

stroke, they placed one skeleton atop a section of a Texas riverbed where they had found fossilized dino footprints (sans tail-dragging marks), giving museum-goers a peephole into how scientific theories emerge.

This double spotlight on the science itself and on how science is "made" is one of the pleasures of a visit here, with many of the exhibits focusing on the current "educated guesses" and the scientists who are making them. An extraordinarily interactive museum, it challenges visitors to figure out which theories make the most sense via computer stations, wall text, videos, soundscapes, and, of course, the artifacts themselves.

Start your visit by exploring the dinosaur rooms on the **fourth floor,** as these get most crowded later in the day. The museum has the largest such collection in the world, and the hot questions surrounding dinosaurs—How did they die out? Did they care for their young? Did they live in organized herds?—are fully explored.

Floors 2 and 3 are diorama driven, with half the floors devoted to the anthropological study of the various peoples of the world; the other half to African and North American mammals. If you're short on time, take the mammal route, which features the poetic work of taxidermist/zoologist/sculptor Carl Akeley, who eventually died in Africa while collecting animals to stuff and display. Akeley pioneered a new technique of sculpting papier maché, which he would then cover with actual animal skins, antlers, and hoofs, often using the animal's bones for structure as well. The results are remarkably lifelike. The exhibit also fulfills his mission to conserve these animals and their environment for future generations—many of the wilderness areas depicted have changed beyond recognition in the past 50 years.

Other highlights include the dazzling **Hall of Minerals,** with its Fabergé-carved gems and the largest star sapphire in the world; the Hall of Ocean Life (with its famed 10-ton blue whale replica hanging from the ceiling); and the new **Spitzer Hall of Human Origins,** an extraordinarily persuasive argument for the theory of evolution.

One of the newest sections of the museum, the **Rose Center for Earth and Space ★★★** has been widely hailed as one of the most architecturally important

5

EXPLORING NEW YORK CITY | Uptown

new buildings in New York—a monumental 120-foot-high glass box enveloping a colossal sphere, which is the new virtual reality theater, the Hayden Planetarium. When you first enter the museum, be sure to get one of the timed tickets to a planetarium show, which is terrific.

Central Park West (btw. 77th and 81st sts.). ℂ **212/769-5100** for information, or 212/769-5200 for tickets (tickets can also be ordered online for an additional $4 charge). www.amnh.org. Suggested admission $19 adults, $14.50 seniors and students, $10 children 2–12; Space Show admission $25 adults, $19 seniors and students, $14.50 children 2–12. Additional charges for IMAX movies and some special exhibitions. Daily 10am–5:45pm except Thanksgiving and Christmas. Subway: B, C to 81st St.; 1 to 79th St.

Cathedral of St. John the Divine ★ CATHEDRAL/ARCHITECTURE

Little-known fact: The largest cathedral in the world is *not* St. Peter's in Rome (which is actually not officially a cathedral), it's St. John the Divine in upper Manhattan. Odder fact: Despite the popish name, it isn't Catholic, it's Episcopalian. Oddest fact: Though construction began on the cathedral in 1892, the building is yet to be completed, and many estimate that it will take another 100 years for that to happen.

All of which makes this a fascinating building to visit, as you'll see a bit of how the ancient cathedrals of Europe might have been built. The 121,000-square-foot structure, a blend of Romanesque and Gothic elements (thanks to the varying tastes of the architects who have worked on it over the past century), is being built without steel, in the classic Gothic manner. To that end, a master stonecutter was brought in from Europe to help train a cadre of American stonecutters in the necessary work in 1979. There's still much work to be done (including a lot of fundraising!). For over a hundred years a temporary dome has kept parishioners dry; that will eventually be replaced. And an unfortunate fire in one portion of the building has also added to the load of work. But what is in place—and there's a lot—is quite beautiful, especially the Rose Window in the apse, the largest in North America.

Services here tend to be among the most musical and progressive in the city. I particularly recommend the New Year's Eve service, featuring original work from some of the best composers in town; and the Blessing of the Animals (on the feast day of St. Francis of Assisi, usually October 4), a ceremony in which New Yorkers bring their pets—ranging from puppies to pythons to thoroughbred horses—to be blessed.

You can explore the cathedral on your own, or on the **Public Tour,** offered 6 days a week; also inquire about the **Vertical Tour** (offered on Wednesdays and Saturdays), which takes you on a hike up the 11-flight circular staircase to the top, for spectacular views.

1047 Amsterdam Ave. (at 112th St.). ℂ **212/316-7490** or 212/932-7347 for tour information and reservations. www.stjohndivine.org. Public Tour $6 adults, $5 seniors and students; Vertical Tour $15 adults, $12 seniors and students. Mon–Sat 7am–6pm; Sun 7am–7pm. Subway: B, C, 1 to Cathedral Pkwy.

Museum of Arts and Design ★ MUSEUM

It's not easy to get a New Yorker's attention, but this museum has done that consistently, and is one of the few museums in town where you'll see more locals than visitors. It draws them in with creative, sometimes wacky, exhibitions on design. One, for example, highlighted the pins worn by former Secretary of State Madeline Albright, another used visitors' sense of smell to delve into how perfumes are created. On the top floor, artists in residence work at their crafts—furniture, textiles, you name it—making the static exhibits below feel that much more vital.

2 Columbus Circle. ℰ **212/299-7777.** www.madmuseum.org. Admission $16 adults, $14 students and seniors, free for high school students with ID and children 11 and under; pay-what-you-wish Thurs 6–9pm. Tues–Sun 10am–6pm; Fri–Sat 10am–9pm. Subway: 1, 2, 3, A, B, C, D to 59th St./ Columbus Circle.

New-York Historical Society ★★ MUSEUM/CULTURAL INSTITUTION NYC's oldest museum (founded in 1804) today feels like its freshest, thanks to a 3-year and nearly $70-million renovation completed in 2011. Now when you enter, there are whiz bang features wherever you look, from an actual Keith Haring ceiling piece over the front desk, to important artifacts embedded in the floor (including a desk clock rescued from the 9/11 site, its hands frozen to the moment the plane hit).

Head first to the superb, 18-minute film, narrated by Liev Schreiber that dramatizes the history of the city in such a compelling fashion, you'll truly feel like you're at the center of the known universe after watching it (which you are, of course). The bulk of the museum is made up of expertly curated temporary exhibits on the intersection of the city's history and world history (recent ones have dealt with Abraham Lincoln's time in NYC and the role Gotham played in World War II). But be sure to put aside enough time to explore the open storage units of the **Henry Luce III Center for the Study of American Culture** (top floors), which are a catalogue of wonders, from the delightful Jerni Collection of toy trains and station houses (kids love it); to one of the world's biggest collection of Tiffany Lamps; to the sculptural models used for the Lincoln Monument in Washington, D.C. You'll also see historic furniture, original Audubon drawings, coins, paintings, silverware, and much more. Use the free audio guide for information on what you're seeing (the headphones are in a bin on the fourth floor). On-site, too: a gift shop and a swank restaurant.

170 Central Park West (at 77th St.). ℰ **212/873-3400.** www.nyhistory.org. Admission $15 adults; $12 seniors, members of the military, and educators; $10 students; children 7–13 $5; free for children 6 and under; pay-what-you-wish Fri 6–8pm. Tues–Sat 10am–6pm (Fri until 8pm); Sun 11am–5pm. Subway: B, C to 81st St.; 1 to 79th St.

Harlem

El Museo del Barrio ★ MUSEUM A showplace for the art of Latin America and the Caribbean. Among its collections are hundreds of pre-Columbian pieces, contemporary and modern paintings and sculptures and, most significantly, 500 Santos de Palo, mostly from Puerto Rico. These hand-carved, wooden saints are very beautiful and well worth a visit. The museum also throws fun parties for every Latin and Caribbean holiday, and hosts changing exhibits.

1230 Fifth Ave (at 104th St.). ℰ **212/831-7272.** www.elmuseo.org. Suggested donation $9 adults, $5 seniors and students; Tues–Sat 11am–6pm; Subway 6 to 103rd St.

Studio Museum in Harlem ★ ART MUSEUM Though it's not a large museum, The Studio Museum is one of the most respected in Gotham, known for presenting challenging, intricate shows of African-American and Caribbean-American art (contemporary and from the 19th and 20th centuries). In addition to

Uptown Attractions

American Folk Art Museum **2**

American Museum of Natural History **6**

Cathedral of St. John the Divine **16**

Children's Museum of Manhattan **7**

Cooper Hewitt National Design Museum **11**

El Museo del Barrio **14**

The Frick Collection **3**

Solomon R. Guggenheim Museum **10**

The Jewish Museum **12**

Metropolitan Museum of Art **8**

Museum of Arts and Design **1**

Museum of the City of New York **13**

Neue Gallery of New York **9**

New York Historical Society **5**

The Studio Museum **15**

Whitney Museum **4**

Sakura Park

W. 125th St.

Grant's Tomb

Morningside Park

15 →

COLUMBIA UNIVERSITY

RIVERSIDE PARK

Broadway

Amsterdam Ave.

Cathedral of St. John the Divine

W. 112 St.

16

W. 110th St. (Cathedral Pkwy.)

*Take the **1** to 110th St. for the Cathedral of St. John the Divine.*

Ⓜ Subway stop

W. 104th St.

16

103 St 1

To Cathedral of St. John the Divine (see inset at left)

15

103 St B-C

Henry Hudson Parkway

Riverside Dr.

RIVERSIDE PARK

West End Ave.

Broadway

Amsterdam Ave.

Columbus Ave.

Central Park West

Manhattan Ave.

W. 100th St.

W. 99th St.

W. 98th St.

W. 97th St.

96 St 1-2-3

W. 96th St.

96 St B-C

W. 95th St.

W. 94th St.

W. 93rd St.

W. 92nd St.

W. 91st St.

W. 90th St.

W. 89th St.

W. 88th St.

86 St 1

W. 87th St.

86 St B-C

86th St.

W. 86th St.

UPPER WEST SIDE

W. 85th St.

W. 84th St.

W. 83rd St.

7

81 St- Museum of Natural History B-C

W. 82nd St.

W. 81st St.

W. 80th St.

79 St 1-2-3

W. 79th St.

6

79th St.

W. 78th St.

W. 77th St.

Riverside Dr.

West End Ave.

Amsterdam Ave.

Columbus Ave.

Central Park West

W. 76th St.

5

W. 75th St.

The Lake

W. 74th St.

W. 73rd St.

72 St 1-2-3

W. 72nd St.

72nd St B-C

W. 71st St.

W. 70th St.

Broadway

W. 69th St.

W. 68th St.

Sheep Meadow

66 St

Lincoln Center

1

W. 67th St.

65th St.

W. 66th St.

2

W. 65th St.

LINCOLN CENTER

W. 64th St.

Freedom Pl.

Henry Hudson Parkway

West End Ave.

Amsterdam Ave.

Columbus Ave.

W. 63rd St.

W. 62nd St.

W. 61st St.

59 St Columbus Circle A-B-C-D-1

W. 60th St.

Columbus Circle

W. 59th St.

1

Hudson River

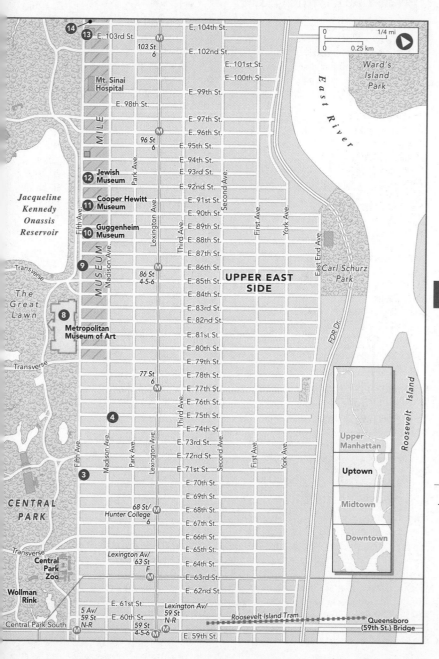

E. 104th St.

E. 103rd St.

14
13

103 St
6

E. 102nd St.

E. 101st St.

E. 100th St.

E. 99th St.

E. 98th St.

Mt. Sinai
Hospital

M
I
L
E

96 St
6

E. 97th St.

E. 96th St.

E. 95th St.

E. 94th St.

E. 93rd St.

Park Ave.

E. 92nd St.

Jewish
Museum
12

Cooper Hewitt
Museum
11

E. 91st St.

E. 90th St.

Lexington Ave.

Guggenheim
Museum
10

E. 89th St.

E. 88th St.

E. 87th St.

Fifth Ave.

Second Ave.

First Ave.

York Ave.

*Jacqueline
Kennedy
Onassis
Reservoir*

Madison Ave.

Third Ave.

East End Ave.

East River

*Ward's
Island
Park*

0   1/4 mi

0   0.25 km

Transverse

M
U
S
E
U
M

86 St
4-5-6

E. 86th St.

E. 85th St.

**UPPER EAST
SIDE**

*Carl Schurz
Park*

9

E. 84th St.

*The
Great
Lawn*

E. 83rd St.

E. 82nd St.

8

E. 81st St.

Metropolitan
Museum of Art

E. 80th St.

FDR Dr.

E. 79th St.

Transverse

77 St
6

E. 78th St.

E. 77th St.

E. 76th St.

E. 75th St.

4

Third Ave.

E. 74th St.

E. 73rd St.

Fifth Ave.

Madison Ave.

Park Ave.

Lexington Ave.

E. 72nd St.

Second Ave.

First Ave.

York Ave.

E. 71st St.

3

E. 70th St.

E. 69th St.

*CENTRAL
PARK*

68 St/
Hunter College
6

E. 68th St.

E. 67th St.

E. 66th St.

E. 65th St.

Transverse

Lexington Av/
63 St
F

E. 64th St.

*Central
Park
Zoo*

E. 63rd St.

E. 62nd St.

**Wollman
Rink**

E. 61st St.

Lexington Av/
59 St
N-R

5 Av/
59 St
N-R

E. 60th St.

59 St
4-5-6

Roosevelt Island Tram

**Queensboro
(59th St.) Bridge**

Central Park South

E. 59th St.

Roosevelt Island

Upper
Manhattan

Uptown

Midtown

Downtown

ENGOYING THE gospel OF HARLEM

There are over 400 churches in Harlem. Some are large and ornate; while others are small, one room churches housed on ground floors of brownstones. And many of those churches, large or small, feature fiery sermons and magnificent gospel services every Sunday.

Gospel tours of these churches have become big business. Mainly frequented by foreign visitors, who line up on Sunday mornings and pay handsomely, there's something uncomfortably voyeuristic about the scene. But, the pastors and the churches that are drawing in the crowds, and their donations, are certainly not complaining. Here are several worth visiting:

- **Abyssinian Baptist Church,** 1230 Fifth Ave at 104th St. *℃* **212/862-7474;** www.abyssinian.org.
- **Canaan Baptist Church,** 132 W. 116th St. *℃* **212/866-0301;** www.cbccnyc.org.

- **First Corinthian Baptist Church,** 1912 Adam Clayton Powell, Jr. Blvd., at 116th St. *℃* **212/864-5976;** www.fcbcsermons.com.
- **Greater Refuge Temple,** 2081 Adam Clayton Powell, Jr. Blvd. *℃* **212/280-5268;** www.greater refugetemple.org.

Most services begin promptly at 11am and seating is on a first come, first serve basis for non-members. Make sure you arrive in plenty of time; there will, most likely, be a line. Tour groups, at some churches get preference to "walk ups." Try calling in advance to find out that particular church's policy.

Service lengths vary, but expect at least 2 hours and up to 3. Most tours leave after the gospel choir and before the sermon and you would think that would be disrespectful, yet because this is a profitable venture for the churches, there are no complaints from the faithful.

two floors of galleries that host changing exhibitions, there's a space right off the lobby for the semi-permanent "Postcards from Harlem" wall, on which famous artists share their own memories of the neighborhood through text, photography, paintings, and drawings.

144 W. 125th St. (btw. Lenox Ave. and Adam Clayton Powell Blvd.). *℃* **212/864-4500.** www.studiomuseum.org. Suggested admission $7 adults, $3 seniors and students, free for children 11 and under, free for all Sun. Thurs–Fri noon–9pm; Sat 10am–6pm; Sun noon–6pm. Subway: 2, 3 to 125th St.

Upper Manhattan

The Cloisters ★★ ART MUSEUM/ARCHITECTURE   An off-shoot of the Metropolitan Museum, the Cloisters is the only museum in the United States devoted wholly to medieval art. And it shows its masterworks in a setting that appears to have been airlifted, utterly intact, from some remote corner of the Pyrenees, or from a castle-lined town in Bavaria.

Opened in 1934, the museum was, in fact, constructed in the United States, but 30% of the architectural elements—columns, pedestals, naves, door frames, exquisite stained glass windows—were salvaged from medieval European structures. It's a stunning mirage—even the land across the river was bought by patron John D.

Rockefeller to thwart development and ensure that the Cloisters' views would forever have a medieval face. At its heart are four cloisters, ancient garden areas centered with a fountain and surrounded by covered walkways of the type that appear in every monastery and abbey in Europe. Off these tranquil gardens are galleries devoted to different periods of art and architecture—a peak-ceilinged Gothic chapel here; a squat, square Romanesque-era hall there—each housing the treasures of that time period.

Though you can see the entire museum in a bit over an hour, pay special attention to the **Unicorn Tapestries,** one of only two full sets with a unicorn theme in the world (the other's in Paris). These richly detailed tapestries can be enjoyed on a number of levels today, just as they were back then. Many scholars see the unicorn as a symbol of Christ, and the hunt to slay it as evocative of the Passion. Others write that the work is a metaphor for courtly love, with the hunt itself courtship, and the last tapestry of the unicorn trapped inside a wedding-ring-like fence symbolizing marriage (despite this captivity, the unicorn does look happy). Whatever you decide, they are strikingly beautiful, an evocative slice of the past.

I highly recommend timing your tour to coincide with one of the curator-led gallery talks or garden walks (usually held midday).

At the north end of Fort Tryon Park. ℰ **212/923-3700.** www.metmuseum.org/cloisters. Suggested admission (includes same-day entrance to the Metropolitan Museum of Art) $25 adults, $17 seniors, $12 students, free for children 11 and under. Nov–Feb Tues–Sun 9:30am–4:45pm; Mar–Oct Tues–Sun 9:30am–5:15pm. Subway: A to 190th St., then a 10-min. walk north along Margaret Corbin Dr., or pick up the M4 bus at the station (1 stop to Cloisters). Bus: M4 Madison Ave. (Fort Tryon Park/the Cloisters).

THE OUTER BOROUGHS

The Bronx

Bronx Zoo ★★★ ZOO   If you count number of animals as well as acreage, The Bronx Zoo is still the largest zoo in the United States, an innovative, unbeatably entertaining place to spend the day. But with over 4,000 animals and 24 exhibits, you need to strategize your time wisely so you can see what you want without meltdowns from the younger set. When I visit with my girls, I most often make a direct path to the **Congo Forest** first, a remarkable exhibit of silverback gorillas that begins with a short film. Once the film is over, curtains dramatically part to reveal floor-to-ceiling windows, with cavorting gorillas galore (unlike other animals at the zoo, the gorillas are always awake if you visit in the daytime; along with the adults there always seem to be half-a-dozen baby gorillas in sight as well). From here we hop over to the nearby "bug carousel" or the butterfly exhibit (a tent with thousands of beautiful butterflies fluttering about your head), or to lunch at nearby Flamingo Park. Then we blow off steam for a bit at the children's zoo—with all the usual farm animals, plus a spider-web jungle gym, and a prairie dog park where children crawl into tunnels and pop their heads up right next to the critters. There are dozens of other animals, a fun monorail ride, feeding shows, and more to keep you entertained.

Tip: To beat the crowds, try to visit on a weekday or on a nice winter's day. In summer, come early in the day, before the heat of the day sends the animals back into their enclosures. Expect to spend an entire day here—you'll need it.

Getting there: Liberty Lines' BxM11 express bus, which makes stops on Madison Avenue, will take you directly to the zoo; call ✆ **718/652-8400.** By subway, take the no. 2 train to Pelham Parkway and then walk west to the Bronxdale entrance.

Fordham Rd. and Bronx River Pkwy., the Bronx. ✆ **718/367-1010.** www.bronxzoo.com. Admission $16.95 adults, $14.95 seniors, and $12.95 for children 3–12; pay-what-you-wish Wed year-round. There may be nominal additional charges for some exhibits. Nov–Mar daily 10am–4:30pm; Apr–Oct Mon–Fri 10am–5pm, Sat–Sun and holidays 10am–5:30pm. Transportation: See "Getting there," above.

New York Botanical Garden ★ GARDEN   An equal to the Brooklyn Botanical Gardens (see below) in both scope and interest, The New York Botanical Gardens boasts the world's largest Victorian greenhouse; a "home gardening" section with classes and demonstrations for all the green thumbs out there; a children's garden and play center; and a 50-acre native forest. If there's any difference between the two gardens—they're both wonderful—it may be the wealth of hands-on programming here. Other than that, if you're interested in visiting just one of these world-class gardens, you have a difficult choice to make.

Getting there: Take Metro-North (✆ 212/532-4900; www.mta.info/mnr) from Grand Central Terminal to the New York Botanical Garden station; the ride takes about 20 minutes. By subway, take the D or 4 train to Bedford Park, then take bus Bx26 or walk southeast on Bedford Park Boulevard for eight long blocks.

200th St. and Kazimiroff Blvd., the Bronx. ✆ **718/817-8700.** www.nybg.org. Admission $10 adults, $5 seniors and students, $1 children 2–12. Free to all Wed and 10am–noon Sat. Extra charges for Everett Children's Adventure Garden, Enid A. Haupt Conservatory, Rock and Native Plant Gardens, and narrated tram tour; All-Garden Pass $20 adults, $18 seniors and students, $8 children 2–12, free children 1 and under (prices change depending on season). Tues–Sun 10am–6pm. Transportation: See "Getting there," above.

Brooklyn

Brooklyn Botanic Garden ★ GARDEN   Right down the street from the Brooklyn Museum, the Brooklyn Botanic Gardens is not only one of those necessary green safety valves, it's also quite an innovative garden in many ways. It was the first in the world to have a "children's garden," allowing local kids to develop green thumbs (it's still here, along with a fun play area for youngsters). There's also a "fragrance garden" for sight-impaired visitors, where everyone is encouraged to sniff and touch the plants; and an authentic Japanese garden, complete with a large pond, pagodas, and plants from that area of the world. The best time of year to visit is spring, when the gardens' many cherry trees are in bloom, though there are seasonal displays, both outdoors and in the on-site greenhouses, year-round.

900 Washington Ave. (at Eastern Pkwy.), Brooklyn. ✆ **718/623-7200.** www.bbg.org. Admission $10 adults, $8 seniors and students (free for seniors Fri), free for children 11 and under. Mar 15–Nov 6 Tues–Fri 8am–6pm, Sat–Sun 10am–6pm; Nov 8–Mar 11 Tues–Fri 8am–4:30pm, Sat–Sun 10am–4:30pm. Subway: Q to Prospect Park; 2, 3 to Eastern Pkwy./Brooklyn Museum.

Brooklyn Museum ★★ ART MUSEUM   Though not as big as the Metropolitan Museum (what is?), this "mini Met"—it covers almost all eras of history in its holdings—is a superb museum on its own terms. Its Egyptian Collection, while not as

The Outer Boroughs | EXPLORING NEW YORK CITY

extensive as the Met's, arguably has more masterpieces. In fact, when an ancient Egyptian piece comes up at auction, dealers often ask, "Is it Brooklyn quality?"—the Brooklyn Museum's collection being the benchmark for this sort of artifact. Among the collection's many wonders are a tiny 5,000-year-old, pre-dynastic terra-cotta sculpture of a woman, which curators have nicknamed "Birdwoman" for her beaklike face, one of the very few intact sculptures from this long-ago era. The Cartonnage of Nespanjetjerenpere is another highlight, a mummy case that looks like it was swiped from the set of *Revenge of the Mummy*, its colors electrically bright and unfaded. I highly recommend renting the audio tour ($3) for this gallery, as it will explain how these works were created, what the symbolism means, and what they reveal about life in ancient Egypt.

Second most popular among the museum's offerings are the Decorative Arts Galleries (on the fourth floor), which re-create important rooms from different eras of American history, including John D. Rockefeller's "Moorish Smoking Room," an extravagantly over-the-top Victorian version of the Middle East, every single bit of space lavishly carved, gilded, inlaid, or embroidered.

Also worth a look: the Museum's American Collection (works by such masters as Albert Bierstadt, Thomas Eakins, Winslow Homer, and Georgia O'Keeffe) and the Elizabeth A. Sackler Center for Feminist Art (permanent and rotating exhibitions of art made by women, including Judy Chicago's famous "The Dinner Party.")

And one final thing that the Brooklyn does better than the Met: party: on the first Saturday of each month, the museum throws open its doors, hires deejays and performers of all sorts, and throws a "First Saturday" fiesta free to the public.

200 Eastern Pkwy. (at Washington Ave.), Brooklyn. ℂ **718/638-5000.** www.brooklynmuseum.org. Suggested admission $12 adults, $8 seniors and students, free for children 11 and under; free to all 1st Sat of the month 11am–11pm. Wed and Sat–Sun 11am–6pm, 1st Sat of the month 11am–11pm, Thurs–Fri 11am–10pm. Subway: 2, 3 to Eastern Pkwy./Brooklyn Museum.

Coney Island ★ ICON/BEACH/AMUSEMENT PARK Honky-tonk paradise, Coney Island has been rescued from extinction a few times (first from developers and most recently from severe Hurricane Sandy damage). Parts of it have been upgraded, but it's still possible to ride some of the classic attractions from times past, including the **Cyclone** (a huge wooden roller coaster, one of the scariest you'll ever ride because you'll do so with the knowledge that nearly a dozen people have been killed on it over the years), and the **Wonder Wheel** (a Ferris wheel with gliding compartments).

If you visit in summer, don't skip the Freak Show, which features the tattooed man, a snake charmer, a man who hammers nails up his nose, and other odd performers. It's one of the last shows of its kind in the U.S., and though it sounds unsavory, it's G-rated. You also have the beach itself here, a motley swatch of sand where gaggles of Brooklynites gather daily in summer to pitch their umbrellas, practice kung fu, listen to boomboxes, picnic, and swim. It's a very social scene, with many different ethnic groups represented, and fascinating in its own way.

Brooklyn. Subway: D, F, N, Q to Coney Island–Stillwell Ave.

New York Aquarium ★ AQUARIUM Badly damaged by Hurricane Sandy, the New York Aquarium was in the process of rebuilding as we went to press (though it had opened to the public). It promises to be the same surprisingly good aquarium it's always been, though currently there's lots of work to be done. That being said, the NY Aquarium is home to hundreds of sea creatures, including California sea lions that perform daily at the Aquatheater. Also basking in the spotlight are Pacific octopuses, sharks, seahorses, black-footed penguins, California sea otters, and a variety of seals. Most impressive: the white beluga whales. Children love the hands-on exhibits at Touch Pool.

502 Surf Ave. (at W. 8th St.), Coney Island, Brooklyn. ✆ **718/265-FISH** (265-3474). www.ny aquarium.com. Admission $9.95. Nov 1–Apr 1 daily 10am–4:30pm; Sept 9–Oct 31 and Apr 2–May 27 Mon–Fri 10am–5pm, Sat–Sun and holidays 10am–5:30pm; May 28–Sept 8 Mon–Fri 10am–6pm, Sat–Sun and holidays 10am–7pm. Subway: F, Q to West 8th St.

New York Transit Museum ★ MUSEUM An underground museum (yes, it's in a former subway station), covering the storied history of the NY City subway system. Best for kids and train nuts, the museum houses a number of handsome vintage subway cars, turnstiles, and the mosaics that used to be in the stations.

Boerum Place and Schermerhorn St., Brooklyn. ✆ **718/694-1600.** http://mta.info/mta/ museum. Admission $7 adults, $5 seniors and children 3–17, free for seniors Wed. Tues–Fri 10am–4pm; Sat–Sun noon–5pm. Subway: A, C to Hoyt St.; F to Jay St.; M, R to Court St.; 2, 3, 4, 5 to Borough Hall.

Prospect Park ★★ PARK Designed by Frederick Law Olmsted and Calvert Vaux after their success with Central Park, this 562 acres of woodland, meadows, and ponds is considered by many to be their masterpiece and the *pièce de résistance* of Brooklyn.

The best approach is from **Grand Army Plaza,** presided over by the monumental **Soldiers' and Sailors' Memorial Arch** (1892) honoring Union veterans. For the best view of the lush landscape, follow the path to Meadowport Arch, and proceed through to the Long Meadow, following the path that loops around it (it's about an hour's walk). Other park highlights include the 1857 Italianate mansion **Litchfield Villa** on Prospect Park West; the **Friends' Cemetery** Quaker burial ground (where Montgomery Clift is eternally prone—sorry, it's fenced off to browsers); the wonderful 1906 Beaux Arts **boathouse;** the 1912 **carousel,** with white wooden horses salvaged from a famous Coney Island merry-go-round (Apr–Oct; rides $2); and **Lefferts Homestead Children's Historic House Museum** (✆ **718/789-2822**), a 1783 **Dutch farmhouse,** with a museum of period furniture and exhibits geared towards kids (hours vary by season; see website for details). There's a map at the park entrance that you can use to get your bearings.

On the east side is the **Prospect Park Zoo** (✆ **718/399-7339**), a modern children's zoo where kids can walk among wallabies, explore a prairie-dog town, and more. Admission is $8 for adults, $6 for seniors, $5 for children 3 to 12. The zoo is open April 1 through November 1 (daily from 10am–4:30pm) and October 31 through March 27 (Mon–Fri 10am–5pm and Sat–Sun and holidays 10am–5:30pm).

At Grand Army Plaza, bounded by Prospect Park West, Parkside Ave., and Flatbush Ave., Brooklyn. ✆ **718/965-8951** (general info), or 718/965-8999 (events information). www.prospectpark.org. Subway: 2, 3 to Grand Army Plaza (walk down Plaza St. West 3 blocks to Prospect Park West and the entrance) or Eastern Pkwy./Brooklyn Museum.

Queens

Louis Armstrong House Museum ★★ HISTORIC HOME/MUSEUM The visitor experience here is as gracious, warm, and intriguing as the man himself, thanks to the marvelous guides (all ex-musicians and jazz historians) who lead visitors through the home every hour on the hour. The only house that this traveling musician ever owned, it was perfectly preserved after the death of his wife Lucille in 1983 (Armstrong himself passed away in 1971), and opened to the public in 2003. The sense that someone still lives here is so eerie that you may find yourself expecting Satchmo to emerge from the kitchen, turn on the stereo, and tell a joke. In the course of your tour, you'll hear about Louis's rags-to-riches history (son of a prostitute, learned to play trumpet in the juvenile detention center, made his name in mobster-owned clubs), and see the fairly modest two-story home that he and his wife lavished with every luxury, from custom-made 24-karat bathroom fixtures to Baccarat chandeliers and a state-of-the-art audio system. The highlight: recordings of everyday life that Armstrong made on his tape-recorder; your guide will play them as you wander through, allowing you to hear the family and visiting musicians talking, laughing, and jamming together.

34–56 107th St., Corona, Queens. ℂ **718/478-8274.** www.louisarmstronghouse.org. Admission $10 adults; $7 seniors, students, and children; children 3 and under free. Tues–Fri 10am–5pm; Sat–Sun noon–5pm; last tour at 4pm. Subway: 7 to 103rd St./Corona Plaza. Walk north on 103rd St., turn right on 37th Ave., turn left onto 107th St., and the house is a half-block north of 37th Ave.

Museum of the Moving Image ★★★ MUSEUM For sheer, unadulterated fun, there's no museum in town that can beat this one. The first museum anywhere to look at TV, film, and video games together (a heretical concept when the museum was opened in 1988), it's not simply an archive of past shows. Instead, it explores the craft and technology behind these arts with startlingly imaginative interactive exhibits, commissioned art works, video sequences and, of course, artifacts. Just how much fun is all this? Well, Citysearch ranked it the best place in the city for a family outing, and *Time Out* magazine called the museum the number one place to go when you're "baked" (and if that doesn't hit all the bases, I don't know what does).

Start your visit with the museum's core exhibit, "Behind the Screen," which explores the many technical issues behind moving images, from explanations of how the eye is tricked into seeing movement in rapidly repeating images, to the intricacies of sound and film editing. You'll have a chance to dub your own voice into such classics as *My Fair Lady,* create original computer animation, transmute the musical score of a famous film scene, and more. Several times a day, working editors, animators, and educators give demonstrations of how these techniques are used on actual productions.

Next, the focus shifts from technical issues to design issues, with exhibits devoted to the make-up, costumes, sets, and publicity stills that help create the image the director (or studio) is looking for. And if you've been harboring a secret yen to play Galactica just one more time, you'll have your chance in the playable video games exhibit.

On the first floor is the museum's full-sized movie theater, which offers included screenings of feature films from around the world, often followed by discussions with the artists involved, including such big names as Glenn Close, Tim Burton, David Cronenberg, and Jennifer Connelly.

The 98,000-square-foot museum is built on the site of Astoria Studio, and this part of Queens was where many of the early American films were made. The overall experience is to see how far we've come in so brief a span of time, and just how powerful is the human imagination.

35th Ave. at 37th St., Astoria, Queens. © **718/777-6800.** www.movingimage.us. Admission $12, $9 seniors and college students with ID, $6 children 5–18, free members and children 5 and under. Wed–Thurs 10:30am–5pm; Fri 10:30am–8pm; Sat–Sun 11:30am–7pm; Fri 4pm–8pm free. Subway: R, M to Steinway St.; N to 36th Ave.

Isamu Noguchi Garden Museum ★ ART MUSEUM

Utterly unique, it's the only museum in the nation to be founded by an artist in his lifetime, dedicated to his work and curated by him. As Noguchi (1904–1988) was a genius in a number of fields—sculpture, architecture, ceramics, furniture design—he was more than up to the task, and created a space that is at once sublimely balanced and (often) rapturously beautiful. On-site are also a small café/bookstore; and an updated Zen sculpture garden (one of the most serene spots in the city). Gallery talks, free with admission and held at 2pm each day, are helpful for those not familiar with Noguchi's work, as they illuminate the complex engineering issues and intentions behind his large, sometimes slab-like, non-representational works.

9–01 33rd Rd. (at Vernon Blvd.), Long Island City, Queens. © **718/204-7088.** www.noguchi.org. Admission $10 adults, $5 seniors and students, pay-what-you-wish first Fri each month from June–Sept 5:30–8pm. Wed–Fri 10am–5pm; Sat–Sun 11am–6pm. Subway: N to Broadway. Walk west (towards Manhattan) on Broadway until Broadway ends at Vernon Blvd.; turn left on Vernon and go 2 blocks.

P.S. 1 Contemporary Art Center ★★ ART MUSEUM

A proving ground for young artists. The work you're going to see here will be challenging, right of the moment, and sometimes downright wacky. "PS 1 is mythological," says Assistant Director Brett Littman. "Wherever I go, people know that there's this crazy building in Long Island City where you see crazy art. They come here to put a notch on their culture belt."

That "crazy building" was once a public school (hence the name), and its somewhat decrepit charm is part of the experience. Because it's not a fancy white box of a space (like its sister institution, the Museum of Modern Art), PS 1 allows its artists to create full-blown, sometimes invasive, installations in the space (one summer several years ago, an artist blasted holes in the brick wall of a gallery). It uses all kinds of unusual spaces to house art, such as the basement boiler room.

The bulk of the work you'll see here will be in changing exhibits, as the museum does not collect art. Instead, visitors are usually greeted with as many as 14 different shows in all parts of the building and, as I've said, some can be quite, well, bizarre. In its retrospective of New York City art several years back, one framed sculpture turned out to be the actual hand of the artist who was sitting on the other side of the wall, personifying her art. Now if that's not worth $10, I don't know what is.

22–25 Jackson Ave. (at 46th Ave.), Long Island City, Queens. © **718/784-2084.** www.ps1.org. Suggested admission $10 adults, $5 seniors and students. Thurs–Mon noon–6pm. Subway: E, M to 23rd St./Ely Ave. (walk 2 blocks south on Jackson Ave. to 46th Ave.); 7 to 45th Rd./Court House Square. (walk 1 block south on Jackson Ave.).

5

The Outer Boroughs

EXPLORING NEW YORK CITY

The **no. 7 train**—which originates in Manhattan at Times Square, makes three stops in that borough, and then snakes, mostly above ground, through the heart of ethnic Queens—is also popularly known as the International Express. Built by immigrants in the early 1900s, the no. 7 IRT (Interborough Rapid Transit) brought those same immigrants to homes on the outer fringes of New York City. That tradition has continued as immigrants from around the world have settled close by the no. 7s elevated tracks. Get off in Sunnyside and see Romanian grocery stores and restaurants; a few stops farther in Jackson Heights, you'll see Indians in saris and Sikhs in turbans; go all the way to Flushing and you'll think you are in Chinatown. You are—Flushing's Chinatown, as big or bigger than Manhattan's. In 1999, the Queens Council on the Arts nominated the International Express for designation as a National Millennium Trail, and that resulted in its selection as representative of the American immigrant experience by the White House Millennium Council, the United States Department of Transportation, and the Rails-to-Trails Conservancy. For more information and for events, visit the **Queens Council on the Arts** website, at www.queenscouncilarts.org (© **347/505-3010**).

ESPECIALLY FOR KIDS

Museums

In addition to the museums specifically for kids detailed below, consider the following, discussed elsewhere in this chapter: The **American Museum of Natural History** ★★★ (p. 138), whose dinosaur displays are guaranteed to wow both you and the kids; the **Museum of the Moving Image** ★★★ (p. 149), where you and the kids can learn how movies are actually made (and play vintage video games); the **Tenement Museum** ★★★ (p. 119), whose weekend living-history program intrigues school-age kids; the **New York Transit Museum** (p. 148), where kids can explore vintage subway cars and other hands-on exhibits; and the **Brooklyn Children's Museum,** 145 Brooklyn Ave. (© **718/735-4400;** www.brooklynkids.org), one of the first such museums in the nation; and **Children's Museum of the Arts**, 103 Charlton Ave (© **212/274-0986;** www.cmany.org), a visual arts-based institution.

Children's Museum of Manhattan ★ MUSEUM   A glitzy affair of changing exhibits that highlight the kiddie zeitgeist of the moment: Red Grooms, Maurice Sendak, and William Wegman's dog art were just a few of the recent exhibit themes. Those with toddlers should go directly to the Child Development Center on the fourth floor, where young 'uns can finger paint to their hearts' delight, play with little stoves, and send rubber balls rocketing down a twisted tube from a loft to the floor (there were days when I never got past this room). Older children will want to take part in the classes and special exhibits, and since these fill up fast, it's important that you stop by the sign up desk right when you enter.

212 W. 83rd St. (btw. Broadway and Amsterdam Ave.). © **212/721-1234.** www.cmom.org. Admission $11 children and adults, $7 seniors, children 1 and under free, free for all on the first Fri of every month from 5–8pm. Tues–Sun 10am–5pm. Subway: 1 to 86th St.

The Museum of Mathematics ★ MUSEUM   When this museum first debuted in 2012, I warned my children that if they didn't behave, I'd take them there. It was no punishment, however, when we finally went. Creatively designed to bring math concepts to life, this little museum (it takes about an hour to see it) has two floors of interactive displays, which will have your kids riding bikes with square wheels, recreating Galileo's experiments, and doing all sorts of other fun numbers games. It's a great new addition for kids under 11.

11 E. 20th St. (near Fifth Ave.). ✆ **212/542-0566.** www.momath.org. Admission $15 adults, $9 seniors and children 2–12. Daily 10am–5pm. Subway: R to 23rd St.

New York City Fire Museum ★ MUSEUM   What kid can resist a big red fire engine roaring by, or a room full of swooping red fire hats? You'll see both in abundance at the New York City Fire Museum, which has one of the largest collections of firehouse memorabilia in the nation. It also has the good sense to hand out a free scavenger hunt map on arrival, which should keep even the most restless of youngsters amused.

278 Spring St. (btw. Varick and Hudson sts.). ✆ **212/691-1303.** www.nycfiremuseum.org. Admission $8 adults; $5 seniors, students, and children. Daily 10am–5pm; Sun 10am–5pm, except Easter, New Year's Day, Christmas, and Thanksgiving. Subway: C, E to Spring St.; 1 to Houston St.

Sony Wonder Technology Lab ★ MUSEUM   It's one big ole' commercial for Sony products, and yes, it dumbs down its explanations of the technology to a sad level at points. But if you happen to be in Midtown with someone, say, under 5 feet tall who loves to press buttons and play computer games, this four-level museum can be a welcome distraction. Advance reservations are recommended as the museum does fill up; expect to spend about 1 hour tops in the museum.

Sony Plaza, 550 Madison Ave. (at 56th St.). ✆ **212/833-8100.** www.sonywondertechlab.com. Free admission. Sun noon–5pm; Tues–Sat 10am–5pm; last entrance 30 min. before closing. Subway: E, M to Fifth Ave.; 4, 5, 6, N, R to 59th St.; F to 57th St.

OUTDOOR ACTIVITIES

Central Park ★★★

Manhattan's 843-acre green oasis is the yin to the city's neon, concrete, and office tower yang. It serves as the city's backyard, its concert hall, its daytime pick-up bar and, in the summer, when dozens don bathing suits to soak up the rays, its green beach. The marvel of the park, besides its size (a full 6% of the total area of Manhattan), is its ability to provide just the right sort of experience for the myriad of very different personalities who think of it as their own. I think it's that chameleon-like quality that makes it such an interesting place for visitors to tour. Seeing it from an outsider's perspective, it's much easier to recognize that the park is a great mirage and paradox.

Because, let's face it, very little here is natural. Every tree, every shrub, every lake and most of the rolling hills were designed, planted, or blasted into existence by landscape architects Frederick Law Olmsted and Calvert Vaux back in the 1850s, and their efforts still shape our experiences today. These two geniuses took a 2½-mile tract of swampland, farms, and suburban towns and created an Arcadia that had no resemblance whatever to what had come before. Below the park, 95 miles

Central Park

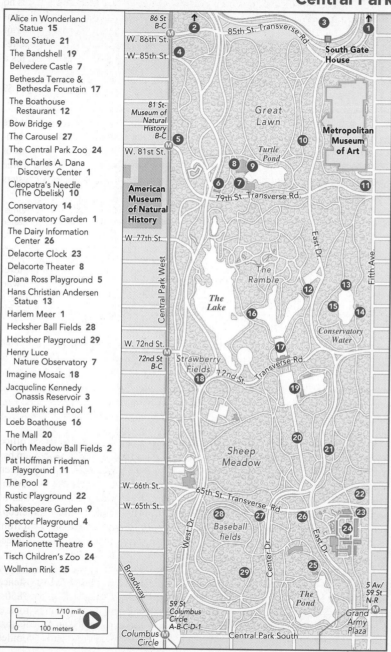

5

EXPLORING NEW YORK CITY | Outdoor Activities

of drainage pipes were installed, many to both fill and periodically empty the four lakes that were created; at ground level the site was transformed using six million bricks, 65,000 cubic tons of gravel, 26,000 trees, and 250,000 shrubs. Even the dirt was imported; the natural topsoil was so poor that 500,000 cubic feet of topsoil was shipped in from New Jersey. As Olmsted once wrote, "Every foot of the park, every tree and bush, every arch, roadway and walk, has been fixed where it is with a purpose."

And what was that purpose? No less than the health of the city. Those who rallied for its creation felt that it was crucial to create a place where New Yorkers could blow off steam, get away from the stresses of urban life. Moreover, Olmsted wanted to create a park that would be a bridge between classes. "There need to be places and time for re-unions," Olmsted wrote, "[where] the rich and the poor, the cultivated and the self-made, shall be attracted together and encouraged to assimilate." Though that didn't happen when the park was first finished—it was too far from the homes of poor New Yorkers for them to visit it—that ideal was realized when the city itself began to wrap around the park, making it finally a true *central* park.

In your own strolls around the park, you'll encounter three different types of landscapes: **pastoral vistas**, such as the Sheep's Meadow, which are meant to invoke a cultivated countryside; **primitive portions** where dense forestation shuts out any view of the city; and the **promenade zones**, which were once used by the city's aristocracy as an extension of their parlors, a place to strut and be seen. An ideal visit here will include all three. I've created a relatively brief list of highlights, along with the activities you can engage in once in the park, that should allow you to do just that. Feel free to ignore the following list altogether and just wander the curving paths of the park, exploring its hidden nooks, surprise vistas, ball fields, and dog runs. There's no right way to see or do this park.

ORIENTATION & GETTING THERE The park runs from 59th Street (also known as Central Park South) at the south end to 110th Street at the north end, and from Fifth Avenue on the east side to Central Park West (the equivalent of Eighth Ave.) on the west side. A 6-mile rolling road, Central Park Drive, circles the park, and has a lane set aside for bikers, joggers, and in-line skaters. A number of transverse (crosstown) roads cross the park at major points—at 65th, 79th, 86th, and 97th streets—but they're built down a level, largely out of view, to minimize intrusion.

A number of subway stops and lines serve the park, and which one you take depends on where you want to go. To reach the southernmost entrance on the west side, take an A, B, C, D, or 1 to 59th Street/Columbus Circle. To reach the southeast corner entrance, take the N or R to Fifth Avenue

Central Park Highlights

Belvedere Castle and the Delacorte Theater ★★ Olmsted and Vaux's "folly" (or fantasy building), this turreted castle sits atop the second-highest elevation in the park. Inside is a nature observatory with good rainy-day activities for children. In front of the castle is the **Delacorte Theater ★★** where the famed **Shakespeare in the Park** is performed, a star-studded and free evening of theater staged in the summer months only. If you decide to take in a show, know that you could end up spending 4 or more hours standing in line to get tickets; they're passed out at 1pm in front of the theater, but depending on the popularity of the show, crowds have been known to show up hours before that, and even camp overnight at the gate to the park. From Belvedere, you'll also look down on the **Great Lawn,** which has gone through a number of incarnations, first as a reservoir and later in the 1930s as "Hooterville," the shantytown where hundreds of homeless families lived out the Depression. Today it's most famous as a concert space: Simon and Garfunkel reunited here in the early 1980s in a widely televised concert.

Enter the park at either 72nd or 79th St. For info on Shakespeare in the Park. (C) **212/539-8500.** www.publictheater.org. Free.

The Carousel ★ A Victorian spinner, this is most children's favorite park stop (it certainly is my daughters'). Though it's not the original carousel (the first burned down in the 1950s), it's a beaut, built in Coney Island in 1908, and featuring some of the tallest merry-go-round horses in the U.S. It's also a much more humane carousel than the original, which was rotated by a blind mule and horse toiling in the basement.

At approximately 65th St., in the dead center of the park. www.centralparkcarousel.com. $2 per ride. Apr–Nov 10am–6pm, Dec–Mar 10am–dusk.

Central Park Zoo/Tisch Children's Zoo ★ ZOO Because of its small size, the zoo is at its best with its displays of smaller animals. The indoor multilevel **Tropic Zone** is a real highlight, its steamy rainforest home to everything from black-and-white colobus monkeys to Emerald tree boa constrictors to a leaf-cutter ant farm; look for the new dart-poison-frog exhibit, which is very cool. So is the large penguin enclosure in the **Polar Circle,** which is better than the one at San Diego's SeaWorld. Despite their pool and piles of ice, however, the polar bears still look sad.

The zoo is good for short attention spans; you can cover the entire thing in 1½ to 2 hours. It's also very kid-friendly, with lots of well-written and illustrated placards that older kids can understand. For the littlest ones, there's the $6-million **Tisch Children's Zoo ★.** With goats, llamas, potbellied pigs, and more, this petting zoo and playground is a real blast for the 5-and-under set.

830 Fifth Ave. (at 64th St., just inside Central Park). (C) **212/439-6500.** www.centralparkzoo.com. Admission $18 adults, $15 seniors, $13 children 3–12, free for children 2 and under. Apr–Oct Mon–Fri 10am–5pm, Sat–Sun and holidays 10am–5:30pm; Nov–Apr daily 10am–4:30pm. Last entrance 30 min. before closing. Subway: N, R to Fifth Ave; 6 to 68th St.

Cleopatra's Needle ★ This handsome obelisk was a gift to the United States from Egypt in 1881, in recognition of the help this country gave in the construction of the Suez Canal. Transporting the 200-ton pillar took 38 days from Alexandria to New York by ship, and then another 144 just to get it from the Hudson River to Central Park. It originally stood at the Temple of the Sun in Heliopolis, and is believed to have been erected in 1600 B.C. The Romans moved it in the 12th century to the front of a temple built by Cleopatra, hence the name. A plaque at the base translates the hieroglyphics.

Near the back of the Metropolitan Museum at roughly 83rd St.

Conservatory Gardens ★★★ The park's only formal gardens are simply stunning, which may be why this is a favorite for wedding photographers. Walk around and you'll notice that each of the gardens' three sections has a different ambiance; one is meant to mimic the gardens of France, another those of Italy, and the third pays tribute to Britain's blossoms.

Enter at Fifth Ave. and 105th St.

Conservatory Waters ★★ Here's the model boat pond where Stuart Little had his fabled race. You can rent a model boat to float around (via remote control), take a look at the Hans Christian Andersen statue (where storytelling takes place on weekends in summer), or visit the Alice in Wonderland statue, an artistic jungle gym for the city's youth.

Enter at 79th St. on Fifth Ave.; the pond is directly uptown of the entrance, down a hill.

The Dairy ★ ARCHITECTURE/TOURS Completed in 1871, this frou-frou laden Gothic structure was an actual dairy set up to give city children access to fresh milk. Today it serves as the park's visitor center, so it's a good place to stop first, to pick up maps. Most of the Central Park Conservancy's free tours start from this point, see below for info on finding their scheduling.

At roughly 65th St., closer to Fifth Ave. (at 64th St., just inside Central Park). ℂ **212/360-2726** for tour info. www.centralparkzoo.com.

The Mall, Bethesda Terrace, and the Loeb Boathouse ★★★ In their original plans for the park, Olmsted and Vaux called the area known today as The Mall "the Promenade," and intended for it to be an "open air hall of reception." Today when you visit you'll be greeted by a grand elm tree-lined walkway bedecked with statues. At its Uptown end is an underused band shell, and west of that is one of the park's premier party places: an unofficial roller-blading rink where regulars dance-skate for hours each weekend to blasting disco music. It's quite a scene.

Bethesda Terrace is at the Uptown end of the mall (just across the road) and is, without a doubt, the architectural heart of the park. You're likely to see a bride or two here, as many use this extraordinarily lovely area of the park as a backdrop for wedding photographs. If you approach it from The Mall, you'll come to a ravishingly carved gate with symbols representing day and night (the side with the witch on a broom is "night"). Take a look as well at the carvings on the stairs down to the fountain area; they represent the four seasons, and no two are alike. Bethesda Fountain was erected to celebrate the opening of the Croton Aqueduct, which finally solved New York's water problems in 1842. Sculpted by Emma Stebbins, the first woman to receive this type of commission from the city, the statue represents the angel Bethesda. She blesses the water with one hand, carrying a lily—the symbol of purity—in the other.

Added to the park in 1874 is **Loeb Boathouse.** This is where you rent the boats that you see bobbing on the lake. It's also the best place in the park to eat, with a decent fast-food counter and a very good restaurant, for which you'll need a reservation. Carrie and Mr. Big, of *Sex and the City,* fell into the water together at the end of a disastrous date on the dock that pushes forward from the café.

At approximately 74th St., off Park Dr. ℂ **212/517-2233.** www.thecentralparkboathouse.com. Boat rentals Apr-Nov $12 1st hr., $2.50 every 15 min. thereafter. A gondola with singing oarsman is often available for $30/hr.

Sheep's Meadow ★ The premier see-and-be-seen spot for New York's teenagers, who turn this expanse of grass into a sunbathing party come spring and summer. They're following a long tradition: This is where New York's hippie "be in," a day of non-political grooviness created by Abbie Hoffman, took place in 1967. The meadow

A word on playgrounds: With a few exceptions, most of the park's 22 playgrounds are located on the rim of the park near the entrances. They tend to pop up every five blocks or so, with some of the more elaborate playgrounds located on the south end of the park (conceived as the children's side of the park because it was nearer to where the lower income families would have lived at the time of the park's opening).

Horse-drawn carriage rides: At the entrance to the park at 59th Street and Central Park South, you'll see a line of horse-drawn carriages waiting to take passengers on a ride through the park or along certain of the city's streets. A ride is about $50 for 20 minutes (plus tip), but I suggest skipping it. Not only are the horses sad-looking, the "tour" you'll get is likely to be filled with misinformation.

Wildlife in the park: Birdwatchers from all over the city flock to the park for the variety of species it hosts, the most coveted sightings being of the endangered red-tailed hawks that make their nest on Woody Allen's Fifth Avenue building (at Fifth Ave. and 74th St.).

got its name in 1864 when park commissioners set sheep to graze here in an attempt to stop the First Division of the NY National Guard from using the meadow as a parade ground (it didn't work). In 1934 the sheep were exiled to Prospect Park in Brooklyn. Between 64th and 68th sts., towards the West Side.

Strawberry Fields ★ A memorial to John Lennon, who was shot to death in front of the Dakota apartment house (1 W. 72nd St.) just across the street from here. A mosaic spells out "Imagine" on the ground; many come here to play music and leave flowers. Enter at 72nd St. and Central Park West and follow the crowds.

Wollman/Trump Rink ★ A wonderfully scenic place to skate, you may remember it from the movie *Love Story*. In the summer, the rink is transformed into a mini-amusement park called **Victorian Gardens**. Enter at Central Park South, across from the Plaza and walk to the rink. Skating Mon–Thurs $11 adults, $5 seniors, $6 children 11 and under; Fri–Sun $17 adults, $9 seniors, $6 children 11 and up. Mon–Tues 10am–2:30pm; Wed–Thurs 10am–10pm; Fri–Sat 10am–11pm; Sun 10am–9pm. Open for skating from late Oct–Apr.

Though the places I list above are just a few of the wonders of the park, there are many others. And many may feel familiar if you're American. Central Park was and remains the most influential piece of landscape architecture in the United States; and many parks around the country were directly copied from this one.

Other Parks in Manhattan

Battery Park ★ PARK At the southernmost tip of Manhattan, Battery Park has been growing kudzu-like for the past several decades and is now really a string of eclectic park spaces that hug the waterfront from just above the original Battery

Park (where the ferry terminal for the Statue of Liberty is located) all the way up to Chambers Street (21 acres in all). At the downtown-most park are a number of stirring war monuments to peruse. Walking uptown from the original battery, you'll encounter expansive lawns, a promenade along the river that runs the length of the park, brand-new playgrounds, and a yacht marina. My favorite parts are the South Cove (on the Esplanade between First and Third places), an artfully varied collection of quays, bridges, and meandering walkways with great river views; and the **Irish Hunger Memorial,** a grassy outcropping direct from Ireland, complete with a real Irish stone fence.

From State St. to New York Harbor. (C) **212/344-3491.** www.thebattery.org. Subway: R to Whitehall St.; 1 to South Ferry; 4, 5 to Bowling Green.

Bryant Park ★ PARK   Just behind the New York Public Library, this park is a welcome respite from the endless high-rises and crushing crowds of Midtown, a 4-acre lawn surrounded by London plane tree–shaded promenades (like the Tuilleries Gardens in Paris), benches, and statuary. It's notable for its extensive programs of public concerts, movies, and even book loans. Weather permitting, a small "reading room" is set up outdoors on the 42nd Street side of the block Monday through Saturday from 11am to 5pm, with movable furniture; kiosks with loaner books, periodicals, and children's books (no library card or ID is required); and free Wi-Fi for those who want to use this tiny outdoor library to get on the Internet. From roughly May through October, the Sixth Avenue end of the park is set up as a stage, where Broadway performers are often invited to give concerts, free movies are shown in the summer (Monday nights), and other events are held. In winter a small "pond" is erected for free ice-skating.

On the 40th Street side is **Le Carrousel** ($2 per ride, June–Oct 11am–8pm; Nov–Jan Sun–Thurs 11am–9pm, Fri–Sat 11am–10pm; Feb 11am–8pm; Mar–May 11am–7pm), an elegant little merry-go-round that spins to the sounds of French cabaret music. A good spot for a picnic, Bryant Park has an excellent sandwich kiosk, 'wich-craft. There are also two pricey, so-so restaurants on the north side of the park (go for drinks, but not dinner).

Behind the New York Public Library, at Sixth Ave. (btw. 40th and 42nd sts.). (C) **212/768-4242.** www.bryantpark.org. Subway: B, D, F, Q to 42nd St.; 7 to Fifth Ave.

Governors Island ★ PARK/HISTORIC SITE   Situated a half-mile south of Manhattan, the 172-acre Governors Island, was, for many years, a Coast Guard installation. Before that, it was an army post for nearly 200 years and played a part in the Revolutionary War. In April 2010, New York City took over. Because it was a military base for so long, few New Yorkers, much less tourists, had visited Governors Island. But that has changed. Much of Governors Island is now a public park and twenty-two acres on the island are already a national monument, centered around two 1812-era fortresses. The island is open to visitors from end of May to October. During that time, you can take a free ferry from the Battery Maritime Building adjacent to the Staten Island Ferry in lower Manhattan. (There is also a ferry from Pier 6 in Brooklyn Bridge Park.) On the island, you can walk or bicycle in a car-free environment and attend any number of activities from jazz concerts to table tennis demonstrations.

℃ 212/440-2200. www.govisland.com. Free. Free ferries depart from Battery Maritime Building (a large green building right next to the Staten Island Ferry terminal), Slip #7, in Manhattan; in Brooklyn free ferries depart from Pier 6, at the foot of Atlantic Avenue; check the website for exact schedules. The island is open every Fri–Sun from end of May–Oct. Subway: 1 to South Ferry; 4, 5 to Bowling Green. Bus: M1. 6, 15.

High Line Park ★★★ PARK   For years, a secret, untamed garden hovered above the cityscape of Chelsea and Hell's Kitchen. Formed from the wild grass, flower, and weed seeds that randomly blew onto the tracks of a 1½ mile abandoned elevated railway, it became a hidden-in-plain-sight oasis for those New Yorkers brave (and limber) enough to scale the trestles. When the city started planning to tear down the historic rail structure (constructed 1929–34), a movement was born to save it and create a "grand public promenade," with easy access from the street, and that has now happened. Beautifully landscaped (in many places with the "weeds" that once grew there naturally), with benches and gourmet food vendors galore, it's become THE place to head on a balmy summer evening for a stroll.

From Gansevoort St. to W. 34th St. (btw. 10th and 11th aves.). ℃ **212/500-6035.** www.thehighline.org. Daily 7am–7pm. Subway: A, C, E, or L to 14th St.

Hudson River Park ★★ PARK   Located at Pier 62 on the Hudson River next to Chelsea Piers, the carousel and skatepark are part of a 9-acre park (which includes the adjacent Pier 63) that is, without exaggerating, an urban miracle. With a Sheeps Meadow-like expanse of grass, marvelous landscaping, and terrific views of the Hudson River, this is an ideal place to bring the kids for a sunny afternoon. Its pride and joy is a custom-designed 36-passenger **carousel** with all the hand-carved animals indigenous to the greater New York City area.

℃ **212/627-2020.** www.hudsonriverpark.org. Carousel $2 per ride. (Children under 42" tall must be accompanied by an adult 18 years or older.) Carousel Sat–Sun 11am–6pm weather permitting. Free skatepark. Skatepark 8am–dusk. Subway: C, E to 23rd St. **Note:** M23 bus will take you almost directly to the entrance of Pier 62.

Riverside Park ★ PARK   Central Park was not the only green space Olmsted and Vaux created in New York City. In fact, many consider Prospect Park (p. 148) and Riverside Park to be their true masterworks. As its name suggests, Riverside Park has always had one advantage over Central Park: glorious river views. Many of the garden-laced promenades make the most of these vistas, as does the lovely boat basin and rotunda area at 79th Street (a hopping bar enlivens evenings at the Boat Basin). As in Central Park, there is a smattering of playgrounds; a skatepark with assorted ramps and half-pipes; and a handful of monuments, including **Grant's Tomb** (at 122nd St., open daily 9am–5pm), the largest mausoleum in the United States at 8,100 square feet. (And the answer to who's buried in Grant's tomb is: No one. Ulysses S. Grant and his wife are not buried; their sarcophagi lie aboveground.)

From 72nd to 158th St (along the Hudson River). www.nycgovparks.org/parks/riversidepark.

Union Square Park ★ PARK/MARKET   The spirit of the 1960s is still very much alive here, though Union Square Park's tradition of political activism goes back to the first Labor Day Parade in 1882, which ended in the park. Since that time, it has become soap box central, a place where orators come on a daily basis to blast whatever

The Little Red Lighthouse

Also known as Jeffrey's Hook Lighthouse, this little red lighthouse located under the George Washington Bridge in Fort Washington Park on the Hudson River was the inspiration for the 1942-children's book classic, *The Little Red Lighthouse and The Great Gray Bridge*, by Hildegarde Swift and Lynd Ward. Built in New Jersey in 1880 and reconstructed and moved to its current spot in 1921, it was operational until 1947. The lighthouse was to be removed in 1951, but because of its popularity there was a public outcry and it was saved. It's now a New York City landmark and on the list of National Register of Historic Places. It's a fun place for the kids to explore and scenic picnic spot in nice weather. It's open to the public, with guided tours by the **New York City Urban Park Rangers** (✆ **212/304-2365**) from spring through fall.

current administration is in power, weighing in on all the big topics of the day A statue of Gandhi, a gift of the Indian people, calmly watches over these proceedings, a fresh wreath of flowers always draped about his neck. Along with the political folk, Union Square hosts the finest **greenmarket** in the city (on the western side of the park) every Monday, Wednesday, Friday, and Saturday. Most days you'll find about 100 vendors hawking locally grown produce, organic wines, cider, flowers, artisan cheeses, even gourmet pickles. It's a lot of fun to visit. Three playgrounds, a dog run, and a very fine equestrian statue of George Washington are also on-site.

From 14th to 17th sts. (btw. Park Ave. South and Broadway). www.nycgovparks.org/parks/union squarepark. Subway: 4, 5, 6, L, N, Q, R to 14th St./Union Square.

Washington Square Park ★★ PARK   This park is nothing if not tuneful and has long been a place for amateur musicians to gather in groups, lugging along instruments for impromptu concerts each weekend (and many weeknights when the weather is nice). The round fountain in the center of the park serves as a stage for a dozen-or-so regular comedians, acrobats, impressionists, and dancers who are good enough to draw crowds of 100 people or more.

Entertaining as well are the intense chess matches played in Washington Square Park from noon to sundown on the southwest corner of the park (the regulars here are real sharks). Children will enjoy the two playgrounds on the north side of the park and watching the bocce ball players practice their ancient game on the south side of the park.

At the southern end of Fifth Ave. (where it intersects Waverly Place, btw. MacDougal and Wooster sts.). Subway: A, C, E, F, M to W. 4th St. (use 3rd St. exit).

ORGANIZED SIGHTSEEING TOURS

Reservations are required for some of the tours listed below, but even if they're not, it's always best to call ahead to confirm prices, times, and meeting places.

Harbor Cruises

Note that some of the lines below may have limited schedules in winter, especially for evening cruises. Call ahead or check online for current offerings.

Bateaux New York ★ The most elegant and romantic of New York's evening dinner cruises, aboard a boat designed for 300 guests with two suites, one dance floor, two outdoor strolling decks, and windows galore. Dinner is a formal, three-course sit-down affair (though the food is just so-so). A live quartet entertains with jazz standards and pop vocal tunes.

Departs from Chelsea Piers, W. 23rd St. and Twelfth Ave. ✆ **866/817-3463.** www.bateauxnewyork. com. 3-hr. dinner cruises around $129 per person. Subway: C, E to 23rd St.

Circle Line Sightseeing Cruises ★★ A New York institution, led by witty, informed guides (many are also actors), the Circle Line takes travelers round the harbor on 3-hour, 2-hour, and 75-minute cruises. The longest makes a complete circle of the city, but I'd recommend the 2-hour tour instead. You'll miss Yankee Stadium and the view of the Palisades (the wooded cliffs of New Jersey) on that one, but all of the other highlights—the Statue of Liberty, the lower Manhattan skyline, the Empire State Building, the Chrysler Building—are included. Make sure to arrive at the dock early because you'll want to grab a good seat: on the right side of the boat, facing inward as you enter (that's the side that faces Manhattan; ask the staff if you're unclear). It can get very chilly on the water, so be sure to dress in layers, or take a seat inside.

In addition, a number of adults-only live music and DJ cruises sail regularly from the seaport from May through September ($20–$40 per person). Depending on the night of the week, you can groove to the sounds of jazz, Latin, gospel, dance tunes, or blues as you sail along viewing the skyline.

Departing from Pier 83, at W. 42nd St. and Twelfth Ave. ✆ **212/563-3200.** www.circleline42.com. Check the website or call for the most up-to-date schedule. 2-hr. cruises $35 adults, $31 seniors, $22 children 3–12, free for children 2 and under. Subway to Pier 83: A, C, E to 42nd St.

The Attack of the Double-Decker Buses

If you were to climb aboard any public bus (cost $2.75), turn to the person next to you, and ask, "What building is that?" you'd probably get a response as informative, accurate, and interesting as what you'll find on the much pricier, hop-on, hop-off bus tours of New York City. I know, I rode a slew of them doing research for this book and was appalled by the poor quality of the guides. I think New York is best appreciated on foot, or on public buses and subways. Not only do you learn more about the city that way, you meet locals, rather than peering at the streets from afar, almost as if you were watching it all on TV. And you'll actually see more than you will if you waste time waiting . . . and waiting . . . and waiting for the next of these hop ons to arrive, rather than just footing it to the next sight. If you insist, the top bus tour is **Gray Line New York** (✆ **800/669-0051** or 212/445-0848; www.newyorksightseeing.com). Tours depart from various locations. Hop-on, hop-off bus tours start at $94 adults for an 8-hour tour, more if you get a 48-hour pass.

When the pedicabs first came on the scene, they were a welcome alternative to the overpriced, stereotypical, and sometimes sad, horse carriage rides. Now, however, the pedicab business has exploded and the pedal-powered machines are so plentiful they have become a nuisance . . . at least to native New Yorkers. Good luck walking along Central Park South and Columbus Circle and avoiding the assault from sales crews trying to lure you onto one of their bikes. Be careful of what you are sold; a quick jaunt can cost you more than a cab ride to the airport. If you do insist on going for a ride, look for one of the original companies, the **Manhattan Rickshaw Company** (© **212/604-4729;** www.manhattanrickshaw.com) where fares range from $20–$40 for a street hail ride; call to arrange a guided tour and make sure you get the rate agreed upon in writing.

Spirit Cruises ★ Spirit Cruises' modern ships are floating cabarets that combine sightseeing in New York Harbor with meals, musical revues, and dancing to live bands. The atmosphere is festive, fun, and relaxed. The buffet meals are nothing special, but they're fine.

Departing from Chelsea Piers, W. 23rd St. and Twelfth Ave. © **866/483-3866.** www.spiritcruises. com. 2-hr. lunch cruises around $50; 3-hr. dinner cruises around $90 per person. Inquire about children's rates. Subway: C, E to 23rd St.

Specialty Tours

CULTURAL ORGANIZATIONS

The **Municipal Art Society** ★ (© 212/935-3960 or 212/453-0050; www.mas.org) offers excellent historical and architectural walking tours. Each is led by a highly qualified guide; topics range from the urban history of Greenwich Village to "Rockefeller Center: Art Deco Masterwork." Tours are $15. Reservations may be required depending on the tour, so it's best to call ahead. The full schedule is available online.

The **92nd Street Y** ★ (© 212/415-5500; www.92y.org) offers a wonderful variety of walking and bus tours, many featuring funky themes or behind-the-scenes visits. Subjects can range from "Carnegie Hall Tour and Tea" to "Jewish Harlem." Prices range from $25 to $100, but many include ferry rides, afternoon tea, dinner, or whatever suits the program. Guides are well-chosen experts. Advance registration is required for all tours.

INDEPENDENT OPERATORS

Big Onion Tours (© 888/806-WALK; www.bigonion.com) are led by local graduate students, most of them studying history, with a few sociologists and literature majors thrown in. The emphasis therefore is on the history of the area you may be visiting—Greenwich Village, Times Square, Central Park—and the lectures tend to be complex, illuminating portraits of those places. My only quibble with these tours is that the talk is often only tangentially related to the building or park you may be

Take the M5: A City Bus That Hits the Highlights

If your feet are worn out from walking, but you still want to see some sights, I suggest hopping on the **M5 bus.** Its route runs from Washington Heights down to the Staten Island Ferry terminal. If you board uptown, around 125th Street and Riverside Drive, and take it downtown, you'll pass landmarks such as Grant's Tomb, Riverside Church, Lincoln Center, Columbus Circle, St. Patrick's Cathedral, Rockefeller Center, the New York Public Library, Empire State Building, Flatiron Building, and Washington Square. And all you need is your MetroCard (or exact coin change) and this trusty guidebook. The bus will move slowly enough that you will be able to consult your book and find the corresponding landmarks.

viewing at the time, so the walking tour can feel more like a classroom lecture than an afternoon's exploration. Adults $25, seniors and students are $20 for these 2-hour tours.

All tours from **Joyce Gold History Tours of New York ★★** (© 212/242-5762; www.nyctours.com) are offered by Joyce Gold herself, an instructor of Manhattan history at New York University and the New School for Social Research, who has been conducting history walks around New York since 1975. Her tours can really cut to the core of this town; Joyce is full of fascinating stories about Manhattan and its people. Tours are offered most weekends March to December and last from 2 to 2½ hours, and the price is $18 per person ($15 for seniors); reservations are not required.

Since 2000, Myra Alperson of **NoshWalks** (© 212/222-2243; www.noshwalks. com), has been leading adventurous, hungry walkers to some of the city's most delicious neighborhoods. From the Uzbek, Tadjik, and Russian markets of Rego Park, Queens, to the Dominican coffee shops of Washington Heights, Alperson has left no ethnic neighborhood unexplored. Tours are conducted on Saturday and Sunday, leaving between 11:30am and 1pm. The preferred means of transportation is subway and the tours generally last around 3 hours and cost about $50. Space is limited, so book well in advance.

On Location Tours (© 212/209-3370; www.sceneontv.com) offers narrated minibus tours through screen history on their "NY TV and Movie Sites"; or, if you want to see Carrie Bradshaw's Big Apple, cut right to the chase and take the company's "Sex and the City Hotspots," Schedules and departure points varies depending on what tour you take and tickets range from $22 to $46. Reservations are required for all tours, as most sell out in advance.

Harlem Spirituals (© 800/660-2166 or 212/391-0900; www.harlemspirituals.com) specializes in gospel and jazz tours of Harlem that can be combined with a traditional soul-food meal. Prices start at $59, $49 for children 5–11, for a "Harlem Gospel" tour, and go up from there based on length and activities/meals. All tours leave from Harlem Spirituals' Midtown office, 690 Eighth Ave. (btw. 43rd and 44th sts.), and transportation is included.

OFFBEAT NEW YORK tours

Elastic City (www.elastic-city.org): Performance art tours of the city's various neighborhoods, which have participants creating poetry in response to the monuments they see, experiencing neighborhoods blindfolded (with a helper to keep them safe), creating art with found objects and doing all sorts of other wacky, creative things. The tour for truly free spirits, it costs $10.

Soundwalk (✆ 212/674-7407; www.soundwalk.com): You don a pair of headphones, and then walk into all sorts of oddball places in the Bronx, Chinatown, the Lower East Side, Times Square, DUMBO, and the Meatpacking District. You might find yourself on the roof of a private building admiring the views or peering into the window of an artist's basement studio, watching her work. For $6, download MP3s on the site or an app on Apple's iPhone store; all you need is an MP3 player or iPhone, map, Metro-Card, walking shoes, and an adventurous spirit, as you'll be taken into places where tourists never go.

Wildman Steve Brill ★

(✆ 914/835-2153; www.wildmanstevebrill.com): If you ever get stranded in Central Park, a tour with Wildman Steve Brill might help you survive. I've seen him in the park, raggedy beard, shorts, hiking boots, and pith helmet, leading groups of eager-eyed followers while instructing them on what flora and fauna they can forage—breaking off a stick of some edible tree and gnawing on it as an example. Brill's Central Park tours occur twice monthly and are not only hilarious, they are educational. If you're lucky, maybe he'll regale you with his tale of his arrest by a park ranger for eating a dandelion. Reservations must be made in advance. Suggested donation is $20 ($15 for children 11 and under)—cash only, exact change.

Big Apple Jazz Tours (✆ 718/606-8442; www.bigapplejazz.com): These tours, hosted by New York jazz expert Gordon Polatnick, are the real deal for jazz buffs. Polatnick's private tours are tailor-made to the jazz interests of his clients. If you're into bebop, he'll show you Minton's Playhouse, the jazz club that was the supposed birthplace of bop. From there he'll take you to other active Harlem clubs that embody Minton's bebop spirit. If you're into the 1960s bohemian Village scene, he'll take you to clubs that represent that golden era of Village jazz clubs. The tour fee is $99 for 4 hours, plus cost of entrance fees, drinks, transportation, and so forth.

SHOPPING

Why do the majority of visitors to New York descend on the city in fall and early winter? They come here to shop. In the run-up to Christmas, Chanukah, Kwaanza, and other big-spender holidays, avid shoppers storm the city because they know that if you can't find it in the Big Apple . . . well, it simply doesn't exist. In this chapter, I attempt to bring some order to the massive number of shopping options in the Big Apple, concentrating on the locally owned shops and shopping experiences that can only be had in NYC.

SHOPPING BY AREA

Often in Gotham, finding what you want has less to do with picking the right store than with choosing the right area in which to shop. Similar types of stores tend to cluster together, making it quite easy for shoppers to flit from one to the next, comparing merchandise and prices. Here, beginning at the bottom of Manhattan and working my way north, is my list of the city's best shopping streets and their areas of specialty.

Downtown

TRIBECA
Duane Street between Greenwich and Hudson Streets: A delightful block of antique and fine furniture stores with such unusual options as Brazilian collectables and "pop" furniture options. *(Subway: 1, 2, 3 to Chambers St.)*

CHINATOWN
Canal Street between Mott and Lafayette: Best for super-cheap knock-off accessories: purses in the style of Kate Spade, watches of all types, beaded jewelry, sunglasses and luggage. If you're planning to buy a T-shirt to commemorate your New York vacation, buy it here for half of what you'd spend in Times Square. *Tip:* Very few stores in this area use price-tags. That's because bargaining is expected so be prepared to walk away if the price seems too high—often the mere gesture of turning towards the door will halve the cost.

For browsing: The fish and herbal markets along **Canal, Mott, Mulberry,** and **Elizabeth Streets** are fun for their bustle and exotica—as well as for the handful of Italian joints still hanging on from the pre-Chinese days when this area was known as Little Italy. *(Subway: 1, 2, 3, 4, 5, 6, N, Q, R to Canal St.)*

If you're looking for specific items or sales, check the daily shopping listings at **www.newyork.citysearch.com, www.timeoutny.com,** and **www.nymag. com** before you leave home. Once you're here, consider picking up the hard-copy magazines: You can find details about the week's sales and newest shops in the "Seeking" and "Shopping" pages of *Time Out New York* or the "Sales & Bargains," "Best Bets," and "Wish List" sections of *New York* magazine.

Other top sources: **www.dailycandy. com,** a newsletter that often lists store openings and the day's hot tips on sale locations; **www.ny.racked.com** and **www.refinery29.com,** list NYC store openings, noteworthy sample sales, and fashion trendspotting.

SOHO, NOHO & NOLITA

Broadway between West Houston and Canal: Club kid central. If you're between the ages of 15 and 29, want affordable, flashy fashions (TopShop, Yellow Ran Bastard)—plus the usual chains (Old Navy, Zara)—this is where to shop. You'll find a similar crop of shops on **Lafayette Street between Houston and Spring,** though head farther uptown on Lafayette and you'll encounter a slew of fine furniture shops.

On the **smaller, side streets** (Spring, Elizabeth, Mott, Mulberry), is an entirely different scene, with local designers setting up shop next to high-fashion consignment stores and such stellar big names as the **Museum of Modern Art Design Store ★,** 81 Spring St. (*©* **646/613-1367**). There also are several hot galleries along West Broadway and sprinkled throughout SoHo. You can find a full list of shops and galleries (most are closed Monday) at www.artseensoho.com. *(Subway: R, Q to Prince St. or 6 to Spring St.)*

THE EAST VILLAGE

9th Street between Second Avenue and Avenue A: New, younger designers tend to pick this street, so you'll find a terrific assortment of "only in New York" fashions, along with shops of designers who have now become a bit more established, vintage stores and bridal boutiques. If you have the time, wander down to St. Marks Place below Second Avenue and 7th Street for similar stores (though not in the same density as 9th Street). St. Marks (the continuation of 8th Street) between Second and Third Avenue is a fun place for teens, filled with vintage stores, cheap sunglasses stands, and t-shirt shops. *(Subway: 6 to Astor Place or L to First Ave.)*

GREENWICH VILLAGE

Bleecker Street between Seventh and Eighth Avenue: Boutique heaven. If cutting-edge style is your thing and you have the pocketbook to support that appetite, the small stores along this block have all the latest fashions, with friendlier service than you'll find Uptown. And oddly, Bleecker Street between Sixth and Seventh Avenues is foodie paradise, selling all the fine cheeses, gelatos, and other goodies that will prevent you from fitting into the fashions an avenue over! *(Subway: A, E, C to 14th St.)*

CHELSEA/MEATPACKING DISTRICT

Far west Chelsea from 14th to 29th streets between Tenth and Eleventh avenues has been transformed into the **Chelsea Art District,** where more than 200 galleries have sprouted up in a once-moribund enclave of repair shops and warehouses. For more on that, see p. 122 and 123 in chapter 5.

UNION SQUARE/THE FLATIRON DISTRICT

Union Square is "big box heaven" with **Whole Foods, Forever 21, Barnes and Noble, DSW (Designer Shoe Warehouse),** and the city's first **Nordstrom Rack** along with other stores. It also is the site of the city's best open food market.

For more mall-type stores, **Fifth Avenue between 14th Street and 23rd Street** is a mecca, mixing home furnishings (Restoration Hardware, EJ Audi) with brand name clothiers (Eileen Fisher, Armani, the Gap). At 23rd is the city's best food store/Italian food court **Eataly** (p. 175), as much a tourist site today as a purveyor of eats from "the Boot."

Midtown

HERALD SQUARE & THE GARMENT DISTRICT

Herald Square—where 34th Street, Sixth Avenue, and Broadway converge—is dominated by **Macy's,** the self-proclaimed "biggest department store in the world," but it's also host to a number of other retailers whose names you'll recognize. (*Subway: 1, 2, 3, B, D, F, M, N, Q, R to 34th St.*)

FIFTH AVENUE FROM 38TH ST. TO 57TH ST.

Window shoppers' paradise, with such grand old beauties as Saks Fifth Avenue, Tiffany's, and Bergdorf Goodman, along with a number of other luxury outlets and flagship stores for Uniqlo, Louis Vuitton and others. For store lists and links to their websites, visit **www.fifthavenuebid.com.** (*Subway: E, M to Fifth Ave/53rd St.*)

Uptown

MADISON AVENUE FROM 57TH ST. TO 79TH ST.

The most expensive retail real estate in the world, which means overpriced baubles and garments for the ultra-rich as far as the eye can see. Along with Barneys New York, you'll find flagship branches for Ralph Lauren, Chanel, Hermès, and Prada. Visit **www.madisonavenuebid.org** for a long list of high-end shops. (*Subway: 6 to 59th, 66th, or 77th sts.*)

THE BIG DEPARTMENT STORES

ABC Carpet & Home ★★★ A museum. A temple. A sanctuary. I can't afford to buy a darn thing at ABC Carpet, except for spiffy soaps, but I sure do love trolling the floors here, as the goods on offer are simply exquisite. You might find children's furniture and bedding fit for Kate and William's kid, throw pillows straight from a high-class harem, and all manner of delightful antique furnishings. Across the street is the multifloor carpet store. The Bronx branch (1055 Bronx River Ave.) offers periodic sales. 881 and 888 Broadway (at 19th St.). www.abchome.com. ✆ **212/473-3000.** Subway: L, N, R, 4, 5, 6 to 14th St./Union Square.

Barneys New York ★★   One week it's on the runways in Paris, the next week it's in the windows of Barneys. Or at least that's how it feels. This is where well-heeled New Yorkers buy their, well, heels . . . and suits and sweaters and other items of apparel, all at outrageous prices. Who knew a pair of shoes could serve as the down payment on a car? *Tip:* Barneys hosts a **warehouse sale** in Chelsea twice a year, featuring discounts of 50% to 80% off the original retail prices. Check the website for sale dates—and arrive early. It's a frenetic scene, but the designer item you score just might be worth it. 660 Madison Ave. (at 61st St.). www.barneys.com. ✆ **212/826-8900.** Subway: N, R to Fifth Ave.

Bloomingdale's ★★★   Classier than Macy's (p. 169) and a bit more logical in terms of layout, Bloomingdales is a shopping behemoth with enough excitement to keep shopaholics occupied for several hours at least. Founded in 1872 as a hoopskirt store, the vast emporium is still in the forefront of fashion with four complete floors just for garments (basement for men's; second, third, and fourth floor for women's). It also sells housewares, furniture, kid's clothing, luggage, kitchen tools, accessories, cosmetics, and jewelry, but its strength are the clothes. Every week Bloomies puts some department, or part of a department, on sale, so be sure to check out local newspapers to see what the buys are when you're here. Weekdays before lunch tend to be the least crowded time to visit, and anyone who purchases over $50 of merchandise is entitled to a free tchotchke at the Visitor's Center, so save your receipts if you have someone not too picky to whom you owe a gift. 1000 Third Ave. (Lexington Ave. at 59th St.). www.bloomingdales.com. ✆ **212/705-2000.** Subway: 4, 5, 6 to 59th St. 504 Broadway (at Broome St.). ✆ **212/729-5900.** Subway: N, R to Prince St.

Century 21 ★   Though it's near-heresy to say so, I count Century 21 as the most overrated store in the city. A four-floor discount department store right across from the World Trade Center site, it made its reputation by selling designer clothing, shoes, and housewares at steeply discounted prices. But though the clothing may say "Calvin Klein," "Mosconi" or "DKNY," I've found that in nine out of ten cases, the really inexpensive offerings look nothing like the goods you'd get from these designers at retail stores. Instead, the fabrics are—to my mind, a sheer opinion—the cheapest polyesters, the colors gaudy, the fit off, and even the labels themselves look different. I suspect this is where designers go to unload the terrible mistakes they've made, or perhaps to peddle lines of cheaper goods, created explicitly for this store and others like it. I'm in the minority on this, as witness to the fact that a new outlet of the store

Take a Shopping Tour

If you want some help in your shopping and feel a bit intimidated by all the options Manhattan has to offer, you might want to consider taking a shopping tour. **Shop Gotham** (✆ **212/209-3370;** www.shopgotham.com) offers walking tours of SoHo and Nolita (Fri– Sat at 11am, Sun at noon, $41) and the Garment Center "Insider" Tour (Wed and Fri at 10am, $67). They can also customize private and group tours like the Sweet Sixteen Shopping Tour. Tours run 2 to 4 hour.

sale SEASONS

These may be obvious to the serious shopper, but for those on the learning curve, here are New York's prime sale seasons:

- **Thanksgiving:** "Black Friday," or the day after Thanksgiving, is the beginning of the holiday shopping season. Many stores inaugurate this high time with major sales. Stores are open wildly early and late.

- **Post-Christmas:** With the Christmas returns and overstocked storerooms come the markdowns.

- **Whites:** Usually in January, this is a sale of linens . . . which these days, are rarely white, but the name persists.

- **January Clearance:** You'll find the European boutiques advertising clearances around the third week of January.

- **Presidents' Day:** This February long weekend brings great deals on winter inventory.

- **Memorial Day:** Promotional sales sail in the last weekend in May.

- **Fourth of July:** Blowouts on bathing suits and summer attire are summoned by the long weekend.

- **Midsummer Clearance:** If there is anything summer-related left on the racks after the Fourth of July, you'll find it on clearance through about mid-August.

opened in 2012 on the Upper West Side. 22 Cortlandt St. (btw. Broadway and Church St.). www.c21stores.com. ℭ **212/227-9092.** Subway: 2, 3, 4, 5, J, M to Fulton St.; A, C to Broadway/Nassau St.; E to Chambers St.; R, W to Cortlandt St. Also at 1972 Broadway (at 66th St.). ℭ **212/518-2121.** Subway: 1 to 66th St., 472 86th St. (at Fourth Ave., Brooklyn). ℭ **718/748-3266.** Subway: R to Bay Ridge.

Lord & Taylor ★★ Flagship of a small chain of department stores, this is New York's overlooked emporium. So when you come here, you won't be battling the crowds as you will at Bloomingdales and Macy's. Still, you experience the best of those two stores: Bloomingdales sense of high style at Macy's discounted rates (thanks to rolling discounts; check the local papers for coupons). This is the store a number of magazine stylists I know head to when they have to populate a fashion shoot on a budget. 424 Fifth Ave. (btw. 38th and 39th sts.). www.lordandtaylor.com. ℭ **212/391-3344.** Subway: F, M to 42nd St.

Macy's ★ With approximately one million items for sale and a huge two-building space that stretches the very long block between Broadway and Seventh Avenue, this, the World's Largest Store, is also one of New York's top tourist attractions. It has some of the best prices of the major department stores, and in general, a higher quality of goods than Century 21, though the fashions here are definitely more middle of the road. The basement is devoted to cookware, of which there's a dazzling variety; the house brand of pots and pans (called Tools of the Trade) may be the best buy, well-made and usually quite inexpensive. And the return policy here is one of the most generous in the city, so mistakes are not irrevocable.

Those are the reasons you should visit. But there are also reasons why you may want to pop a valium before you attempt it. The vast scale of Macy's and the huge crowds it attracts are its Achilles heel, as there's no other place in New York quite so confounding to shop. There's never a salesperson around when you need one; on sale days the masses can be crushing; and even native New Yorkers get lost here, wandering for half an hour at a time trying to get to the right department. At Herald Square, W. 34th St., and Broadway. www.macys.com. ☏ **212/695-4400** or 212/494-7300. Subway: B, D, F, N, Q, R, 1, 2, 3 to 34th St.

Saks Fifth Avenue ★★ Despite the fact that it's now a chain, there's still definite glamour to the original Saks Fifth Avenue. It's a classic, and unlike Macy's, its size is manageable. As for its prices. . . . They may not be within the realm for many people, but even browsing here is a delight and the cosmetics on the first floor include many brands that you simply won't find elsewhere in the U.S. 611 Fifth Ave. (btw. 49th and 50th sts.). www.saksfifthavenue.com. ☏ **212/753-4000.** Subway: B, D, F, Q to 47th–50th sts./Rockefeller Center; E, F to Fifth Ave.

RECOMMENDED STORES
Antiques & Collectibles

New York has such a bounty of excellent—and pricey—antique stores that it seems churlish to highlight one above the rest. Instead, I'll send you to the blocks off **Broadway, specifically 10th and 11th streets,** where a dozen stores thrive, specializing in French and American Art Deco pieces, Asian antiques and lamps from all eras. One block up is the well-regarded **Kentshire Galleries** (37 East 12th St.), a specialist in 18th and 19th century English antiques. Antique hunters will also want to troll **East 59th, 60th,** and **61st streets** around Second Avenue, not far from the **Manhattan Art and Antiques Center,** at 1050 Second Ave. between 55th and 56th streets (☏ **212/355-4400;** www.the-maac.com), where about two dozen high-end dealers line the street and spill over onto surrounding blocks. Fans of midcentury furniture and Americana with a twist should browse **Lafayette Street** in SoHo/NoHo.

Beauty

C. O. Bigelow ★★★ The oldest apothecary shop in the nation (it was founded in 1838), Bigelows has become known for its huge range of beauty supplies, carrying European and Japanese products that aren't available anywhere else in the U.S. Some of the products are quite unusual (like "frownies," an 1800's stick 'em on cure for frown lines which claims to train the wrinkles to go in another direction as you sleep). Even if you don't need to buy, stop by to browse under the Victorian gas chandeliers (converted to electric, but still lovely). 414 Sixth Ave. (btw. 8th and 9th sts.). www.bigelow-chemists.com. ☏ **212/533-2700.** Subway: A, C, E, F, M to W. 4th St.

Kiehl's ★ Founded in 1867 as an apothecary shop—its specialty back then were such magic potions as "Money Drawing Oil"—it's switched to more modern snake oil, facial creams, and cleansers, in the 1960s, and has been wildly popular ever since. The best two things about shopping here are the historic décor (the original chandeliers are still in use) and the generous gift of numerous small samples with each purchase. 109 Third Ave. (btw. 13th and 14th sts.). www.kiehls.com. ☏ **212/677-3171.** Subway: L, N, R, 4, 5, 6 to 14th St./Union Square.

Ricky's ★ A punky, funky chain of cosmetics stores that go beyond the typical "Duane Reade" selection of beauty products into wigs, hair dyes for every shade of the rainbow, body glitters, and shampoos even your stylists never heard of. It's also great for souvenirs and small gifts, as it has a number of silly toys and grooming products for adults and kids. All in all, there are 16 stores in all parts of the city. 44 E. 8th St. (at Greene St.). www.rickysnyc.com. ✆ 212/254-5247. Subway: N, R to 8th St. Also at 466 Sixth Ave. (at 11th St.). ✆ 212/924-3401. Subway: A, B, C, D, E, F to W. 4th St. 112 W. 72nd St. (btw. Columbus Ave. and Broadway). ✆ 212/769-3678. Subway: 1, 2, 3 to 72nd St. 728 Ninth Ave. (btw. 49th and 50th sts.). ✆ 212/245-1265. Subway: C, E to 50th St.

Ray's Beauty Supply ★★ Where New York's actors come to get all their makeup—the variety here is mind-blowing: 32 varieties of false eyelashes from Liza Minelli spiky to Jennifer Lopez furry, 200 different blushes, countless eye shadows and professional quality brushes, hair dryers, and other beauty gizmos. The prices here are often 40% to 75% less than what you'd find elsewhere. 721 Eighth Ave at 45th St. www.raysbeautysupply. ✆ 800/253-7793. Subway: 1, 2, 3, N, R to Times Square.

Books

In addition to the following, don't forget the giant **Scholastic Store** (557 Broadway, between Prince and Spring sts.; ✆ 212/343-6166; www.scholastic.com/sohostore) in SoHo for children's books and events.

Barnes and Noble ★★★ This famous chain—largest in the nation—was founded in NYC, and the massive original store seems to carry every book ever published. Here's a wonderland for bibliophiles, of which numerous branches are found throughout the city and its suburbs. As for its birthplace: that is at the corner of Fifth Avenue and 18th Street. Consult www.bn.com for locations. ✆ 212/253-0810. Subway: L, N, R, 4, 5, 6 to 14th St./Union Square.

Books of Wonder ★★ Do you remember the charming bookstore in the Meg Ryan romcom *You've Got Mail?* It was inspired by Books of Wonder (Meg even worked here briefly to train for the role), and the real thing is just as magical (and jam-packed with great kiddie reads) as the cinematic store. In fact, I'd say that the story-reading sessions combined with the cupcake counter, will make an avid reader out of even the most book-phobic of kids. 18 W. 18th St. (btw. Fifth and Sixth aves.). www.booksofwonder.com. ✆ 212/989-3270. Subway: L, N, R, 4, 5, 6 to 14th St./Union Square.

Drama Book Shop ★ As much clubhouse as bookstore, this is where many in NY's theatrical community head between rehearsals and auditions. Not surprisingly, it's filled with scripts (including those of all the shows on Broadway, if you want that kind of souvenir), plus a myriad of books about the art and craft of theater. On site, too: a small stage for performances and panels. 250 W. 40th St. (btw. Eighth and Ninth aves.). www.dramabookshop.com. ✆ 212/944-0595. Subway: A, C, E to 42nd St.

Forbidden Planet ★★ Know anyone who lives in a fantasy world? This is where you should buy their gift. Forbidden Planet specializes in all of the "geek" obsessions: sci-fi, horror, Japanese anime, comic books, and fantasy games. That includes figurines from such cult classics as *Buffy the Vampire Slayer* and *Star Wars;* gaming implements; and more such ephemera. 840 Broadway (at 13th St.). www.fpnyc.com. ✆ 212/473-1576. Subway: L, N, R, 4, 5, 6 to 14th St./Union Square.

Idlewild Books ★★★   This innovative travel bookstore makes perusing the shelves intuitive by mixing guidebooks with works of history, memoirs, and other titles about the destination in question. It also boasts one of the most knowledgeable, cheery staffs in the city. A gem. 12 W. 19th St. (off Fifth Ave.). www.idlewildbooks.com. ℂ **212/414-8888.** Subway: N, R to 23rd St.

Kitchen Arts & Letters ★   A superb cookbook store. Along with titles from the standard celeb chefs are out-of-print, rare and even foreign language books, all just brimming with recipes and advice. 1435 Lexington Ave. (btw. 93rd and 94th sts.). www.kitchen artsandletters.com. ℂ **212/876-5550.** Subway: 6 to 96th St.

McNally Jackson Books ★   Many bookstores post recommendations from their staff, but few are as right on as the ones here. A great place to find that book for the plane home, or just take a break from the shopping madness of Soho (there's a nice café on-site). 52 Prince St. (btw. Lafayette and Mulberry sts.). www.mcnallyjackson.com. ℂ **212/274-1160.** Subway: N, R to Prince St.; 6 to Spring St.

The Mysterious Bookshop ★   Another specialty book dealer; do you need a clue as to what's sold here? Didn't think so. Though you should know the store has both antique and current mystery novels, as well as a club for collectors. 58 Warren St. (at W. Broadway). www.mysteriousbookshop.com. ℂ **212/587-1011.** Subway: 1, 2, 3, A, C, E to Chambers St.

Rizzoli ★★★   The prettiest bookstore in New York City—truly, it looks like a film set—it's also chockablock with fabulous art books, the type of massive tomes (on architecture, dance, fashion, you name it) that really dress up a room. And for those who like to, well, read, there are hundreds of other titles as well in this three-story store. 31 W. 57th St. (btw. Fifth and Sixth aves.). www.rizzoliusa.com. ℂ **212/759-2424.** Subway: N, R to Fifth Ave.

The Strand ★★★   Grungy, maddeningly disorganized, stuffy and crowded, the Strand is nonetheless one of New York's premier bookstores, a place that rivals the legendary "Library at Alexandria" in its scope and variety. Its motto is "Eight Miles of Books" and it certainly feels like it has that many when you visit; best of all, many of

OPEN FOR business?

Hours can vary significantly from store to store—even different branches of the Gap can keep different schedules in this city!

Generally, stores open at 10 or 11am Monday through Saturday; 7pm is a common closing hour. Both closing and opening hours tend to get later as you move downtown, with some East Village stores keeping their gates down until 1pm, and staying open until 8pm or

later. In the Financial District, some stores close for the entire weekend (this is the only part of the city, however, where that happens).

All of the big department stores are open 7 days a week, with many staying open until 9pm on Thursdays.

Nervous you'll show up and nobody will be there to sell? Call ahead or go on the Internet to double-check hours.

these are "front list" books that are ordered directly from the publisher at a substantial discount (sometimes as much as 50%). Those looking for rare books should look no farther: The Strand has the largest collection in the city, with dozens trading in each day. 828 Broadway (at 12th St.). www.strandbooks.com. ℂ 212/473-1452. Subway: L, N, Q, R, 4, 5, 6 to 14th St./Union Square.

Clothing & Shoes

Brooks Brothers ★ Yes, it's a chain, but this is where it started and the store is a classic, all burnished woods, seas of ties, and sales ladies in pearls. 346 Madison Ave. (at 44th St.). www.brooksbrothers.com. ℂ **212/682-8800.** Subway: S, 4, 5, 6, 7 to 42nd St./Grand Central. Also at 1934 Broadway (at 65th St.). ℂ **212/362-2374.** Subway: 1 to 66th St. and 1 Liberty Plaza. ℂ **212/267-2400.** Subway: 2, 3, 4, 5, A, C, J, M, Z to Broadway/Nassau St.

Huminska ★★ For women only, but women of all sizes (a rarity). Huminska specializes in miraculously flattering dresses. Many are in a faux wrap pattern that hides the lumpy bits, and they come in all sorts of patterns and colors. If you're looking for new staples for your work and going out wardrobe, this is where to head. 248 Mott St. (btw. Houston and Prince sts.) www.huminska.com. ℂ **212/477-3458.** Subway: 6 to Bleeker or Spring.

Jeffrey New York ★ For its chicer-than-thou clientele, it's either here or Barneys. As you might imagine, price is no object for this crowd. An outlet of the revered Atlanta mega-boutique, it offers shoes, accessories, and make-up, along with the cutting edge clothing. 449 W. 14th St. (near Tenth Ave.). www.jeffreynewyork.com. ℂ **212/206-1272.** Subway: A, C, E, L to 14th St.

Jill Anderson ★★ Classic cuts (think Audrey Hepburn), in a range of luxurious fabrics and colors, that somehow make everyone look better than when they walked in. And hallelujah, she has petites that actually fit small women, and extra larges that are generous enough for the plus-sized ladies among us. A shop for women only. 331 E. 9th St. (btw. First and Second aves.). www.jillanderson.com. ℂ **212/253-1747.** Subway: 6 to Astor Place.

Meg ★★ You may not have heard of designer Meghan Kinney, but she's been a fixture in Manhattan for the past decade thanks to this little boutique. Taking her inspiration from Martha Graham, her designs have a fluidity to them which is quite unique. I also like her use of kicky, unusual fabrics and the fact that though the look is young, it doesn't look foolish on her middle-aged clients. Worth a visit. 312 E. 9th St. www.meg shops.com. ℂ **212/260-6329.** Subway: 6 to Astor Place.

Searle ★★ Buy a winter coat here, and you'll never have to buy another. That isn't an exaggeration. High quality, beautifully cut, and wonderfully warm, these are good winter investments. Searle also have other clothes, but the women's outerwear is what makes this place such a find. 635 Madison Ave. (at 59th St.). www.searlenyc.com. ℂ **212/750-5153.** Subway: 4, 5, 6, N, R to 59th St. Also at 1051 Third Ave. (at 62nd St.). ℂ **212/838-5990.** Subway: 4, 5, 6, N, R to 59th. 1296 Third Ave. (at 74th St.). ℂ **212/717-5200.** Subway: 6 to 77th St. 1124 Madison Ave. (at 84th St.). ℂ **212/988-7318.** Subway: 4, 5, 6 to 86th St.

Tip Top Shoes ★ Here's where you come when your feet start complaining about all the walking you've been doing in NYC. Tip Top specializes in shoes that are comfortable, but don't look nerdy. And the prices aren't bad at all. A full selection for both men and women. 155 W. 72nd St. (btw. Broadway and Columbus). www.tiptopshoes.com. ℂ **212/787-4960.** Subway 1, 2, 3 to 72nd St.

Topshop and Topman ★ Looking for a statement piece? Head to the "Tops," for very creative accessories, tee's, flirty dresses, and mod menswear. You can't buy your entire wardrobe here—some of it's just plain odd and the quality varies greatly—but if you're looking for just the right thing to go clubbing in, you've likely come to the right place. 478 Broadway (at Broome St.). www.topshopnyc.com. ℂ **212/966-9555.** Subway: 6 to Spring St.

Uniqlo ★★ You have to be cut slim to fit into some of these Japanese fashions, but if you can wear them, the values are extraordinary. Uniqlo offers fitted corduroys, pencil skirts, printed tee's, cashmere sweaters in every shade of the rainbow, and suits dignified enough to wear to work, all for prices that are a third what you'd pay elsewhere in the city. 666 Fifth Ave. (at 53rd St.). www.uniqlo.com. ℂ **877/486-4756.** Subway: E, F to Fifth Ave.; B, D, F, Q to 47th–50th sts./Rockefeller Center. Also at 31 W. 34th St. (btw. Fifth and Sixth aves.). Subway: B, D, F, N, Q, R to 34th St./Herald Square. 546 Broadway (btw. Prince and Spring sts.). Subway: N, R to Prince St.

JUST KIDS

Jane's Exchange ★ They grow so fast! That's why this consignment store just for kids makes so much sense. The clothes are lightly used (some look like they've never been worn), very cute, and highly affordable. 191 E. 3rd St. (near Avenue B). www.janesexchangenyc.com. ℂ **212/677-0380.** Subway: L to First Ave.

Shoofly ★★ Sophisticated European shoes and clothing are the hallmarks of this small but expertly curated shop. There's also a good toy collection. 42 Hudson St. (btw. Duane and Thomas sts.). www.shooflynyc.com. ℂ **212/406-3270.** Subway: 1, 2, 3 to Chambers St.

Space Kiddets ★★★ My daughters love this place for its hip kids wear—including dozens of patterned t-shirts and fancy jeans. I like going for the friendly staff. Prices are on the high side, but they're tempered by frequent sales (announced on the website). 26 E. 22nd St. (btw. Broadway and Park Ave.). www.spacekiddets.com. ℂ **212/420-9878.** Subway: N, R to 23rd St.

VINTAGE & CONSIGNMENT CLOTHING

Beacon's Closet ★★ A worthy excuse to trek out to Brooklyn, Beacon's trades in both trendy and vintage clothes, brought in by the fashionistas of this hip, artsy neighborhood. Very few items cost more than $20 and the selection is huge, housed in a 5,500-square-foot store. 88 N. 11th St. (in Williamsburg). www.beaconscloset.com. ℂ **718/486-0816.** Subway: L to Bedford St.

Housing Works Thrift Shop ★ Do-gooder shopping: not only will you find terrific buys on all of the top designers, but part of what you spend will go to help a homeless person living with HIV or AIDS. Along with designers such as Calvin Klein, Perry Ellis, and Diane Von Furstenberg, these stores carry wedding gowns and furniture. There are now 12 outlets around the city, but I always have the best luck at this one. 306 Columbus Ave (btw. 74th and 75th St.). www.housingworks.org. ℂ **212/579-7566.** Subway: 1, 2, 3, B, C to 72nd. St.

Ina and Ina Men's ★★★ This is where the *Sex and the City* costume department resold its clothes once the series ended. Though those costumes are now long gone (they sold out in 2 hours flat), there's no other place in the city where you'll be able to achieve "Carrie's" look as affordably, replicating that character's haute but wacky sensibility. The men's part of the store has equivalently daring clothing for guys. There are now three outlets, but the one I list here has the best selection for both genders. 15 Bleeker St. (at Elizabeth St.). www.inanyc.com. (✆ **212/228-8511.** Subway: 6 to Spring St.

Michael's ★★ You'll find one-of-a-kind couture clothes (Gucci, Prada, Escada) at deep discounts here, including wedding gowns. It also has the largest selection of hats and purses of any of the consignment houses. 1041 Madison Ave., 2nd Floor (btw. 79th and 80th sts.). www.michaelsconsignment.com. (✆ **212/737-7273.** Subway: 6 to 77th St.

Edibles

Chelsea Market ★★★ In 1997, what had been the old Nabisco factory went from cranking out oreos to housing a dozen of the city's most gourmet-level food vendors. Still the largest of the city's food malls, it's a delightful mix of restaurants and stores, all housed in the now industrial-chic shell of the old factory. Among the culinary stars on premises are **Jacques Torres Chocolates, Amy's Bread** (wonderful baked goods); **One Lucky Duck** (astonishingly good raw vegan take-out food); **Fat Witch Bakery** (primo brownies); **The Lobster Place** (just what it sounds like), and much more. 75 Ninth Ave (btw. 15th and 16th sts.). www.chelseamarket.com. (✆ **212/243-6005.** Subway: A, C, E to 14th St.; L to Eighth Ave.

Eataly ★★★ I LOVE Eataly. There, I said it. Sure, it's overcrowded and a tad pretentious. But Mario Batali's Italian food hall, which is split between half-a-dozen restaurants; and shops selling all sorts of comestibles; is a game changer. Not only has it raised the level of what locals expect when they shop (there's a vegetable butcher who will prep your greens for free! And row upon row of imported dried pastas in every shape imaginable!) but it has introduced the city to a broader range of Italian food. One restaurant is all vegetarian, for example, and the rooftop is an Italian beer garden. Come to eat, come to shop, but just come. I guarantee you'll enjoy the bustle and foodie frenzy of Eataly. 200 Fifth Ave. (at Broadway). www.eataly.com. (✆ **212/229-2560.** Subway: N, R to 23rd St.

Murray's Cheese's ★★★ Cheese is the new wine, attracting obsessive devotees who, like oenophiles, can spend hours tasting, musing, comparing. And Murray's is at the epicenter of this movement. A cavernous emporium with over 250 varieties of cheese from all over the world and multiple tasting stations, Murray's has a fanatical following (in fact, the *New York Times* once ran a story about a lawyer who takes off every Thursday just to work behind the counter there for fun). As of 2013, Murray's now has an attached restaurant, every dish featuring cheese. 254 Bleeker St. (btw. Sixth and Seventh Aves.). www.murrayscheeses.com. (✆ **212/243-3289.** Subway: A, B, C, D, E, F, M to West 4th St.

Zabar's ★ Featured in films by Woody Allen, this is undoubtedly New York's most famous grocery/deli, an iconic New York emporium, but one that has—to my

NYC IS chocolate city

With this many chocolate makers in town, the Big Apple could be renamed the Big Bonbon. Many sweet shops around the city now turn out homemade chocolates in every variety that are so good, the stores, like four-star restaurants, are bona fide destinations.

What I like best about **Jacques Torres Chocolate ★★★**—besides the fact that Jacques Torres is a dashingly handsome Frenchman who likes to cook (making him every woman's dream guy)—is its owner's willingness to blend common ingredients with splendid chocolates. He does this, for example, with two breakfast cereals—plain bran flakes and Cheerios—and the results are exquisite. You'll also want to pick up a can of his extraordinarily rich hot chocolate ($16 for an 18-oz. tin; the "Wicked" version is slightly spicy), which puts Hershey's to shame. The chain has several locations today, including one Uptown at 285 Amsterdam Ave., at 73rd Street, and 350 Hudson St., at King Street, in the Hudson Square neighborhood (✆ **212/414-2462**). The 66 Water St. shop in DUMBO, Brooklyn, lets you watch chocolate being made—just don't neglect his nearby **Ice Cream Store** at no. 62. (✆ **718/875-1269;** www.mrchocolate.com).

Just east of the Metropolitan Museum of Art is the Madison Avenue incarnation of the Paris import **La Maison du Chocolat ★**, 1018 Madison Ave., at 78th Street (✆ **212/744-7117;** www.lamaisonduchocolat.com). This boutique takes its chocolate very seriously, proffering possibly the best pure chocolate you've ever tasted. They abhor any bitterness in their chocolate and make it a point to claim that they use nothing stronger than 65% cocoa. If you're downtown, stop by their shop at 63 Wall St. (✆ **212/952-1123**), or duck into the Midtown 30 Rockefeller Center store (✆ **212/265-9404**).

One of the oldest chocolate shops in the city is the 1923-established **Li-Lac Chocolates ★★**, 40 Eighth Ave., at Jane Street (✆ **212/924-2280;** www.li-lacchocolates.com), home to new batches of handmade fudge daily. Nearby is Allison Nelson's sublime **Chocolate Bar ★**, 19 Eighth Ave., at West 12th Street (✆ **212/366-1541;** www.chocolatebarnyc.com). Try the superdark 72%—so rich you might speak in tongues after a few bites.

More unconventional chocolate is found at **Kee's Chocolates ★★**, 80 Thompson St., near Spring Street (✆ **212/334-3284;** www.keeschocolates.com), where owner Kee Ling Tong makes her own unique creations 7 days a week, like mango green tea and Thai chili.

A final suggestion: **Bond Street Chocolate ★**, 63 E. 4th St. (✆ **212/677-5103;** www.bondstchocolate.com), for chocolate in much more innovative forms—like miniature skulls and the "divine collection" of Virgin Mary, Jesus, and Ganesh chocolate statues. Bond has lots of darks on the menu, as well as unusual flavors like tequila, elderflower, and absinthe truffle.

mind—declined a bit in recent years. I wouldn't make a special visit to see it, but if you're in the neighborhood, stop by for a bit of lox, or the famed lobster salad. More interesting nowadays are the competitively priced housewares and cookware on the second floor. 2245 Broadway (at 80th St.). www.zabars.com. ✆ **212/787-2000.** Subway: 1 to 79th St.

SWEETS

Dylan's Candy Bar ★ Dylan Lauren (the daughter of designer Ralph Lauren) created this wonka-esque palace of sugar, and it's turned into a bona fide tourist attraction over the years. I won't deny a visit to this shiny, sherbet-colored emporium is fun—heck, just seeing that many different varieties of gummy bears in one place is enough to keep my daughter's grinning for days—but I always leave feeling a bit queasy. 1011 Third Ave. (at 60th St.). www.dylanscandybar.com. ℂ **646/735-0078.** Subway: 4, 5, 6, N, R to 59th St.

Economy Candy Store ★★ A better candy experience, I think, can be had at the old-fashioned Economy Candy. Founded in 1937, and little changed since, it's the place to go for all of those penny candies you can't find anywhere else, plus classic treats like bubble gum cigars (remember those?) and wax lips. The halvah and house-dipped chocolates are also quite good. A trip down a very sweet memory lane. 108 Rivington St. (btw. Delancey and Norfolk sts.). www.economycandy.com. ℂ **212/254-1531.** Subway: F to Delancey St.

Electronics

The Apple Store ★ That humongous glass cube across from the Plaza Hotel is actually the biggest Apple Store in the world (at 18,000 square feet). It opened in early 2006, and only closed when Hurricane Sandy shuttered the entire city (it's open 24/7). Along with the genius bar, is a 46-seat theater and more than a dozen Internet-connected computers loaded with games—geek paradise. Apple has opened several other branches, including one in Grand Central Station. 767 Fifth Ave. (at 59th St.). www.apple.com. ℂ **212/336-1440.** Subway N, R to Fifth Ave. Also at 89 E. 42nd St. (at Park Ave.). ℂ **212/284-1800.** 103 Prince St. (at Greene St.). ℂ **212/226-3126.** Subway: R to Prince St. 401 W. 14th St. ℂ **212/444-3400.** Subway: L to 8th Ave.

B&H Photo & Video ★★★ I know people who visit New York City *just* to shop at B&H. Not only is it the largest camera store in the United States, it also boasts the best prices in the country (and that's a rarity for NYC). But you'd be mistaken if you think the store is just for shutterbugs; it's also tops for most everything electronic, from computers to mixing boards to chargers. So grab a number and be ready when it's called; the staff is extremely knowledgeable if sometimes a bit impatient (*Note:* B&H is closed on Saturdays.) 420 Ninth Ave. (at 34th St.). www.bhphotovideo.com. ℂ **800/606-6969** or 212/444-6615. Subway: A, C, E to 34th St.

Gifts & Stationary

Alphabets ★★ Kitsch heaven! In the market for a talking Pee Wee Herman doll, Simpson's chess set, Curious George T-shirt, or a lighter embossed with pictures of the Rat Pack? You're in the right place. For those with more "grown-up" sensibilities, Alphabets sells luxurious French soaps, fine wood jewelry boxes, lovely linens, and much more. 115 Avenue A (at E. 7th St.). www.alphabetsnyc.com. ℂ **212/579-5702.** Subway: F to Second Ave.

Evolution Nature Store ★ Who knew that there'd be a market for freeze-dried mice, stuffed piranhas, and pendants made from butterfly wings? Apparently the mad scientists behind Evolution did, and in 1993 they opened this mesmerizing store cum museum, where you can spend an engrossing hour staring at perfectly preserved skeletons (all types of animals), pristine fossils, stuffed creatures, and bugs encased in plastic. A great place to take the kids. 120 Spring St. (at Greene St.). www.evolutionnyc.com. ☎ **212/952-3195.** Subway: N, R to Spring St.

Kate's Paperie ★★ Silly as it may seem, I always feel my pulse quicken whenever I venture into Kate's, the largest purveyor of exotic papers in the city (the store has over 4,000 different types from 40 countries). While Kate's is not cheap, it carries smaller items—hot wax presses, tiny books, pretty collections of stationery—that are perfect for gifts, and hey, you don't need to travel elsewhere to buy the card! Four other outlets available; see website for addresses. 435 Broome St. (btw. Broadway and Crosby St.). www.katespaperie.com. ☎ **212/941-9816.** Subway: N, R to Prince St.

Pearl River ★★★ If you're like me, Pearl River will unleash yens you never knew you had. You'll walk into this blockwide two-story department store dedicated to goods imported from Asia, and suddenly realize how much you desperately need lacquered chopsticks, or a silk brocaded mandarin shirt, or that industrial-sized bag of rice crackers. It happens every time. Part of the seduction is the grand size of the place; the bright colors, intricate designs, and silky textures of the clothes; a dazzling number of choices. And prices are reasonable in the extreme. I have found lovely silk shirts marked down to just $15, a wedding-gift-worthy hand-glazed Japanese bowl going for just $25, and fun lamps for a mere $14.50. And if all the shopping tires you out, simply retire to the mezzanine tearoom for a tea break—green tea, of course. 477 Broadway (at Grand St.). www.pearlriver.com. ☎ **212/431-4770.** Subway: R, W to Prince; 6 to Spring.

Home Design & Housewares

Broadway Panhandler ★★ High quality cookware at serious discounts is the draw here. In business since 1976, Broadway Panhandler consistently undercuts "suggested retail pricing" on such top brands at Boedum, All Clad, Emile Henry by a good 40% or more. There are also such unique (and possibly giftworthy) items as silicone glove potholders, aprons in all patterns, silicone "food loops" that you can use to truss and then cook food in, and fancy blown-glass olive oil "drizzlers." 65 E. 8th St. (btw. Broadway and University Place). www.broadwaypanhandler.com. ☎ **866/266-5927.** Subway: N, R to 8th St.

Fish's Eddy ★ Want to bring home a set of dishes with the NY skyline on them? You'll find those here, along with a slew of equally peppy, original plateware. Those who like vintage styles for modern tableware—like soda fountain and pint glasses—will find them here. 889 Broadway (at 19th St.). www.fishseddy.com. ☎ **877/347-4733.** Subway: L, N, R, Q, 4, 5, 6 to 14th St./Union Square.

Jonathan Adler ★ Remember that short-lived reality competition show on interior design? Adler was one of the judges, and you'll see why his taste was taken so seriously at his delightful store. Come here if you're looking for snazzy throw pillows, frames, lamps, and other small furnishings. (Check the website for more locations.) 47 Greene St. (at Broome St.). www.jonathanadler.com. ☎ **212/941-8950.** Subway: N, R to Canal St. Also at 1097 Madison Ave. (btw. 83rd and 84th sts.). ☎ **212/772-2410.** Subway: 6 to 86th St.

Jewelry & Accessories

Doyle & Doyle ★ Run by certified gemologist Elizabeth Doyle and her sister Irene (a veteran of the diamond trade), Doyle & Doyle specializes in Georgian,

Edwardian, and Art Deco-era jewelry, which are shown to beautiful effect in display cases mounted on the wall (like fine paintings). Even if you're not buying, this is a fun store to visit. 189 Orchard St. (btw. Houston and Stanton sts.). www.doyledoyle.com. ✆ **212/677-9991.** Subway: F to Second Ave.

Jill Platner ★ Ultra-modern designs, mixed with unusual materials (many pieces are strung on a Gore-Tex-like thread called Tenara) make Jill Platner the go-to place for people who like to make a statement with their accessories. All the pieces are made in NYC, and happily, many sell for well-under $100. 113 Crosby St. (btw. Houston and Prince sts.). www.jillplatner.com. ✆ **212/324-1298.** Subway: N, R to Prince St.

Lunessa ★★ This tiny Soho store, with its gem bar and wondrously friendly staff, make jewelry shopping a heckuva lot of fun. First off, using that gem bar, they'll help you design your own piece. Or you can choose one of the elegant, delicate creations by owner Elise Perelman. 100 Thompson St. (near Prince St.). www.lunessacom. ✆ **917/305-0510.** Subway: N, R to Prince St.

Tiffany & Co. ★★ This is the original, and whether or not you decide to pose in front of it nibbling a croissant or not, you'll enjoy visiting the elegant, multilevel store. Its goods range well beyond jewelry, by the way; many brides register here for fabulous tableware and stemware. Happily, everything you buy comes wrapped in the store's iconic robin's egg blue box. 727 Fifth Ave. (at 57th St.). www.tiffany.com. ✆ **212/755-8000.** Subway: N, R to Fifth Ave. Also at 37 Wall St. (btw. William and Broad sts.). ✆ **212/480-4587.** Subway: 2, 3 to Wall St.

Tourneau Time Machine ★ Welcome to the world's largest watch store, giving the lie to the idea that nobody wears watches anymore. Somebody must be buying the 8,000 different styles that come from about 100 brands and are displayed here with a dazzle that's noteworthy! 12 E. 57th St. (btw. Fifth and Madison aves.). www.tourneau.com. ✆ **212/758-7300.** Subway: N, R to Fifth Ave. Also at 510 Madison Ave. (at 53rd St.). ✆ **212/758-5830.** Subway: E, M to Fifth Ave–53rd St. 10 Columbus Circle (the Shops at Columbus Circle). ✆ **212/823-9425.** Subway: A, B, C, D, 1 to Columbus Circle.

Museum Stores

Metropolitan Museum of Art Store ★★★ Like something you've seen at the museum? It's likely you'll be able to bring it home . . . in the form of a mug, or a

The Diamond District

West 47th Street between Fifth and Sixth Avenues is the city's famous Diamond District. They say more than 90% of the diamonds sold in the United States come through this neighborhood first, so there are some great deals to be had if you're in the market for a nice rock or other fine jewelry. The street is lined with showrooms; and you'll be wheeling and dealing with the largely Hasidic dealers, who are friendly enough but can be tough negotiators. For a complete introduction to the district, including smart buying tips, point your Web browser to **www.diamond district.org.** FYI, virtually all of these dealers are open Monday through Friday only.

piece of jewelry, or a print for your wall. The Met is expert at turning the stars of its vast collection into lovely items for daily life. Also notable is the extraordinary collection of art books and posters for sale. 1000 Fifth Ave. (at 82nd St.). www.store.metmuseum.org. ℂ **212/570-3894.** Subway: 4, 5, 6 to 86th St. Also at Rockefeller Center, 15 W. 49th St. ℂ **212/332-1360.** Subway: B, D, F, M to 47th–50th sts./Rockefeller Center. On the mezzanine level at Macy's, 34th St. and Sixth Ave. ℂ **212/268-7266.** Subway: B, D, F, N, Q, R to 34th St./Herald Square.

MoMA Design Store ★★★   Many of the iconic furniture items displayed at the Museum of Modern Art are sold here, in licensed reproductions, meaning you could take home an Eames recliner or Frank Lloyd Wright chair. The shop also has more affordable items, from nifty toys for kids to beautiful pieces of contemporary jewelry to swank and unusual cutlery. A true treasure trove. Also in Soho. 44 W. 53rd St. (btw. Fifth and Sixth aves.). www.momastore.org. ℂ **212/767-1050.** Subway: E, F to Fifth Ave.; B, D, F, Q to 47th–50th sts./Rockefeller Center. Also at 81 Spring St. (at Crosby St.). ℂ **646/613-1367.** Subway: 6 to Spring St.

New York Transit Museum Store ★   Hip NYC souvenirs are on sale here, like cufflinks made from old subway tokens or mouse pads with the subway map on them. And you can buy these oddities right as you're leaving town, since the store is in Grand Central Station. Grand Central Terminal (on the main level, in the shuttle passage next to the Station Master's office), 42nd St. and Lexington Ave. www.transitmuseumstore.com. ℂ **212/878-0106.** Subway: 4, 5, 6, 7, S to 42nd St./Grand Central.

Toys

American Girl Place ★   Sigh. Will you be able to avoid this place if you're traveling with a girl under the age of 8? Probably not, though many people find the experience underwhelming and overcrowded (despite the fact that this is a 43,000-square-foot store). To "do" the whole experience, you'll want to eat at the café, get a doll makeover at the salon, and head to the on-site theater. 609 Fifth Ave. (at 49th St.). www.americangirl.com. ℂ **800/247-5223.** Subway: B, D, F, M to 47th–50th sts./Rockefeller Center.

FAO Schwarz ★★   Another required stop for those with children, but slightly less painful than American Girl Place. Yes, the massive toy store has every type of game, bauble and stuffed animal under the sun, and seeing them all in one place is kinda fun . . . even for grown-ups. *Warning:* There's a soda fountain on-site and sugar highs and shopping are a dangerous combination. 767 Fifth Ave. (at 58th St.). www.fao.com. ℂ **212/644-9400.** Subway: N, R to Fifth Ave. or 4, 5, 6 to 59th St.

Kidding Around ★★★   The antithesis of Time Square's Toys "R" Us, this store stays away from all of those annoying beeping, buzzing, and flashing toys. Instead the focus is on playthings that the child manipulates herself, hopefully learning something in the process. Prices are fair, and the shop has a number of unusual toys such as rubber horseshoes ($11, hey you can play in the living room), soap-making kits, and all kinds of dazzling costumes. 60 W. 15th St. (btw. Fifth and Sixth aves.). www.kiddingaroundnyc.com. ℂ **212/645-6337.** Subway: F to 14th St.

WALKING
TOURS

n the pages ahead, you supply the feet and the eyes, and I supply the commentary. I've picked two neighborhood walks that will envelop you in the sweep of the city's history, architecture . . . and gossip. The first of them, a tour of Lower Manhattan, the oldest area of New York City, obviously has the most historical resonance. But the second, a Harlem tour, touches on Revolutionary War history, along with 20th-century issues. I'm willing to bet that one of these itineraries will be the highlight of your visit. And if you happen to be a resident, a walking tour of one of these special areas of Manhattan is a fine exercise for natives, too.

WALKING TOUR 1: HISTORIC LOWER MANHATTAN

GETTING THERE:	**Take subway 4 or 5 to Battery Park, walk from there into Battery Park and towards the river.**
START:	**Battery Park, stand at a spot where you can see the river.**
FINISH:	**The 9/11 Memorial**
TIME:	**1½ to 2 hours**
BEST TIMES:	**Weekdays during the daytime, so that you can take in the hustle and bustle of the area.**

Not only is this the most historic part of the city—New York reached no further than Wall Street for its first 100 years of existence—it also affords the best overview of architectural styles in the city. Buildings range from jazzy Art Deco structures, to pseudo-Greek temples, to the soaring glass rectangles of the "International Style" heyday, one rubbing up against the other like guests at a fantastic costume party where Martha Washington cha-chas uninhibitedly with Donald Trump. All the sites inhabit a compact, eminently walkable area.

More importantly, Lower Manhattan is the area of the city that has seen the most tragedy, having endured not one but four terrorist attacks over the years (I describe them below), terrible fires, and a cruel occupation by the British during the Revolutionary War that left the city in rubble. The scars of these events, the weight of the tears shed, and the lives lost, give this area a resonance and presence unlike those found in most other areas of the United States.

1 Battery Park

Look out at the river. It's the reason this great city was built. When Henry Hudson and his crew of 16 sailed up it in 1609, mistakenly thinking they'd find Asia at its mouth, little did they know they were setting into motion a chain of events that would still be shaping lives over 400 years later. It was Hudson's reports about the trading possibilities of the area (particularly for valuable animal pelts), plus his amazement at the great natural harbor here, that spurred the Dutch to create settlements in the area. They guessed, rightly it turned out, that the harbor of New York would be the linchpin that would connect Europe (via the Atlantic Ocean) with the interior of this vast and wealthy continent (via the Hudson River. Later, after the building of the Erie Canal, which connected the Hudson with the Great Lakes, NYC became the most powerful city in the nation.)

Walk towards the circular stone building known as:

2 Castle Clinton

Though it doesn't look like much now, this circular structure (it was taller in some earlier incarnations) has, over the years, been at the center of New York life. In 1807, the "West Battery," as it was then called, was built as a fort on a landfill island in the water off Manhattan to ward off British invasions; it never saw action—the Brits attacked Washington, D.C. instead, during the War of 1812. In 1823, the federal government ceded the site (renamed Castle Clinton in 1817, in honor of the city's mayor, De Witt Clinton) to the city, and it became an extremely popular entertainment center called Castle Gardens (the "Swedish Nightingale," Jenny Lind, was a headliner here in 1850) until 1855, when the space was transformed once more into the city's first immigrant processing center. Over eight million new arrivals, a full two-thirds of those who came to the United States at this time, spent their first hours in the United States here registering their names with the government, exchanging money, and getting information on jobs, medical care, and lodgings. In 1890, the vast number of immigrants—and the growing problem of outsiders scamming them—necessitated a move to a larger and more easily patrolled space, Ellis Island. The famed architectural team of McKim, Mead and White then stepped in and transformed the site into the nation's first aquarium, visited by about 90 million people until it was moved in 1941 to Coney Island. After the site stood empty for many years, the National Parks Service took it over and restored the Castle Clinton of the original fort.

Walk back inland stopping at the:

3 Large Flagpole

You'll see it right at the entrance to the park and at its base is a bas relief sculpture depicting the historic scene of Dutch official Peter Minuet "buying" Manhattan from Native American residents in order to consolidate the Dutch colony in one easily defended spot.

Just how the "sale" of the island went down is still a matter of controversy. It happened in 1626, and most likely the "sellers" were the Canarsie tribe who, according to a letter by Dutch merchant Pieter Schage, let the island go for 60 guilders (the equivalent of $24). But did the Indians know they were selling the island, or did they think that they were simply accepting shiny trinkets as part

Walking Tours: Downtown

1. Look at the River
2. Castle Clinton
3. Large Flagpole
4. National Museum of the American Indian
5. Bowling Green Park
6. Fraunces Tavern
7. Goldman Sachs Building
8. Stone Street
9. Mill Lane
10. Hanover Square
11. Wall Street
12. 40 Wall Street
13. Federal Hall
14. The NY Stock Exchange
15. 1 Wall Street
16. Trinity Church
17. Canyon of Heroes
18. National 9/11 Memorial

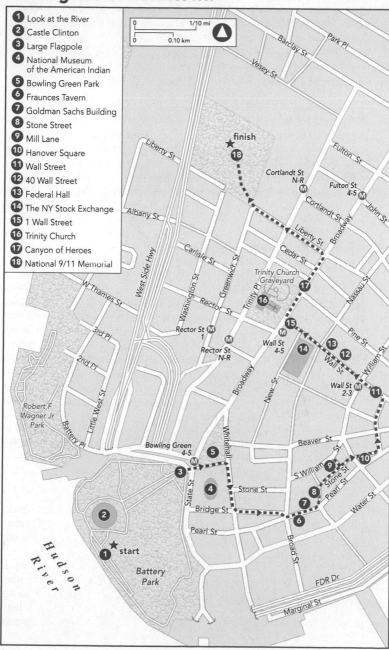

of a welcome ceremony? And were the Canarsie even in a position to sell it, as it had long been a communal hunting ground, used by a number of tribes? We'll never know the truth of the matter or even if it happened on this spot, but this is the one place in Manhattan where the most infamous real estate deal in history is memorialized.

As for Peter Minuit, he was recalled from his post in Manhattan in 1631 (much to his dismay), but returned on behalf of the Swedish government in 1638 to set up a rival "New Sweden" colony on the Delaware River.

Walk further inland to the plaza in front of the:

4 National Museum of the American Indian

The original Dutch fort stood in just this place. But what you see in front of you is a building of just as much significance. Designed by Cass Gilbert, this was one of the most important structures in the city when it was built—the Alexander Hamilton U.S. Customs House. Before 1913, when the federal government instituted the personal income tax, the federal government's revenue came almost entirely from customs on goods imported into the States. And a full 75% of this revenue came from the Port of New York, where it was processed in this appropriately grand Beaux Arts colossus, completed in 1907, and comprising over 450,000 square feet of interior space.

It's a wedding cake of an edifice, with dozens of bright white sculptures adorning the gray granite facade. Daniel Chester French was the sculptor—he also did the moving sculpture of Lincoln at the Lincoln Memorial—and his choice of symbols could be used as a treatise on the prejudices of Victorian America. The four women seated at the front represent the four "great" continents of the world. From left to right as you look at them, they are Asia, the Americas (South America, barely present, is tellingly represented by the Aztec-like structure that North America has her foot on), Europe, and Africa. America and Europe look full of vigor and purpose, but Asia has her eyes closed (perhaps in meditation?), and Africa—in a metaphor for her lack of vision and power?—is in a deep slumber. America is sheltering a new immigrant who crouches to her left, and the immigrant is pushing forward a wheel with wings on it, those of the Roman god Mercury, the divine overseer of commerce (a comment, some think, on the essential role immigrants were playing in the expanding economy).

At the top of the building are 12 more figures, this time meant to represent the great trading nations of history: Greece, Rome, Phoenicia, Genoa, Venice, Spain, Holland, Portugal, Denmark, England, France, and Belgium. Why Belgium, you ask? The official story is that during World War I, "vandals" carved BELGIUM across the shield of the figure that had originally been "Germany." No explanation has ever been given on how vandals could surreptitiously make such a big change to one of the most visible and heavily guarded buildings in the city.

If you have the time, go inside the building for a peek at the marvelous WPA murals in the rotunda (depicting the great conquistadors, ironic as the building now houses the National Museum of the American Indian); the staircase on the right as you enter (meant to evoke the look of the inside of a nautili shell); and in what is now the study center of the museum, the elaborate, imposing rows of teller windows where merchants would pay their Customs taxes.

Turn around and walk into:

5 Bowling Green Park

This was the city's first official park (est. 1733). Had you been a soldier during the British Colonial era, you would have been stationed at the fort that once stood here, Fort George, and likely you'd have passed your leisure time lawn bowling where the park now stands (hence the name Bowling Green Park).

On July 9, 1776, the Declaration of Independence was read aloud (near City Hall) and a small battalion of agitated colonists marched here to behead the statue of King George that stood in the center of the park. It had been erected just 5 years previously by many of these same men, in gratitude for the king's part in repealing the odious Stamp Act (the one that provoked the "no taxation without representation" movement). Though it can't be proven, legend has it that the lead statue was then melted down and used for cannon balls and bullets in the war against the British. The gate that rings the park is the original, one of the few Colonial structures of any sort left in Manhattan (when it was first erected, its spokes had royal crowns at their tips; these, too, were destroyed by the colonists).

Look north to the great skyscrapers that now shadow the park. On your left, the building with the Egyptian motif (5 Broadway) was the headquarters of the White Star shipping line. It is here that distraught relatives came to learn the fate of their loved ones after the sinking of the Titanic (there's a famous photo of a stricken Jacob Astor exiting the building after learning that his son had perished). Across the street, to your right, is the former headquarters of Standard Oil, the company that made John D. Rockefeller his millions. As you step back out of the park you should be able to see the elaborate oil lamp at the top.

Walk out of the park, going towards the museum and then walking on the side of the museum on Whitehall Street until you reach Bridge Street. Turn on to it and walk to Broad Street. Take a right and in front of you will be:

6 Fraunces Tavern

The bad news first: This is not what Fraunces Tavern actually looked like, but a hopeful reconstruction completed in 1904 and based on the architectural styles of the period (about 40% of the building is original). Nonetheless, it was here that the Sons of Liberty met on dozens of occasions to discuss plans for evicting the British. Once the Revolutionary War was over, Fraunces Tavern was the place where George Washington delivered his famous "Farewell to the Troops" and where Alexander Hamilton set up his first Office of the Treasury.

On a more sobering note, in 1975 Fraunces Tavern was bombed by the Armed Forces Puerto Rican National Liberation Front. Four people were killed and dozens injured. The choice of this site for the bombing had dual reasons: Not only is it a symbol of American ideals, it is one of the few important historic buildings in New York that has a Caribbean connection, as Samuel Fraunces was an immigrant from the West Indies.

Look behind you to see the:

7 Goldman Sachs Building

Directly across the street from the tavern is the headquarters of Goldman Sachs, the massive glass and brownstone skyscraper that cuts Stone Street in two. When it was being constructed, crews found the foundations of old **Governor Lovelace's Tavern,** another Colonial-era watering hole, and briefly seat of the Colonial government. In a compromise with local archaeologists, part of the site was left open with a glass-viewing pane atop it. If you walk around the perimeter of the skyscraper in the same direction that you've been going, you should be able to see these excavations through glass panels in the sidewalk (they're at the end of the rows of benches, one under the colonnade, one in the open air). Take a moment to read the plaques and gaze down.

Continue to walk north, curving around the Goldman Sachs building until you spot:

8 Stone Street

Here you'll have a remarkably accurate snapshot of what the city looked like in about 1837. This narrow winding street (it's the next street west from Pearl Street) was the first to be paved in New Amsterdam and the only street that is thought to still be where the Dutch colonists originally placed it. All of the buildings were constructed in the period immediately following the great fire of 1835, which devastated the city, wiping out 20 square city blocks. Many blamed the volunteer firefighters of the time who, working in rival squads for cash payment, spent more time fighting one another than fighting the flames (Martin Scorsese's 2002 film, Gangs of New York, dramatically re-creates a similar firefighter battle).

The buildings we see today are classic Greek Revival structures of straight up-and-down brick with granite bases. They were built as counting houses and warehouses for local merchants. **57 Stone St.,** you'll notice, has a very Dutch steplike gable, added in 1908 by architect C. P. H. Gilbert as a nostalgic nod to New Amsterdam.

Continue to the middle of the street and then step to the left onto:

9 Mill Lane

Mill Lane has the distinction of being the shortest street on Manhattan (and yes, there was once a mill here). Folk tradition had it that it was here that Peter Stuyvesant, the Dutch Director-General of New Amsterdam, signed a treaty of surrender when the British invaded. Thanks to recently uncovered documents, we know that historic act actually happened at Stuyvesant's farm, which was in what is today the East Village. Stuyvesant surrendered unwillingly, having torn to pieces the first letter sent by the British warship commander. City leaders then pieced the letter painstakingly back together. Upon seeing the favorable terms it presented the colonists (they would be allowed to keep their land and businesses), 93 leading citizens—including Stuyvesant's 17-year-old son, a traitorous young fogey—demanded that Stuyvesant surrender the colony to the British. Stuyvesant did so, but mourned the loss of the colony for the rest of his life.

Take a Break ☕

Grab a sweet treat at the patisserie, **Financier** ★ (62 Stone St.; 8am–8:30pm; $3–$5 for coffee and pastries). There are both indoor and outdoor tables, and every French delicacy you could want—from fruit tarts to Napoleons just oozing cream. Espresso, cappuccino, and soft drinks are also available.

At the end of Stone Street lies:

10 Hanover Square

One of the only places in New York City to retain its "royalist" title after the American Revolution, it was named for the House of Hanover, from which the era's British monarchy was descended. Once the center of the social and political life of the city, this was where the colony's first newspaper was published. The cotton exchange dominated one corner. When he was still considered a respectable citizen, notorious pirate Captain Kidd lived here in bourgeois splendor with his wife (they were known for their grand dinner parties). India House, on the west side of the square, is a perfectly preserved example of a brownstone banking house from the 1850s.

Continue walking to the uptown point of the triangle that is Hanover Square and hook a left onto Hanover Street. Walk until you come to:

11 Wall Street

You are now standing at what was the boundary of the city during Dutch Colonial times. If you had been alive then, you'd be staring at a 9-foot-high wooden wall erected to keep out British invaders, who, it was thought (wrongly) would be more likely to invade by land than by sea. To your right, when you face north, would have been the largest slave market in the United States (approximately at the corner of Pearl and White Streets), a bastion of inhumanity that held more auctions than any other in the U.S. in the 18th century. Slavery was not fully outlawed in New York until 1827, making it one of the last two northern states to do so.

Take a left and walk to:

12 40 Wall Street

New York's greatest monument to thwarted ambitions. Architect William Van Alen had a dream: He wanted to build the tallest building in the world, taller than the Woolworth Building (which held the record from 1917 to 1930). Problem was, his former partner and archrival H. Craig Severance had the same aspirations, and in the summer of 1929, at the height of the bubble that preceded Black Tuesday (the great stock market crash), they began a "race to the top," Van Alen at 40 Wall St., and Severance at the Chrysler Building. In a record 11 months, Van Alen completed 40 Wall St., then the Bank of Manhattan building, certain that the Chrysler building was completed and his structure would be the tallest. But once Van Alen finished construction, Severance administered the *coup de grâce* that he'd been hiding in the elevator shaft of his building: the Chrysler Building's iconic, Art Deco spire, which added an unbeatable 125 feet onto the building. I can only imagine that Van Alen felt some small measure of satisfaction when the

7

WALKING TOURS | Historic Lower Manhattan

Chrysler's title was snatched from it one short year later by the Empire State Building. Take a moment to gaze up at 40 Wall; it's still an impressive achievement and a beautiful building, with all of the ziggurat-like stepbacks (cascading layers) of the prototypical late '20s skyscraper.

Keep walking in the same direction until you get to the corner of Wall Street and Broad Street. Our next stop is:

13 Federal Hall

The most historically significant piece of land in the city, Federal Hall is a quintessential Greek Revival edifice, a modified version of the Parthenon (can't get much more Greek than that!), completed in 1842. Note the statue of George Washington; it was here, perhaps on the very spot where the statue now stands, that George Washington took the oath of office to become president (though not in this actual building, but in an earlier one located on this spot).

That momentous occasion would be enough to secure its place in history, but matters just begin there: The Bill of Rights was drawn up in this former British City Hall (transformed into "Federal Hall" when the Brits quit the city); the famous Zenger Trial (which helped secure freedom of the press) took place in a court in the hall; and before the Revolutionary War, the Stamp Act Congress met here and railed against "taxation without representation." Head inside to see the magnificent rotunda, one of the loveliest public spaces in the city.

Note the austere, somewhat anonymous-looking building across the street from the hall; it was the headquarters of banker J. P. Morgan (the window of his former office is above the flagpole). If you look closely at the side of the building that faces Federal Hall, you'll notice that it is pocked with small indentations. These are the scars of the Financial District's first terrorist attack, which occurred in 1920. One bright and sunny morning (isn't it odd that these events always seem to occur on beautiful days?), a horse and carriage loaded with explosives parked here. Moments later a huge explosion shook the street, killing 31 people and wounding scores more. The blast was so powerful that all that was ever found of the horse was a horseshoe, and the police used this piece of evidence to trace the blacksmith who made it. He had vague recollections of shoeing the horse of an Italian man, and on this scanty piece of evidence the police (and press) decided that the blast must have been the work of Italian anarchists. No one was ever charged with the crime.

Next walk towards:

14 The New York Stock Exchange

You are now gazing at the most famous (some would say infamous) financial institution in the world. The building's towering columns, crowded ornamental pediment, and huge flag trumpet louder than any opening bell that this is a place of incomparable might and prestige (interestingly, it's a much more imposing building than the government's plainer Federal Hall across the street). In front of the Stock Exchange is a scraggly buttonwood tree, meant to invoke the buttonwood that New York's first traders stood under in 1792 when they met to begin brokering the Revolutionary War debt—the first stock market in America.

Continue crosstown on Wall Street towards Broadway until you arrive at:

15 1 Wall Street

Take a moment to gaze at this absolutely stunning Art Deco building, once one of the priciest addresses in the city. The beautifully fluted, curtainlike limestone of the facade; the spider web pattern of the cathedral window above the entry; and the sumptuous, soaring lobby, remind us of a time when such excess and exquisite workmanship were the norm for places of business (which were, literally, in the heady times before the Stock Exchange crash, conceived as temples of commerce).

Cross the street to:

16 Trinity Church

For a full description of the history and architecture of Trinity Church, go to p. 117. Do wander the graveyard here, in addition to going inside the church; it has the remains of Alexander Hamilton and other notables.

Exit the graveyard and look uptown on Broadway as you are now in the:

17 Canyon of Heroes

Look down as you amble along at the brass plates with names and dates listing the ticker tape parades that have been held along this swatch of Broadway. Had you been here on one of those occasions in the 1930s or '40s, the crowds around you would have been shoulder to shoulder, and above your head, hundreds would have been standing at the windows, showering the street with the long paper ribbons of stock market quotations that spewed from their machines, marking the dance of the stock market. Read the plates. The catalogue of names is an interesting retread of American history and political alliances; along with athletes, astronauts, and presidents, you'll find parades for the American hostages released from Iran (1982), pianist Van Cliburn (1958), and the controversial President Sukarno of Indonesia (1956).

Walk up town on Broadway, turn left on Liberty Street and follow the signs to the:

18 9/11 Memorial

Be sure to reserve advance tickets online so that you can skip some of the lines at this iconic memorial. For more information, see p. 119.

WALKING TOUR 2: **HARLEM**

GETTING THERE:	**Take the 2 or 3 subway to 125th Street.**
START:	**Walk downtown to 120th Street and Malcolm X Boulevard (also known as Lenox Avenue).**
FINISH:	**The Apollo Theater, 253 W. 125th St.**
TIME:	**1 hour**
BEST TIMES:	**Daylight hours**

More than in any other place in the city, you need to have a strong imagination and social sense to really enjoy touring Harlem. The tragic fact is that much of what made this area unique, lively and . . . well, Harlem, during the fabled Jazz Era (aka The

Harlem Renaissance), crumbled beneath the wrecking ball decades ago. What you now see here—the wide avenues, the rows of brownstones, the elegant apartment buildings—are somewhat an accident of history, the physical face of an area that housed a people, but wasn't necessarily "of" that people (I'll explain below). But despite all this, Harlem remains the African-American capital of the United States (sometimes called the "capital for Africans throughout the world"), a one-of-a-kind area with much to recommend it. Architect and author Zevilla Jackson Preston best sums up the appeal of the area in the book HarlemWorld, in which she writes, "Ultimately it is the energy on the street, the beat on the street—all of the beautiful black people on the streets—that make the experience unique."

Harlem was settled by a number of different groups over the years—Dutch farmers first, followed by their British counterparts, then poor Irish and Italian immigrants. But development of the area only took off in the years just prior to 1904, when the city's first subway line opened, a 9½-mile snaking tunnel, connecting Lower Manhattan with points as far north as 145th Street. In anticipation of this event, an unprecedented housing boom hit the neighborhood, with developers slapping up Victorian row house after row house for the crowds of upwardly mobile immigrants—middle-class Jews and Germans, primarily—they were certain would soon flood this newly commutable neighborhood. What they didn't anticipate were recessions and panics in 1893, 1907, and 1910, which deflated the housing market; and badly affected the development of large numbers of homes on the Upper West Side.

Because of these miscalculations, property owners were left with hundreds of unrentable homes and soon began doing what nobody else had done in the history of the United States: renting or selling brand-new, often beautifully appointed buildings to the race that had, until that point, always made do with the tumble-down, ghetto housing no other group would accept. In 1905, a pioneering real estate agent named Philip Payton persuaded a white landlord to rent him 31 W. 133rd St. so that he could re-lease it to African Americans. The landlord accepted the offer because Payton promised to pay far more than the going rate, a substantial $5 more per tenant per month (a lot of money in those days). Several other white landlords panicked and bought the buildings in order to evict the black tenants, but by then it was too late. Payton had the funding to buy several other buildings, and black migration into the area began in earnest.

So what you'll see in Harlem today are homes and businesses that were not created by or for African Americans. These lovely buildings, however, did allow for a standard of living and security, primarily in the 1920s, '30s, and '40s, that was unprecedented for African Americans in the United States.

Another thing you won't see in Harlem today are the Jazz Era nightclubs and theaters for which the area was famed. Tragically, those historic sites were torn down. But we will visit places where the great figures of Harlem, men and women such as Langston Hughes, Malcolm X, Mother Hale, and Adam Clayton Powell, Jr. lived, worked and made history.

A note about this tour: Harlem is the largest neighborhood in Manhattan by far, stretching from approximately 116th Street all the way up to the river. There's no way to see it all in one walk, so I've devised a tour that gives you a taste of the area's history from different eras. I'd urge you to go back, and see such historic gems as Striver's Row, Sugar Hill, and the home of Alexander Hamilton.

Walking Tour: Harlem

❶	Mt. Olivet Baptist Church
❷	Hale House
❸	4-16 West 122nd St.
❹	Mount Morris Park
❺	55 West 125th Street
❻	The Former Home of Poet Langston Hughes
❼	Collyer Park
❽	The Corner of Adam Clayton Powell Jr. Boulevard and 125th Street
❾	Blumstein's Department Store
❿	The Apollo Theater

1 Mt. Olivet Baptist Church

Stand across the street (120th St. and Malcolm X Blvd., aka Lenox Ave.) so that you can get a better look at this prominent Harlem Church (over the years, Presidential candidate Howard Dean and former Venezuelan President Hugo Chavez have addressed the congregation). If you look closely you'll notice something that one doesn't usually see on the façade of a church: several Stars of David. This church epitomizes the neighborhood's transformation over the years; it was built (in 1907) to be the neighborhood's first synagogue. The architect, the first Jewish architect licensed in New York State, based its design on that of the

Second Temple in Jerusalem, which had just been excavated, making worldwide headlines. Remember the name Louis Blumstein, a prominent member of this congregation, as he'll reappear later in this walking tour.

Walk uptown on Broadway, turn left on 122nd Street, and turn left until you reach 152 W. 122nd St. which is:

2 Hale House

We jump forward now a century to 1969 when an act of kindness changed the lives of thousands of children. A young woman named Lorraine Hale was driving on 146th Street when she saw a drugged-out mother nodding off on the street, her 2-month old baby almost slipping from her arms. Ms. Hale got out of the car and told the mother she needed to get treatment and that she could leave the baby with her own mother—Clara McBride Hale—while she got sober. The next day the drug-addicted mother did just that, and soon hundreds of babies were being left with "Mother Hale," who pioneered methods of treating babies born with addictions (and also took in a lot of HIV-positive babies).

This all happened during the 1960s, '70s, and '80s, a period of steep decline for Harlem, a time when many landlords stopped maintaining and even abandoned the buildings in the neighborhood (in 1960, a census showed only 50% of the housing in Harlem to be deemed sound, as opposed to 85% elsewhere in the city). Harlem became synonymous with urban decay, and Hale House, though a controversial institution later, was one of its few rays of hope. You can read more about the house and its mission on the plaque at the door.

Walk back to Malcolm X Boulevard, cross the street and walk east on 122nd Street until you get to:

3 4–16 West 122nd Street

This is not a famous building, but a very beautiful one and a good example of the kind of talent that was enlisted to build Harlem's brownstones when the neighborhood was first being developed. This one is by architect William Tuthill, who went on to design Carnegie Hall later in his career. Like many Gotham brownstones, the main entrance is on the second, not the ground, floor. Why? It's a tradition left over from when the Dutch settled Manhattan. A people from a sea-level land, prone to flooding, it was their tradition to place the more important rooms above ground level, locating the kitchen and servants quarters below.

Look towards the park at the east end of the street. It used to be called:

4 Mount Morris Park

Named for General Roger Morris, this park was created in honor of the very first American victory in the Revolutionary War. It was in the vicinity of where you're standing now, on September 16, 1776, that George Washington engaged in what he called a "brisk little skirmish" with the Redcoats. Just 1 month earlier, the largest British expeditionary fleet in history had sailed into New York Harbor, bringing with it 21,000 troops, a full 40% of all the men engaged by the Royal Navy at that time. In quick order, these trained soldiers slaughtered approximately 2,800 American militiamen at the Battle of Brooklyn, forcing Washington to escape Brooklyn under cover of night and hightail it to the northern reaches of Manhattan. At the small battle on this site, called the Battle of Washington Heights, enemy buglers taunted the colonists by playing the call that traditionally ended a foxhunt. Enraged, Washington called for reinforcements and drove the Redcoats back to what is now the Upper West Side. It was the first time his soldiers had won an engagement and did much to boost morale. Today, the park is known as Marcus Garvey Park, in honor of the founder of the Universal Negro Improvement Association.

Walk back to Malcolm X Boulevard and walk uptown to:

5 55 West 125th Street

Former President Bill Clinton had his first office, after he left the presidency, on the top floor of this high-rise building. You may remember that he decided to move to Harlem after a public outcry over the taxpayer-supported rent on his proposed Carnegie Hill office space (a whopping $850,000 per year, more than all of the other presidential offices combined). Alas, he's no longer headquartered here, but it was an appropriate choice: Harlem is one of the Business Empowerment Zones his administration created, and you'll see all around you signs of the prosperity that policy engendered.

Walk West to Fifth Avenue, turn uptown and walk to 127th St., Turn east and walk to 20 E. 127th St.:

6 The Former Home of Poet Langston Hughes

Hughes bought this brownstone in 1947, likely with the royalties he received for writing the libretto to the Broadway musical "Street Scene." His was an open house, with other writers, musicians, and friends from the neighborhood dropping by at all hours. He was particularly known for his kindness to the children of the neighborhood; he called the garden in front of his house "The Children's Garden" and let the little ones plant whatever they wanted to there. It was in this house that he wrote his famous book length poem, *Montage for a Dream Deferred*. Some decades after his death in 1967, the house was turned into a poetry center, but unfortunately, it was forced to close in 2007, due to lack of funding.

Walk back to Fifth Avenue and continue uptown to the corner of 128th Street. Here you'll see:

7 Collyer Park

Are you a fan of the TV show *Hoarders*? Here lived the original hoarders, a pair of reclusive brothers who lived in this home from the 1880s until their deaths in 1947. Though rumors swirled about their compulsive behavior, nobody knew the extent of their hoarding until both were found dead in their home, surrounded by 140 tons of stuff, including books, musical instruments, towering stacks of newspapers, baby carriages, guns, furniture, and all manners of junk. All were set with booby traps to ward off outsiders. It took over a year to clear out the house, which was eventually razed, as it was rotting on its foundations. If you need a rest, you can sit in this pretty pocket park for a moment before moving on.

Walk back to Malcolm X Boulevard and walk downtown to 125th Street. Turn right (West) and if you have time, stop at the Studio Museum (p. 141) to see the art. If not, proceed on to:

8 The Corner of Adam Clayton Powell Jr. Boulevard and 125th Street

Abuzz with history, this intersection is one of the most important in Harlem. Look over first at the windswept northwest corner, where the statue of Adam Clayton Powell, Jr., Harlem's first African American Congressman, stands. This is also the spot where Malcolm X spent many long hours lecturing to Harlem residents on behalf of the Nation of Islam. His message—"We are blacks first and everything else second"—was such a powerful one, and he was such an effective orator, that before he left the NOI that organization had nearly half a million members (it dwindled rapidly after his resignation). His message, which rejected non-violence and condemned integration as cultural suicide, was a controversial one that went directly against the goals of the NAACP, the largest civil rights organization of the time.

Now, look across the street at the tall white building with geometric patterns climbing up its façade, the former Hotel Theresa. If your olfactory glands have any imagination, you may detect a hint of Cuban cigar smoke in the air. In 1960, a young Fidel Castro was scheduled to speak at the United Nations, but no hotel in town would take him and his contingent. After he threatened to set up camp on the lawn of the United Nations, the government ordered the city hotels to accommodate him, but Castro got into an argument with the hotel he had picked, the Shelburne. So, after a conversation with Malcolm X, he moved up here to the Hotel Theresa. It was a dramatic gesture, and one he hoped would show his solidarity with Black Americans (and perhaps encourage a few to register with the Communist Party). Repeated clashes between the pro- and anti-Castro forces outside the hotel kept the 258-police contingent assigned to Castro busy. On his second day at the Theresa, Nikita Khrushchev came to visit, and his police contingent plus Castro's created the greatest show of force Harlem had ever witnessed (to this day it hasn't been matched).

Four years later, when Malcolm X broke with the Nation of Islam to found his own Organization of Afro-American Unity (open to people of all religions), he held his press conference at the Theresa and soon afterwards moved his offices here. When he was assassinated in 1965, just one year later, this is where crowds gathered to mourn until they were dispersed by the police.

Walk further West until you get to 147 W. 125th St., the former:

9 Blumstein's Department Store

When it opened its doors in 1900, this was the neighborhood's largest and most exclusive store, built at a cost of $1 million (notice the beautifully worked copper ornamentation on the facade, a mix of Art Deco and Spanish Renaissance in its patterning). And yes, it was owned by Louis Blumstein, whom we met at the beginning of this tour.

In 1934, the Urban League began a campaign, spearheaded by Reverends John H. Johnson and Adam Clayton Powell, Jr., to boycott and picket the store until it changed its hiring practices. Up until that point, though the vast majority of its clientele was African American, Blumstein's refused to hire any black store clerks (a particularly maddening policy as this was the Great Depression and jobs were scarce). The action lasted 2 months, with picketers carrying signs with the simple but effective request DON'T BUY WHERE YOU CAN'T WORK. Blumstein's finally relented, hiring 34 African-American women as clerks. Dr. Martin Luther King, Jr., often spoke of this strike in his speeches, as an example of the power of non-violent protest.

In 1958, Dr. King himself was at the center of history at Blumstein's. He was seated at a table signing copies of his book *Strides Towards Freedom* when an African-American woman named Izola Ware Curry got to the front of the line. After asking, "Are you Martin Luther King?" she pulled a letter opener out of the book she was carrying. Shouting "You Communist, you Communist!" she stabbed him in the chest. Dr. King was rushed to Harlem Hospital with the blade still in (had it been removed he would have bled to death) and underwent surgery. The next morning, the *New York Times* reported that had King sneezed, he would have died, as the blade was touching his aorta. From his hospital bed, King issued a letter of forgiveness to Wade, who was committed to an insane asylum for the act (she had had a long history of mental instability).

Walk further West until you get to 147 W. 125th St.:

10 The Apollo Theater

For years 125th Street was known as the "Great Black Way," in comparison to Broadway's "Great White Way." This was the theater district of Harlem. Only a few of these great show palaces still exist, but right in front of us is the most famous and influential: The Apollo Theater (253 W. 125th St.). A whites-only burlesque house until 1934, it changed its policy and its lineup, becoming a music hall in January of that year and introducing the legendary "Amateur Night" a few months later. Among the many big names who jumpstarted their careers at Amateur Night: Sarah Vaughn, Lauryn Hill, James Brown, and most famously Ella Fitzgerald, who was planning to dance but fortuitously changed her mind backstage right before she went onstage. Amateur night continues here every Wednesday at 7:30pm, and it's as raucous as ever, with wild cheers for the performers the audience enjoys and painfully cruel shouts and boos for those who get the axe. If they're offering tours, do take one (see p. 206 for more information on that).

NEW YORK CITY ENTERTAINMENT & NIGHTLIFE

I t isn't a boast but a plain fact: from opera to jazz, from nightclubs to bars, from concert recitals to theater and dance, New York offers the greatest variety and sheer quantity of evening entertainment in America.

It's a dizzying but important subject because most visitors enjoy New York's nightlife to the same extent they enjoy its daytime sightseeing. And in New York, unlike most other American cities, the sidewalks aren't "rolled up" when darkness descends. In the Big Apple (one of the only cities in the country that operates its public transportation throughout the night), the bright lights stay on until 4am and you owe it to yourself to take in all the after-dark excitement.

To make them easy to peruse, I've grouped the nighttime opportunities in this chapter by entertainment category.

THE NYC THEATER SCENE

You can traipse the entire Metropolitan Museum of Art, attend a Yankees game, and ascend to the top of the Empire State Building, but you can't really say you've *done* New York until you spend an evening at the theater. It's an essential element in a NYC vacation, like going to the beach in Hawaii or slurping pasta in Italy. And though every 3 years or so some major critic issues an obituary declaring New York theater is dead, somehow the corpse continues to rise from its glittering grave, producing Pulitzer Prize-winning plays, fine new musicals, and theatrical events of all sorts that just may, when done well, shift your perspective an iota, give you a peephole into another culture, or perhaps illuminate, for 2 fleeting hours, the human condition.

Ticket Tactics

Let's start with a trade secret that no one in the theater industry wants you to know: Only suckers and out-of-towners pay full price for most Broadway and Off-Broadway shows (see the box on p. 197 for an explanation of the difference between the types of theater). I'd say that, on average, only five or six shows *per year* get away with charging full price for their seats

THEATER basics

There are three types of theaters in NYC: Broadway, Off-Broadway, and Off-Off-Broadway:

Broadway shows: Tend to be performed in the Times Square area (the one exception being the shows at Lincoln Center). They cost, without a discount, between $77 for a balcony seat (as little as $65 at some plays), to $157 for an orchestra seat, all the way up to $350 for a so-called "premium" seat at certain musicals.

Off-Broadway shows: Are performed in venues all over town, with a good many now clustered in the Union Square area. Top prices for Off-Broadway musicals rarely go above $100, with plays topping out (usually) at $89. Off-Broadway theaters are much smaller than those on Broadway, pay less to cast and crew, and are thus able to present more controversial, less commercial plays and musicals. Many of the recent Pulitzer Prize drama winners began as Off-Broadway shows.

Off-Off-Broadway shows: Are staged in very small theaters, often featuring experimental works or actors' showcases. These productions also play in theaters all over town; some of the best-known venues are PS 142, The Performing Garage, and Here. Although you'll rarely see these shows advertised or even reviewed in the *New York Times*, they will be listed in the *Village Voice* and *Time Out* magazine.

Schedule: Broadway and most Off-Broadway shows perform eight times a week, most commonly Tuesday through Sunday, though some do play on Monday (instead of Tues or Sun). Matinee (daytime) performances are usually presented at 2pm on Wednesday and Saturday, and 3pm on Sunday. Evening performances take place 8pm Wednesday through Saturday, 7pm on Tuesday night. And if a show is geared towards families, evening performances may be at 7pm on other nights of the week, as well.

eight shows per week. For the other 60-or-so productions, discounts *are the norm,* not the exception. Don't believe anyone who tells you otherwise.

BUYING TICKETS ONLINE

Booking tickets before you arrive in New York City is the most time-effective strategy. You're able to schedule your time in advance, get early dinner reservations. and not waste any of your previous vacation hours standing in line at box offices or ticket brokers. To do so at a discount, try **Playbill.com** or **Theatermania.com,** both of which require free registration to see the discount codes; or **BroadwayBox.com,** which is open to all and doesn't require registration. In general, discounts will range from 35% to 50% off, though a handling fee will be tacked onto the cost of your ticket, varying by venue (it can come to as much as $10).

If you're a total theater maven, and planning to see as many shows as you can handle, or someone who comes into NYC regularly to see theater, consider joining the "Gold Club" at TheaterMania. It costs $99 a year, and entitles the participant to even more deeply discounted shows (usually those who join are rewarded with a pair of free Broadway tickets). Other theater ticket clubs include **Audience Extras,** for $115 a year (www.audienceextras.com), and **Play-by-Play,** for $115 a year (www.play-by-play.com).

For the big hits, shows like "Book of Mormon" or "Matilda," you can use the sites above (though they won't be able to provide you with a discount), or you can deal directly with **Telecharge** (© **212/239-6200;** www.telecharge.com) or **Ticketmaster** (© **212/307-4100;** www.ticketmaster.com), both of which handle Broadway and Off-Broadway shows and most concerts. I don't recommend going through a broker not listed in this book, as their ticket prices can be outrageous. Usually, if you plan far enough ahead, it's possible to get tickets to even the most popular shows through the sources listed here.

GETTING YOUR TICKETS ONCE YOU'RE IN NYC

Tickets are sold directly at **theater box offices,** and by using them, you don't have to pay the service charge (though you rarely get a discount this way, unless you have a code from one of the websites above). However, by going to the box office, you may be able to score better seats. Often, on the day of performance, the "house seats" that are reserved for the use of the cast and crew (who pass them along to family members, friends, and investors), are sold to the general public. And these are primo seats, in the center and near the stage.

You should also try the **Broadway Concierge & Ticket Center,** run by the League of American Theatres and Producers (the same people behind www.livebroadway.com, above) at the **Times Square Visitor's Center,** 1560 Broadway, between 46th and 47th streets (Mon–Fri 9am–7pm; Sat–Sun 8am–8pm; hours subject to seasonal changes; www.timessquarenyc.org). They may have tickets for otherwise sold-out shows, both for advance and same-day purchase, and charge only about $5 extra per ticket.

Last but certainly far from least, is the discount-ticket **TKTS Booth.** Its main branch is located on 46th Street, between Broadway and Seventh Avenue (hours: Mon and Wed–Sat 3pm–8pm, Tues 2pm–7pm, and for matinees only Wed and Sat 10am–2pm and Sun 10am–2pm). It also has a Brooklyn outlet (at 1 MetroTech Center at the corner of Jay Street and Myrtle Avenue Promenade in Brooklyn, hours: Mon–Sat 11am–6pm), and one at the South Street Seaport in Manhattan (at the corner of Fulton and South sts., hours: Mon–Sat 11am–6pm, Sun 11am–4pm). TKTS presents a greater breadth of shows than do the online discounters, but you pay for that choice with your time (during busy periods the wait in line can be up to an hour). Those who do brave the line are often rewarded with $45 seats to Off-Broadway plays and $75 seats at big Broadway musicals.

But there are ways to **"game" the TKTS line,** including:

o **Go to the TKTS in Brooklyn or at the South Street Seaport.** You'll rarely wait longer than 20 minutes at either outlet, and at both you can purchase matinee tickets the day before a show (at the Times Square booth, ticket purchases are day-of-show only). The only downside at these two outlets: No day-of-matinee tickets are sold.

o **Don't go early.** Tickets are released from the theaters to the booths throughout the day, so you don't necessarily increase your chances of getting the show you want by going early in the day, or waiting in line before the booth opens. Instead, go when it's most convenient.

o **Go to the theater on a Monday or Tuesday night,** the slowest nights of the week. You'll encounter almost no line and will have a much bigger selection than usual.

o **Pick a play instead of a musical.** TKTS has one dedicated window for plays only, and its line is always shorter.

Warning: Do not buy from the **scalpers** who roam up and down the line at TKTS. A few may be legitimate—say, a couple from the 'burbs whose companions couldn't make it for the evening—but they could be swindlers passing off fakes for big money. It's not a risk worth taking.

Here are a few additional methods of garnering discounts or getting into sold out shows:

Rush Tickets: A number of Broadway and Off-Broadway theaters have taken to offering "rush tickets" for the first row of seats on the day of a show. The average price is $25 for these neck-benders (it's preferable to be a couple of rows back—the sightlines are better and there's less danger of being spit on by performers). The rules and methods for their sale vary by show; sometimes these seats are only available to students, while in other cases any member of the public can get them (call the theater in advance to ask). In the past, these seats were given out on a first-come, first-served basis, but recently a number of the theaters have adopted a more humane lottery method.

Standing Room: Sold-out shows offer "standing room" tickets on the day of the show only, to about 10 people per show (depending on the size of the theater). They are sold at 10am when the box office opens, and for the really popular shows a line will form an hour earlier for these "standing spots" at the back of the house. The cost of these non-seats range from $15 to $25, again depending on the show.

Student and youth discounts: Although Broadway theaters won't care how old you are or what you do, a number of the Off-Broadway houses do sell specially priced seats (sometimes for as little as $15) to students and those under 30. While some do this on the day of show only, others allow these theatergoers to purchase in advance with the correct identification. Among the theaters that usually discount in this way are the New York Theater Workshop, the Pearl Theater Company, and The Roundabout Theater Company. You'll also occasionally find $5 tickets to Off-Broadway shows for teenagers (and their chaperones) at a wonderful website called **High Five** (www.high5tix. org). If you're traveling with a teen, check the site before buying any tickets.

CHOOSING THE RIGHT SHOW TO SEE

I'll admit it: I'm a walker. If I accidentally pick an awful show, I leave at intermission rather than fork out extra money to the babysitter so that I can sit through something dull. It doesn't happen that often because over the years, I've formulated the following rules to help me choose which shows to see.

Skip the long-running Broadway musicals: There should be an expiration date on Broadway musicals, just as there is on milk. After about 2 years, they turn sour.

Here's why: The first cast usually leaves around the 1-year mark, and then a second cast is announced to much fanfare. When it comes to the third go-round, the big-name actors aren't willing to take over the roles, so they get lesser-known pros in the parts. These second-tier actors aren't any less talented, but because they have no clout they never get to rehearse with the director and put their own mark on the role. Instead, they are "put in" by a stage manager, and are expected to re-create what the previous actor did; that can lead to wooden, dull performances. The chorus, which usually stays with the show for a few years, simply becomes bored and starts sleepwalking through their performances. That's why you'll often see a better show if you go to a newer one.

You can find out how long a show has been on by calling the theater; asking the folks at the TKTS booth; looking at Telecharge.com (which lists when shows opened); or checking *The New Yorker* magazine, which lists "long-running" shows separately in its theater section.

Beware the "un-nominated" Broadway shows: It doesn't matter which shows win a Tony Award—that's pretty much a crapshoot. But the nominating committee, which is made up of distinguished theater professionals—actors, writers, producers, and the like—is savvy about theater and usually does a good job rewarding the most interesting shows with nominations in late May. If a new play, musical, or revival can't manage to get a nod (and in some years there's very little competition for nominations), take it as a sign that your theater dollars may be better spent elsewhere. Each show that gets nominations will trumpet that fact in their ads (but don't punish the Off-Broadway shows, as only Broadway shows are eligible for the Tonys). A good source for this type of information is the Telecharge.com site, which lists nominations and awards for each show.

Do some research before you buy: The Web is a treasure trove of information, including past reviews of shows. Instead of going blindly to the TKTS line (see above), surf to **www.nytimes.com, www.timeout.com/newyork,** or **www.nymag.com** before you get to New York and pick a show that's garnered a fair number of good reviews. While the reviewers aren't always right (and lately, I think the *New York Times* critics have been really off in their recommendations; you can read synopses of chief reviewer Ben Brantley's views at **www.didhelikeit.com**), at least by reading up you'll have a better idea of what the shows are about.

Avoid "Juke Box" Musicals: *Mamma Mia* set off a frenzy of shows that simply take the catalogue of some famous pop composer and then string songs together with a silly, inorganic story. In most cases you'll hear better renditions of these songs at your local theme park—don't go!

CONSIDER SEEING AN OFF-BROADWAY SHOW

Because of the huge financial pressures on Broadway producers, they usually (but not always) stick with tried-and-true formulas, revivals, or shows with a clear marketing hook. For anything slightly edgy or even intellectual, you often need to go to the smaller Off-Broadway theaters (see the "Theater Basics" box, p. 197). These theaters also tend to charge substantially less for tickets, sometimes shaving $25 to $50 off the cost.

Although I can't guarantee that you'll always see a great show, the following Off-Broadway theater companies consistently produce exciting, award-winning productions. They are:

o **New York Theatre Workshop** (79 E. 4th St., between Second Ave. and the Bowery; ℂ **212/460-5475;** www.nytw.org; subway: 6 to Astor Place). An intellectually heady and sometimes avant garde company. **Biggest hits** include: *Once* (Tony Award), *Rent* (Pulitzer Prize), *Quills,* and *Mad Forest.*

o **Playwrights Horizons** (416 W. 42nd St., between Seventh and Eighth aves.; ℂ **212/564-1235;** www.playwrightshorizons.org; subway: 1, 2, 3, N, R, S to Times Square or A, E, C to 42nd St.). Dedicated to nurturing the art of the writer (lyricists and librettists as well as playwrights), Playwrights has always had a great eye for

KIDS TAKE THE STAGE: family-friendly THEATER

Broadway theaters do not allow children under the age of 5 to attend, nor do they give discounts to kids (with the exception of the Kids Night On Broadway discount program, go to www.kidsnightonbroadway.com; discounts are usually only offered in February). But beyond Broadway is affordable, often mesmerizing theater that's aimed squarely at the pre-puberty crowd, with dozens of offerings each week. The following organizations, in particular, present a roster of consistently challenging and entertaining family shows.

The **New Victory Theater,** 229 W. 42nd St., 10th Floor, between Seventh and Eighth avenues ((℃ **646/223-3010;** www.newvictory.org), books shows from around the U.S. and abroad that are inventive and smart enough for the entire family to enjoy. One musical that made its debut here even moved to Broadway (now how about that for a kiddie show?). Past offerings have included quality puppet shows, acrobatic and circus troupes, "new vaudeville" acts, and theater pieces.

The **Swedish Cottage Marionette Theatre** (℃ **212/988-9093;** www.centralpark.org or www.cityparksfoundation.org) puts on marionette shows for kids at its 19th-century Central Park theater throughout the year. Reservations are a must.

While David Mamet hardly seems like a playwright for the kiddies, the "Atlantic for Kids" series is making a go of it at the **Atlantic Theater Company,** 336 W. 20th St., between Eighth and Ninth avenues (℃ **212/645-8015;** www.atlantictheater.org), which Mamet co-founded with Academy Award–nominated actor William H. Macy.

Every summer, the marvelous touring theater company **Theaterworks USA** (www.theaterworksusa.com) presents a summer of free theater for kids at the Lucille Lortel Theater. Musicals written and performed by up-and-coming Broadway talents, they are among the most delightful shows in town, for people of all ages.

Look for Young People's Concerts and Kidzone Live!, in which kids get to interact with orchestra members prior to curtain time, at the **New York Philharmonic** (www.nyphil.org/education; p. 204). Also check to see what's on for the entire family at **Carnegie Hall** (www.carnegiehall.org; p. 204), which offers family concerts at prices as low as $6; plus the CarnegieKids program, which introduces kids ages 3 to 6 to basic musical concepts through a 45-minute music-and-storytelling performance. For kid-friendly classical music, see what's on at **Bargemusic** (p. 203), which presents occasional chamber-music concerts geared for kids. And don't forget Jazz for Young People, Wynton Marsalis's stellar family concert series and curriculum at **Jazz at Lincoln Center** (www.jalc.org/educ; p. 211).

talent, producing the works of Stephen Sondheim, Christopher Durang, A. R. Gurney, and Wendy Wasserstein. **Biggest hits include:** *Clybourne Park* (Tony Award), *Driving Miss Daisy* (Pulitzer Prize), *Sunday in the Park with George* (Pulitzer Prize), *The Heidi Chronicles* (Pulitzer Prize).

o **The Public Theater** (425 Lafayette St., off Astor Place; ℃ **212/564-1235;** www.publictheater.org; subway: 6 to Astor Place). A strong emphasis on American playwrights, especially Asian-, Latin-, and African-American writers, has kept this theater relevant and popular since 1967. In all, Public Theater productions have been awarded 40 Tonys (for shows that moved to Broadway) and 138 Off-Broadway or "Obie" awards. **Biggest hits include:** *A Chorus Line* (Pulitzer Prize), *Hair* (Tony Award), *Bring in 'Da Noise, Bring in 'Da Funk* (Pulitzer Prize), *Topdog/Underdog* (Pulitzer Prize).

o **Signature Theatre** (555 W. 42nd St.; ℂ **212/244-PLAY** [222-7529]; www. signaturetheatre.org; subway: A, E, C to 42nd St.). Devotes each season to just one playwright, who gets to choose which works he or she wants represented. Because the theater picks only established playwrights to showcase, the productions are often peopled by these bigwigs' big-name actor friends, meaning that star-gazing is virtually guaranteed. **Biggest hits include:** *Burn This* (with Edward Norton) and *The Fifth of July* (with Robert Sean Leonard and Parker Posey).

o **The Vineyard Theatre** (108 E. 15th St., off Union Square; ℂ **212/353-0303;** www.vineyardtheatre.org; subway: 4, 5, 6, N, R to Union Square.). The Vineyard may well be the biggest risk-taker of the major Off-Broadway theaters, presenting out-and-out performance art alongside less far-out plays and musicals. When they're good, they're great; and when their shows miss the mark, they're still usually intellectually intriguing. **Biggest hits include:** *Avenue Q* (Tony Award), *Three Tall Women* (Pulitzer Prize), and *How I Learned to Drive* (Pulitzer Prize).

CLASSICAL MUSIC, OPERA & DANCE

New York has grown into one of the world's major opera, music, and dance centers. The season generally runs September through May, but there's usually something going on at any time of year.

Opera

Metropolitan Opera ★★★ Everything about attending an opera here is grand—from the entrance you'll make past hanging Chagall murals to the world-class singers you'll hear (such as Renee Fleming) to the pomp and glitz of the productions themselves. The lovely little secret about the Met is that the cheap seats get the best sounds. Sit in the theater's ground floor section and you may have trouble making out the words, but buy a "family circle" seat, and the voices will float up to you in all their crystalline clarity. The Met makes 200 $20 rush tickets available for Monday through Thursday shows, 2 hours before curtain (get in line early!); 50 of them are set aside for seniors 65 and older, and can be obtained by calling the main number (proof of age required). *Warning:* Don't show up late, unless you want to watch the first act on a video screen in the basement; the Met does not seat latecomers. At the Metropolitan Opera House, Lincoln Center, Broadway and 64th St. ℂ **212/362-6000.** www.metoperafamily.org. Subway: 1 to 66th St.

New York City Opera ★★ The Met's sister company is an institution with a mission. Make that three missions, actually: to champion American singers (Beverly Sills got her start here), to perform contemporary or forgotten operas (though not exclusively), and to serve as the "People's Opera," as former Mayor Fiorella

LINCOLN CENTER: A one-stop-shop FOR CULTURE

Lincoln Center (a complex of giant theaters on the west side of Manhattan, flanking Columbus Avenue between 62nd and 65th Streets) hosts everything from major symphonic premieres to the Big Apple Circus to Fashion Week. It's most famous for its presentation of classic works of music, dance, opera, film and theater, and towards that end houses a number of permanent companies, as well as playing host to the world's leading performing arts organizations of all kinds.

Resident companies include: The **Chamber Music Society of Lincoln Center** (✆ 212/875-5788; www.chambermusicsociety.org); the **Film Society of Lincoln Center** (✆ 212/875-5600 for an automated schedule or 212/875-5601 for the box office; www.filmlinc.com); and **Lincoln Center Theater** (✆ 212/362-7600; www.lct.org), the latter of which houses both a well-respected Broadway and Off-Broadway theater.

For details on the **Metropolitan Opera,** the **New York City Ballet, the Juilliard School,** the phenomenal **New York Philharmonic,** and the **American Ballet Theatre,** which takes up residence here every spring, see "Classical Music, Opera & Dance," in this chapter.

Most of the companies' **major seasons** run from about September or October to April, May, or June. Summer brings outdoor/indoor events like **Midsummer Night's Swing,** with partner dancing, lessons, and music on the plaza in July; August's **Mostly Mozart** fest; and **Lincoln Center Festival,** which invites top troupes from across the globe to perform, both indoors and outdoors.

Tickets for performances at Avery Fisher and Alice Tully halls can be purchased through **CenterCharge** (✆ 212/721-6500) or online at **www.lincolncenter.org** (click on "Event Calendar"). Tickets for all Lincoln Center Theater performances can be purchased thorough **Telecharge** (✆ 212/239-6200; www.telecharge.com).

Terrific, 1-hour **guided tours** of Lincoln Center will take you into the bowels of the complex, and sometimes even into rehearsals.

Tours start at 10:30am and 4:30pm at the David Rubinstein Atrium on Broadway (between 62nd and 63rd streets).

LaGuardia, a founder, put it, by keeping prices reasonable. Now this is opera, of course, so premium orchestra seats won't be cheap, but they top out at about a third less than what you'd pay at the Met for similar seats. In 2011, due to financial challenges, City Opera abandoned its lease at Lincoln Center to become a traveling company, dividing its productions between the Brooklyn Academy of Music and City Center. Various locations. ✆ **212/870-5570** (information or box office), or 212/307-4100 for Ticketmaster. www.nycopera.com.

Classical Music

Bargemusic ★   This small theater (125 seats), set on an actual barge, moored near the Brooklyn Bridge, has big views of the Manhattan skyline and acoustics to die for. Pianissimos are more piano here and fortissimos molto-loud, even when played by a solo piano or string quartet. This is one of the few truly intimate stages in the city, and the prices are intimate, too, starting at just $35 a pop. At Fulton Ferry Landing (just south of the Brooklyn Bridge), Brooklyn. ℂ **718/624-2083** or 718/624-4061. www.bargemusic.org. Subway: 2 or 3 to Clark St.; A to High St.; F to York St.

Carnegie Hall ★★ More than 100 years ago, Tchaikovsky himself presided over the opening performance of Carnegie Hall, just one of a legion of great musicians who have graced this famous stage. Today, you'll see such stars as Joshua Bell, Anne Sophie-Mutter, YoYo Ma, The Vienna Symphony, and more—all drawn by the unsurpassed acoustics and the honor of playing this magnificent hall (you can tour it during the daytime; call for info). Ticket prices ricochet up and down, depending on the day of the week, the act and, of course, the theater area in which you choose to sit. 154 W. 57th St. at Seventh Ave. ℂ **212/247-7800.** www.carnegiehall.org. Subway: N, Q, R to 57th St.

New York Philharmonic ★★★ Constantly reinventing itself, the nation's oldest orchestra recently hired one of the youngest musical directors working today, native New Yorker Alan Gilbert. He's shaken things up, in a good way, instituting both a composer-in-residence program and an artist-in-residence program. The latter has attracted serious star power: Pianist Emmanuel Ax was in residence in 2013, and pianist Yeffim Bronfman takes the seat in 2014. Philharmonic tickets range from about $26 to $130, with rush tickets available to students (with ID at pickup) and seniors (63 and older) when the box office opens at 10am Monday through Saturday and at noon on Sunday. A number of concerts feature pre-show talks and meet-the-artist events, and tend to be quite intimate and informative. There are also kids' concerts and free concerts in NYC parks over the summer. At Avery Fisher Hall, 10 Lincoln Center Plaza, Broadway at 65th St. ℂ **212/875-5656.** www.nyphil.org. Subway: 1 to 66th St.

Dance

American Ballet Theater ★★ ABT features more of an emphasis on story ballets than the New York City Ballet—*Coppelia, Swan Lake, Sleeping Beauty*—and tends to produce more bravura stars than NYCB (where the emphasis is on ensemble work). Currently, ABT has a raft of Latino leapers who are thrilling audiences with the artistry and sheer physical prowess of their dancing. At the Metropolitan Opera House (in Lincoln Center). ℂ **212/477-3030.** www.abt.org. Subway: 1 to 66th St.

City Center ★★ Alvin Ailey, the American Ballet Theater, and Paul Taylor perform here, along with other major dance companies. You'll understand why, once you've attended a show in this splendid, Moorish-revival space (formerly a temple). In the basement are the stages of the excellent Manhattan Theatre Club. 131 W. 55th St. (btw. Sixth and Seventh aves.). ℂ **212/247-0430** or 212/581-1212. www.citycenter.org. Subway: F, N, Q, or R to 57th St.; B, D, or E to Seventh Ave.

Dance Theater Workshop ★ Hipper and smaller, DTW cocoons its audiences in dance, from the performance clips that often play near the box office, to the "Meet the Artist" programs after shows, to the wine and snack gatherings at the on-site café, usually attended by the performers after the show. You'll see top talent here, with an emphasis on "flavor-of-the-moment" emerging stars, some of whom have staying power (Bill T. Jones started here, as did David Parsons), and some of whom will ultimately succumb to the unfortunate economics of modern dance (a field in which only a handful of artists are able to make a living). 219 W. 19th St. (btw. Sixth and Seventh aves.). ℂ **212/691-6500.** www.dtw.org. Subway: 1 to 18th St.

ATTEND A tv TAPING

Though it may seem odd to take time out of your vacation to do what you do at home—watch TV—it's the behind-the-scenes elements that make the experience here: the scurrying grips and cameramen, the "warm-up act" before the show, and seeing what the host does when the camera isn't on.

Attending tapings is a very popular activity, so it's important that you request tickets in advance, *far* in advance. In fact, 6 months ahead of time is not too early for a cult hit such as *The Colbert Report*. If you can't plan that far ahead, or are rejected for an advance seat, all hope is not lost—stand-by seats are distributed for most shows. To snag one of these, you'll need to get up early and do a lot of waiting around, but many people on the stand-by list do get in. **One warning:** Stand-by tickets are given out by person, not by couple, so if you're traveling with someone else, both of you have to brave the line to attend the show.

Some shows to try and see:

- *The Daily Show with Jon Stewart:* www.thedailyshow.com/tickets
- *The Colbert Report:* www.colbert nation.com/tickets
- *Good Morning America:* http:// abcnews.go.com/GMA
- *Late Night with David Letterman:* www.cbs.com/shows/late_show/ tickets/or in person at the theater
- *Live with Kelly and Michael:* http://dadt.com/live/get-tickets. html
- *Saturday Night Live:* send email in August only to snltickets@ nbcuni.com
- *The View:* http://abc.go.com/ shows/the-view/tickets

To see the **Today Show,** simply get up at dawn and head over to Rockefeller Center. You'll see where the crowds are that day.

Joyce Theater ★★   The blockbuster modern dance shows tend to play the Joyce and it's not hard to see why: It's simply the best space in the city to see dance—there's not a bad seat in the house. In this renovated, Art Décor-era movie theater, audience sits slightly above the dancers, meaning that you won't be seeing just the feet, or just the bodies—you'll get the whole picture. In past years, this is where Pilobolus has played, as well as the Parson's Dance Company, Jennifer Muller, and Merce Cunningham. In 2015, the Joyce will move, probably, to a Frank Gehry-designed theater on the site of the former World Trade Center. 175 Eighth Ave. (at 19th St.). ℂ **212/242-0800** for tickets, or 212/691-9740 for theater. www.joyce.org. Subway: A, C, or E to 14th St.; 1 to 18th St. Joyce SoHo at 155 Mercer St. (btw. Houston and Prince sts.). ℂ **212/431-9233.** Subway: R to Prince St.; 6 to Bleecker B, D, F, or M to Broadway/Lafayette.

New York City Ballet ★★★   NYCB was founded by Lincoln Kirstein and the 20th century's greatest ballet choreographer, George Balanchine. And it is for Balanchine's work that you still attend performances at the New York City Ballet; his choreography is the staple here and remains as diamond-sharp, elegant, and moving as when they were first performed, some as many as 50 years ago. Balanchine's version of *The Nutcracker* is a holiday classic and one of the most difficult tickets to get each Christmas season. At the David H. Koch Theater at 20 Lincoln Center Plaza, Broadway at 64th St. ℂ **212/870-5570** or Center Charge 212/721-6500. www.nycballet.com. Subway: 1 to 66th St.

LANDMARK MULTI-USE VENUES

Apollo Theater ★★ Is there a more resonant place in all of Manhattan to listen to blues, jazz, or pop music than the legendary Apollo Theater? To me, it's a thrill just to walk past the collage of all of the greats who've played here and then take a seat in this lovely, surprisingly intimate theater (built in 1914, it looks much bigger on TV). Perhaps most famous for launching the careers of Ella Fitzgerald, Aretha Franklin, and Duke Ellington, it still is the venue of choice for all sorts of celebrities from James Brown to Bill Cosby. But Amateur Night on Wednesday remains the headline attraction, a gladiatorial music demonstration where the winners may emerge stars and the losers are skewered with the unkindest of boos and shouted insults. 253 W. 125th St. (btw. Adam Clayton Powell and Frederick Douglass blvds). ℂ **212/531-5300** or -5301. www.apollo theater.com. Subway: B or D to 125th St.

Beacon Theatre ★★ They really knew how to build theaters back in the 1920s: Every seat at this Art Deco landmark has a good view, and the acoustics are remarkable. Which may be why this is such a favorite of the touring bands who make this their New York home. While you won't get the mega-names, you will see talented stars either on the way up or down, names such as ZZ Top, Willie Nelson, Bonnie Raitt, Clay Aiken, and Journey. Prices vary widely by show and seat. 2124 Broadway (at 74th St.). ℂ **212/465-6500.** www.beacontheatre.com. Subway: 1, 2, or 3 to 72nd St.

Brooklyn Academy of Music ★★★ Outside of Manhattan, BAM is the finest of the multi-use facilities. In fact, it may well be the best place in the United States for challenging, inventive, and acclaimed international productions of music, dance, performance art, and theater. It's at BAM where you'll see the latest theater opus from Brit director Peter Brooks, Phillip Glass's newest symphony, or Bill T. Jones/Arnie Zane Dance company in performance.

Along with the large **BAM Opera House** and the smaller **BAM Harvey Theater,** the organization has a dedicated movie theater (The **BAM Rose Cinema**) for art films and a café space where up-and-coming talent perform. I've never been disappointed by anything I've seen here, though occasionally I've had difficulty getting a seat. It may be the most consistently exciting venue in New York, and the 35-minute-long train ride it takes to get here from Manhattan is well worth the effort. (For those squeamish about using the subway late at night, a BAM bus picks up theatergoers after performances are over and brings them to a choice of 15 locations in Manhattan, for a one-way bus fare of $7; info on the website). *For penny pinchers:* Discounts are sometimes offered to students and seniors, so inquire when purchasing a ticket. 30 Lafayette Ave. (off Flatbush Ave.), Brooklyn. ℂ **718/636-4100.** www.bam.org. Subway: 2, 3, 4, 5, M, N, Q, or R to Pacific St./ Atlantic Ave.

Joe's Pub ★★★ It's hard to classify just what Joe's Pub is, beyond a very handsome space, in a landmark building, that hosts performances, and serves strong cocktails and pub food. Its show roster is so all over the map that one can't really say "this is a world music club" or "this is a cabaret," or "this is a rock and roll hall." It's been all those things and more over the years, hosting spoken-word artists, rising singer/ songwriters, jazz bands, pop stars, you name it. All I can tell you is the quality of the

PARK IT! shakespeare, MUSIC & OTHER FRESH-AIR FUN

As the weather warms, New York culture goes outside to play. Here are some top picks:

o **Shakespeare in the Park,** an offering of the Public Theater (see p. 154), casts big stars (Meryl Streep, Jesse Tyler Ferguson) in elaborate, outdoor productions at the outdoor Delacorte Theater in Central Park (near 79th Street in the Center of the Park). Tickets are free, but hard to come by. Either sign up for the daily, online lottery (at **www.public theater.org**) or get on the line in the park. Tickets there are distributed at the theater free on a first-come, first-served basis (two per person) at 1pm on the day of the performance. Would-be theater goers usually line up 3 to 4 hours in advance of the show, but for big hits, people have been known to camp overnight in the park!

o **New York Philharmonic** and the **Metropolitan Opera.** Free concerts are held beneath the stars on Central Park's Great Lawn and in parks throughout the five boroughs. For schedules, call the Philharmonic at ✆ **212/875-5656** or the Metropolitan Opera at ✆ **212/362-6000.** The Philharmonic maintains a list of their upcoming gigs at **www.nyphil. org;** look under "Concerts & Tickets."

o **SummerStage,** at Rumsey Playfield, midpark around 72nd Street, features concerts, primarily, of all types. Over the years, they've featured everyone from the Indigo Girls to Patti Smith to the Martha Graham Dance Company. The season usually runs from mid-June through August. Big-name shows usually charge admission, but often tickets are free (donations always encouraged). For info, visit **www.cityparksfoundations.org/ summerstage.**

The biggest free summer arts spectacular is way downtown, where the **River to River Festival** inundates lower Manhattan in June and July. Stages spring up at indoor and outdoor spots like the South Street Seaport, Battery Park, and the World Financial Center, showcasing live dance, readings, and a smattering of virtually every kind of music you can think of. Information at **www.rivertorivernyc.com.**

talent, whatever it may be, is always high, and the room is wonderfully festive. Too vague? Here's a list of past performers to give you a taste of what you might be in for: Leonard Cohen, David Byrne, fashion designer Isaac Mizrahi, monologist Mike Daisy, Alicia Keys, Dolly Parton, Wynton Marsalis. Confusing, right? But in a good way. 425 Lafayette St. (btw. Astor Place and 4th St.). ✆ **212/539-8778** or 212/967-7555 for advance tickets. www.joespub.com. Subway: 6 to Astor Place.

Roseland ★   There's nothing old-fashioned about the events that take place at this iconic, 1919 ballroom. They range from circuit parties to concerts to conventions. In recent years, some of the performers who have graced the stage here (the house can

Tickets for events at all larger theaters as well as at Hammerstein Ballroom, Roseland, Irving Plaza, B.B. King's, and S.O.B.'s can be purchased through **Ticketmaster** (℮ **212/307-7171;** www.ticketmaster.com).

Advance tickets for an increasing number of shows at smaller venues—including Bowery Ballroom, Mercury Lounge, Jazz Standard, and others—can be purchased through **Ticketweb** (℮ **866/468-7619;** www.ticketweb.com). Do note, however, that Ticketweb can sell out in advance of actual ticket availability. Just because Ticketweb doesn't have tickets left for an event doesn't mean it's completely sold out, so be sure to check with the venue directly. You can also visit **www.live nation.com** for tickets, if you're not automatically directed there by the websites of Roseland, the Apollo, and many others.

Even a sold-out show doesn't mean you're out of luck. There are usually a number of people hanging around at showtime, trying to get rid of extra tickets for friends who didn't show, and they're usually happy to pass them off for face value. You'll encounter pushy professional scalpers, too, who peddle forgeries for exorbitant prices and are best avoided (you'll probably know who the professionals are when you see them). Be aware, of course, that all forms of resale on-site are illegal.

hold up to 3,200 standing) included Beyonce, Nikki Minaj, Björk, and Jason Mraz. Advance tickets can be purchased at the **Fillmore New York at Irving Plaza** box office (see below) without the Ticketmaster service fee. 239 W. 52nd St. (btw. Broadway and Eighth Ave.). ℮ 212/777-6800 or 212/307-7171 for Ticketmaster. www.roselandballroom.com. Subway: C, E, or 1 to 50th St.

Symphony Space ★★ For many years, this has been where the National Public Radio Show "Selected Shorts" taped. But that's just the beginning of the offerings at this always busy theater. It also hosts yearly readings of James Joyce's *Ulysees*, dance performances, world music concerts, and a wonderful series called "New Voices," which features new musical works from Broadway composers (and would-be Broadway composers). The theater has two stages and a small café where cabaret performances and open mic nights often take place. 2537 Broadway (at 95th St.). ℮ 212/864-1414. www.symphonyspace.org. Subway: 1, 2, or 3 to 96th St.

LIVE ROCK, JAZZ, BLUES & MORE

If you're in town to see one of the mega-concerts, you probably already know to go to **Radio City Music Hall** (www.radiocity.com), **Madison Square Garden** (www.madisonsquarden.com), or nearby **Jones Beach** (www.jonesbeach.com). For slightly smaller, but still very rewarding, concerts with artists like Toshi Reagon, Erasure, or The Cowboy Junkies, your best strategy is to see what's on the roster at the following well-respected venues:

- **Bowery Ballroom,** 6 Delancey St. (at Bowery). © **212/533-2111.** www.boweryballroom. com. Subway: F to Delancey St.; J, M, or Z to Bowery.
- **Highline Ballroom,** 431 W. 16th St. (btw. Ninth and Tenth aves.). © **212/414-5994.** www. highlineballroom.com. Subway: A, C, E, or L to 14th St.
- **Irving Plaza,** 17 Irving Place (1 block west of Third Ave. at 15th St.). © **212/777-1224** or 212/777-6800. www.livenation.com/irving-plaza-tickets-new-york/venue/47. Subway: L, N, Q, R, 4, 5, or 6 to 14th St./Union Square.
- **Knitting Factory,** 361 Metropolitan Ave., Williamsburg, Brooklyn (at Havemeyer St.). © **347/529-6696.** http://bk.knittingfactory.com. Subway: L to Bedford Ave.; G to Metropolitan-Grand.
- **Music Hall of Williamsburg,** 66 N. Sixth St., Williamsburg, Brooklyn (btw. Kent and Wythe aves.). © **212/260-4700.** www.musichallofwilliamsburg.com. Subway: L to Bedford Ave.
- **Terminal 5,** 610 W. 56th St. (btw. Eleventh and Twelfth aves.). © **212/260-4700.** www.terminal5nyc.com. Subway: A, B, C, D, or 1 to 59th St./Columbus Circle.

Local Rock & Rockabilly Clubs

Part of the fun of going out and hearing live music in Manhattan is discovering new talent; and just hanging out while someone eager and young plays. For that type of experience, I recommend the following neighborhood clubs:

Arlene's Grocery ★ The longest-running music club on the Lower East Side— the Strokes were discovered here—Arlene's Grocery looks like a typical neighborhood *bodega* from the outside (hence the name). But inside you aren't going to find any groceries. Instead, there's a spacious bar with cozy seating nooks towards the back; and a lower-level club, with a big seatless pit for the audience, sided by a few tables and chairs. Grungy, loud, and dark, it's the epitome of a rock club, and rock is what you'll get here, usually five or six acts per night for a flat cover charge (usually $10). 95 Stanton St. (btw. Ludlow and Orchard sts.). © **212/995-1652.** www.arlenesgrocery.net. Subway: F to Second Ave.

Bitter End ★ Bob Dylan, Linda Ronstadt, Arlo Guthrie, Melissa Manchester . . . all of the big names of the '60s and '70s played The Bitter End, and the club still has the posters to prove it, so old they can't really be called "yellowing," they're now a permanent deep woodsy brown. This is no nostalgia club, though: The Bitter End continues to act as a tryout house for new singer-songwriter types (primarily), many of whom are quite talented. 147 Bleeker St. (btw. Thompson St. and LaGuardia Place). © **212/673-7030.** www.bitterend.com. Subway: A, B, C, D, E, F to W. 4th St.

Mercury Lounge ★★ You visit Mercury Lounge because of the talent of its booker: If there's a band playing in and around New York City that's on the edge of hitting it big, you're going to hear them here. It's just a shame that the room they have to play in isn't more comfortable. With very few seating options, it's not a great place to hang out. Still, if the music is your main priority, this is the place to hit. 217 E. Houston St. (at Essex St./Avenue A). © **212/260-4700.** www.mercuryloungenyc.com. Subway: F to Second Ave.

Rockwood Music Hall ★★ A fun, smaller place (but with two stages you can move between), it features good funk music, country rock, and up-and-coming local artists. Low key, inexpensive, and cool. 196 Allen St. (at East Houston). ✆ **212/477-4145.** www.rockwoodmusichall.com. Subway: F to Second Ave.

Rodeo Bar ★ For country, rockabilly, and even New Orleans–style jazz, Rodeo Bar gives the best imitation of a roadhouse in New York City, rustling up bands with names like *The Dixieland Swingers* and *Angry John and the Killbillies* for live music shows 7 nights a week. There's never a cover charge, and they don't even seem to have a system in place to make sure you buy a drink, probably because you'll feel kinda silly hanging out in a room with peanut shells all over the floor, without a cold one in your mitt. Patrons who pony up for a Tex-Mex meal get a seat right in front of the band, but even if you're just drinking, you can see the show from the bar stools in the back (it's also broadcast on TVs around the room). 375 Third Ave. (at 27th St.). ✆ **212/683-6500.** www. rodeobar.com. Subway: 6 to 28th St.

Jazz, Blues, Latin & World Music

Big-name jazz clubs can be really fun in New York, and likewise, expensive. Music charges and bar-tab/drink minimums can vary dramatically, depending on who's playing; beware especially of a dinner requirement at some, even for a late show. Call ahead or ask the host so you know what you're getting into. Reservations are almost always essential at top spots.

Bill's Place★ A real, honest-to-goodness speakeasy—patrons even have to bring their own booze—this tiny club was started in 2005 in the same historic Harlem brownstone where Billie Holiday was discovered (singing in a previous club there at the age of 17). It's a tiny place, so reservations are required and costs are low (a $20 donation is requested). Performances Friday and Saturday nights only, but by some great old timers who know how to bend a note. 148 W. 133rd St. (btw. Lenox and Seventh aves.). ✆ **212/281-0777.** www.webbmmpr.com/billsplace.html. Admission $15. Subway: 3 to 135th St.

Birdland ★★ Birdland is the second-grandest dedicated facility in the city for jazz, after Jazz at Lincoln Center (p. 211). The huge, 4,000-square-foot amphitheater has dignified gray carpets covering both the floors and walls, and is decorated throughout with black-and-white pictures of the great jazz performers. Though this is not the original Birdland where Coltrane played, it still presents top acts. In fact, if your idea of jazz is a small battalion of men blowing horns, this is where to come, as the large space is able to accommodate big bands that other venues (other than the concert halls around town) simply can't fit. My favorite night is Monday, when Jim Caruso's Cast Party takes place, and Broadway stars from nearby theaters stop by to sing standards and trade wisecracks. 315 W. 44th St. (btw. Eighth and Ninth aves.). ✆ **212/581-3080.** www.birdlandjazz.com. Subway: A, C, or E to 42nd St.

Blue Note ★ The Blue Note has the most corporate feel of all the clubs (perhaps because it's now a chain, with four clubs in Japan and one in Italy). Tables are jammed together, the bar area is even more crowded, and the second floor is given over to a huge souvenir stand of such kitschy items as jazz golf balls and bubble-head figurines of musicians. But it still attracts some genuine talent, so it can't be overlooked, and it does have a terrific late-night series for newcomers. Ticket prices vary widely and can go as high as $45 plus drinks; it's cheaper at the bar (though I'd recommend avoiding

JAZZ AT lincoln center: NOT ACTUALLY AT LINCOLN CENTER

You've heard of food courts? This is the "Jazz court," a massive, three-theater facility with a mini-museum on-site, that has been wedged into the Uptown corner of the city's premiere mall, The Time Warner Center.

Its centerpiece is the **Rose Hall,** a concert hall in the round (usually, though it can also be configured as a standard proscenium theater), with remarkable acoustics and a splendidly be-bop look created by huge boxes of light that change color throughout the night—from subtle creams to striking autumn leaf colors—forming a glowing crown around the performance space. Some seats are actually behind the musicians, giving real aficionados a chance to check out the fingering as the musicians perform. This is where Wynton Marsalis, the center's director, struts his stuff in concert with the Lincoln Center Jazz orchestra. Programs here are primarily focused on swing and New Orleans–style jazz. Though the hall can be intimidating,

Marsalis does his best to keep the informal jazz vibe, encouraging the audience to clap along and call out; usually by the end of the evening, they're doing just that.

The **Allen Room,** the center's second largest space, has a configuration that can be switched to accommodate a dance floor, a seven-tier amphitheater, or cocktail-table seating. Whatever the look, it's a splendidly beautiful room with a wall of glass behind the performing space, lending to the music a Central Park backdrop. **Dizzy's Club Coca Cola** is the most traditional of the theaters, a smaller cocktail and dinner jazz club (again with that transcendent view of Columbus Circle and the park), and the only one of the three facilities to operate year-round, serving as a showcase for some of the younger talents in jazz (called the "upstarts"). In the Time Warner Center (at Broadway and 60th St.). ℰ **212/258-9800.** www.jalc.org. Subway: 1, A, E, C to 59th St.

Live Rock, Jazz, Blues & More

the bar at all costs; you're too far from the music here and the atmosphere is like Grand Central Station at rush hour). 131 W. 3rd St. (at Sixth Ave.). ℰ **212/475-8592.** www.bluenote. net. Subway: A, B, C, D, E, or F to 4th St.

Iridium ★   Iridium tends to attract a slightly older crowd, drawn by earlier shows (the first performance of the night is at 8pm rather than 9pm), better-quality food than at most clubs, and a more intimate setting that allows patrons to get up close and personal with the performers. And what performers they are: Herbie Hancock, Jose Feliciano, Arturo Sandoval, Mose Allison, and saxophonist Houston Person have graced the stage here in recent years. 1650 Broadway (at 51st St.). ℰ **212/582-2121.** www.iridium jazzclub.com. Subway: 1 to 50th St.

S.O.B.'s ★★   To my mind, this is the single most joyous place you can visit between the hours of 8pm and 2am. A large club decorated with fake palm trees and giant parrots, it specializes in the music that you'd find in the places where, well, you'd find parrots and palm trees: India (great *bangra* or Indian pop music parties), the Dominican Republic, Trinidad, Cuba, Puerto Rico, Jamaica, and Brazil. Its "Brazil Show" (scheduled every Saturday) is the longest-running party in New York, featuring throbbing music and a bravura stage show of samba dancing and *capoeira* (a dancelike Brazilian martial art). Admission ranges from $10 to $25. 204 Varick St. (at Houston St.). ℂ **212/243-4940.** www.sobs.com. Subway: 1 to Houston St.

The Village Vanguard ★★★ Though it turned 75 years old in 2010, The Village Vanguard still has the youngest spirit of any of the jazz clubs in town, consistently featuring the best of the new talents and cutting-edge jazz. It also looks the most like a jazz club *should* look, to my mind. You enter a red door and descend a steep staircase to a battered, triangular room, cluttered with posters and pictures of all the greats who played and recorded albums here (Mingus, Davis, Monk, Marsalis). The club has also showcased folkies such as Pete Seeger and Harry Belafonte over the years, but today it's strictly jazz and its prices are among the most reasonable: a $25 cover, plus one drink most nights. *One warning:* The sightlines can be problematic, so get here early to nab a front table. 178 Seventh Ave. S. (just below 11th St.). ℂ **212/255-4037.** www.village vanguard.com. Subway: 1, 2, or 3 to 14th St.

CABARET

An evening spent at a sophisticated cabaret just might be the quintessential New York night on the town. It isn't cheap: Covers can hit $100 at the Carlyle (see below), and require two-drink or dinner-check minimums. Always reserve ahead, and get the low-down when you do. The best of the remaining cabaret rooms (a number have closed in recent years) are:

Café Carlyle ★★ You come here for the big stars of the cabaret world: Judy Collins, Betty Buckley, Barbara Cooke and the like. So the shows are terrific, the setting elegant, but being in this rarified atmosphere will be pricey: admission ranges from $75 to $125 plus a drink minimum. Value-minded cabaret fans can save by reserving standing room (which usually results in a spot at the bar) for $50. On most Mondays, Woody Allen joins the Eddy Davis New Orleans Jazz Band on clarinet to swing Dixie-style ($145 cover). At the Carlyle Hotel, 35 E. 76th St. (at Madison Ave.). ℂ **212/744-1600.** www. thecarlyle.com. Closed July–Aug. Subway: 6 to 77th St.

54 Below ★★ Relatively new on the scene, and, yes, underground on 54th Street, this is Broadway's cabaret. What that means is the vast majority of performers are playing hooky from their real jobs at the big Broadway houses nearby. They're often trying out new material, giving the shows a joyously loose feel, but because the talent is so stellar—Patty Lupone, Sherie Renee Scott, Tony-winner Norbert Leo Butz, and composers Lynn Ahrens and Stephen Flaherty (of *Ragtime* and *Once On This Island*) all took the stage here in 2013—it never feels like a rehearsal. And the club itself is charming, with a 1930s speakeasy décor, much better food than necessary, and great sightlines. A winner! 254 W. 54th St. (btw. Eighth Ave. and Broadway). ℂ **646/476-3551.** www.54below.com. Subway: C, E to 50th St.

STAND-UP COMEDY

Here's the dirty little secret about most comedy clubs (with two exceptions, see below): In order for comics to make a living, they need to play at more than one comedy club in an evening. So you'll often see a very similar show, from club to club. That being said, the clubs below have the most stringent talent-bookers, and therefore the funniest comics on tap. Most clubs charge a cover, along with a two-drink minimum. Reservations recommended.

Carolines on Broadway ★ Unlike the clubs below, Carolines builds its shows around headliners, folks you might see on a sitcom or in a film. Among Caroline Hirsch's regulars are Dave Chapelle, Colin Quinn, Kathy Griffin, Gilbert Gottfried, and a lot of *Saturday Night Live* alumni. 1626 Broadway (btw. 49th and 50th sts.). *C* **212/757-4100.** www.carolines.com. Subway: N or R to 49th St.; 1 to 50th St.

Comedy Cellar ★ When Jerry Seinfeld, Robin Williams, Ray Romano and other equally famous, New York-based comedians decide to "try out" material in front of an audience, they usually drop into this basement room in the Village. On nights when these "biggies" don't make an appearance (and their sets are never advertised in advance), newer headliners take the stage. In general, the comedy is more "blue" (read: vulgar) than at Carolines or Gotham. 117 MacDougal St. (btw. Bleecker and W. 3rd sts.). *C* **212/254-3480.** www.comedycellar.com. Subway: A, B, C, D, E, F, or M to W. 4th St. (use 3rd St. exit).

Gotham Comedy Club ★★ With more elbow room and a booker who picks the "cleaner" comics, Gotham tends to get an older, more sophisticated crowd than the other clubs. And sometimes the talent can be stellar. Comedy Central tapes *Live at Gotham* here with rotating hosts, Tuesday is set aside for new talent, and gay and lesbian comics take the stage Wednesdays at Homo Comicus. Call ahead for reservations. 208 W. 23rd St. (btw. Seventh and Eighth aves.). *C* **212/367-9000.** www.gothamcomedy club.com. Subway: F, N, or R to 23rd St.

Upright Citizens Brigade Theatre ★★★ In 1996, four "missionaries" of improv comedy came to New York from Chicago and founded this theater. Dedicated to the art of "long form improvisation," in which performers riff on one or two subjects for up to half an hour, the troupe's appreciation for the absurd, along with their smart, fearless performing style, quickly made them a hit among jaded young New Yorkers. So much so that Comedy Central created an "Upright Citizens Brigade" TV show. Alumni of the theater include Tina Fey, Seth Myers, and Amy Poehler, and sometimes they come back to perform. With tickets that range from free to $12, a show here will always be less expensive than at the more standard comedy clubs in town. 307 W. 26th St. (btw. Eighth and Ninth aves.). *C* **212/366-9176.** www.ucbtheatre.com. Subway: 1 to 23rd St. UCBeast: 153 E. 3rd St. (btw. Avenues A and B). *C* **212/366-9231.** http://east.ucbtheatre.com. Subway: F to Second Ave.

BARS, COCKTAIL LOUNGES & DANCE CLUBS

Of the many thousands of bars in Gotham, I've chosen a dozen or so either because they'll (likely) be utterly different from those you'd find in your own hometown; or because they're the kind of places where you can easily meet and mingle with locals. Obviously, this is just a small selection, so if you see a watering hole that intrigues you, head in and belly up to the bar!

AUTHOR! AUTHOR! WHERE TO hear THE SPOKEN WORD

As the home base of the American news media, New York is matched only by London in the number of free or inexpensive lectures and readings that take place each evening, year-round. The folks in charge of creating buzz for a new book, product, or even a policy decision know that by getting it in front of the opinion makers here, they have a better chance of getting their message out to the rest of the world. You become their witting audience, not just by attending a lecture but by becoming part of the opinion-making machine (for all the good and the bad that implies).

By the way, readings can be some of the most inexpensive and entertaining events in New York. Many readings are free; most others charge only a small cover.

Thorough weekly listings can be found in *Time Out New York's* "Books" section. there's almost always a major author in town reading at one of the local Barnes & Noble stores (www. bn.com) and Brooklyn bar Pete's Candy

Store (p. 221) for readings and discussions. The Moth's live storytelling performances (www. themoth.org) are another New York phenomenon, often with celebrities doing cameos among the "regular" storytellers.

o **The 92nd St. Y ★★** at Lexington Avenue (**© 212/415-5740;** www.92y.org; subway: 4, 5, or 6 to 96th St.). The top venue in the city for lectures and "conversations" of all types, the 92nd Street Y (originally called the Young Men's Hebrew Association) has been a fixture of the Jewish community since 1845. And though a number of programs are devoted to Jewish topics, the vast range of talks (open to all) in a Monday, Tuesday, and (sometimes) Thursday lecture series are more far-reaching, covering issues of health, politics, gastronomy, ecology, and the arts. Some of the

Tribeca

Tribeca is an curious mix of dive bars left over from the pre-DeNiro era when this was a seedy industrial zone, and the current wave of über-high-end lounges where $18 drinks are the standard.

Bubble Lounge ★ As you might have guessed from the name, this cushy bar specializes in champagne drinks for those with champagne tastes (many cocktails are a whopping $16, and the bar menu includes caviar). Still, if you're in a celebratory mood—and appropriately dressed—this might be a good choice. 228 W. Broadway (btw. Franklin and White sts.). © 212/431-3433. www.bubblelounge.com. Subway: 1 to Franklin St.

Brandy Library ★★ Scholars of, well, booze will appreciate this swank, leather-swathed bar which is set up like a library, but has bottles rather than books on the shelves. If you sit down at a table, you'll be handed a cocktail menu that's a good 2-inches thick, listing tastings of all the world's finest whiskeys, brandys, rums, you name it. Along with just getting a draught of one, tasting flights are offered for those distinguished guests who have spoken here include Nobel laureate Elie Wiesel, newsman Dan Rather, actor Alan Alda, domestic diva Martha Stewart, and comedian Steve Martin.

○ **Nuyorican Poets Café ★,** 236 E. 3rd St., between Avenues B and C (℃ **212/505-8183;** www. nuyorican.org; subway: F to Second Ave.). Since 1989, the Nuyorican has presented poetry, drama, music, and film. The raucous, energetic **Poetry Slams** (the café fields a championship Slam Team) "perform" poetry as a sport: Aspiring stars show up and throw down their work in front of a mixed crowd and three teams of audience judges, who score them on the poetry and presentation. The Friday slams begin around 10pm (cover charge $10) and feature an invited slam poet. Slam Opens are held most Wednesdays ($8

cover). The storefront bar gets crowded quickly, so get there early on Slam nights.

○ **KGB ★,** 85 E. 4th St., between Second and Third avenues (℃ **212/505-3360;** www.kgbbar. com; subway: F to Second Ave.; 6 to Astor Place). This second-floor bar (sadly not wheelchair-accessible) in an old East Village brownstone was once a Ukrainian social club and is decorated with vintage Communist memorabilia. There's never a cover, so it's affordable to refresh your drink often for the readings held almost every night of the week starting at around 7pm. It's a tiny bar, holding perhaps 40 to 50 comfortably, and double that for a hot reader, with theme nights curated by individual writers for poetry, mystery tales, science fiction, and other genres.

who want to sample some of the more esoteric brands. 16 N. Moore St. (at Varick St.). ℃ **212/941-0142.** Subway: 1 to Franklin St.

Walker's ★ Part sports bar (four TVs flank the walls, and football helmets grace the bar) and part nostalgia trip, thanks to the vintage posters on the wall and the pressed tin ceiling, this is the least pretentious place in the 'hood to down a brewsky and a burger. Friendly, not too pricey: what more could you want? 25 N. Moore St. (at Varick St.). ℃ **212/941-0142.** Subway: 1 to Franklin St.

Chinatown & Nolita

Winnie's ★ Up for an adventure? How about a night of Cantonese karaoke at Chinatown's premier dive bar? The drinks here will knock you for a loop (especially the house special "Hawaiian Punch"), but so will much of the howling, er, I mean, singing. Still, if you're up for something silly, different and inexpensive, Winnie's delivers. 104 Bayard St. (btw. Baxter and Mulberry sts.). ℃ **212/732-2384.** Subway: J, M, N, Q, R, Z, or 6 to Canal St.

Mother's Ruin ★   A premiere pick-up joint, with sneaky cocktails that taste less potent than they are (especially those made with the slushy machine), a genetically blessed crowd, and wonderfully tasty bar snacks—that's Mother's Ruin in a nutshell. If you want to hang with the beautiful people, head here (the look of the place is clean and pretty, too, with large windows and a classic pressed tin ceiling). 18 Spring St. (btw. Mott and Elizabeth sts.). ℂ **212/219-0942.** Subway: 6 to Spring St.

The Lower East Side

You won't be short of choices when it comes to LES (Lower East Side) bars, especially in the vicinity of Rivington and Allen streets. Here are two of my favorites.

PKNY ★★   Of course, New York has a tiki bar. We have every other sort of bar and restaurant, so why not? And this one's a hoot, with bamboo-fenced walls, a thatched ceiling and a slack-guitar soundtrack. Every drink comes with a cheerful little hat or umbrella of some sort, but for once, that's not to distract you from the taste. Here the mai tais, zombies, punches, and scorpion bowls are downright delish: never cloying or too sweet, and always topped with the freshest of fruits. 49 Essex St. (btw. Hester and Grand sts.). ℂ **212/777-8454.** www.pk-ny.com. Subway: F, J, M or Z to Delancey/Essex St.

The Box ★★   New York nightlife at its raunchiest, the Box is a Belle Epoque-styled bar/theater, with a Gen Y mentality. Guests arrive around midnight for drinking, dancing and mingling; a burlesque show starts at 1am, always featuring topless dancers and usually some kind of oddball magician, acrobat, transsexual performers or comedian. It can be a lot of fun, though it's definitely R-rated. 189 Chrystie St. (btw. Stanton and Rivington). ℂ **212/982-9301.** www.theboxny.com. Subway: F to Second Ave.

The Ten Bells ★★★   You become 10 times cooler just by walking into this sexy, very European bar that seems entirely candle-lit (though it's not) and has an extraordinary selection of wines and sherries by the glass, from small producers across Europe and the U.S. The seemingly all-French waitstaff will help you select the right vino, and since this is a place you'll want to linger, you may also go for one of the tapas, or cheese plates. As for the clientele: They're an unusually stylish group of folks of all ages, which is unusual for a NYC bar. I think the European jazz soundtrack, kept at a conversation-enhancing level, may be why Ten Bells is popular across generations. 247 Broome St. (btw. Ludlow and Orchard sts.). ℂ **212/228-4450.** www.thetenbells.com. Subway: F, J, M or Z to Delancey/Essex St.

SoHo

Pegu Club ★★★   A refreshingly adult place to start or end an evening, Pegu has an elegant décor, meant to evoke the 19th century officer's club in Burma, for which it's named. The sophisticated cocktails, many of which are made with house-infused liqueurs and bitters, are designed by owner and famed mixologist Audrey Saunders, formerly of Bemelman's Bar in the Carlyle Hotel. 77 W. Houston St., 2nd Floor (at W. Broadway). ℂ **212/473-PEGU [473-7348].** www.peguclub.com. Subway: A, B, C, D, E, F, or M to W. 4th St.

Pravda ★★   Vodka is Czar at this Russian-themed basement lounge, which serves 21 different brands from all parts of the potato-distilling world (cheers Moldova!). You sling them back in a curved-ceiling cellar alongside cyrillac signs posted on the walls and surrounded by chic Soho-types lounging in armchairs and plush circular leather booths. Upstairs is a smaller bar area where things get even more USSR-era; everyone smokes up here, damn the law! By the way, the bar snacks are mighty, fine, too. 281 Lafayette St. (just south of Houston St.). © **212/226-4944.** http://pravdany.com. Subway: F, B or D to Broadway/Lafayette St.; R to Prince St.; 6 to Bleecker St.

The East Village

Death & Company ★★★   The cocktails here are as colorfully named as the bar itself—like the "Scallywag" which mixes five different types of rum (including a 75-year-old one) with two types of bitters, vanilla syrup, and "demarar" syrup; or the perfectly balanced "Mortal Enemy," which blends Dorothy Parker gin with crème de cacao, black current cordial, absinthe, and fresh lime juice. They're all works of liquid art, and can be enjoyed in a civilized fashion, as the bouncer at the door stops letting people in when all the seats are taken; and the music is more likely to be tango or Dixieland jazz than pop. 433 E. 6th St. (btw. First Ave. and Avenue A). © **212/388-0882.** www. deathandcompany.com. Subway: 6 to Astor Place.

Decibel ★★   A gritty, underground sake bar, Decibel has become a center of social life for many of the ex-pat Japanese living in New York City. In fact, most of the clientele are Japanese, the soundtrack is Japanese rock, and the bar food can be exotic (dried squid, anyone?). But all are welcome, and if you feel a bit out of place when you enter this Tokyo transplant, you'll relax once you tuck into any of the 30-odd sakes on offer here each evening. A real experience. 240 E 9th St. (btw. Second and Third aves.). © **212/979-2733.** www.drinkgoodstuff.com. Subway: 6 to Astor Place.

McSorely's Old Ale House ★   If you're a man's man (which I'm obviously not), you'll like New York's oldest continuously operating pub (est. 1854), and one that famously kept out women until a lawsuit in 1970 ended the bigotry (it was a landmark case that ultimately outlawed discrimination in all public places in the city). With sawdust on the rough wooden floor; yellowing photos, and newspaper clips chronicling all of the famous people who got smashed here (Abraham Lincoln was one of them); and a jumble of relics in every nook and cranny (the handcuffs hanging from the ceiling once belonged to Houdini); it's an evocative place to hang out . . . if you're smart enough to visit before 4pm in the afternoon. After that point it gets ugly—kind of like the frat parties I pretended to like in college—with out-of-towners jammed together tighter than in a rush-hour train, shouting over the din. 15 E. 7th St. (btw. Bowery and Second Ave). © **212/473-9318.** Subway: 6 to Astor Place.

PDT ★★★   The name stands for "Please Don't Tell" and is meant to speak to the exclusivity of this bar, which hides in the back of a hot dog stand (you enter through a hidden door in the old-fashioned phone booth—no, really!); and requires a reservation. The owners say it's because they don't want an over-crowded bar, so once the seats and stools are spoken for (the reservations line opens at 3pm), they turn would-be patrons away. It's a lot of rigramarole to get a drink, I admit, but the cocktails here are so unusual and tasty (many created on-site from liquor that's been specially doctored inhouse), and the scene so urbane once you're in, well, it's worth it. And the bar snacks—high quality hot dogs and tater tots—hit the spot. 113 St. Marks Place. (btw. Avenue A and First Ave.). © **212/614-0386.** www.pdt.nyc. Subway: L to First Ave.

Zum Schneider ★★   Ignore the views of the New York cityscape from the large plate-glass windows here and you could be in a beer hall off some gritty side street in

Munich. The beers pack as much of a punch (be careful, unusual German beers such as Kolsch have a higher alcohol content than you may be used to), the bratwurst has that same snap, and if you stick around long enough—till, say, 2 or 3am—revelers here are likely to hop on top of the benches and boogie, just like they do across the pond. It's a fun, loud place with dozens of beers, a rock and hip-hop soundtrack, and a party spirit. Did you ever think you'd be going to a genuine German beer garden when you booked your NYC vacation? 107 Ave. C (at 7th St.). ☏ **212/598-1098.** www.zumschneider.com. Subway: F to Second Ave.; L to First Ave.

The Village & Chelsea

Employees Only ★★★   The place to come if you take your cocktails seriously. A crack staff of veteran bartenders man the place, squeezing their own juices daily and infusing liquors with interesting additions, such as lavender (in the gin) and herbes de Provence (in the vermouth), which they then mix into some of the most bizarre but delicious drinks in town. Upping the festivity factor is a psychic who does readings in the front, and a cute garden out back for those sultry summer nights. 510 Hudson St. (btw. Christopher and W. 10th sts.). ☏ **212/242-3021.** www.employeesonlynyc.com. Subway: 1 to Christopher St.

The Half King ★★   Owned by journalist Sebastian Junger (author of "The Perfect Storm"), this classic British-style pub draws a lot of literary types and occasionally hosts reading. Low-key and cozy, it's the perfect place to down a pint after exploring the nearby galleries. 505 W. 23rd St. (at Tenth Ave.). ☏ **212/462-4300.** www.thehalfking.com. Subway: C or E to 23rd St.

The Other Room ★★   This is the place to come if you take your wine and beer seriously. There's no hard stuff served, but you will find an abundance of unusual ales, beers, and wines. The bar itself is sleek and simple, with a good amount of art dotted about, and a local crowd of Villagers both gay and straight. A low-key, friendly bar, the place focuses on conversation and good brew (or vino). 143 Perry St. (btw. Washington and Greenwich sts.). ☏ **212/645-9578.** www.theotherroom.com. Subway: A, C, E to Spring St.

The Flatiron District & Union Square

Birreria ★★   Meet the Italian beer garden, a sweeping space on the 14th floor of the building that houses the food court Eataly (see p. 175, it's part of that eating group). When the weather is nice, the retractable ceiling is pulled back to reveal the sky, a rarity in New York nightlife. Home-brewed, unfiltered, naturally carbonated cask ales (you'll see the massive vats as you enter) are part of the appeal, though you can also try unusual Italian wines, which are stored in large wooden barrels behind the bar. Along with a buzzing bar scene are long, group tables for diners. 200 Fifth Ave. (at 23rd St.). ☏ **212/229-2560.** www.eataly.com. Subway: N, R to 23rd St.

Old Town Bar ★   People have been tippling here since 1892 and that includes during Prohibition; if you check under the seats in the high-backed booths, you'll see the hiding spaces for bottles. The appeal of Old Town is easy to see; yes, it's a little run down (it could use a new paint job), but with its 14-foot-ceilings, its memorabilia-laden walls and its Belle Epoque décor, there are few places as quintessentially "olde New York." Sit near the dumb waiter, so you can watch the staff hand crank the food

Bars, Cocktail Lounges & Dance Clubs

NEW YORK CITY ENTERTAINMENT & NIGHTLIFE

and dishes up and down like they did a century ago. 45 E. 18th St. (off Broadway). *(2)* **212/529-6732.** www.oldtownbar.com. Subway: 4, 5, 6, L, N, Q, R to Union Square.

Times Square & Midtown West

Carnegie Club ★ Live music, cathedral-height ceilings, and a swellegant décor make this one of Midtown's few truly classy watering holes. The only downside—which some will consider a plus—this is a cigar bar, so get ready for smoke curling around your martini glass and head there. 156 W. 56th St. (btw. Sixth and Seventh aves.). *(2)* **212/957-9676.** www.hospitalityholdings.com. Subway: F or Q to 57th St.

Morrell Wine Bar & Café ★★ The premiere wine bar in the city, Morell offers over 2,000 types of wine, many available by the glass. Although it can get crowded—it's in the heart of Rockefeller Center, after all—the scene never feels overly touristy, and the people-watching, especially from the sidewalk tables (open in good weather), can't be beat. 1 Rockefeller Plaza (at 49th St.). *(2)* **212/262-7700.** www.morrellwinebar.com. Subway: B, D, or F to 47th–50th sts./Rockefeller Center.

The Rum House ★★ You don't expect to find a place that's both this hip and this unpretentious right in the heart of Times Square, but here it is. Re-opened in 2011 in the Edison Hotel, this classic, old-time watering hole serves up a mean cocktail and decent bar food. On some nights, a live pianist adds to the ambiance, softly playing hits from the days of Gershwin and Irving Berlin. 228 W. 47th St. (btw. Broadway and Eighth Ave.). *(2)* **646/490-6924.** www.edisonrumhouse.com. Subway: A, C or E to 42nd St.

Russian Samovar ★ Infused vodkas are the draw here (my favorite is the dill), which you sample carefully, as they serve them straight. I'm also a big fan of the borscht; it somehow makes a lovely side to the tipples (or a pre-theater meal). Many nights, a live pianist will be accompanying your drinking. 256 W. 52nd St. (btw. Eighth Ave. and Broadway). *(2)* **212/757-0168.** www.russiansamovar.com. Subway: 1 to 50th St.

Swing 46 ★★ Gotham's active swing dance community supports this wonderful supper club (though you can come to dance without eating), which means there's live music here six nights a week (Mondays a DJ takes over) and locals Lindy Hop, jitterbug, waltz, and freestyle well into the wee hours. Don't know how to swing dance? Lessons are offered early in the evening most nights. "Nice casual" is the dress code (so no sneakers or jeans); music charges are $12, and $15 Friday and Saturday. 349 W. 46th St. (btw. Eighth and Ninth aves.). *(2)* **212/262-9554.** www.swing46.com. Subway: C or E to 50th St.

Midtown East

The Campbell Apartment ★★★ For an F. Scott Fitzgerald experience in New York, head here and drink the types of cocktails that Zelda over-imbibed: tall fruity drinks in oddly shaped glasses with such names as "Flappers Delight" and "Prohibition Punch." The "apartment" was once the office of tycoon John W. Campbell, who turned this 60-foot-long room into a replica of a Florentine palazzo, inlaying the ceiling and adding an ornate balcony. Visit on a weekend, early afternoon, or late evening when the commuting hordes will have already sloshed onto Metro-North (a train to the suburbs), leaving you free to enjoy this elegant space in peace. Proper attire required: which means no athletic gear, shorts, or torn jeans. In Grand Central Terminal, 15 Vanderbilt Ave. *(2)* **212/953-0409.** www.hospitalityholdings.com. Subway: S, 4, 5, 6, or 7 to 42nd St./Grand Central.

Upper West Side

Prohibition ★   A neighborhood bar, with better-than-average bar food, a pool table in the back room, and live music every night of the week (usually funk or R&B). The staff is friendly, as are the patrons, and the Prohibition-era style murals and decor hit just the right note. This really fun joint attracts a crowd that ranges from people in their 20s all the way to those in their 40s and 50s. 503 Columbus Ave. (btw. 84th and 85th sts.). ℂ 212/579-3100. www.prohibition.net. Subway: 1 to 86th St.; B or C to 86th St.

Stone Rose Lounge ★   For moguls and the models they squire, this is a "see and be seen" bar. Owned by a bar mogul (Randy Gerber) and his model wife (Cindy Crawford), Stone Rose is an elegant, noisy, huge (5,000-square-foot) bar with floor-to-ceiling windows. Try to nab a seat near them for one of the loveliest views in New York: Columbus Circle at night, lit up, with fountains spraying and Central Park slumbering in the background. In the Time Warner Center, 10 Columbus Circle, 4th floor. ℂ 212/823-9970. www.gerbersbars.com/stonerose. Subway: 1, A, B, C, D to Columbus Circle.

Upper East Side

Bemelman's Bar ★★★   Put on the ritz at this iconic bar, decorated with murals by Ludwig Bemelman, the illustrator behind the famous "Madeline" children's books. How plush is this? The ceiling is covered by 24-karat gold leaf, and the bar is made of a rare black granite. Live jazz plays as you tipple, to account for a $15 cover charge on top of the already pricey drinks here. 35 E. 76th St. (on Madison Ave.). ℂ **212/744-1600.** Subway: 6 to 77th St.

Lexington Bar and Books ★   It takes a moment to register and then you suddenly realize why the atmosphere at Lexington Bar and Books is at once decidedly strange and deeply familiar: people are smoking (!) and no one is turning them in to the police. That's because Lexington Bar and Books is one of the few "cigar bars" in the city with a special license allowing cigar smoking—and cigarettes by extension. So if you've been longing for the days of a cocktail with a cig, here's the place to come, though you'll have to dress up: This is a highly patrician bar, with a crowd in their later 30s and 40s, and a dress code requiring jackets in winter and collared shirts year-round. 1020 Lexington Ave (at 73rd St.). ℂ **212/727-3902.** Subway: 6 to 77th St.

Harlem

Bier International ★   Take the word "International" seriously. On my last visit, this buzzing nightspot had 10 German beers; 2 from Belgium; 1 each from France, the Czech Republic, and Great Britain; and 2 from NYC. And those were just the beers on tap. The bottle list is even more extensive. It's all served in an airy, chic-industrial space with breeze-catching tables on the sidewalk outside. 2099 Frederick Douglass Blvd. (btw. 113th and 114th sts.). ℂ **212/876-8838.** www.bierinternational.com. Subway: B, C to Cathedral Pkwy./110th St.

Corner Social ★   Truly one of the most social places in the neighborhood, this newish bar (it opened in late 2012) has become an open-to-all, always jumping, hangout, thanks to its better-than-usual bar food and friendly waitstaff. One of the most welcoming joints in Harlem. 321 Lenox Ave (at 126th St.). ℂ **212/510-8552.** www.corner socialnyc.com. Subway: 2, 3 to 125th St.

67 Orange Street ★★   Named for the address of the first black-owned bar in the city (it's confusing, I know, as this isn't on "Orange Street"), this tiny, super-hip cocktail haven serves up creative libations, often made with home infused liquors (I had an excellent Manhattan made with cigar-smoke infused bourbon), and bearing such tongue in cheek names as "The Color Purple" and "Cleopatra's Lust." The bar can be hard to find, as the windows are totally covered with drapes, so look for the address. 2082 Frederick Douglass Blvd. (at 113th St.). ✆ **212/662-2030.** www.67orangestreet.com. Subway: B, C to Cathedral Pkwy./110th St.

Brooklyn

It would take an entire book to list all of the spectacular outer-borough haunts, but here's a small, subway-friendly sampling of the can't-miss variety.

Brooklyn Bowl ★★   Yes, it's a bowling alley, but you don't have to hit the pins to have a delightful night out here. A massive space with an updated carny décor, and a wide selection of beers, cocktails, and food, this is a great place just to come and hang out. Live DJ's spin catchy music on the nights bands aren't playing. 61 Wythe Ave., Williamsburg (btw. N. 11th and N. 12th sts.). ✆ **718/963-3369.** www.brooklynbowl.com. Subway: L to Bedford Ave.; G to Nassau St.

Maison Premier ★★   Channeling the spirit of New Orleans—think Garden District *not* Bourbon Street—this oyster and cocktail bar is a wonderfully elegant place to while away an evening. And while you don't have to pay homage to the "green fairy" to hang here, it is interesting to take a gander at the working replica absinthe fountain, based on the one that once graced Crescent City's Olde Absinthe House. 298 Bedford St. (near First St.), Williamsburg, Brooklyn. ✆ **347/335-0446.** www.maisonpremiere.com. Subway: L to Bedford St.

Pete's Candy Store ★★   It seems appropriate that grown-up games should be the focus of a bar in a former candy store. You come here if you love pub quizzes, spelling bees, and other contests of the beer-buzzed-brain. Pete's also hosts lectures and live music, making this little neighborhood joint a primo place not just for a frosty mug, but for serious entertainment. Something goes on here every night of the week (see the website for a current schedule). 709 Lorimer St. (btw. Richardson and Frost sts.), Williamsburg, Brooklyn. ✆ **718/302-3770.** www.petescandystore.com. Subway: L to Lorimer St.

Tatiana ★★   Acrobats! Showgirls! Crooners! Tatiana is a Las Vegas-meets-Vladivostok experience, a Russian supper club where the meal is an endless feast (of Russian and Continental foods), the vodka flows freely and ex-pat Russians of all ages boogey until dawn. It's not cheap, but going here may well be your most memorable, if weird, night in New York. 3152 Brighton 6th St. (at the boardwalk), Brighton Beach, Brooklyn. ✆ **718/891-5151.** www.tatianarestaurant.com. Subway: B, Q to Brighton Beach.

The Shanty ★★★   This is New York City's first distillery since Prohibition and through one large, glass wall of the bar, drinkers can see the giant vats where the owners are creating both gin and whiskey. Alan Katz is one of those co-owners and he was, for many years, the host of "The Cocktail Hour" on Martha Stewart radio, so you know the mixology here is world class (the drink menu changes with the seasons, but always includes liquors distilled on property). Ask nicely, and they'll take you on a tour of the distillery. 79 Richardson St. (at Leonard St.), Williamsburg, Brooklyn. ✆ **718/878-3579.** www.nydistilling.com. Subway: L to Lorimer St.

GETTING beyond THE VELVET ROPE

There's nothing that will transport you back to the worst day of high school quicker than facing the gatekeeper at the door of a New York dance club. It's a humbling, depressing experience (especially if you don't get in), but there are ways to increase your odds of spending more time in the club than on the sidewalk.

1. **Choose your companions carefully.** Large groups of men have little chance of getting into a club together, so if you're traveling in a pack of guys, split up until you get inside the club. Women have a better chance of getting in, as do couples.

2. **Dress the part.** Look at the celebrity magazines and see what they're wearing when they sashay past the ropes. Usually it's an upscale casual look, but that will change season to season. Avoid suits at all costs, the same for "business casual," and if you plan to wear sneakers, make sure they're clean.

3. **Make nice.** The "chooser" at the door has been entrusted by the owner to create a cool "mix" of people inside the club, so though you may not get in right away, you could be picked in 15 minutes, especially at a larger club, when they need more redheads, or tall women, or perhaps when the moon goes into Jupiter (I don't think even the gatekeepers have a clear idea of what they're looking for). You'll blow your chances, however, if you give the all-powerful guy at the door any argument or attitude. Instead, wait

patiently with a smile on your face, chatting with your companion, and you just might get in. Never wait more than 15 minutes at a club that can hold less than 500 (and would therefore be considered "exclusive") or half an hour at a larger place; at that point, it's pretty clear that they won't pick you.

4. **Call in advance for a reservation.** Some dance clubs have restaurants attached, and those who dine get automatic entry, later in the evening, to the dance club. You can also reserve a table at a club in advance for you and your guests, but be careful: Those who get a table are required to take "bottle service," which means you buy a bottle of liquor for you and your companions that can easily cost upwards of $300. Another ploy is to call in advance and ask for a bar reservation; it's not as surefire a method but sometimes it works (it all depends on how many advance reservations come in).

5. **Never admit to being a tourist.** Clubs are where the worst New York snobbery comes to the fore. It's sad but true: They really don't want tourists. That doesn't mean you shouldn't go; just don't attempt to get in by telling them it's your "last night before you go back to Alabama."

6. **Say you're there to meet the deejay.** This is my trickiest tip, but it actually works. Go to the club's website in advance, find out who the deejay will be that night, and say that you're meeting him or her inside.

Dance Clubs

No New York trends fluctuate quite as much as the club scene. So remember: Finding and going to the latest hot spot is not worth agonizing over. Clubgoers spend their lives obsessing over "the Scene." But this is New York, and there are so many choices no one club is the empirical best. Instead of giving you a random list of the clubs that were hot at the moment, I'm going to suggest picking up a copy of *Time Out New York,* which will list the best parties of the week. Go to the one that most intrigues you.

Additional online sources that might score you reduced admissions or place you on a guest list for select clubs, include **www.clubplanet.com** and **www.sheckysnightlife. com.** Many clubs offer the guest-list sign-up service on their websites, too. No matter what, call ahead, because schedules change constantly and can do so at the last minute.

Note: New York nightlife starts late, of course. With the exception of places that have scheduled performances, dance floors stay almost empty until midnight.

THE GAY & LESBIAN SCENE

Though the stats are shaky, most experts estimate that New York City is home to the largest gay population in North America, if not the world. All in all, there are about 70 major bars and nightclubs to suit every taste, wardrobe, and fetish, but the party only starts there. I'd recommend that you check out such publications as *Next* (www. nextmagazine.com), the lesbian-centric *GO* (www.gomag.com), *The Blade* (available in gay bars), and the more mainstream *Time Out* **magazine** (on newsstands) for listings of these clubs as well as the innumerable dance parties, go-go and drag shows, gay knitting circles (yes, really), and other happenings that take place every week at dozens of venues around the city. Of course, in many New York bars, clubs, cabarets, and lounges are mixed with both gay and straight clientele (especially in 'hoods like the Village, Chelsea, and Hell's Kitchen).

Boxers ★   Yes, that's the outfit the bartender was wearing the night I visited, but the name of the joint also refers to the fact that this is a sports bar, with 11 massive TVs lining the walls, and huge photos of rippled men engaged in all sorts of games on the walls. Hell's Kitchen is the latest hot spot for gay nightlife, so expect a toned, young crowd here, up for a party. A big perk: The lovely roof bar. 742 Ninth Ave. (at 50th St.). © **212/942-1518.** www.boxersnyc.com. Subway: C, E to 50th St.

Candle Bar★   Possibly the oldest, continuously operated gay bar in the city (opinions differ, but that's what patrons here claim), this is a proud, old-fashioned dive, down to the Donkey Kong machine in the corner, right next to the pool table. "This is where everybody doesn't quite know your name," a regular told me."But they'll act like they do." A great, low-key hang that's friendly for people of all ages. 309 Amsterdam Ave. (btw. 74th and 75th sts.). © **212/799-0062.** Subway: 1, 2, 3 to 72nd St.

Cubby Hole ★★   Early in the evening, The Cubby Hole gets a mixed crowd from the neighborhood of men and even straight women, but by 11pm it's strictly "lipstick lesbians" and club girls rocking out to the jukebox. It's a fun scene and the decor is hilarious, with literally hundreds of paper animals and fish, Chinese lanterns, and plastic flying pigs dangling from the ceiling. 281 W. 12th St. (at W. 4th St.). © **212/243-9041.** www.cubbyholebar.com. Subway: A, C, E, or L to 14th St.

Flaming Saddles Saloon ★★★   Yeehaw! Welcome to "Coyote Ugly" for gay men (and the many women who show up to watch the hot, shirtless bartenders hoof it on top of the bar every 40 minutes or so). The soundtrack is country western and the mood exuberant. 739 Ninth Ave. (btw. 52nd and 53rd sts.). © **212/713-0481.** www.flaming saddles.com. Subway: 1 to Houston.

Henrietta Hudson ★ Dominated by a large pool table (always in use) in the center room and two bars, this divey bar hosts dancing many nights and seems especially popular among Latina and African-American women. See the website for special theme nights (Wednesdays is Salsa Night). 438–444 Hudson St. (at Morton St.). ℭ **212/924-3347.** www.henriettahudson.com. Subway: 1 to Houston St.

The Eagle ★★ For "bears," "cubs," and the boys who love them, this dungeon-like club is the epicenter of the leather scene in New York. Forgot your chaps? Not a problem—the Eagle has a tiny "leather goods" store in the elevator for all your codpiece and whipping needs. (There's also a quite civilized roof garden on the 3rd floor, open in good weather.) 554 W. 28th St. (btw. Tenth and Eleventh aves.). ℭ **646/473-1866.** www. eaglynyc.com. Subway: C, E to 28th St.

The Monster ★★★ A fabulous Art Deco space, once home to El Chico (a former flamenco cabaret whose murals still adorn the walls), The Monster has two faces. Upstairs is a piano bar with a crowd of show-tune-crazy regulars; downstairs a groovy discothèque with go-go boys, weekend tea dances, and the most popular Latin Night in the city. The Monster experienced a resurgence of popularity recently, and now is hot, hot, hot! 80 Grove St. at Sheridan Square. ℭ **212/924-3558.** www.manhattan-monster.com. Subway: 1 to Christopher St.

Therapy ★★ A chic, candle-lit, two-floor bar that attracts a "pretty boys in Barney's shirts" crowd of buff 20- and 30-some-things for casual cruising. You could come here and meet the love of your life, or just have a drink. It's also where the ladies from Rue Paul's Drag Show often perform. 348 W. 52nd St. (btw. Eighth and Ninth aves.). ℭ **212/397-1700.** www.therapy-nyc.com. Subway: C, E to 50th St.

XL ★ Set in The Out Hotel (p. 47), on many nights this is one of the sweatiest, writhingest dance floors in the city. While some locals sniff that it's too "bridge and tunnel" (that is, filled with non-New Yorkers), others think of it as the hottest dance party in the city. 512 W. 42nd St. (at Tenth Ave.). ℭ **212/239-2999.** www.xlnightclub.com. Subway: A, C, E, or L to 42nd St.

SPECTATOR SPORTS

For details on the New York City Marathon and the U.S. Open tennis championships, see the "New York City Calendar of Events," in chapter 9.

BASEBALL With two baseball teams in town, you can catch a game almost any day, from Opening Day in April to the beginning of the playoffs in October.

For information on pricing and availability of tickets for the Metropolitans, call the **Mets Ticket Office** at ℭ **718/507-TIXX** (507-8499), or visit http://newyork.mets.mlb. com.

Yankee Stadium is, as it has always been in every incarnation, in the Bronx. (Subway: C, D, 4 to 161st St./Yankee Stadium). For single-game tickets, contact **Yankee Stadium** (ℭ **718/293-4300;** http://newyork.yankees.mlb.com). You can also buy Mets and Yankees tickets by contacting **Ticketmaster** (ℭ **800/745-3000;** www.ticketmaster. com), visiting the stadium on the day of the game, or trying online resale sites such as **StubHub** (www.stubhub.com).

BASKETBALL There are two pro hoops teams that play in New York at **Madison Square Garden,** Seventh Avenue, between 31st and 33rd streets (ℭ **212/465-6741,** or

800/745-3000 for tickets; www.thegarden.com or www.ticketmaster.com; Subway: A, C, E, 1, 2, 3 to 34th St.). The **New York Knicks** (© **877/NYK-DUNK** [695-3865] or 212/465-JUMP [465-5867]; www.nba.com/knicks) are the NBA team from NYC. They play from November through mid-February. The second is the accomplished WNBA team the **New York Liberty** (© **212/564-9622;** www.wnba.com/liberty); its season falls in the summer months, beginning in late May.

FOOTBALL   Both the New York Giants and the New York Jets play in the Meadowlands Stadium. It's located not in New York City, but in East Rutherford, New Jersey. *Note:* This stadium will host the Super Bowl in 2014, the first cold-weather stadium ever to host this classic.

ICE HOCKEY   NHL hockey is represented in Manhattan by the **New York Rangers,** who play at Madison Square Garden (© **212/465-6741;** http://rangers.nhl.com or www.thegarden.com; Subway: A, C, E, 1, 2, 3 to 34th St.). Rangers tickets are hard to get, so plan well ahead; call © **800/745-3000,** or visit **www.ticketmaster.com** for online orders.

PLANNING YOUR VISIT TO NEW YORK CITY

9

As with any trip, a little preparation is essential before you start your journey to NYC. This chapter provides a variety of planning tools, including information on how to get there, how to get around within the city once there, and when to come. And then, in a mainly alphabetical listing, we deal with the dozens of miscellaneous resources and organizations that you can turn to for help.

GETTING THERE

By Plane

Three major airports serve New York City: **John F. Kennedy International Airport** (JFK, ℂ **718/244-4444;** www.panynj.gov/airports/jfk.html) in Queens, about 15 miles (and about 1 hr. driving time) from Midtown Manhattan; **LaGuardia Airport** (LGA, ℂ **718/533-3400;** www.panynj. gov/airports/laguardia.html), also in Queens, about 8 miles (30 min.) from Midtown; and **Newark Liberty International Airport** (EWR, ℂ **973/961-6000;** www.panynj.gov/airports/newark-liberty.html) in nearby New Jersey, about 16 miles (45 min.) from Midtown New York. Almost every major domestic airline serves at least one of the New York–area airports; most serve two or all three.

GETTING INTO TOWN FROM THE AIRPORT

Since there's no need to rent a car in New York, you're going to have to figure out how you want to get from the airport to your hotel and back.

For transportation information for all three airports (JFK, LaGuardia, and Newark), the website **www.panynj.gov/airports** is best for up-to-the-minute news; click on the airport at which you'll be arriving.

The Port Authority runs staffed Ground Transportation Information counters on the baggage-claim level at each airport, where you can get information and book various kinds of transport. Most transportation companies also have courtesy phones near the baggage-claim area.

Generally, travel time between the airports and Midtown by taxi or car is 45 to 60 minutes for JFK or Newark, 20 to 35 minutes for LaGuardia. Always allow extra time, especially during rush hour or peak holiday travel times, and if you're taking public transportation.

FINDING A good AIRFARE INTO NYC

Book at the right time. Sounds odd, but you can often save a good amount by booking your airfare 42 days in advance of departure. That figure comes from a study of thousands of airfares that the Airlines Reporting Corporation undertook in 2012. Book much earlier or later than that and you won't have access to the lowest-priced seats, as the airlines only release them when they have an idea of how the plane is selling. Book too close to departure and the airline knows they've "got you" and will charge more.

Fly when others don't and take an itinerary the business travelers don't want. Those who fly midweek and midday, and who stay over a Saturday night generally pay less than those who fly at more popular times

Do a smart web search: Such search engines as DoHop.com and Momondo.com will search all of the discount sites as well as the airline sites directly, so that you get a broader and more impartial search. The only airline that won't come up is Southwest Airlines, so be sure to search it separately, as it now flies into LaGuardia Airport.

Don't be particular about airports: Go to whatever airport is offering the cheapest fares, instead of choosing one of the three airports over the other. That's my honest advice. None of the three New York City Airports are more or less convenient to the city than the others (although LaGuardia is somewhat closer), and they all have equally lousy records for delays and lost luggage.

SUBWAYS & PUBLIC BUSES Unfortunately, for a major international city, New York's public transit options to and from our airports are disappointing, but not impossible to navigate. Give yourself an extra hour for travel delays—such as waiting for the right Rockaway-bound A train to get you to the JFK Airport-bound AirTrain station (see the box "AirTrains to Newark & JFK" below). If you're traveling through LaGuardia, you'll have to catch the M60 bus either on 125th Street in Harlem, or just down the elevated-subway stairs at the N or Q-train Astoria Boulevard station in Queens.

The subway *can* be more reliable than taking a car or taxi at the height of rush hour, but *a few words of warning:* This isn't the right option for you if you're bringing more than a single piece of luggage or if you have young children in tow, since there's a good amount of walking, including stairs, and usually a subway car that's too crowded for excess baggage.

TAXIS Despite significant rate hikes the past few years, taxis are still a quick and convenient way to travel to and from the airports. They're available at designated taxi stands outside the terminals, with uniformed dispatchers on hand during peak hours at JFK and LaGuardia, around the clock at Newark. Follow the GROUND TRANSPORTATION or TAXI signs. There may be a long line, but generally those lines move quickly. Fares, whether fixed or metered, do not include bridge and tunnel tolls ($4–$6, if applicable) or a tip for the cabbie (15%–20% is customary). They do include all passengers in the cab and luggage—never pay more than the metered or flat rate, except for tolls and a tip (8pm–6am a 50¢ surcharge also applies on New York yellow cabs). **Taxis have a limit of four passengers,** so if there are more in

AIRTRAINS TO NEWARK & JFK:
cheap BUT NOT HASSLE-FREE

It's a terrible shame that none of the New York-area airports have decent train service.

Best is **AirTrain Newark,** which connects Newark-Liberty International Airport with Manhattan via a monorail/rail link. At **Newark International Airport Station** passengers must transfer to a **NJ Transit** train and often there's a significant time-gap between the arrival of the monorail, and the departure of the train into the city (despite the posted arrival times for the trains).

All AirTrains heading to. NJ Transit will deliver you to New York Penn Station at 33rd Street and Seventh Avenue, where you can get a cab or transfer to the subway or bus.

A one-way trip costs about $15.50 total, if you factor the $2.50 subway fare to Penn Station, and $13 for the AirTrain (partly served by NJ Transit) from Penn

to Newark Airport. NJ Transit trains run at least six times an hour from 6am to 9pm and four times an hour from 9pm to midnight (there is no service from 2–5am), and depart from their own lobby/waiting area in Penn Station; you can check the schedules on monitors before you leave the airport terminal, and again at the train station. NJ Transit tickets can be purchased from vending machines at both the air terminal and the train station (no ticket is required to board the AirTrain). The one-way fare is $13 (children 4 and under ride free; for ages 5 to 11, as well as seniors and disabled riders, the fare is $8.75). On your return trip to the airport, the AirTrain is far more predictable, time-wise, than subjecting yourself to the whims of traffic.

Note that travelers heading to points beyond the city can also pick up Amtrak

your group, you'll have to take more than one cab or try and hail a minivan taxi. For more, see "By Taxi," p. 235.

- **From JFK:** A flat rate of $52 to Manhattan (plus tolls and tip and a 50¢ N.Y. state tax) is charged. The meter will not be turned on and the surcharge will not be added.
- **From LaGuardia:** There's no set fare, but you can expect the meter to run about $30, plus tolls and tip.
- **From Newark:** The dispatcher for New Jersey taxis gives you a slip of paper with a flat rate ranging from $50 to $75 (toll and tip extra), depending on where you're going in Manhattan, so be precise about your destination. New York yellow cabs aren't permitted to pick up passengers at Newark. The yellow-cab fare from Manhattan to Newark is the meter amount plus $15 and tolls (about $69–$75, perhaps a few dollars more with tip). Jersey taxis aren't permitted to take passengers from Manhattan to Newark.

PRIVATE CAR & LIMOUSINE SERVICES Private (or "livery") car and limousine companies provide convenient 24-hour door-to-door airport transfers for roughly the same cost as a taxi. The advantage they offer is that you can arrange your pickup in advance and avoid the hassles of taxi lines. Call at least 24 hours in advance and other NJ Transit trains at Newark International Airport Station to their final destinations.

The service from JFK into the city is even worse. A few bumpy years after opening in 2003, at a cost of nearly $2 billion, **AirTrain JFK** is operating somewhat more efficiently. It's only $5 if you take a subway to the AirTrain, $13 if you take the Long Island Rail Road—but what you save in money you'll lose on time getting to the airport. From Midtown Manhattan, the ride can take anywhere from 40 minutes to over an hour, depending on your connections. Only a few subway lines connect with the AirTrain: the A, E, J, and Z; the E, J, Z to Jamaica Station and the Sutphin Blvd.–Archer Ave. Station; and the A to Howard Beach. The latter is the fastest option for most people.

A word of warning for both AirTrains: If you have mobility issues, mountains of luggage, or a bevy of small children, skip the AirTrain. You'll find it easier to rely on a taxi, car service, or shuttle service that can offer you door-to-door travel.

For more information on AirTrain Newark and connection details, call ℂ **888/EWR-INFO** (397-4636), or go online to **www.panynj.gov.** For connections to trains, contact **NJ Transit** (ℂ **973/275-5555;** www.njtransit.com) or **Amtrak** (ℂ **800/USA-RAIL** [872-7245]; www.amtrak.com).

For more information on AirTrain JFK, go online to **www.panynj.gov.** For connection details, click on the links on the website or MTA's site, **www.mta.info/mta/airtrain.htm.**

(even earlier on holidays), and a driver will meet you near baggage claim (or at your hotel for a return trip). You'll probably be asked to leave a credit card number to guarantee your ride. You'll likely be offered the choice of indoor or curbside pickup; indoor pickup is more expensive but makes it easier to find your driver (who usually waits in baggage claim carrying a sign with your name on it). You can save a few dollars if you arrange for an outside pickup; call the dispatcher as soon as you clear baggage claim and then take your luggage to the designated waiting area, where you'll wait for the driver to come around, which may take anywhere from 10 to 30 minutes. Besides the wait, the downside is that curbside can be chaotic during prime deplaning hours.

Vehicles range from sedans to vans to limousines and tend to be clean and comfortable. Prices vary slightly by company and the size of car reserved; toll and tip policies are the same. (*Note:* Car services are *not* subject to the flat-rate rule that taxis have for rides to and from JFK.) Ask when booking what the fare will be and if you can use your credit card to pay for the ride so there are no surprises at drop-off time. There may be waiting charges tacked on if the driver has to wait an excessive amount of time due to flight delays when picking you up, but the car companies will usually check on your flight to get an accurate landing time.

If you're traveling to a borough other than Manhattan, call **ETS Air Service** (📞 **718/221-5341**) for shared door-to-door service. For Long Island service, call **Classic Transportation** (📞 **631/567-5100;** www.classictrans.com) for car service. For service to Westchester County or Connecticut, contact **Connecticut Limousine** (📞 **800/472-5466** or 203/974-4700; www.ctlimo.com).

If you're traveling to points in New Jersey from Newark Airport, call **Olympic Airporter** (📞 **800/822-9797;** www.olympic-limo.com) for Ocean, Monmouth, Middlesex, and Mercer counties, plus Bucks County, Pennsylvania; or **State Shuttle** (📞 **800/427-3207;** www.stateshuttle.com) for destinations throughout New Jersey.

Additionally, **New York Airport Service** express buses (📞 **877/599-8200;** www.nyairportservice.com) serve the entire New York metropolitan region from JFK, Newark, and LaGuardia, offering connections to the Long Island Rail Road; the Metro-North Railroad to Westchester County, upstate New York, and Connecticut; and New York's Port Authority terminal, where you head for New Jersey.

The two companies with the best reputations are **Carmel** (📞 **866/666-6666;** www.carmellimo.com) and **Legends** (📞 **888/LEGENDS** [534-3637] or 718/788-1234; www.legendslimousine.com); but **Allstate** (📞 **800/453-4099** or 212/333-3333; www.allstatelimo.com) and **Tel-Aviv** (📞 **800/222-9888;** www.telavivlimo.com) also are recommended. (Keep in mind, though, that these services are only as good as the individual drivers—and sometimes there's a lemon in the bunch. If you have a problem, report it immediately to the main office.)

These car services are good for rush hour (no ticking meters in rush-hour traffic), but if you're arriving at a quieter time of day, taxis work fine.

Warning: When you leave the terminal, you may be approached by a private car driver trying to get a fare back to Manhattan, or a driver without a taxi/livery license looking to make some extra money. It's illegal, as well as more expensive than waiting in line or calling for a livery cab. Their prices are almost always a lot more than what a reserved car or yellow cab would be, and you may be taken advantage of if the driver thinks you're a NYC newbie. Don't negotiate with them. Grab a cab, order a livery car, or take a bus or shuttle.

PRIVATE BUSES & SHUTTLES   Buses and shuttle services provide a comfortable and less expensive (but usually more time-consuming) option for airport transfers than do taxis and car services.

SuperShuttle and **NYC Airporter** serve all three airports; **Olympia Trails/Coach USA** serves Newark. These shuttles are great surface-road alternatives during peak travel times because the drivers usually take lesser known streets that make the ride much quicker than if you go with a taxi or car, which will virtually always stick to the traffic-clogged main route.

The familiar blue vans of **SuperShuttle** (📞 **800/258-3826;** www.supershuttle.com) serve all three area airports, providing door-to-door service to Manhattan and points on Long Island every 15 to 30 minutes around the clock. You don't need to reserve your airport-to-Manhattan ride; just go to the ground-transportation desk or use the courtesy phone in baggage claim and ask for SuperShuttle. Hotel pickups for your return trip require 24 to 48 hours' notice; you can make your reservations online. Fares run from about $13 to $28 per person, depending on the airport, with discounts available for additional riders in the same party.

NYC Airporter (ⓒ **718/777-5111;** www.nycairporter.com) buses travel from JFK and LaGuardia to the Port Authority Bus Terminal (42nd St. and Eighth Ave.), Grand Central Terminal (Park Ave. btw. 41st and 42nd sts.), and Penn Station (Seventh Ave. btw. 31st and 32nd sts.). Look for the airport's ground transportation desk (there's one in every terminal) or the uniformed personnel of the Airporter outside. Buses depart the airport every 20 to 30 minutes (depending on your departure point and destination) between 5am and 11:30pm. One-way fare from JFK to Manhattan is $16, $29 round-trip; from LaGuardia it's $13 one-way and $23 round-trip. The bus also runs between Newark and JFK and LaGuardia airports. A shuttle bus from the initial stops to Midtown hotels can be added at no additional charge.

Olympia Airport Express (ⓒ **877/863-9275;** www.coachusa.com/olympia/ss.newarkairport.asp) provides service every 15 minutes (every 30 minutes from 6:45am to 11:15pm) from Newark Airport to Bryant Park (at 42nd St. and Fifth Ave.), the Port Authority Bus Terminal (on 42nd St. btw. Eighth and Ninth Aves.), and Grand Central Terminal (on 41st St. btw. Park and Lexington Aves.). Call for the exact schedule for your return trip to the airport. The one-way fare runs $16, $28 round-trip; $5 one-way for members of the military.

By Bus

Busing to and from New York City from major East Coast cities has become the single most cost-effective way to get into town. A number of companies offer frequent, regular service between most of the major cities in the East (and as far west as Buffalo and Toronto) for a fraction of what you'd pay by train or plane. From Philadelphia, the average ride might range from $10 to $20; for the other two cities you'll pay $15 to $30, but there are times when specials reduce the fares to just $1. The companies to call include:

○ **Megabus** (ⓒ **877/GO2-MEGA** [462-6342]; www.megabus.com)
○ **Boltbus** (ⓒ **877/BOLTBUS** [265-8287]; www.boltbus.com)
○ **Vamoose** (ⓒ **212/695-6766;** www.vamoosebus.com)
○ **DC2NY** (ⓒ **888/888-DCNY** or 202/332-2691; www.dc2ny.com)

By Train

Amtrak (ⓒ **800/USA-RAIL** [872-7245]; www.amtrak.com) runs frequent service to New York City's Penn Station, on Seventh Avenue between 31st and 33rd streets, where you can get a taxi, subway, or bus to your hotel.

If you're traveling to New York from a city along Amtrak's Northeast Corridor—such as Boston, Philadelphia, Baltimore, or Washington, D.C.—Amtrak may end up being faster than flying (when you factor in time getting to the airport and getting through security), especially on the high-speed *Acela* trains. The Acela Express trains cut travel time from D.C. down to 2½ hours, and travel time from Boston to a lightning-quick 3 hours.

GETTING AROUND THE CITY

Because most travelers confine themselves to Manhattan, I will, as well, in this section. Those traveling to the outer boroughs can be confident, however, that public transportation—subways, buses, ferries, or some combination of the three—can get you anywhere you wish to go in the city proper, whether it be the sandy shores of Brighton Beach, Brooklyn, or Yankee Stadium in the Bronx. The city's transportation network is run by the Metropolitan Transportation Authority (aka the MTA); maps and schedules for NYC's myriad transportation options can be found at www.mta.info. You can also key in your itinerary at www.hopstop.com, a terrific site and app that will give you complete directions, including how far you'll walk to get to the station and whether you'll also need to take a bus. Hopstop also estimates taxi fares, a handy trick.

Subway

I wish I could confine my transportation advice to just three words—"**take the subway**"—and be done with it. To my mind, the NYC subways, 110 years young in 2014, are the single most efficient, rapid, easy, and affordable way to get just about anywhere you'd want to go in Manhattan, with the exception of some of the far eastern sections of the Upper East Side (and that will change once the Second Avenue subway is completed); and crosstown above 59th Street. It runs 24 hours a day, 7 days a week, and yes, it gets crowded at rush-hour (roughly from 8 to 9:30am and from 5 to 6:30pm on weekdays), but even then it's still the fastest way to get from point A to point B.

But because of the starring role the subways have played in action films set in New York over the years, with squinty-eyed thugs menacing grandmothers on graffiti-riddled trains, many visitors are scared to go underground.

That fear is unwarranted. Not only is the graffiti gone, thanks to the persistent efforts of those invisible transit cops (you rarely see one, but there are 3,000 of them keeping order underground and on the buses, often in plain clothes), the subways are safer than ever.

Of course, that doesn't make them Disneyland. Though the cars are heated in winter and air-conditioned in summer, the platforms are not, and they often feel 10 degrees colder than the city streets in winter, and 10 degrees hotter in summer. Pickpockets remain a problem, as they are in Paris, London, and every other city where large numbers of people jam together in small spaces. So remember to move your wallet to a place where you can keep track of it before boarding the train (if you're wearing pants, the front pocket is usually best).

PAYING YOUR WAY

A SingleRide subway fare (available only at vending machines) is $2.50 (half price for seniors and those with disabilities), and children under 44 inches tall ride free (up to three per adult). To that, you'll need to add a $1 fee for the subway card itself (add time or money onto your card and there will be no additional fee). Once you're in the system, you can transfer freely to any subway line that you can reach without exiting your station. MetroCards also allow you a **free transfer** between bus and subway within a 2-hour period.

MetroCards are usually purchased at the ATM-style vending machines now located in every subway station, which accept cash, credit cards, and debit cards; from a

MetroCard merchant, including corner delis and drugstores; Hudson News, at Penn Station and Grand Central Terminal; or at the MTA information desk at the **Times Square Information Center,** 1560 Broadway, between 46th and 47th streets.

MetroCards come in a few different configurations:

Pay-Per-Ride MetroCards can be used for up to four people by swiping up to four times (bring the entire family). You can put any amount from $5 (for two rides) to $100 on your card. Every time you put $8 or more on your Pay-Per-Ride MetroCard, it's automatically credited 15%—in other words, spend $20 and you get a free ride, plus a 50¢ balance. You can refill your card at any time until the expiration date on the card, usually about a year from the date of purchase, at any subway station.

Unlimited-Ride MetroCards, which can't be used for more than one person at a time or more frequently than at 18-minute intervals, are available in two values: the **7-Day MetroCard,** which allows you 7 days' worth of unlimited subway and bus rides for $30; and the **30-Day MetroCard,** for $112. They go into effect the first time you use them—so if you buy a card on Monday and don't begin to use it until Wednesday, Wednesday is when the clock starts ticking on your MetroCard. Seven- and 30-day MetroCards run out at midnight on the last day. Unlimited-ride MetroCards cannot be refilled.

Tips for using your MetroCard: The MetroCard swiping mechanisms at turnstiles are the source of much grousing among subway riders. If you swipe too fast or too slow, the turnstile will ask you to swipe again. If this happens, *do not move to a different turnstile,* or you may end up paying twice. If you've tried repeatedly and really can't make your MetroCard work, tell the token booth clerk; chances are good, that you'll get the movement down after a couple of uses.

If you're not sure how much money you have left on your MetroCard, or what day it expires, use the station's MetroCard Reader, usually located near the station entrance or the token booth (on buses, the fare box also will display this information).

Mass Transit Fares in New York City

SUBWAYS, MTA BUS

Fare Type	Full*	Reduced*
Base Pay-Per-Ride MetroCard Fare	$2.50	$1.25
Minimum purchase for new MetroCard	$5	$5
Cash (Bus only)	$2.75	$1.25
Single-Ride Ticket	$2.75	N/A
UNLIMITED-RIDE METROCARD		
7-day	$30	$15
30-day	$112	$56

* Reduced-fare customers who do not have a reduced-fare MetroCard pay $2.50 at a subway station booth for a round-trip.

** Reduced fare is not available during peak periods, 6–10am and 3–7pm weekdays.

USING THE SYSTEM

As you can see from the full-color subway map of most of Manhattan on the inside back cover of this book, the subway system basically mimics the lay of the land above

If you're not sure how to get, say, from the Museum of Natural History to the Brooklyn Bridge, you might want to visit **www.hopstop.com**. Offering navigation help on several major U.S. subway systems, the useful widget can tell you how to get from one place to the other underground. (It also gives you a comparison for time/cost using a taxi or car service.) You can modify your request by specifying "more walking" or "fewer transfers".

---

ground, with most lines in Manhattan running north and south, like the avenues, and a few lines east and west, like the streets.

To **go up and down the east side of Manhattan** (and to the Bronx and Brooklyn), take the 4, 5, or 6 train.

To travel **up and down the West Side** (and also to the Bronx and Brooklyn), take the 1, 2, or 3 line; the A, C, E, or F line; or the B or D line.

The N, R, and Q lines first **cut diagonally across town** from east to west and then snake under Seventh Avenue before shooting out to Queens.

The **crosstown** S line, called the Shuttle, runs back and forth between Times Square and Grand Central Terminal. Farther downtown, across 14th Street, the L line works its own crosstown magic.

Express trains often skip about three stops for each one they make; express stops are indicated on subway maps with a white (rather than solid) circle. Local stops are usually about nine blocks apart.

Directions are almost always indicated using "uptown" (northbound) and "downtown" (southbound), so be sure to know what direction you want to head in. The outsides of some subway entrances are marked UPTOWN ONLY or DOWNTOWN ONLY; read carefully, as it's easy to head in the wrong direction or get stuck on the wrong platform.

By Bus

Since buses can get stuck in traffic and stop every couple of blocks, rather than the eight or nine blocks that local subways traverse between stops (unless you catch a "Limited" bus), they're much less useful than the subway. I recommend using them only if you have to travel east to west; note that you can combine a bus ride with a subway ride at no additional cost (the transfer has to take place within 2 hours of the time you first boarded either the subway or the train).

PAYING YOUR WAY

Like the subway fare, a SingleRide **bus fare** is $2.75, half price for seniors and riders with disabilities, and free for children under 44 inches (up to three per adult). The fare is payable with a **MetroCard** or **exact change** (excluding pennies). And they do mean *change:* Bus drivers don't make change, and fare boxes don't accept dollar bills or pennies. You can't purchase MetroCards on the bus, so have them ready before you board.

USING THE SYSTEM

You can't flag a city bus down—you have to meet it at a bus stop. **Bus stops** are located every two or three blocks on the right-side corner of the street (facing the direction of traffic flow). They're marked by a curb painted yellow and a blue-and-white sign with a bus emblem and the route number or numbers, and usually an ad-bedecked bus shelter.

Almost every major avenue has its own **bus route.** They run either north or south: downtown on Fifth, uptown on Madison, downtown on Lexington, uptown on Third, and so on. There are **crosstown buses** at strategic locations all around town: 14th, 23rd, 34th, and 42nd (east- and westbound); 49th (westbound); 50th (eastbound); 57th (east- and westbound); 66th (eastbound across the West Side on 65th St., through the park, and then north on Madison, continuing east on 68th to York Ave.); 67th (westbound on the East Side to Fifth Ave., and then south on Fifth, continuing west on 66th St., through the park and across the west side to West End Ave.); and 79th, 86th, 96th, 116th, and 125th (east- and westbound). Some bus routes, however, are erratic: The M104, for example, turns at Eighth Avenue and 41st St. and goes up Broadway to West 129th St.

Most routes operate 24 hours a day, but service is infrequent at night. During rush hour, main routes have "Limited" buses, identifiable by the red card in the front window; they stop only at major cross streets.

In 2011, the MTA also added new **Select Bus Service** ("SBS") on the M15 line, heading north on First Avenue and south on Second Avenue, as well as the M34 across 34th Street. For the first time, these buses let passengers save time by paying at the bus shelter before boarding, with inspectors on board verifying tickets. The stops are at the same 9 or 10 block intervals as Limited lines (more at **www.mta.info/nyct/sbs**).

Most city buses are equipped with wheelchair lifts, making buses the city's most accessible mode of public transportation. Buses also "kneel," lowering down to the curb to make boarding easier.

By Taxi

Cabs can be hailed on any street, provided you find an empty one—often simple, yet nearly impossible at 5pm when the taxi drivers change shifts. They're pricey, but can be convenient if you're tired or are not sure how to find an address. Don't assume they'll be quicker than the subway or walking, though. In Midtown at midday, you can often walk to where you're going more quickly thanks to traffic.

Official New York City taxis, licensed by the Taxi and Limousine Commission (TLC), are yellow, with the rates printed on the door and a light with a medallion number on the roof. You can hail a taxi on any street. *Note:* In 2013, a city law was

When you're waiting on the street for an available taxi, look at the **medallion light** on the top of the coming cabs. If the light is out, the taxi is in use. When the center part (the number) is lit, the taxi is available—this is, when you raise your hand to flag the cab. If all the lights are on, the driver is off-duty. Taxi regulations limit the number of people permitted to take a cab to four, so expect to split up if your group is larger.

passed creating a new fleet of apple green taxis/livery cars, which will pick up passengers in the outer boroughs and upper Manhattan. Like yellow cabs, they will be hailable, but unlike the yellow ones they will not be allowed to pick up passengers below 110th Street in Manhattan (though they'll be allowed to drop off passengers there). As we go to press, the details of their fare structure has not yet been worked out.

The **base fare** on entering the cab is $2.50. The **cost** is 50¢ for every ⅕ mile or 40¢ per 60 seconds in stopped or slow-moving traffic (or for waiting time). There's no extra charge for each passenger or for luggage. However, you must pay **bridge or tunnel tolls.** You'll also pay a **$1 surcharge** between 4 and 8pm and a **50¢ surcharge** after 8pm and before 6am. A 15% to 20% tip is customary. All taxis are now equipped with a device that allows you to pay by credit card.

The TLC has posted a **Taxi Rider's Bill of Rights** sticker in every cab. Drivers are required by law to take you anywhere in the five boroughs, to Nassau or Westchester counties, or to Newark Airport. They are supposed to know how to get you to any address in Manhattan and all major points in the outer boroughs. They are also required to provide air-conditioning and turn off the radio on demand. Smoking in the cab is not allowed.

You are allowed to dictate the route that is taken. It's a good idea to look at a map before you get in a taxi. Taxi drivers have been known to jack up the fare on visitors who don't know better by taking a circuitous route between points A and B. Don't be afraid to speak up.

On the other hand, listen to drivers who propose an alternate route. These guys spend 8 or 10 hours a day on these streets, and they know where the worst traffic is, or where Con Ed has dug up an intersection that should be avoided. A knowledgeable driver will know how to get you to your destination efficiently.

Another important tip: **Always make sure the meter is turned on at the start of the ride.** You'll see the red LED readout register the initial $2.50 and start calculating the fare as you go. I've witnessed unscrupulous drivers buzzing unsuspecting visitors around the city with the meter off, and then overcharging them at drop-off time.

For all driver complaints, including the one above, and to report lost property, call ℂ **311** or 212/NEW-YORK (639-9675; outside the metro area).

By Bicycle

Believe it or not, New York is a great bicycling city. Already the number of designated bike routes and lanes, including some major protected bike lanes painted green and with their own traffic signals, has mushroomed under Mayor Bloomberg—part of his vision for a more sustainable transportation network.

In 2013, it got even better with the city's rollout of the **Citibike** system (http://citibikenyc.com). Following the successful examples set by cities like Paris, Montreal, and Washington D.C., the city's program charges $9.95 a day ($25 per week), with unlimited free trips that clock in at less than 30 minutes (beyond that, a half-hourly rate kicks in). The freestanding, solar-powered racks dot many streets across the five boroughs, each holding around a dozen sturdy bikes outfitted with lights and tough tires. It's been a huge success.

For a current map of the ever-expanding city bike-lane network, visit the NYC DOT webpage at **www.nyc.gov,** or **www.nycbikemaps.com.** Alas, helmets are not provided at these stands; it's a smart idea to bring your own.

By Car

Forget driving yourself around the city. It's not worth the headache. Traffic is horrendous, and parking even more problematic.

If you do arrive in New York City by car, park it in a garage (expect to pay at least $25–$45 per day) and leave it there for the duration of your stay. If you drive a rental car in, return it as soon as you arrive and rent another when you leave.

Just about all of the major car-rental companies have multiple Manhattan locations.

Traveling from the City to the Suburbs

The **PATH** system (℘ **800/234-7284;** www.panynj.gov/path) connects cities in New Jersey, including Hoboken and Newark, to Manhattan by subway-style trains. Stops in Manhattan are at the World Trade Center, Christopher and 9th streets, and along Sixth Avenue at 14th, 23rd, and 33rd streets. The fare is $2.25 one-way.

New Jersey Transit (℘ **973/275-5555;** www.njtransit.com) operates commuter trains from Penn Station, and buses from the Port Authority at Eighth Avenue and 42nd Street, to points throughout New Jersey.

The **Long Island Rail Road** (℘ **511;** www.mta.info/lirr) runs from Penn Station, at Seventh Avenue between 31st and 33rd Streets, to Queens (ocean beaches, Citi Field [the new home of the New York Mets], Belmont Park) and points beyond on Long Island, to even better beaches and summer hot spots such as the Hamptons. You can also connect to the Fire Island ferry from the LIRR.

Metro-North Railroad (℘ **212/532-4900;** www.mta.info/mnr) departs from Grand Central Terminal, at 42nd Street and Lexington Avenue, for areas north of the city, including Westchester County, the Hudson Valley, and Connecticut.

BY BUS

Greyhound (℘ **800/231-2222** in the U.S.; ℘ **001/214/849-8100** outside the U.S. with toll-free access; www.greyhound.com) is the sole nationwide bus line. Greyhound buses (and buses from many other regional lines) arrive at the Port Authority Bus Terminal (625 8th Avenue at 42nd St.; ℘ **212/502-2200;** www.panynj.gov/bus-terminals/port-authority-bus-terminal.html).

WHEN TO GO

"Anytime you like" is the short answer. New York is a 12-month, 24-hour destination and there's always something exciting going on here.

Significantly, New York does not experience the real extremes of temperature of a Minneapolis or Phoenix. Yes, we get snowstorms and 10-degree weather, but rarely for more than a day or two, with the snow usually scooped into graying piles overnight. We also have heat waves, but it's unusual for the temperature to break 100°F for more than 4 or 5 days each summer, though it will be a sticky heat when it hits and none too pleasant. In general, this type of extreme heat occurs only in late July and August, with the most blustery and bitterly cold days falling in January and February, and occasionally December. (Of course, in this age of global warming, you never know what will happen.)

If you want to know what to pack just before you go, check the Weather Channel's online 10-day forecast at **www.weather.com**; and maybe compare it to the local NY1 forecast at **www.ny1.com/weather.**

Culture, too, is a year-round exercise. Most of the major plays, musicals, and art shows debut between September and May, so those who like to be on culture's cutting edge visit then. In the summer months NYC teems with arts events as the city transforms itself into an outdoor theater/concert hall, with dozens of free shows—from Shakespeare in the Park to Shakespeare in the Parking Lot—crowding the calendar and delighting penny-pinchers. All of the major art institutions participate in this summer free-for-all, with the Museum of Modern Art sponsoring concerts in its sculpture garden, the Metropolitan Opera bringing music to the parks, and dozens of other institutions, large and small, established and unknown, jumping on the alfresco bandwagon.

So what it all comes down to, in my mind, is cost, and here there is a *major* difference between seasons. Persons who visit in the slower months pay the right amount for their lodging, and those who come when the city is crowded—and here I'm going to sound like the clichéd New Yorker—get screwed.

So when are prices the most moderate? Deep winter, in the months of January (after the 4th) and February, it's not at all unusual to find a lovely room for as little as $109 a night. Visit in the fall, especially October, November, and December, and that same room, in the same hotel, could cost upwards of $300 a night. Spring is also pricey, albeit slightly less so than in the fall, and prices drop into a middle range in the summer. Room rates over Christmas, New Year's, the New York Marathon, and Thanksgiving reach their pinnacles for the year. If you must visit at those times, get ready to pay a good $50 more than even the pricey fall rates.

New York's Average Temperature & Rainfall

	JAN	FEB	MAR	APR	MAY	JUNE	JULY	AUG	SEPT	OCT	NOV	DEC
Daily Temp. (°F)	38	42	50	61	71	79	84	83	75	64	54	43
Daily Temp. (°C)	3	6	10	16	22	26	29	28	24	18	12	6
Days of Precipitation	11	10	11	11	11	10	11	10	8	8	9	10

New York City Calendar of Events

When planning your vacation, you may want to consider the special events or yearly festivals that might be occurring during the time of your visit. I've included a very limited sampling below of what I consider to be the "visit-worthy" events. As I can make no claims to psychic abilities, I can't include all of the nifty happenings that haven't yet been announced, so this is an incomplete list. To get a complete picture, pick up a copy of

Time Out magazine when you arrive. The "Around Town" section will leave you dizzy—usually there are upwards of 150 interesting events happening any one week. For a more selective listing, buy the current **New Yorker** magazine, which devotes the first tenth of its pages to its picks for the most intellectually stimulating or artistically important events of the week. For the most complete listings, go to the New York City Convention & Visitors Bureau's site **www.nycgo.com.**

JANUARY

New York Boat Show. Yachts to pontoon boats to canoes are all on display at the **Jacob K. Javits Convention Center,** usually from New Year's Eve through the second week of the New Year. Call *(C)* **212/984-7007** or visit **www.nyboatshow.com.**

Winter Restaurant Week. A misnomer, because this gourmet shindig actually lasts 2 weeks (reappearing in summer for another 2; see below), this is the time of year when cheap foodies can try out the city's best restaurants for as little as $25 at lunch, $35 at dinner, for three courses at each meal. Some participating restaurants in 2013 included standouts like A Voce, The Dutch, and EN Japanese Brasserie. Call *(C)* **212/484-1222** for info, or visit **www.nycgo.com.** You can make reservations starting 2 weeks in advance. Late January/early February.

Chinese New Year. Based on the lunar calendar, Chinese New Year always falls sometime in January or February, with 2 weeks of parades, festive meals, and special performances staged throughout Chinatown's streets, and along East Broadway. Visit **www.explorechinatown.com**, or call the **NYCVB hot line** at *(C)* **212/484-1222** or the **Asian American Business Development Center** at *(C)* **212/966-0100.** Chinese New Year falls on January 31 in 2014, and it's the Year of the Horse.

FEBRUARY

Fashion Week. Early February is when American designers parade their new lines for the press and big department store buyers. It's impossible to get tickets to the runway shows (they go to the likes of Gwyneth Paltrow and Madonna). I only mention Fashion Week here because the

event can tie up rooms at the Midtown hotels, raising prices (better to stay Downtown or Uptown when the fashionistas are in town).

Westminster Kennel Club Dog Show. I've always found it funny that Fashion Week—that parade of "Best in Breed" women—should be followed directly by a dog show. At least at the dog show, they're upfront about the purpose of the spectacle. The winnowing from just cute to anatomically awesome takes place the second weekend of the month at **Madison Square Garden.** With over 2,500 pooches appearing, it's quite the scene. Check the website **www.westminsterkennelclub.org** for further info. Tickets are available starting in mid-October via **Ticketmaster** (*(C)* **866/858-0008;** www.ticketmaster.com). Mid-February.

MARCH

The Pier Antiques Show. Never heard of it? Then you obviously aren't into antiques and collectibles, as this is one of the largest shows in the world for folks who care about old stuff. Taking place on the Passenger Ship Terminal Piers for a weekend mid-month, the show draws literally hundreds of treasure seekers. Call *(C)* **293/732-6642** or visit **www.pierantiqueshow.com** for this year's dates, plus a calendar of additional shows. Usually mid-March, and again in mid-November.

St. Patrick's Day Parade. Thanks to one of the largest Irish-American populations in the United States, St. Paddy's is an enormous event in NYC, rivaling only New Year's Eve for its displays of public inebriation. Every pub in town throws a party, and in the afternoon, all of 150,000 marchers parade down Fifth Avenue from 44th to 86th streets, starting at

11am. Call ☏ **718/231-4400** or visit **www.nycstpatricksparade.org.** March 17.

APRIL

New York International Auto Show. Here's the irony: You don't need a car in New York, yet this is the largest car show in the U.S. Held at the Javits Center, many concept cars show up that will never roll off the assembly line but are fun to dream about. Call ☏ **800/282-3336** or visit **www.autoshowny.com** or **www.javitscenter.com**. Early to mid-April.

Easter Parade. No floats, no marching bands, just ordinary people in extraordinary hats mark Easter in one of the city's most low-key but charming celebrations. Most spend the afternoon strolling up and down in front of St. Patrick's Cathedral, but Fifth Avenue from 57th Street all the way down to 45th is closed to traffic from 11am to 4pm, with the greatest number of chapeaus in evidence around noon. Easter falls on April 20th in 2014.

Tribeca Film Festival. Founded by Robert DeNiro and Jane Rosenthal in 2002, this little film festival has quickly grown into one of the most influential in the nation. You'll see films from all over the world here, from big studio pictures to tiny independent productions from places such as Slovakia and Dubai. And unlike other film fests, this one is truly for all ages, with a nifty street fair on the second weekend (usually featuring a zoo and rides), as well as children's films throughout the 2-week event, which usually run from the last week in April into the first week of May in the past 3 years. To learn more, visit www.tribecafilm.com/festival.

MAY

Fleet Week. About 10,000 Navy and Coast Guard personnel are "at liberty" in New York for the annual Fleet Week at the end of May. Usually from 1 to 4pm daily, you can watch the ships and aircraft carriers as they dock at the piers on the west side of Manhattan, tour them with on-duty personnel, and watch some dramatic exhibitions by the U.S.

Marines. Even if you don't take in any of the events, you'll know it's Fleet Week because those 10,000 sailors invade Midtown in their starched white uniforms. It's wonderful—just like *On the Town* come to life. Call ☏ **877/957-SHIP**, or visit **www.intrepidmuseum.org.** Late May.

JUNE

Belmont Stakes. The final event in horse racing's grand trifecta of events (the Kentucky Derby and The Preakness are the first two). Any horse able to win all three instantly enters the record books and his owner becomes a multi-millionaire, thanks to the breeding fees he'll be able to collect for the rest of that horse's life. Folks arrive at this jolly, crowded event in Queens before the actual race so they can view the horses and socialize. For information, call ☏ **516/488-6000** or visit **www.nyra.com.** Early June.

Gay Pride Weekend. More than just a parade (though the naughty, outrageous, rambunctious parade is still at the heart of the festivities), NY's pride weekend draws men and women from across the U.S. for a weekend of lectures, dances, and rallies. Learn more at www.nycpride.org.

Mermaid Parade. A smaller, nautically themed, daytime version of Greenwich Village's Halloween Parade, the Mermaid Parade takes place towards the end of June each year in Coney Island. Founded in 1983, the parade has the same kind of homegrown ambience and raunch as its Greenwich Village counterpart. Along with the ball that follows, featuring performances by local burlesque acts, the event is a heckuva a lot of fun. Get details at www.coneyisland.com or call ☏ **718/372-5159.**

Restaurant Week. Late June (see "January," above).

JULY

Macy's Fourth of July Fireworks. Start the day amid the crowds at the Great July 4th Festival in lower Manhattan, and then catch Macy's fireworks extravaganza over New York Harbor. It's the country's largest pyrotechnic show on Independence Day, and huge barges launch the fireworks from the Hudson or East Rivers. Call ℂ **212/484-1222** or the Macy's Visitor Center at 212/494-3827; **www.macys.com/fireworks.**

Several Festivals at Lincoln Center. The **Lincoln Center Festival** celebrates the best of the performing arts from all over—theater, ballet, contemporary dance, opera, nouveau circus performances, even puppet and media-based art. Recent editions have featured performances by Le Théâtre du Soleil, the Royal Opera, the Royal Ballet, and actors Ralph Fiennes, Liam Neeson, and Alan Cumming. Schedules are available in the spring, and tickets go on sale in May or early June. Call ℂ **212/875-5000,** or visit **www.lincoln centerfestival.org/festival.** An outdoor festival of artists at Lincoln Center, with free performances, runs through the end of August. The **Mostly Mozart Concert,** an indoor offering, brings master musicians from all over the world to play the music of the 18th-century master. Also part of the fun outdoors at Lincoln Center at this time of year is **Midsummer Night's Swing:** evenings of big-band swing, salsa, and tango under the stars to the sounds of top-flight bands. Dance lessons are offered with purchase of a ticket (for single or multiple nights).

AUGUST

Harlem Week. The world's largest black and Hispanic cultural festival actually spans almost the entire month, to include the Harlem Jazz and Music Festival and the New York City Children's Festival. Expect a full slate of music, from gospel to hip-hop, and lots of other festivities. Call ℂ **877/427-5364,** or visit **http://harlemweek.com.** Throughout August.

New York International Fringe Festival (FringeNYC). Held in a variety of downtown venues and park spaces for a crowd looking for the next underground hit (as in *Urinetown,* which went from the Fringe to Broadway in 2001), this arts festival presents alternative as well as traditional theater,

musicals, comedy, and all manner of performance. Hundreds of events are held at all hours over about 10 days. Suffice it to say that the quality can vary wildly Call ℂ **212/279-4488** for information, or 866/468-7619 to purchase tickets; or visit **www.fringenyc.org.** Mid- to late August.

U.S. Open Tennis Championships. For one brief, bright-tennis-whites moment each year at the end of August (and into September), the city becomes a center for international sport with the start of the U.S. Open, one of tennis' four Grand Slam events. For full information call ℂ **866/OPEN-TIX** (673-6849; it's always busy) or 718/760-6200 well in advance; visit **www.usopen.org** or **www. usta.com** for information. Two weeks around Labor Day.

SEPTEMBER

Fashion Week. Part 2 of the event mentioned above, and yes, it sends hotel rates soaring. Try and avoid visiting the week if you can (details on dates at www.mbfashion week.com)

New York Film Festival. Legendary hits like *Pulp Fiction* and *Mean Streets* both had their U.S. premieres at the Film Society of Lincoln Center's 2-week festival, a major stop on the film-fest circuit. Screenings are held in various Lincoln Center venues; advance tickets are a good bet always, and a necessity for certain events (especially evening and weekend screenings). Call ℂ **212/875-5600** (for recorded information), or 212/875-5601 for box office information; or check out **www. filmlinc.com/nyff.** Two weeks from late September to early October.

OCTOBER

Greenwich Village Halloween Parade. Men in drag, women in drag, zombies dancing to Michael Jackson's *Thriller*—all these apparitions and more made their appearance at recent parades, and you'll see there if you attend. This is New York's most outrageous event and the largest Halloween parade in the world. Some locals spend all year working on their costumes; if you dress up, you can march, too. For information on how to do that, and for the parade routing (which changes), call the *Village Voice* parade hot line at ✆ **212/475-3333,** ext. 14044, or visit **www.halloween-nyc.com.** To snag a viewing spot in Greenwich Village along the parade route, you'll need to show up at about 5pm (2 hr. before the parade starts) . . . or have a nice dinner and show up at 9pm to view the second half. The crowd will have thinned by then, and because the event usually doesn't end until close to 11pm, you'll have more than enough time to enjoy it. October 31.

NOVEMBER

Holiday Trimmings. Starting the day after Thanksgiving (and often even before that), the entire city dresses up for Christmas, stringing lights, hanging tinsel, and inserting the computer chips into all of the moving figurines that have, of late, hijacked the windows of the city's large department stores. The best street to see the trimmings, by far, is **Fifth Avenue, between 39th and 59th streets.** Along with the spectacular windows at the big department stores—**Saks Fifth Avenue, Lord & Taylor, Bergdorf Goodman,** and **Tiffany's**—you'll also want to admire the massive fir tree at Rockefeller Center (off Fifth Ave., at 51st St., lit in late November; go to www.rockefellercenter.com for more details). The windows at **Macy's** (34th St. at Broadway) are also deservedly famous, as is the indoor winter wonderland display at the heart of which is a Santa, waiting to hear your tots' Christmas wishes (just like in *Miracle on 34th Street*). **Madison Avenue, between 55th and 60th streets,** is also worth a stroll, and if you have the time, drop by **Bloomingdales** (Lexington Ave., between 59th and 60th sts.) for its yearly display.

Chanukah is also a big deal in this city, with the largest Jewish population outside of Israel. On Fifth Avenue at 59th Street, a giant menorah—at 32 feet it's the largest in the world—is lit each year on the first night of Chanukah and for 7 nights thereafter. On the first and final evenings, steaming *latkes* (potato pancakes) are distributed at sunset, and live music accompanies the electric candle-lighting. The dates for Chanukah shift according to the Hebrew calendar. Call ✆ **212/736-8400** for more information.

New York City Marathon. Some 30,000 runners from around the world participate in the largest U.S. marathon, and more than a million fans cheer them on as they follow a route that touches all five New York boroughs and finishes at Central Park. Call ✆ **212/423-2249** or 212/860-4455, or visit **www.nyrr.org,** where you can find applications. First Sunday in November.

Radio City Christmas Spectacular. This New York tradition now starts well before Thanksgiving, and it's still as extravagantly kitschy as ever, with laser-light shows, onstage ice-skating, horses, camels and, of course, the fabulous Rockettes, executing their 300-plus kicks per show. Shows run approximately 7 days a week, with six daily performances (on many dates) starting at 9am and going until 10pm. For information, call ✆ **212/465-6225,** or visit **www.radiocitychristmas.com;** you can also buy tickets at the box office or via Ticketmaster's **Radio City Hot Line** (✆ **866/858-0007),** or visit **www.ticketmaster.com.** Throughout November and December.

The Pier Antiques Show. Mid-November (see "March," above).

Macy's Thanksgiving Day Parade. The procession starts at Central Park West and 77th Street and finishes at Herald Square at 34th Street, a much-beloved national tradition. Huge hot-air balloons in the forms of Rocky and Bullwinkle, Snoopy, the Pink Panther, Bart Simpson, and other cartoon favorites are the best part. The night before, you can usually see the big blow-up on Central Park West at 79th Street; call in advance to see if it will be open to the public. Call ✆ **212/484-1222** or Macy's Visitor Center at 212/494-3827. Thanksgiving Day.

The Nutcracker. Ballet impresario George Balanchine's masterpiece. The music is by Tchaikovsky, and half the cast is under 15, culled from New York City Ballet's famous dance school at Juilliard. Your children will love it, though it's an expensive treat. The show sells out early, so make your reservations in October if you can, when the seats first go on sale. Call *©* **212/496-0600,** or go online to **www.nycballet.com**. Late November through early January.

DECEMBER

Christmas Traditions. In addition to the *Radio City Christmas Spectacular* and the New York City Ballet's staging of *The Nutcracker* (see "November," above), traditional holiday events include the National Chorale's singalong performances of Handel's *Messiah* at **Avery Fisher Hall** (*©* **212/875-5030;** www.lincolncenter.org) for a week before Christmas. The *Messiah* is also staged in many churches and other venues throughout the city during December. Check local listings.

New Year's Eve. The biggest party of all is in Times Square, where raucous revelers count down the year's final seconds until the ball drops at midnight at 1 Times Square. This one, in the cold surrounded by thousands of tipsy revelers all penned in by NYPD barricades, is a masochist's delight. Be sure to use the restroom before you wedge yourself in. Call *©* **212/768-1560** or 212/484-1222, or visit www.timessquarenyc. org. December 31.

Runner's World Midnight Run. Enjoy **fireworks** followed by the New York Road Runners Club's annual run in **Central Park,** which is fun for runners and spectators alike; call *©* **212/860-4455,** or visit **www.nyrr. org.** December 31.

Brooklyn's fireworks celebration. Head to Brooklyn for the city's largest New Year's Eve **fireworks** celebration inside Prospect Park (and supervised by the FDNY). Call *©* **718/965-8999,** or visit **www.prospect park.org.** December 31.

New Year's Eve Concert for Peace. The Cathedral of St. John the Divine is known for its annual concert, whose past performances have included singer Judy Collins, Forces of Nature Dance Company, and the world premiere of *Songs of War, Remembrance, and Hope* by Glen Cortese. The evening culminates in the passing of a candle flame while the audience of thousands sings "This Little Light of Mine." For tickets, call *©* **212/316-7540** or go online to **www.stjohndivine. org.** December 31.

Public Holidays

Banks, government offices, post offices, and many stores, restaurants, and museums are closed on the following legal national holidays: January 1 (New Year's Day), the third Monday in January (Martin Luther King, Jr., Day), the third Monday in February (Presidents' Day), the last Monday in May (Memorial Day), July 4 (Independence Day), the first Monday in September (Labor Day), the second Monday in October (Columbus Day), November 11 (Veterans Day/Armistice Day), the fourth Thursday in November (Thanksgiving Day), and December 25 (Christmas). The Tuesday after the first Monday in November is Election Day, a government holiday.

[Fast FACTS] NEW YORK CITY

Area Codes There are four area codes in the city: two in Manhattan, the original **212** and **646;** and two in the outer boroughs, the original **718,** plus **929** and **347.** Also common is the **917** area code, which is assigned to cellphones. All calls between these area codes are local calls, but you'll have to dial 1 + the area code + the seven digits for all calls, even ones made within your area code.

Business Hours In general, **retail stores** are open Monday through Saturday from 10am to 6 or 7pm, Thursday from 10am to 8:30 or 9pm, and Sunday from noon to 5pm (see chapter 6). **Banks** tend to be open Monday through Friday from 9am to 5pm, with many open Saturday mornings, and some now even open on Sundays.

Customs **What You Can Bring into the U.S.** Every visitor more than 21 years of age may bring in, free of duty, the following: (1) 1 liter of wine or hard liquor; (2) 200 cigarettes, 100 cigars (but not from Cuba), or 4.4 pounds of smoking tobacco; and (3) $100 worth of gifts. These exemptions are offered to travelers who spend at least 72 hours in the United States and who have not claimed them within the preceding 6 months. It is forbidden to bring into the country almost any meat products (including canned, fresh, and dried meat products such as bouillon, soup mixes, and so forth). Generally, condiments including vinegars, oils, spices, coffee, tea, and some cheeses and baked goods are permitted. Avoid rice products, as rice can often harbor insects. Fruits and vegetables are prohibited as well. Customs will allow produce depending on where you got it and where you're going after you arrive in the U.S. International visitors may carry in or out up to $10,000 in U.S. or foreign currency with no formalities; larger sums must be declared to U.S. Customs on entering or leaving, which includes filing form CM 4790. For details regarding U.S. Customs and Border Protection, consult your nearest U.S. embassy or consulate, or **U.S. Customs and Border Protection (www. cbp.gov).**

What You Can Take Home from the U.S. If you're an international visitor, for information on what you're allowed to bring

home, contact one of the following agencies:
U.S. Citizens: U.S. Customs & Border Protection (CBP), 1300 Pennsylvania Ave. NW, Washington, DC 20229 (℗ **877/227-5511;** www.cbp.gov).
Canadian Citizens: Canada Border Services Agency, Ottawa, Ontario, K1A 0L8 (℗ **800/461-9999** in Canada, or 204/983-3500; www.cbsa-asfc.gc.ca).
U.K. Citizens: HM Revenue and Customs, Crownhill Court, Tailyour Road, Plymouth, PL6 5BZ0 (℗ **300/200-3710;** www.hmrc. gov.uk).
Australian Citizens: Australian Customs Service, Customs House, 5 Constitution Ave., Canberra City, ACT 2601 (℗ **1300/363-263;** from outside Australia, 612/9313-3010; www.customs.gov.au).
New Zealand Citizens: New Zealand Customs, 1 Hinemoa St., Harbour Quays Box 2218, Wellington, 6140 (℗ **0800/428-786;** from outside New Zealand, 649/927-8036; www.customs.govt.nz).

Disabled Travelers New York is more accessible to travelers with disabilities than ever before. The city's bus system is wheelchair-friendly, and most of the major sightseeing attractions are accessible. Even so, always call first to be sure that the places you want to go to are fully accessible and lifts are operational.

Most hotels are ADA compliant, with suitable rooms for travelers who use wheelchairs as well as those with other disabilities. But before you book, **ask lots of questions based on your needs.** Many city hotels are in older buildings that have been modified to meet requirements; still, elevators and bathrooms can be on the small side, and other impediments may exist. If you have mobility issues, you'll probably do best to book one of the city's newer hotels, which tend to be more accommodating. At **www.access-able.com,** you'll find links to New York's best accessible accommodations (click on "World Destinations"). Some Broadway theaters and other performance

9

PLANNING YOUR VISIT TO NEW YORK CITY | Business Hours

venues provide total wheelchair accessibility; others provide partial accessibility. Many also offer lower-priced tickets for theatergoers with disabilities and their companions, though you'll need to check individual policies and reserve in advance.

Hospital Audiences, Inc. (☎ 212/575-7676; www.hainyc.org) arranges attendance and provides details about accessibility at cultural institutions as well as cultural events adapted for people with disabilities. Services include "Describe!," which allows visually impaired theatergoers to enjoy theater events; and the invaluable **HAI Hot Line** (☎ 212/575-7676), which offers accessibility information for hotels, restaurants, attractions, cultural venues, and much more.

Museums: In New York, the general rule is: the larger the museum, the more extensive the facilities for persons with disabilities. For example, the Metropolitan Museum of Art offers free rental of standard and extra-wide wheelchairs at all of its coat-check stands, regular sign-language and touch tours for the deaf and blind, attended elevators, and accessible bathrooms and water fountains. In smaller museums, such as the Museum of the Chinese in the Americas, you'll find fewer such amenities, so call first for information.

Doctors   If you get sick, consider asking your hotel concierge to recommend a local doctor—even his or her own. This will probably yield a better recommendation than any toll-free telephone number would.

There are also several walk-in medical centers, like **Beth Israel Medical Group,** 55 E. 34th St., between Park and Madison avenues (☎ 212/252-6000), for nonemergency illnesses. The clinic is open Monday through Sunday from 8am to 8pm.

The **NYU Downtown Hospital** offers physician referrals at ☎ 212/312-5000. You can also try the emergency room at a local hospital. Many hospitals also have walk-in clinics for emergency cases that are not life threatening; you may not get immediate attention, but you won't pay the high price of an emergency-room visit.

Pack **prescription medications** in their original containers in your carry-on luggage. Also bring along copies of your prescriptions in case you lose your pills or run out. Don't forget an extra pair of contact lenses or prescription glasses.

If you have dental problems on the road, a service known as **1-800-DENTIST** (☎ 800/336-8422) will provide the name of a local dentist. Also see "Hospitals," later in this section.

Drinking Laws   The legal age for purchase and consumption of alcoholic beverages is 21; proof of age can be requested at bars, nightclubs, and restaurants, especially if you're graced with youthful looks. Liquor and wine are sold only in licensed stores, most of which are now open 7 days a week. Liquor stores sometimes are closed on holidays. Beer can be purchased in grocery stores and delis 24 hours a day, except Sunday before noon. Last call in bars is at 4am, though many close earlier. Do not carry open containers of alcohol in your car or any public area that isn't zoned for alcohol consumption. The police can fine you on the spot.

Driving Rules   See "Getting Around," earlier in this chapter.

Electricity   Like Canada, the United States uses 110 to 120 volts AC (60 cycles), compared to 220 to 240 volts AC (50 cycles) in most of Europe, Australia, and New Zealand. Downward converters that change 220–240 volts to 110–120 volts are difficult to find in the United States, so bring one with you.

Embassies & Consulates   All embassies are in the nation's capital, Washington, D.C. Some consulates are in major U.S. cities, and most nations have a mission to the United Nations in New York City. To find where your embassy is, check **www.embassy.org/embassies**.

Emergencies For all emergencies—a fire, police, or health emergency—call **911.**

Family Travel Good bets for the most timely information include the "Weekend" section of Friday's *New York Times,* which has a section dedicated to the week's best kid-friendly activities; and the weekly *New York* magazine, which has a full calendar of children's events in its listings section. *Big Apple Parent* is usually available, for free, at children's stores and other locations in Manhattan.

The first place to look for babysitting is in your hotel (better yet, ask about babysitting when you reserve). Many hotels have babysitting services or will provide you with lists of reliable sitters. If this doesn't pan out, call the **Baby Sitters' Guild** (ⓒ **212/682-0227;** www.babysittersguild. com). The sitters are licensed, insured, and bonded, and can even take your child on outings.

Hospitals The following hospitals have 24-hour emergency rooms. Don't forget your insurance card.

Downtown: New York Downtown Hospital, 170 William St., between Beekman and Spruce streets (ⓒ 212/312-5106 or 212/312-5000) and **Beth Israel Medical Center,** First Avenue and 16th Street (ⓒ 212/420-2000).

Midtown: Bellevue Hospital Center, 462 First Ave., at 27th Street (ⓒ 212/562-4141); **New York University Langone Medical Center,** 550 First Ave., at 33rd Street (ⓒ 212/263-7300); and **Roosevelt Hospital,** 425 W. 59th St., between Ninth and Tenth avenues (ⓒ 212/523-4000).

Upper West Side: St. Luke's Hospital Center, 1111 Amsterdam Ave., at 114th Street (ⓒ 212/523-4000); and **Columbia Presbyterian Medical Center,** 630 W. 168th St., between Broadway and Fort Washington Avenue (ⓒ 212/305-2500).

Upper East Side: New York Presbyterian Hospital, 525 E. 68th St., at York Avenue (ⓒ 212/746-5454); **Lenox Hill Hospital,** 100 E. 77th St., between Park

and Lexington avenues (ⓒ 212/434-2000); and **Mount Sinai Medical Center,** 1190 Fifth Avenue at 100th Street (ⓒ 212/241-6500).

Insurance For information on traveler's insurance, trip cancellation insurance, and medical insurance while traveling, please visit **www.frommers.com/tips.**

Internet & Wi-Fi New York is rife with Wi-Fi (wireless fidelity) "hotspots" that offer free Wi-Fi access or charge a small fee for usage. A good directory of free hotspots in the city can be found at **www.openwifinyc. com.** Many of the city's parks and major plazas offer free Wi-Fi through various sponsor-carriers. Some subway stops also now offer Wi-Fi, as do all the Starbucks in the city.

Your hotel may also provide Wi-Fi or broadband access in your room, sometimes for a hefty daily fee. It's always surprised us that the higher-end hotels are the ones who charge for Internet access, while the budget places are more likely to use free Internet as a selling point.

FedEx Office (www.fedex.com/us/office/ services/computer/index.html) has free Wi-Fi at most locations, as well as computers you use for 30¢ per minute. There are dozens of locations around town.

Legal Aid While driving, if you are pulled over for a minor infraction (such as speeding), never attempt to pay the fine directly to a police officer; this could be construed as attempted bribery, a much more serious crime. Pay fines by mail, or directly into the hands of the clerk of the court. If accused of a more serious offense, say and do nothing before consulting a lawyer. In the U.S., the burden is on the state to prove a person's guilt beyond a reasonable doubt, and everyone has the right to remain silent, whether he or she is suspected of a crime or actually arrested. Once arrested, a person can make one telephone call to a party of his or her choice. The international visitor should call his or her embassy or consulate.

LGBT Travelers   In truth, gay and lesbian travelers need very little special advice when it comes to New York City. With one of the largest and most politically active gay populations in the world, and dozens of gay bars and clubs (see chapter 8 for more on the city's nightlife options), you should feel welcomed and accepted in the Big Apple. After all, this is where the Broadway musical was born, right?

Traditionally, the gay community of New York has been centered around Christopher Street in the West Village, but in the last decade it's expanded to Chelsea and Hell's Kitchen. If you're a bar-hopper, these are the three areas you'll want to explore, though there are gay bars in every neighborhood of Manhattan, just as there are gay people in every neighborhood. For more complete listings of bars and special events than you'll find in this tome, go into any gay bar or store and pick up a copy of *Gay City News* (www.gaycitynews.com) and the free magazines **Next (www.nextmagazine.com)** and **GO magazine (www.gomag.com),** which is lesbian-oriented. You'll also find lots of information on their websites. Much of the same information is available via standard websites. Another good resource is *Time Out* (available on newsstands), which has a large section devoted to gay and lesbian events and festivities.

Mail   At press time, domestic postage rates were 33¢ for a postcard and 46¢ for a letter. For international mail, a first-class letter of up to 1 ounce costs $1.10; a first-class postcard costs the same as a letter. For more information go to **www.usps.com**.

If you aren't sure what your address will be in the United States, mail can be sent to you, in your name, c/o General Delivery at the main post office of the city or region where you expect to be. (Call ✆ **800/275-8777** for information on the nearest post office.) The addressee must pick up mail in person and must produce proof of identity (driver's license, passport, and so on). Most post offices will hold mail for up to 1 month, and are open Monday to Friday from 8am to 6pm, and Saturday from 9am to 3pm.

Always include zip codes when mailing items in the U.S. If you don't know the zip code, visit www.usps.com/zip4.

Medical Requirements   Unless you're arriving from an area known to be suffering from an epidemic (particularly cholera or yellow fever), inoculations or vaccinations are not required for entry into the United States.

Money & Costs   Frommer's guidebooks list exact prices in the local currency. However, rates fluctuate, so before departing consult a currency exchange website such as **www.xe.com** to check up-to-the-minute rates.

New York City can be one of the most expensive destinations in the United States (and the world). You can pay more for lodging, dining, and transportation than almost anywhere else; however, in this book, we steer you to the best values for your money at every level.

In terms of how much to bring: not that much in cash. You never have to carry too much cash in New York, and while the city's pretty safe, it's best not to overstuff your wallet (although always make sure you have at least $20 in cash for small purchases).

ATMs   In most Manhattan neighborhoods, you can find a bank with *ATMs* (automated teller machines) every couple of blocks. Most delis, many restaurants and clubs, and other stores have an ATM on premises, so if you need cash quickly, you're probably never more than about 100 feet away from one. (Though keep an eye on the fees imposed for using the ATM; they will go on top of whatever fee your bank charges; and note that in some bars and clubs, where you can't leave once you've paid your admission, the withdrawal fee is hefty.)

WHAT THINGS COST IN NEW YORK CITY	US$
Cab from JFK airport to Manhattan (plus tolls)	52.00
Single full-fare subway or bus ride	2.75
7-Day Unlimited-Ride MetroCard for bus or subway	30.00
Massage (50 min.) at Elizabeth Arden Red Door Spas	135.00
Bicycle rental Central Park (1 hr.)	15.00
Ticket to a N.Y. Yankees game (Terrace)	85.00
Pint of beer (draft pilsner or lager)	7.00
Cup of coffee in a cafe or bar	2.50
Coca-Cola in a café or bar	3.00
Cocktail in a bar	14.00
Bottle of water	1.00–2.00
Tube of toothpaste	5.99
Admission to Museum of Modern Art	25.00
Movie ticket	14.00
Walking Tour	15.00
Discount Ticket to a Broadway Show	65.00–75.00
Full-price to a Broadway show (orchestra)	135.00

9

Newspapers & Magazines There are three major daily newspapers: the *New York Times,* the *Daily News,* and the *New York Post.* There are also two free daily papers, *AM-New York* and *Metro,* usually distributed in the morning near subway stations and in self-serve boxes around town.

If you want to find your hometown paper, visit **Universal News & Magazines,** at 234 W. 42nd St., between Seventh and Eighth avenues, and 977 Eighth Ave., between 57th and 58th streets. Other good bets include the **Hudson News** dealers, located in Grand Central Terminal, at 42nd Street and Lexington Avenue, and Penn Station, at 34th Street and Seventh Avenue.

There are several weekly and biweekly newspapers and magazines (such as the glossies *New York Magazine* and *Time Out New York*), as well as the *Village Voice* and *Gay City News,* which are excellent sources of information about events, dining, and attractions in the city. We list them and their websites throughout the book.

Packing The most important item in your suitcase will be a pair of very, very comfortable shoes, because your dogs are gonna be barking! This is a walking city, and what with getting from place to place and trudging through the marble halls of the Metropolitan Museum of Art or the American Museum of Natural History, a springy, supportive pair of shoes is essential (you may want to bring two pairs to increase your feet ease). Other than that, fill your suitcase with what pleases you most at home: Very few actual New Yorkers have the budget or time to dress like the ladies on *Sex and the City,* and unless you plan on going to the theater, the opera, or a very fancy restaurant, casual clothes should suffice.

Dressing appropriately for the weather is also key, so be sure to check the chart on p. 238 for the average temperatures at various times of the year. Those visiting in the fall and spring months (mid-September to mid-Novemver, and mid-March to mid-May) are advised to bring clothes that you can layer, as a balmy afternoon can turn chilly once the sun goes down.

Passports To enter the United States by air, international visitors must have a valid passport that expires at least 6 months later than the scheduled end of your visit.

Note: U.S. and Canadian citizens entering the U.S. at land and sea ports of entry from within the western hemisphere must now also present a passport or other documents compliant with the Western Hemisphere Travel Initiative (WHTI; see www.getyouhome.gov for details). Children 15 and under may continue entering with only a U.S. birth certificate, or other proof of U.S. citizenship.

Australia **Australian Passport Information Service** (✆ **131-232,** or visit www.passports.gov.au).

Canada **Passport Office,** Department of Foreign Affairs and International Trade, Ottawa, ON K1A 0G3 (✆ **800/567-6868;** www.ppt.gc.ca).

Ireland **Passport Office,** Frederick Buildings, Molesworth Street, Dublin 2 (✆ **01/671-1633;** www.foreignaffairs.gov.ie).

New Zealand **Passports Office,** Department of Internal Affairs, 109 Featherston St., Wellington, 6011 (✆ **0800/225-050** in New Zealand or 04/463-9360; www.passports.govt.nz).

United Kingdom Visit your nearest passport office, major post office, or travel agency or contact the **HM Passport Service,** Peel Building, 2 Marsham St. 89 Eccleston Square, London, SW1P 4DF (✆ **0300/222-0000;** www.gov.uk/government/organisations/hm-passport-office).

United States To find your regional passport office, check the U.S. State Department website (http://travel.state.gov/passport) or call the **National Passport Information Center** (✆ **877/487-2778**) for automated information.

Police Dial ✆ **911** in an emergency; otherwise, call ✆ **646/610-5000** (NYPD Switchboard) for the number of the nearest precinct. For nonemergency matters, call ✆ **311.**

Safety The FBI consistently rates New York City as one of the safest large cities in the United States, but it is still a large city and crime most definitely exists. So trust your instincts and take the same precautions you'd take in any large city (don't flash your money or carry too much of it at one time; stay in well-lit, crowded areas).

Senior Travel New York subway and bus fares are half price ($1.25) for people 65 and older. Many museums and sights (and some theaters and performance halls) offer discounted admittance and tickets to seniors, so don't be shy about asking. Always bring an ID card, especially if you've kept your youthful glow.

Many hotels offer senior discounts, but they may not be as good as the regular discounts one gets through bargain websites, so always check before pulling out your AARP card.

Smoking Smoking is prohibited on all public transportation; in the lobbies of hotels and office buildings; in taxis, bars, and restaurants; and in most shops. In 2011, smoking was banned in all NYC parks and beaches.

Subway Safety Tips In general, the subways are safe, especially in Manhattan. There are panhandlers and questionable characters like anywhere else in the city, but subway crime has gone down to 1960s levels. Still, stay alert and trust your instincts. Always keep a hand on your personal belongings.

When using the subway, **don't wait for trains near the edge of the platform** or on extreme ends of a station. During non-rush hours, wait for the train in view of the token-booth clerk or under the yellow DURING OFF HOURS TRAINS STOP HERE signs, and ride in the train operator's or conductor's car (usually in the center of the train; you'll see his or her head stick out of the window when the doors open). Choose crowded cars over empty ones—there's safety in numbers.

Student Travel There are student discounts at almost every museum in New York, so student travelers should bring their school IDs with them.

Taxes Sales tax is 8.875% on meals, most goods, and some services. **Hotel tax** is 5.875%. **Parking garage tax** is 18.375%. The United States has no value-added tax (VAT) or other indirect tax at the national level. Every state, county, and city may levy its own local tax on all purchases, including hotel and restaurant checks and airline tickets. These taxes will not appear on price tags.

Telephones Generally, hotel surcharges on long-distance and local calls are astronomical, so you're better off using your **cellphone** or a **public pay telephone.** Many convenience stores and drugstores sell **prepaid calling cards** in denominations up to $50; for international visitors these can be the least expensive way to call home. Many public pay phones at airports now accept American Express, MasterCard, and Visa credit cards. **Local calls** made from most payphones cost 25¢ or 50¢ (no pennies, please).

That said, there aren't as many payphones on the streets of New York City as there used to be, because of the prevalence of cellphones, and the ones that are there are often out of order.

To make a **local call** in one of the five boroughs, **dial 1,** followed by the area code and the seven-digit number. Most long-distance and international calls can be dialed directly from any phone. **To make calls within the United States and to Canada,** dial 1. **For other international calls,** dial 011, followed by the country code, city code, and the number you are calling.

Calls to area codes **800, 888, 855, 877,** and **866** are toll-free. However, calls to area code **900** (chat lines, bulletin boards, "dating" services, and so on) can be expensive—charges of 95¢ to $3 or more per minute. Some numbers have minimum charges that can run $15 or more.

For **reversed-charge or collect calls,** and for person-to-person calls, dial the number 0 then the area code and number; an operator will come on the line, and you should specify whether you are calling collect, person to person, or both. If your operator-assisted call is international, ask for the overseas operator.

For **directory assistance** ("Information"), dial **411** for local numbers and national numbers in the U.S. and Canada. For dedicated long-distance information, dial 1, then the appropriate area code plus **555-1212.**

Mobile Phones. Just because your cellphone works at home doesn't mean it'll work everywhere in the U.S. (thanks to our nation's fragmented cellphone system). It's a good bet that your phone will work in New York City, but take a look at your wireless company's coverage map on its website before heading out. There's also the savvy option of using your smartphone's **Skype** app at Wi-Fi hotspots for free and very cheap calling.

If you need to stay in touch at a destination where you know your phone won't work, rent a phone that does from **National Geographic Talk Abroad Services** (© **800/287-5072;** cellularabroad. com) or a rental-car location, but beware that you'll pay $1 a minute or more for airtime.

You may even consider purchasing a cheap, pay-as-you-go phone in many locations (including convenience stores) throughout the city.

If you're not from the U.S., you'll be appalled at the poor reach of the **GSM (Global System for Mobile Communications) wireless network,** which is used by much of the rest of the world. Your phone will probably work in most major U.S. cities; it definitely won't work in many rural areas. And you may or may not be able to send SMS (text messaging) home.

Time The continental United States is divided into **four time zones:** Eastern

Standard Time (EST), Central Standard Time (CST), Mountain Standard Time (MST), and Pacific Standard Time (PST). Alaska and Hawaii have their own zones. For example, when it's 9am in Los Angeles (PST), it's 7am in Honolulu (HST), 10am in Denver (MST), 11am in Chicago (CST), noon in New York City (EST), 5pm in London (GMT), and 2am the next day in Sydney.

Daylight saving time (summer time) is in effect from 1am on the second Sunday in March to 1am on the first Sunday in November. Daylight saving time moves the clock 1 hour ahead of standard time.

Tipping   In hotels, tip **bellhops** at least $1 per bag and tip the **chamber staff** $1 to $2 per day (more if you've left a big mess). Tip the **doorman** or **concierge** only if he or she has provided you with some specific service (for example, calling a cab for you or obtaining difficult-to-get theater tickets). Tip the **valet-parking attendant** $1 every time you get your car.

In restaurants, bars, and nightclubs, tip **service staff** and **bartenders** 15% to 20% of the check (or you can simply double the tax on the check which will be 16%), tip **checkroom attendants** $1 per garment, and tip **valet-parking attendants** $1 per vehicle.

As for other service personnel, tip **cab drivers** 15% of the fare; tip **skycaps** at airports at least $1 per bag ($2–$3 if you have a lot of luggage); and tip **hairdressers, barbers,** and **massage therapists** 15% to 20%.

Toilets   You won't find many public toilets or restrooms on the streets in New York City, but they can be found in hotel lobbies, bars, restaurants, museums, department stores, and railway and bus stations. Large hotels and fast-food restaurants are often the best bet for clean facilities.

Public restrooms are available at the visitor centers in Midtown (1560 Broadway, btw. 46th and 47th sts.; and 810 Seventh Ave., btw. 52nd and 53rd sts.). You can find relief at the New York Public Library's main building on Fifth Avenue just south of 42nd Street. Grand Central Terminal, at 42nd Street between Park and Lexington avenues, also has clean restrooms. There are staffed bathrooms open from early in the morning until fairly late at night in the Times Square subway station (closer to Seventh Ave.). Your best bet on the street is Starbucks or another city java chain—you can't walk more than a few blocks without seeing one. You can also head to hotel lobbies (especially the big Midtown ones) and department stores such as Macy's and Bloomingdale's. On the Lower East Side, stop into the Lower East Side BID Visitor Center, 54 Orchard St., between Hester and Grand streets (weekdays 9:30am–5:30pm, weekends 9:30am–4pm).

Visas   The U.S. State Department has a **Visa Waiver Program (VWP)** allowing citizens of the following countries to enter the United States without a visa for stays of up to 90 days: Andorra, Australia, Austria, Belgium, Brunei, Czech Republic, Denmark, Estonia, Finland, France, Germany, Greece, Hungary, Iceland, Ireland, Italy, Japan, Latvia, Liechtenstein, Lithuania, Luxembourg, Malta, Monaco, the Netherlands, New Zealand, Norway, Portugal, San Marino, Singapore, Slovakia, Slovenia, South Korea, Spain, Sweden, Switzerland, Taiwan, and the United Kingdom. (**Note:** This list was accurate at press time; for the most up-to-date list of countries in the VWP, consult **http://travel.state.gov/visa**.)

Even though a visa isn't necessary, in an effort to help U.S. officials check travelers against terror watch lists before they arrive at U.S. borders, visitors from VWP countries must register online through the Electronic System for Travel Authorization (ESTA) before boarding a plane or a boat to the U.S. Travelers must complete an electronic application providing basic personal and travel eligibility information. The Department of Homeland Security recommends filling out the form at least 3 days before traveling. Authorizations will be valid for up to 2 years or until the traveler's passport expires, whichever comes first. Currently, there is a $14 fee for the online application.

9

PLANNING YOUR VISIT TO NEW YORK CITY | Visas

Existing ESTA registrations remain valid through their expiration dates. **Note:** Any passport issued on or after October 26, 2006, by a VWP country must be an **e-Passport** for VWP travelers to be eligible to enter the U.S. without a visa. Citizens of these nations also need to present a round-trip air or cruise ticket upon arrival. E-Passports contain computer chips capable of storing biometric information, such as the required digital photograph of the holder. If your passport doesn't have this feature, you can still travel without a visa if the valid passport was issued before October 26, 2005, and includes a machine-readable zone; or if the valid passport was issued between October 26, 2005, and October 25, 2006, and includes a digital photograph. For more information, go to **http://travel. state.gov/visa**. Canadian citizens may enter the United States without visas, but will need to show passports and proof of residence.

Citizens of all other countries must have (1) a valid passport that expires at least 6 months later than the scheduled end of their visit to the U.S.; and (2) a tourist visa.

For information about U.S. Visas go to **http://travel.state.gov** and click on "Visas." Or go to one of the following websites:

Australian citizens can obtain up-to-date visa information from the **U.S. Embassy Canberra,** Moonah Place, Yarralumla, ACT 2600 (② **02/6214-5600**) or by checking the U.S. Diplomatic Mission's website at **http://canberra.usembassy. gov/visas.html**.

British subjects can obtain up-to-date visa information by calling the **U.S. Embassy Visa Information Line** (② **09042-450-100** from within the U.K.

at £1.23 per minute; or ② **866/382-3589** from within the U.S. at a flat rate of $20 and is payable by credit card only) or by visiting the "Visas to the U.S." section of the American Embassy London's website at **http://london.usembassy.gov/visas. html**.

Irish citizens can obtain up-to-date visa information through the **U.S. Embassy Dublin,** 42 Elgin Rd., Ballsbridge, Dublin 4 (② **1580-47-VISA** [8472] from within the Republic of Ireland at €2.44 per minute; **http://dublin.usembassy.gov**).

Citizens of **New Zealand** can obtain up-to-date visa information by contacting the **U.S. Consulate General,** Citigroup Center, 23 Customs St., East Auckland CBD (② **649/887-5999; http://newzealand. usembassy.gov**).

Visitor Information NYC & Company runs the Official NYC Information Center at 810 Seventh Ave. (at 53rd St.), New York, NY 10019. You can call ② **800/ NYC-VISIT (692-8474)** to request the *Official NYC Guide* detailing hotels, restaurants, theaters, attractions, events, and more. The guide (and a New York City map) is free and will arrive in 7 to 10 days. You can also download it online on the company's website, **www.nycgo.com**, where you will find a wealth of free information. To speak with a live travel counselor, call ② **212/484-1222,** which is staffed weekdays from 8am to 6pm EST, Saturday and Sunday from 8am to 5pm EST.

For visitors from the U.K., the NYC & Company office is located at Colechurch House, 1 London Bridge Walk, London, SE1 2SX (② **020/7367-0900**). You can download or order the Official NYC & Company visitor guide online at **www. nycgo.com**.